FINAL CUTS

The Last Films of 50 Great Directors

NAT SEGALOFF

Final Cuts: The Last Films of 50 Great Directors
© 2013 Nat Segaloff. All Rights Reserved.

No part of this book may be reproduced in any form or by any means, electronic, mechanical, digital, photocopying or recording, except for the inclusion in a review, without permission in writing from the publisher.

Excerpts from non-authorial interviews and other material appear under a Fair Use Rights claim of U.S. Copyright Law, Title 17, U.S.C. with copyrights reserved by their respective rights holders.

Many of the designations used by manufacturers to distinguish their products are claimed as trademarks or service marks. Where those designations appear in this book and the publisher was aware of such a claim, the designations contain the symbols ®, SM, or TM. Any omission of these symbols is purely accidental and is not intended as an infringement.

Because this page cannot legibly accommodate all the copyright notices, the notices appear at the back of the book in a section titled "Credits," which constitutes an extension of the copyright page.

Published in the USA by:
BearManor Media
PO Box 1129
Duncan, Oklahoma 73534-1129
www.bearmanormedia.com

ISBN 978-1-59393-233-6

Printed in the United States of America.
Cover design by Christopher Darling.
Book design by Brian Pearce | Red Jacket Press.

Table of Contents

Preface/Acknowledgments ...7
Foreword................................ 13
Robert Aldrich...................... 17
Robert Altman..................... 23
Dorothy Arzner 29
James Bridges..................... 37
Richard Brooks 45
Frank Capra......................... 53
Charles Chaplin 59
George Cukor 65
Michael Curtiz..................... 73
Cecil B. DeMille 79
Edward Dmytryk 85
Blake Edwards 91
Victor Fleming 95
John Ford 101
John Frankenheimer.......... 107
Samuel Fuller 113
D.W. Griffith....................... 121
Howard Hawks................... 127
Alfred Hitchcock 131
John Huston....................... 137
Elia Kazan.......................... 143
Stanley Kramer 151
Stanley Kubrick................. 159
David Lean 167
Sidney Lumet 173
Rouben Mamoulian 179

Joseph L. Mankiewicz 187
Leo McCarey...................... 195
Vincente Minnelli................ 203
Sam Peckinpah.................. 209
Arthur Penn 217
Michael Powell 223
Otto Preminger 231
Nicholas Ray 237
Michael Ritchie 245
Martin Ritt.......................... 251
John Schlesinger............... 257
Donald Siegel.................... 263
George Stevens................. 271
Preston Sturges................. 277
Frank Tashlin 283
King Vidor.......................... 289
Raoul Walsh 297
Orson Welles..................... 303
William Wellman................ 311
Billy Wilder......................... 317
Robert Wise 323
William Wyler..................... 329
Peter Yates 337
Fred Zinnemann................ 345
Selected Bibliography 351
Credits 357

For James Bridges and Jack Larson

"I feel cheated. I just feel cheated of all the great things he woulda done that I'm never gonna see."

— JIMMY J, *SEPTEMBER 30, 1955*
SCREENPLAY BY JAMES BRIDGES

Preface/ Acknowledgments

Considering how hard they had to fight to make their first films, no wonder most directors hang on as long as they can before making their last. The reasons a career ends vary: Some directors die or become infirm; some rack up too many flops to get financing; some can't find backing for projects they want to do and can't summon interest for those that are offered. And some just get tired of the Hollywood bullshit.

But many great filmmakers find themselves shut out of a system they once dominated. A chilling example of this: In the mid-1980s, Arthur Penn (*Bonnie and Clyde, The Miracle Worker, Night Moves*) attended a preview of a new blockbuster with his son, Matthew. When it was over, studio representatives handed out survey forms to the audience that asked, "Did you like the ending?" "Should the ending be happier?" "Was the hero likable?" It was filmmaking by popular vote, Matthew recalled, "and Dad looked me with this smile that he had, particularly when it was something bad that involved him, and said, 'That's it for me.' And he was right. During the last twenty years of his life he got to make only one more feature film."[1]

It was grotesque that such a celebrated director — one who arguably revolutionized cinema — could sire a new generation of filmmakers and yet be kept from making another film himself, but there's a long list of directors who outlived their filmographies. Orson Welles took acting jobs and plowed his salary into his own pictures. Fred Zinnemann had to recite his credits to studio tyros too young to know them and too lazy to look them up. Billy Wilder found himself interviewed, awarded, and quoted for the last 21 years of his life, but never hired, even though his career included *Some Like It Hot, The Apartment, Lost Weekend, Irma La Douce,* and *Sunset Boulevard.* "I didn't suddenly get stupid," he once said.

1. Comments at Arthur Penn memorial, January 15, 2011.

There are talented directors whose first films were also their last. Two that tragically come to mind are Steve Gordon (*Arthur*, 1981) and Barbara Loden (*Wanda*, 1970), both of whom earned acclaim for their debuts but who died without encores, Gordon the year after his hit, Loden after battling Hollywood and cancer for ten years.

Some who were successful in other movie disciplines retreated after one directorial turn: writers Robert Riskin (*When You're in Love*, 1937), Ernest Lehman (*Portnoy's Complaint*, 1972), and George S. Kaufman (*The Senator Was Indiscreet*, 1947); actors Peter Sellers (*I Like Money*, 1961) and Dom DeLuise (*Hot Stuff*, 1979); choreographer Patricia Birch (*Grease II*, 1982); cinematographers John Alonzo (*F.M.*, 1978) and William A. Fraker (*The Legend of the Lone Ranger*, 1981); and, most memorably, renaissance man Charles Laughton (*Night of the Hunter*, 1955).

This book chronicles the last films of fifty great directors who had substantial careers before. In many cases the reason is purely physical: Filmmaking is so demanding that it's predominately a young person's craft. Even though older, more experienced directors can operate more efficiently, the stamina to stand for fourteen hours a day, command a crew, engage actors, and wield the immense mechanism of production demands an endurance that few possess in their later years. For every Hitchcock, Altman, Buñuel, Bergman, Huston, or Eastwood who works into his 70s or 80s there are scores more who hang up their megaphones in their 60s. A few years can make an enormous difference on the set, not to mention in getting insurance or prying budgets from nervous studio executives half the director's age. (In what other art form is youth more valued than maturity?) "There comes a time," wrote *The New York Times'* Bosley Crowther in his lament over Charles Chaplin's *A Countess From Hong Kong*, "when one wishes quietly that there were some polite and gentle way to prevent or restrain great artists…from hammering away at their old crafts after they have reached a certain plateau of accomplishment or age."[2] (Crowther's statement becomes ironic when one notes that he lost his job nine months later when he missed the critical boat on *Bonnie and Clyde*.)

Most of what follows is being collected for the first time. When the filmmakers in this book began their careers, production news was provided to studio-controlled fan magazines and was spun, if not wholly invented, to feed the system at the expense of history. By the time of these final films, however, motion picture scholarship had become established

---

2. *New York Times*, March 26, 1967.

and archivists were preserving the documents of movie companies and those who worked for them. Remarkably little of the material that follows has been explored beyond perfunctory citations in the penultimate chapters of various biographies.

All of the directors in these pages created estimable bodies of work. Most were products of the studio system in its heyday who found themselves unable to adapt to the independent financing, production, and distribution circus that replaced it in the 1960s. Some, like Robert Altman, John Huston, and Orson Welles were already fiercely independent and simply entered a new creative phase. Even directors who were known for their bravado, like Howard Hawks, William Wellman, Raoul Walsh, and George Stevens faced, at some point, a fatal disconnect with their public.

The stories behind these films are as touching as they are varied. George Cukor heard the clock ticking while he was making *Rich and Famous* (1981). Not only was he then the oldest working member of the Directors Guild of America, but production stopped every afternoon so the eighty-one-year-old director could take a nap. Robert Altman hid his cancer while he was rushing to finish *A Prairie Home Companion* (2006). Alfred Hitchcock's 1976 *Family Plot* was moderately successful but his dear friend Lew Wasserman, who ran the studio, prevailed on him to prepare another film even though both men knew it would never be made. Director William Wyler took on *The Liberation of L.B. Jones* in 1969 because it was a provocative story about racial intolerance, but Wyler's World War II hearing loss compromised his speed and he fell behind schedule until his loyal crew conspired to cover for him with the studio.

There is a perception that late films are less interesting than those made in a director's prime. Not so; fully half of the titles in this book won plaudits on their initial release and even today would make current filmmakers envious. Joseph L. Mankiewicz earned Oscar® nominations with *Sleuth* (1973); David Lean left movies with a knighthood and fresh acclaim for *A Passage to India* (1984); Samuel Fuller made such a powerful statement about racism in *White Dog* (1982) that his studio was afraid to release it; and Orson Welles, unable to get financing for his ambitious dramatic works, combined documentary and fiction so well in *"F" for Fake* (1973) that he paved the way for reality TV. The ultimate phoenix is John Huston. The durable director of *The Maltese Falcon* and *Key Largo* had dropped out of the pantheon with *Phobia* (1980), *Victory* (1981), and *Annie* (1982). Yet in 1984 he reclaimed his spurs with *Under the Volcano* and confirmed it in 1985 with *Prizzi's Honor*, finally bowing out in 1987 with the sublime (and posthumously released) *The Dead*.

In order to be included in this book, which is admittedly U.S.-centric, a director must meet four criteria:

He has to be dead

The last film has to have been a scripted theatrical feature

He must have enjoyed a substantial career

There must exist sufficient documentation to tell the story of making the film.

Alert readers will by now have cringed at the over-use of the pronoun *he*. This is not solely a matter of grammar. Regrettably, only one woman — Dorothy Arzner — was both prolific and well enough documented to include. Even Ida Lupino, the movies' second-most-celebrated female director during the studio era, veered into television after a number of remarkable early features, and her last film, *The Trouble with Angels* (1966), was a work-for-hire over which she had scant control. Living female directors such as Kathryn Bigelow, Mimi Leader, Jane Campion, Julie Dash, Plyllida Lloyd, Amy Heckerling, Julie Taymor, and Mira Nair are, one hopes, nowhere near the end of their careers, and are therefore happily, if ironically, excluded.[3] The same is true for Asian, Native American, and African-American filmmakers. The careers of African-American directors such as Oscar Micheaux,[4] Henry Hampton, Gordon Parks, Jr., and Gordon Parks, Sr. were either too brief or too undocumented;[4] and current directors of color — Antoine Fuqua, the Hughes brothers, Robert Townsend, Carl Franklin, John Singleton, Melvin van Peebles, Michael Schultz, Tyler Perry, and Spike Lee, for example — are very much alive.

By limiting the contents to fifty I've had to leave out many major figures whose work I respect but for whom I didn't have space, access, research, or personal affinity. If there is ever a *Final Cuts II*, this may change.

The stories that follow remind us of how much of what goes into making a movie never appears on the screen, primarily the posturing and positioning (let's call it bullshit, shall we?) within the corporate art form known as motion pictures. Every film is a struggle even before the

---

3. Norah Ephron died after this manuscript closed.
4. Micheaux is well represented by Patrick McGilligan's *Oscar Micheaux: The Great and Only: The Life of America's First Black Filmmaker*. New York: HarperPerennial, 2007.

camera rolls, and it's astonishing how many obstacles are placed in the way of experienced and talented filmmakers by people who are neither. As one reads these accounts one begins to see that if as much energy was spent *making* movies as on *thwarting* them, film history would be different. And probably better.

Acknowledgment goes to Howard Prouty, Barbara Hall, and the staff of the Margaret Herrick Library of the Academy Foundation of the Academy of Motion Picture Arts and Sciences for generous access to a wealth of special material, much of it hitherto unexplored. Thanks to Peggy Alexander and the staff of the UCLA Performing Arts Special Collections for their archival work, and the WGA Shavelson-Webb Library, Karen Pedersen, director.

Loving thanks to those who kept me focused during this necrology and the years that led up to it: my indomitable agent, Agnes Birnbaum of Bleecker Street Associates, Inc.; Ami and Ivanna Lahmani and their children Adam and Joseph-Benjamin. And a special shout-out to BearManor's passionate publisher, Ben Ohmart, and editor Sandra Grabman.

Thanks also to friends and facilitators, past and present, now and gone: Leslie Agnew, David Austin, Jack Baker, Claire and Donovan Brandt (Eddie Brandt's Saturday Matinee), Michael Bright, Scott Bushnell, Terry "Ilsa" Byrne, Eileen Cushing, Christopher Darling, Jean Porter Dmytryk, Karl Fasick, Carl Ferrazza, David M. Forbes, A. Alan Friedberg, Murry Frymer, Karen Golden; Hope Goldsmith, Gary Goldstein, Jane Badgers Harris, Arnold Herr, Dana Hersey, Ed Hettstrom, Edith Horne, Larry Jackson, Nico Jacobellis, Saul Kahan, Mike Kaplan (the younger), Mike Kaplan (the elder), David Kleiler, Barry Krost, Christine LaMonte, Jane Lanouette, Jack Larson, Michael Lennick, Paul A. Levi, Alice and Leonard Maltin, John Markle, Janet Maslin, Myron Meisel, Stephen M. Mindich, James Robert Parish, Arthur and Peggy Penn, Matthew Penn, Scott Peterson, JD and Susan Pollack, Jim Ringle, Deac Rossell, Nat Rudich, Henry Santoro, Nancy Seltzer, Larry Silverman, Clark Smidt, Jim "Hotspell" Spellmeyer, Richard Stanley, Judy Stark, Allan Taylor, Teller, and Bill Weber.

Four disclaimers. 1) This book is full of spoilers; the oldest title is eighty years ago and if you haven't seen it by now it's your own fault. 2) The year of a film's release is included only if it's germane to the storytelling. 3) Much of the information is drawn from trade papers such as *Variety* and *The Hollywood Reporter*. In recent years these papers of record have abandoned their historic duty to report the minutiae of show business in favor of running puff pieces; as such, they have become practically useless for scholarship. 4) In footnotes you'll see the phrases *Interview with the author* and *Conversation with the author*. The first indicates that the material is from my formal interview while the second comes from social chats that are subject to the vagaries of memory. Weight should be given to the former, attention to the latter.

Nat Segaloff
Los Angeles

Foreword

From 1970 to 1975 I was a studio publicist. Part of my job was setting up interviews for touring celebrities with the entertainment press. Then, from 1976 to 1991, I switched sides and worked as one of the self-same entertainment press, often speaking to people I'd worked for a few years earlier. The professions never overlapped but the relationships did, and some of the information and insights in these pages come from the intimacy that I enjoyed with a remarkable number of filmmakers, many who are now gone. I do not pretend to be objective; try passing joints with Robert Altman and not be seduced by his charisma and intellect; sit across from Arthur Penn and realize that this is the man who changed American cinema; smile at being called "kid" by John Huston during the last poker game he would ever play; or commiserate with James Bridges about how hard it was to fire a star from a movie that only got financing because that star agreed to be in it.

Crossing from one side of the street to the other carried risks, such as when a producer I'd worked for as a publicist asked me to help him promote a film and I had to decline by explaining that I was there to review it. Then there was the time a film company treated me badly on a press junket because the TV station I represented wasn't important enough. The next day I bumped into the company's executives while I was having breakfast with an old friend from my publicity days who also happened to have directed that company's biggest hit of the previous year. Boy did I get apologies.

One of my mentors, the late journalist and novelist Gregory Mcdonald, once told me that "there are no wrong questions," and he was right. When you have a microphone or note pad in your hand you can ask anything. Just as amazingly, your interview subject usually feels compelled to answer.

"Is it true that somebody once asked to see a script of *M*A*S*H* while you were filming it and it took you half an hour to find one?" I asked Robert Altman, trying to untangle the rumor that he and his actors made it up as they went along. "Probably," Altman said, but then he clarified,

"When you're making a movie, by the time you get to the set, you know the script so well that you don't need the pages you're going to shoot that day." Then he added that the script supervisor certainly had a copy if they needed it. As for the film's blood and profanity — the first studio release to use the "F" word — Altman said, "The whole point of [M*A*S*H] was to do that film in such incredibly bad taste that you would have everybody laughing because nothing could be in worse taste than war itself. These bodies that people blow up and then send back in a helicopter and say, 'fix this' like a carburetor. It wasn't intellectual, it was visceral."

Martin Ritt and I shared stories of the Blacklist — I as a scholar, he as a victim — but, despite numerous pleas on my behalf, I could never persuade him to let me write his biography. "Look, Nat," he'd say in that gravely, world-weary voice, "Every time I make a film, the shitheels come out of the woodwork" — "shitheels" to Marty were the right-wingers like Hilton Kramer who made a career out of recalling the long-settled past — "and I don't want my family or me to have to go through it between pictures, too." I thought of that when I was chatting with Cliff Robertson, who had been blacklisted in Hollywood, not for his politics but because he caught Columbia Pictures chief David Begelman forging a check in his name.

Because I was a freelancer, and therefore had no publisher to protect me, I made it a point to tape record almost all my interviews from 1972 on. Those tapes, plus assorted videos and lots of paperwork, are now in my UCLA Performing Arts Special Collection. Call it luck, foresight, or paranoia, but that material informed this book. I can only hope that future scholars access it and remember that, while there are no wrong questions, some of the answers might need a little explaining.

I said at the outset that no director plans on a particular movie being his last, at least not while he's making it. I should add that today it's become hard to make even a second one. "In the old days they used to *help* a producer make a film," John Houseman once told me. "Now they *dare* him." The directors in this book displayed a combination of skill, gumption, and luck. But they also had the good fortune to work at a time when Hollywood was interested in making movies instead of "product" and original thought was considered an asset, not a risk. The studio system flourished because it made movies that audiences paid to see, not because clever accountants fabricated profits by laying off the risk on ancillary markets. "What's truly important," a director I won't name told me, "is the asses in the theater seats, not the assholes in the studio suites."

In a business that wants to be an art form, creative tension gets the juices flowing. Perhaps directors *should* treat each film as if it could be their last. That way it might be good enough that it won't be.

Robert Aldrich directing ...*All the Marbles*.

ROBERT ALDRICH
The Tough Get Going

Delicate is not a word that settles upon Robert Aldrich; most of his films have all the subtlety of a nuclear explosion, which, in fact, is exactly how he ended *Kiss Me Deadly*. Yet his work is neither ham-fisted nor accidental. Let's call it assertive, much like the man himself, and the combination of his personality and the precision with which he made his pictures left an entertaining and sometimes startling legacy.[5]

Aldrich's biggest hit was the 1967 World War II action picture *The Dirty Dozen*, in which a team of convicted felons is offered clemency if they will launch a suicide mission to kill a cadre of vacationing Nazis in a bold attempt to disrupt the German High Command just before D-Day. At the time he directed it, Aldrich was barely fifty, at the peak of his powers, and the violent ensemble drama showed it.

Ironically, Aldrich had come to the movies from an economics background and in that capacity entered Hollywood filmmaking as a clerk at RKO. His training at that chronically cash-strapped studio led him to become a production manager and assistant director which, contrary to its title, has less to do with actors than in making crews adhere to schedules. Among the directors he assisted were Joseph Losey, Charles Chaplin, Robert Rosson, Lewis Milestone, and William Wellman. This gave Aldrich a respect for budgets and an insider's knowledge of how to stretch them. He had to leave features to become a director — on

---

5. It was the late critic Stuart Byron who called this to my attention. A former publicist himself, he took me to task for not pushing Aldrich's 1973 *Emperor of the North Pole* as an auteurist work. "Look at the placement of the people in his shots," Stuart said. "In each one you can tell the relationship of the characters to each other and to their setting. Only Hitchcock does it as well." He was right. And *Emperor of the North* (Fox later took off *Pole* because they thought audiences would think it was about Eskimos) is a stunning film.

Republic Pictures' TV series *China Smith* (1952) — but was lured to MGM in 1953 where he directed *The Big Leaguer*. It was his next film, however, that set his career trajectory: *World for Ransom* (1954) on which he used some of his cast and crew from the *China Smith* TV show to turn out the feature more cheaply.[6] He grouped them in a company he called Associates and Aldrich, notably according his collaborators first billing.

Two Burt Lancaster action hits followed: *Apache* and *Vera Cruz*, both 1954 and both building his box office clout. But it was *Kiss Me, Deadly* in 1955 that established Aldrich as a powerhouse. Scripted by A. I. "Buzz" Bezzerides from Mickey Spillane's "Mike Hammer" private eye novel, it uses the stock structure of a man, a blonde, her death, and his quest to find out why. Only this time the motive isn't Mafia (as in the book), it's espionage, and the penalty isn't merely death, it's atomic annihilation. Because the prize that the bad guys are after is a box containing a critical mass of fissionable material, and, when it's opened, all Hell breaks loose. When United Artists released the film in America they shortened the ending to make it look as though Mike Hammer (Ralph Meeker) and his secretary Velda (Maxine Cooper) perished in the explosion. Only when Aldrich's personal print found its way to the Directors Guild of America after his death in 1983 was the missing footage restored that showed them escaping.

Kiss Me, Deadly, with its no-nonsense style, would typify Aldrich's best work, and when he veered from it, the work suffered. *The Big Knife* (1955), for example, was a wordy, histrionic film of Clifford Odets' wordy, histrionic play about a movie actor weighing the risks of career compromise. Aldrich's next outing, *Autumn Leaves* (1956), with Joan Crawford being romanced by closet maniac Cliff Robertson, presaged his 1960s macabre duo, *Whatever Happened to Baby Jane?* and *Hush…Hush, Sweet Charlotte*. In those gothic dramas he showed not only that he could handle dueling divas but that he could play the audience like a harp.[7] Between those hits, he directed *The Garment Jungle* and *The Angry Hills*, which are more notable for the fights he had with the studio over cuts and credits than for what he went through shooting them.

The last eighteen years of his career taught the combative Aldrich an important lesson: Everybody on the other side of the camera is the enemy.

---

6. Alfred Hitchcock later did the same thing when he shot *Psycho* in 1960 using the crew from his *Alfred Hitchcock Presents* TV series. He also paid them less.

7. There is ample reportage elsewhere of the combat between Bette Davis and Joan Crawford in *Baby Jane*, the veracity of which may be inferred from the lack of combat reported between Davis and her *Charlotte* co-star, Olivia DeHavilland, who replaced Crawford.

He was particularly critical of actors who threw their weight around behind the scenes or held up production. But he didn't discriminate; he had little time for studio executives who thought they could do his job better.[8] And when he was flush with money after *The Dirty Dozen* he set up his own studio so he wouldn't have to take orders from anybody.

The year was 1967 and it was auspicious, for that was the year of *Bonnie and Clyde, The Graduate, Valley of the Dolls, In the Heat of the Night, Cool Hand Luke, The Battle of Algiers, Elvira Madigan, In Cold Blood, I am Curious (Yellow), Point Blank, Robbery, Quatermass and the Pit, Ulysses, Two for the Road,* and *Who's That Knocking at My Door?* After those innovative pictures the Production Code would be modernized into the MPAA's (Motion Picture Association of America) letter-based rating system, and movies would enter the adult age.

Aldrich was one of the first to avail himself of the new screen freedom. First in *The Legend of Lylah Clare*, with Kim Novak as a sensuous movie star, and then with *The Killing of Sister George*, about a doomed lesbian relationship (both 1968), he pushed the industry's boundaries and buttons. Two remarkable war/antiwar films — *Too Late the Hero* (1970), which he also wrote, and *Ulzana's Raid* (1972) — show that Aldrich was at ease talking to a generation of moviegoers that shared his nihilism. *Ulzana's Raid*, in particular, is an unflinching look at military regulations in conflict with experience and pragmatism.

It was the financial failure of 1973's *Emperor of the North*, however, that threw Aldrich for a loop. A stylized Depression-era story of a wise old hobo (Lee Marvin), a mouthy young one (Keith Carradine), and the sadistic train conductor (Ernest Borgnine) who has sworn to keep them both off his express, it sent the director scrambling for something less didactic. And it paid off: back-to-back successes of *The Longest Yard* (1974) and *Hustle* (1975), both with Burt Reynolds, once again gave Aldrich ammunition. He chose to spend it with the very actor who first caused him to distrust actors — Burt Lancaster — on *Twilight's Last Gleaming* (1977), a well-intentioned but on-the-nose polemic about a general (Lancaster) who threatens to start World War III unless the President (Charles Durning) confesses the secret agreements leading up to the Vietnam war. It was the right message at the wrong time; American audiences were fed up with real war and, three months after its unsuccessful release, they would be flocking to see the fictional belligerence of *Star Wars*.

---

8. Author's conversation with Alan Sharp, screenwriter of *Ulzana's Raid*.

But the rustiest nail in Aldrich's creative coffin would be 1977's *The Choirboys*, in which he let his boldness of subject — out of control cops — cross over into sheer vulgarity in a homophobic, sexist, frat house of a movie adapted from Joseph Wambaugh's bestseller. Where Wambaugh, a former Los Angeles cop, used irony and understatement to pillory aberrant policeman, Aldrich could find no screen counterpart, so he just let fly.

...All the Marbles (1981) rose out of the ashes of the MGM Grand Hotel and Casino in Las Vegas, and that's not a metaphor. On December 5, 1973 MGM's then-owner, Kirk Kerkorian, opened the bigger and better complex on the site of several previous casinos, naming it after one of the studio's most prestigious films. On November 21, 1980 a fire started in the hotel's casino restaurant that quickly spread and took the lives of 85 people. For years rumors circulated that the fire was set by the Mob as a warning to Kerkorian to stay out of Atlantic City, where he had floated his intentions. By July of 1981 the Grand was rebuilt bigger and better.[9] Kerkorian never broke ground in Atlantic City.

Cynicism suffuses...*All the Marbles*. In broad strokes — and it was conceived with both broads and stroking in mind — a wily but hapless manager (Peter Falk) guides a female wrestling tag-team called the California Dolls (Vicki Frederick and Laureen Landon) along a low-rent arena circuit until they get their big break in a grudge match against their arch rivals, the Toledo Tigers, held at — ta-DAAA — the MGM Grand Hotel and Casino in Reno. The last half hour of the film is the match, told more or less in real time, with the MGM logo in practically every shot.

Second unit shooting (establishing shots and drive-bys) went first, from November 5 through 14, 1980, under veteran cinematographer Joseph Biroc.[10] Principal photography ran November 14 to February 24, 1981 on locations from Youngstown and Akron, Ohio to Chicago to Los Angeles to Reno to Las Vegas.

...All the Marbles is a film in conflict with itself. As a work of cinema it is pure Aldrich: muscular direction, strong visual storytelling, and kinetic editing all set in a world whose days are eternally cloudy and whose nights seethe in gaudy neon. As a work of drama, however, Mel Frohman's script (also worked on, sans credit, by Michael Barrie, Rich Eustis, and Jim Mulholland)[11] is adrift in creating knowable people. Peter Falk's Harry Sears never progresses beyond explaining that his immi-

---

9. In 1985 it was sold to Bally's and a biggerer and betterer MGM Grand opened in Las Vegas in 1997.
10. Biroc papers, Academy of Motion Picture Arts and Sciences (AMPAS).
11. per *IMDb.com*

grant father raised him on Will Rogers, Clifford Odets, and *The New York Times*; Vicki Frederick's Iris is a pill junkie who goes cold turkey near the end; and Laureen Landon's Molly smokes and finally fights back. That's it. There are plenty of dialogue scenes in the film's first half but they do little to build character, so that by the time the Dolls rassle the Tigers there is nothing emotional at stake, only the $10,000 purse. Thus no matter how hard Frederick and Landon work — and they go the distance, particularly in their matches, which were advised by World Women's Champion Mildred Burke — there is no sense of exhilaration, only relief when the credits roll at 113 minutes. Perhaps the Aldriches — Robert's son William was producer — saw this coming, which is why the script was worked on by a succession of writers, none of whom was able to infuse it with human interest.

Or maybe, like professional wrestling, it was just too sleazy to attract the carriage trade but not violent enough for the mouth-breathers.... *All the Marbles* pulled a disappointing $6.5 million domestic gross but reportedly did much better on the international market where action trumps character and where the film's title was changed to the no-nonsense, straight-up moniker *The California Dolls*.

In its way, it was perfect Aldrich.

Robert Altman in his pre-digital days.

ROBERT ALTMAN
Going for Broke

Every Robert Altman film threatened to be his last. In a career that spanned 36 features, countless TV episodes, and several short subjects (some of which were home movies), he only scored commercial success a handful of times, hardly the track record that Hollywood rewards. What saved him were his low budgets, major stars who yearned to work with him, the critics, and, of course, the quality of the work itself. As for the critics, their fervor was sometimes so fierce as to become scandalous, as when *The New Yorker*'s Pauline Kael reviewed Altman's *Nashville* while it was still editing because its official release was scheduled during her sabbatical and she wanted her remarks on the record.

But Altman didn't care about Hollywood. Barely tolerant of the studio types that he initially had to court in order to get financing (he once remarked that there were many of them he wouldn't want to sit down to lunch with), he nurtured his reputation as a rebel. When someone described him as a cult director, he famously responded, "What is a cult? It just means not enough people to make a minority."[12] Yet even though he was admired and his films were celebrated for their overlapping dialogue, offbeat casting, casual plotting, and wandering camera, they had virtually no influence on other filmmakers. Nobody could make an Altman film but Altman.

Born in Kansas City, Missouri and educated at a combination of Catholic and military schools, Altman joined the Air Force immediately after World War II and flew B-24 bombers. His first marriage (1946-49) to LaVonne Elmer brought him to Los Angeles where he tried to sell scripts but, when he couldn't crack the still-entrenched studio system,

---

12. Conversation with the Author.

they divorced and he returned to Kansas City in 1950. There he made an uncountable number of industrial films and commercials until he could return to Hollywood, which he did in 1956. By then he had assembled the financing to write, produce, and direct an independent dramatic film, *The Delinquents*.[13] This gained the attention of Norman Lloyd and Joan Harrison, who produced Alfred Hitchcock's television show, and they engaged Altman to direct a pair of episodes. Other television followed, a lot of it, so much that Altman claimed he took his first studio feature, *Countdown* (1968), "Just to get out of television."[14] Based on William W. Spencer's novel *The Pilgrim Project*, in which NASA sends a lone astronaut on a suicide mission to the moon to beat the Russians there, it introduced what would become Altman's signature style: overlapping dialogue, events happening organically rather than being contrived, and actors who were *behaving* rather than *acting*. (It didn't hurt that those actors included Robert Duvall, James Caan, and Michael Murphy.)

Still, it didn't distinguish him; when he was handed *M*A*S*H* in 1969 he was either the fifteenth, sixteenth, or seventeenth director that Twentieth Century-Fox tried to entice. The only reason he got as much freedom as he did to make it was that the studio was distracted at the time by their bigger budget war picture, *Patton*. On its release in 1970, *M*A*S*H* captured the zeitgeist of the anti-Vietnam war movement and returned almost $38 million in rentals on a $3.5 million negative cost, $10 million more than *Patton* with its $12 million budget. Yet it was *Patton* that got the Oscars®. ("That was a different war," Altman shrugged.[15])

M*A*S*H's success was bittersweet to its director, who insisted he'd signed a flat rate contract and never shared in its immense revenues. "Fox has made over a billion dollars off me," he said in 1983, referring not only to the feature but to its long-running spin-off television series, which he detested, "and they've never even sent me a case of champagne."[16] Regardless, its earnings conferred a decade of opportunity that made him the most celebrated director of the New Hollywood even though, at forty-five, he was twice as old as the film students who were poised to take over the business. His films that followed — *McCabe & Mrs. Miller* (1971), *Images* (1972), *The Long Goodbye* (1973), *Thieves Like Us*

---

13. The film starred Tom Laughlin, whose later fame as "Billy Jack" led the owners of *The Delinquents* to reissue that film and claim that it inspired Laughlin's character.
14. Conversation with the Author. Altman later admitted that the picture had some good things in it.
15. Interview with the Author for WSBK-TV, Boston, 1983.
16. Ibid.

(1974), and *California Split* (1974) — form an unequalled artistic run in American cinema and, as if they weren't enough, were capped in 1975 by *Nashville*.

The same year that *Nashville* was lauded, however, saw the release of *Jaws*[17] and, with it, a shift to a blockbuster mentality and the not-unrelated beginning of the end of America's flirtation with auteurs. Altman survived, largely through the patronage of Fox which, though it may not have sent him Dom Perignon, gave him budgets to make the risky *3 Women* (1977), *A Wedding* (1978), *Quintet* (1979), *Perfect Couple* (1979), and *Health* (1980). During this period he also produced films for other directors, such as Alan Rudolph (*Welcome to L.A.*, 1976) and Robert Benton (*The Late Show*, 1977). The party ended in 1980 with *Popeye*. A quirky musical adaptation of the spinach-eating comic strip sailor, it became a clash of egos among the Disney and Paramount studios who financed it, producer Robert Evans, composer Harry Nilsson, and screenwriter Jules Feiffer. *Popeye* was Robin Williams' first film and nearly Robert Altman's last; he returned from location in Malta to find that his production company, Lion's Gate, had been robbed of much of his editing and audio equipment.[18] Soon after, he relocated to New York, got involved in theatre (*Come Back to the 5 and Dime, Jimmy Dean, Jimmy Dean*, which he later filmed), and made movies by assembling independent financing.[19] Although he deigned to shoot the occasional film in Los Angeles (notably in 1992's *The Player*, a poison pen letter to the industry he love-hated), he came to regard himself as a world filmmaker who did as he pleased.[20]

By the time *A Prairie Home Companion* came his way in 2005, he hadn't worked in three years. After finishing *The Company* (released in 2003), Altman had wanted to do *Paint*, set in the cut-throat world of the New York art scene, but script and cast never gelled. Meanwhile the radio *APHC*'s Garrison Keillor had been itching to write a movie script and contacted Altman through Altman's lawyer, George Sheanshang, who later became Keillor's lawyer, and who connected them with another client, Bill Pohlad of River Road Entertainment. When producer John Penotti of Greene-Street Films and distributor Bob Berny of Picturehouse stepped

---

17. It bears mentioning that *Jaws* is, first and foremost, a brilliant use of pure cinema that arguably became a bigger box office success because of its filmmaking skill.
18. A different Lions Gate than today's full service mini-major.
19. "I live there because there's a good restaurant," he told the Author. "My house."
20. In 1995 he received a heart transplant, something he revealed publicly only when he received a career Oscar® on March 5, 2006 "in recognition of a career that has repeatedly reinvented the art form and inspired filmmakers and audiences alike."

in, a deal was born. Altman and Keillor immediately bonded thanks to their shared Midwestern backgrounds.[21] It will also be noted that none of the participants was connected with a Hollywood studio.

Inspired by the enduring American Public Media (*nee* Minnesota Public Radio) variety show created by Keillor in 1974 and aired almost continually ever since (with a two year break from 1987-1989), the film was written by Keillor from a story by him and Ken La Zebnik. Its gimmick is that the radio station that carries *APHC* has been bought by a Texas conglomerate and the broadcast that comprises the film may be its last. As the usual eclectic collection of entertainers and others gathers, we get a sense of the passing of tradition as well as the idea that looking into the past isn't as constructive as facing the future.

As he filmed it, Altman was diagnosed with leukemia. It's easy to read his disease into the film's attitude, for it displays little of the dry humor for which he and Keillor were known. The star-heavy ensemble included Meryl Streep, Lily Tomlin, Lindsay Lohan, Virginia Madsen, Kevin Kline, Woody Harrelson, John C. Reilly, Tommy Lee Jones, musical guest stars, and actual show personnel. As with all Altman ensemble films there are plots and subplots unified both by a common theme (the passing of an era) and an event (the last show). Cast members perform their songs live, and Altman directed from a wheelchair while wearing an oxygen cannula. Paul Thomas Anderson (*Boogie Nights*) was hired as standby director in case Altman couldn't finish. The short, efficient shooting schedule ran from June 29 through July 28, 2005 in *APHC's* Fitzgerald Theatre in St. Paul, Minnesota. It was enabled by using two, and sometimes three, Sony digital cameras instead of film. The sensitivity of the digital equipment allowed Altman to shoot without cumbersome lighting. He also had everyone on wireless microphones and never told anyone who'd be on camera at any given time.

Actors loved Altman and, according to Tommy Lee Jones (who played the killer mogul), he loved them back. "He has respect for acting and looks on it as a significant part of the process," Jones said, "as opposed to an inconvenience that has to be gotten out of the way somehow so one can go about the real job of cinema."[22]

Altman died on November 20, 2005 after completing the editing and his signature complex sound mix. After early festival screenings, it was released on June 9, 2006. With a budget estimated at $10 million it

---

21. Patrick Z. McGavin, *Screen International*, August 19, 2005.
22. Production notes.

grossed more than twice as much theatrically and, with the after-market, almost certainly went into profits, which is as worthy an epitaph as its good reviews.

If anybody other than Robert Altman had made *A Prairie Home Companion* it would never have been made in the first place. The director's deceptively easygoing style was in sync with Keillor's relaxed self-assurance (that occasionally veers into smugness). Altman continues a cinematic trick he pioneered in *M*A*S*H*, in which he zooms into a character's face and holds the shot long after you'd think he should have cut away. The effect is to isolate the character within a group, invading his privacy and his thoughts. In this and other ways, Altman was a brilliant manipulator, so much so that everyone who worked with him seldom felt manipulated. Studio executives, however, seemed immune to his charms (perhaps they sensed the underlying hostility), but cast and crew willingly submitted because they trusted him and felt secure taking risks.

Because of this, it's hard to ever find a bad performance in an Altman film, an observation he once explained by offering the advice, "Hire good actors." He then elaborated: "By the time we get working and start shooting they know what kind of film we're going to make, they know what their contribution is to be. I don't restrict the actors; I allow them to do what they can do and what they will do; in fact, I insist on it."[23] To achieve this he became a consummate reader of people's moods, and, despite the ego normally ascribed to directors, he usually described his work with *we, us* and *our* — in the collective, rather than the royal sense — referring to the creative community he nurtured.

If the coolness of *A Prairie Home Companion* is a far cry from the ribaldry of *M*A*S*H*, the irony of *Nashville*, the cynicism of *The Player*, or the existential brilliance of *The Long Goodbye* and *McCabe and Mrs. Miller*, it's still a miracle that an 80-year-old filmmaker could pull a visual statement out of a 30-year-old radio show and bring it to the screen with rounded characters and mature themes when directors one third his age were busy remaking TV shows they were too young to have seen and comic books their mothers threw away when they left for film school.

As Billy Wilder said as he left Ernst's Lubitsch's funeral, but which also applies to Robert Altman, "No more Altman. Worse, no more Altman films."

---

23. Interview with the Author, op. cit.

DOROTHY ARZNER
First in Line

"I went out with the big studio era," said Dorothy Arzner with less bitterness than might be expected from the first woman to make a name for herself as a Hollywood director. "I wouldn't say I left it. It left me also."[24]

Although a handful of women had directed movies before her — Lois Weber, Alice Guy Blaché, Isa May Park, Ruth Ann Baldwin, Elizabeth Pickett[25] — it's Arzner who is most often cited as the first woman to build a track record within the male-dominated studio system. Scholars may disagree on whether her films presage modern Feminist doctrine, but there is little question that she addressed casting, tonal, and thematic statements that were later codified by the Women's Movement. She made, as Karyn Kay and Gerald Peary wrote, "personal films featuring strong female protagonists" and "worked in Hollywood at a time when women directors were not allowed."[26] It was Arzner's direction of Katharine Hepburn in *Christopher Strong* (1933) that brought the star's steely core into view after George Cukor showed her sensitive side in the previous year's *A Bill of Divorcement*. Under her guidance in *Craig's Wife* (1936), Rosalind Russell's career trajectory was redefined. She allowed Irene Dunne to reveal a sense of humor in *Theodora Goes Wild* (1936) after the versatile actress had been mired in weepies like *Back Street* (1932) and *Magnificent Obsession* (1935). And she turned the serene Merle Oberon into an action hero in *First Comes Courage* (1943). Yet it is also *First Comes Courage* that

---

24. Dorothy Arzner, UCLA Special Collections, Oral History Project interview.
25. Ally Acker. *Reel Women: Pioneers of the Cinema 1896 to the Present*. New York: Continuum Publishing Company, 1991.
26. Karyn Kay and Gerald Peary, "Interview with Dorothy Arzner," first published in *Cinema* (U.S.) in 1970, and in the co-authors' *Woman and Cinema: a Critical Anthology*. New York: Dutton, 1977.

marked Arzner's final theatrical feature despite a successful commercial track record and her acceptance by the male moguls who hired her.

Arzner began her career, like many working women of her era, as a secretary. Born in 1900[27], she waited tables in her father's Hollywood restaurant and went to the University of Southern California with the goal of being a doctor (not, please note, a nurse). "I wanted to be like Jesus," she said: "'Heal the sick and raise the dead,' instantly, without surgery, pills, et cetera."[28] When that notion died, she declared for movies and won a job as script typist at $15 a week with William C. DeMille at Famous Players. Before long she realized that what she really wanted to do was direct "because he [sic] was the one who told everyone else what to do."[29]

Six months later she was in the cutting room of Realart, the low-rent subsidiary of Paramount Pictures, which is what Famous Players-Lasky had become, editing 52 pictures in two years. Her innovative cutting of the Rudolph Valentino bullfighting movie *Blood and Sand* (1923) and James Cruze's landmark western epic *The Covered Wagon* (1923) made her invaluable to Paramount, but after she co-wrote, edited, and was script supervisor on Cruze's 1926 *Old Ironsides* — all without credit — she knew it was time to rebel. Holding a job offer from Columbia's Harry Cohn, for whom she had written scripts between Paramount jobs, she pressured Paramount head B. P. Schulberg into letting her direct a picture for him.[30] The result, *Fashions for Women* (1927), was a hit, and, thereafter, so was she. People liked her. "No one gave me trouble because I was a woman," she later recalled. "Men were more helpful than women."[31]

Over the next sixteen years she directed nineteen more pictures, in whole or part, mostly for Paramount, but also for RKO, Goldwyn, MGM, and, finally, Columbia. Guiding such major actresses in addition to Hepburn, Russell, and Dunne as Clara Bow, Sylvia Sidney, Ruth Chatterton, Claudette Colbert, Lucille Ball, Maureen O'Hara, and Joan Crawford, Arzner — according to critic Mary Murphy, and she's not alone — "changed the image of women onscreen. In the wild and experimental days after the transition to sound, Arzner captured with unique force the emotional reality of women alone and in relationships with friends, lovers, roommates, and rivals. Her women were full characters."[32]

27. Some sources say January 3, 1897.
28. Kay and Peary, op. cit.
29. Kay and Peary, ibid.
30. Kay and Peary, ibid.
31. Kay and Peary, ibid.
32. Mary Murphy, *Los Angeles Times*, January 24, 1975.

Add Kay and Peary, "She deserves the feminists' applause for she has documented the lives of all women in the complex struggle for career, independence, integrity, and love."[33] At the time she was working, however, Arzner doesn't seem to have had such an agenda, although it's hard to know for sure, as the gears of the publicity machine were not turning in her direction. Nor, for that matter, did they favor anybody other than stars; "Lasky Names Woman Director" is how the trades covered Arzner's Paramount hiring. Movies remained a men's club.

"Maybe producers felt safer with men," Arzner opined in a 1976 interview. "They could go to a bar and exchange ideas more freely…Today, of course, even the stars are all men. When men do put women in pictures, they make them so damned sappy, weeping all over the place, that it's disgusting."[34]

Craig's Wife broke that mold. Harriet Craig (Rosalind Russell) dominates her rich husband (John Boles) in her climb to the top. Although Russell reportedly tried to get out of doing the film, it won her acclaim and stardom, and the picture itself drew critical appreciation even though it was not a moneymaker. Arzner saw Russell's character not as a hard-nosed aggressor but as "a woman who is ultimately regenerated."[35] Unfortunately, Harry Cohn, the similarly aggressive ruler of Columbia Pictures, thought women should be passive and pure, and the film's bare commercial break-even did little to change his sexist mind. Nevertheless, in 1942 he okayed the production of *First Comes Courage* and brought Arzner back from RKO where she had just directed *Dance, Girl, Dance* (1940) with Maureen O'Hara and Lucille Ball.

Adapted by George Sklar and scripted by Lewis Meltzer and Melvin Levy from Elliott Arnold's 1942 novel *The Commandos*, it was slated for production at the very end of that year, first under that title, then with the title changed to *Attack By Night*.[36] The studio synopsis provided to press at the time makes *First Comes Courage* (its final title as of May 24, 1943) sound like wartime morale-lifting fare: Nicole (Merle Oberon) lives in the Nazi-occupied Norwegian town of Stavik.[37] Her neighbors loathe her for consorting with the Commandant of the German garrison, Major

33. Karyn Kay and Gerald Peary, *Dorothy Arzner*, Films By Women/Chicago, 1974.
34. Source uncertain; possibly *The New York Times*, August 30, 1976. The photocopy in Arzner's AMPAS file is incomplete but the font appears to be the one used by the *Times*.
35. Murphy, op. cit.
36. *IMDb.com* cites Harry Joe Brown as adapter and Sklar as co-screenwriter with Meltzer and Levy but Academy records of June 4, 1943 and MPAA records of June 15, 1943 do not.
37. Changed from France to Norway to capitalize on public interest in occupied Norway. (*Hollywood Reporter*, December 29, 1942.)

Dichter (Carl Esmond), but they don't know that she is using her friendship to gain secrets that she conveys to the British via the local optician, Dr. Aanrud (Fritz Leiber), who writes her dispatches with invisible ink on the eyeglasses of Norwegian fishermen. Aanrud warns Nicole that, if Dichter ever suspects her, he, Aanrud, will arrange for the Nazi's execution. This comes to pass, but not before Dichter pressures Nicole into marriage, which she accepts, thinking it will maintain her cover.[38] On their honeymoon, however, he reveals his plan to murder her. Fortunately, Colonel Allan Lowell (Brian Aherne), who was Nicole's lover when he lived in Stavik before the war, is the Commando who is sent to kill Dichter. He does, but is wounded by Nazis and taken to a prison hospital. Nicole, with the help of a nurse who happens to be in the underground, helps him escape, and as he prepares to sail to England he asks Nicole to join him. She refuses, preferring to stay in Norway and be a patriot, but he swears they shall reunite at war's end.

Arzner scholars in subsequent years have reappraised *First Comes Courage* and remarked less on its stock plot points (which the film's contemporary critics noted unenthusiastically) than in their cinematic execution.[39] More about this later.

The 40-day shoot began on December 31, 1942, with interiors at Columbia and exteriors, in part, on Mt. Wilson. This involved a dramatic stunt in which Otto Mazetti, a former circus tumbler (and brother of actor Richard Talmadge, who later emigrated to the USSR, where he became a star), doubled for Ahern in falling "over a jagged precipice" onto the roof of a shack some forty feet below.[40]

Despite the "conventionally developed plot,"[41] some attention was given to authenticity. Studio craftsmen built five perfect models of Norwegian sailing ships as miniatures for the film, including a model of Roald Amundsen's The Gjoa. Actual Commandos from Vancouver Island in Victoria, B.C. played themselves using tactics "so revolutionary that they must be kept secret for months to come" (or at least until the film was released). And just to make sure that no actual Norwegians were offended by the suggestion that there might be collaborators among them, E. Wessel Klausen, the picture's technical adviser, announced that ninety-five percent of Norway's 2,900,000 residents were loyal to the Allies and, of those, only two percent were Quislings. (As Norway was

38. The official sanctions their wedding rings upon a copy of *Mein Kampf*.
39. Columbia press notes, May 27, 1943.
40. This and three following items were publicity factoids from Columbia's pressbook.
41. *Variety*, December 2, 1943.

still under Nazi occupation at the time, that still left 2,900 to worry about).

A week before the end of the shooting schedule, Arzner fell ill with pneumonia and was forced to leave the production, so director Charles Vidor took over. According to the film's cinematographer, Joseph Walker, Vidor showed up on the set one day and announced, "Arzner's off the picture. Cohn thinks the thing's a dud. He's not about to spend any more money on it. My orders are to finish it in fast order."[42] When Arzner recovered, she left the studio and took her feature film career with her. The picture was released on July 29, 1943, but this date is arguable because most reviews appeared in December of 1943, noting that the film had been shot a year earlier.

Scholars Kay and Peary, who secured a rare late interview with Arzner, state that Vidor directed the final scenes and offer extensive supportive comment in their *Chicago 74* piece lauding Arzner's inventiveness prior to that. These touches include the camera following a child's handball falling to the ground and being kicked by booted Nazi soldiers; a woman medic bravely choosing death over treason; and sudden bursts of violence in otherwise serene settings. There are others, too: foreshadowing Oberon's and Ahern's relationship by dissolving between them drinking cups of coffee; but especially Oberon's performance, which is assured and staged to reflect her character's strength. But these went largely unremarked at the time. *The Los Angeles Times* said only "Some scenes…suffer from overstressing" and notes that audience members laughed at them.[43] *Variety* said that its "situations are too static to permit above average performances."[44] Columnist Dorothy Manners, however, writing for the *Los Angeles Herald-Examiner*, praised "the entire sequence involving the capture of Commando Aherne, his imprisonment in a Nazi prison hospital, and the subsequent "exciting escape engineered by her ladyship and one of the patriot nurses."[45] *Commonweal* admitted that "the melodrama gets pretty thick" but praised Arzner for "[knowing] how to build up cinema in an exciting style, and the film's editor [Viola Lawrence] uses cross-cutting to keep you on the edge of your chair…The principals in the cast never warm up to all the heroism except for one scene that vibrates with theater as Nicole and Dichter tell each other off after the wedding."[46]

42. Joseph B. Walker and Juanita Walker. *The Light on Her Face*. Hollywood, CA: The American Society of Cinematographers Press, 1991.
43. Edwin Schallert, *Los Angeles Times*, December 2, 1943.
44. *Variety*, op. cit.
45. Dorothy Manners, *Los Angeles Herald-Examiner*, December 2, 1943.
46. No byline, *Commonweal*, September 10, 1943.

First Comes Courage is either the summation of Arzner's studio career or an aberration. Her biographer, Judith Mayne, believes that it differs only somewhat in that Oberon/Nicole is not a grounded woman but exhibits "mythic heroism." She's not just a woman trying to survive at work but is a patriot on a mission. Nevertheless, "*First Comes Courage* twists the gender conventions with the war/spy game, and in the process, celebrates women's work, not *as* love and romance, not as a *substitute* for love and romance, but as what makes everything else possible."[47]

After she recovered, Arzner directed war training films for the WACs and moved into industrials after the war. She also produced some 50 Pepsi commercials for her friend Joan Crawford, who was then married to Alfred N. Steele, the CEO and Chairman of the Pepsi-Cola Company. She taught at UCLA for four years in the 1960s (where one of her students was Francis Ford Coppola) and retired to La Quinta, near Palm Desert, California. On January 25, 1975 the Committee of Women Members of the Directors Guild of America — of which Arzner was the first female DGA member — celebrated her with a tribute hosted by Ida Lupino. Katharine Hepburn sent a wire that read, "Isn't it wonderful you've had such a great career when you had no right to have a career at all."

Arzner died at her home on October 1, 1979. Her *Daily Variety* obituary coldly reported "No survivors, no services"[48] but in fact she is survived by, so far, three generations of women filmmakers who got through Hollywood's door, in part, because Arzner kicked it open with her talent and the ability to wield it.

---

47. Judith Mayne. *Directed by Dorothy Arzner*. Bloomington and Indianapolis, Indiana: The University of Indiana Press, 1994.
48. *Daily Variety*, October 4, 1979.

James Bridges.

JAMES BRIDGES
Gentleman Jim

Nobody in Hollywood expected *Bright Lights, Big City* to be James Bridges' last film. MGM was romancing the 52-year-old filmmaker to write and direct their modern western, *Road Show*; he and Larry McMurtry had the backing to make *Desert Rose*, about a Las Vegas showgirl and her daughter; he was writing *The Occupation of Paris* remembering the time the Army took over his Paris (Arkansas) hometown during World War II; and Clint Eastwood had taken a liking to his and Peter Viertel's script of *White Hunter, Black Heart*, drawn from Viertel's 1953 *roman-à-clef* about John Huston making *The African Queen* in 1951. But in 1992 Bridges developed cancer.

A soft-spoken Southerner, Bridges came to Hollywood in his 20s to pursue acting but found his voice as a playwright through the mentoring of John Houseman and Norman Lloyd, who was then producing the Alfred Hitchcock television show. The Hitchcocks led to other TV shows in the early 60s and then to writing the theatrical feature *The Appaloosa* (1966) for director Sidney J. Furie but, more importantly, for its star, Marlon Brando. It was, however, his intelligent script for *Colossus: The Forbin Project*, from D. F. Jones' novel about an alliance between American and Russian super-computers that achieve world peace by holding the human race captive, that gave him the career momentum to direct and write *The Baby Maker* in 1970. A frank but non-sensationalized drama about a surrogate mother who becomes too close to the parents who hire her, it gave Bridges, by then 34, the reputation as a director who knew how to handle young actors. "I really enjoy working with people who have not, as Kazan says, once they become successful, have turned into wax fruit," Bridges explained. "When I did that film a lot of offers came in."[49]

---

49. Interview with the Author, October 28, 1978.

Before *Baby Maker* was released, he had become house writer to veteran directors Robert Wise and Mark Robson in The Filmmakers Group, a boutique company set up at Universal. There, instead of making his own films, he found himself rewriting Joan Micklin Silver's Vietnam home front drama *Limbo* (a.k.a., *Women in Limbo;* 1972) for Robson and advising Wise on projects like *The Hindenburg* and *Two People*. Bridges felt yoked. It was *The Paper Chase* (1973), based on John Jay Osborn's novel about first-year Harvard Law students, that put him back on track. Timothy Bottoms and Lindsay Wagner (whom he'd met on *Two People*) headed an ensemble that included Edward Herrmann, James Naughton, David Clennon, and Blair Brown, many of whom were beginning their careers. But it was Bridges' casting of John Houseman as the imperious contracts professor Charles W. Kingsfield, Jr. (after James Mason, Melvyn Douglas, John Gielgud, Paul Scofield and others passed on it) that earned the film its greatest acclaim. It also earned Houseman an Oscar® for his performance and a whole new career essentially playing himself.

Bridges didn't do too badly, either. "When *The Paper Chase* came out I was offered an incredible number of films," he recalled, "but I never found anything I really wanted to do. There were things that I wanted to do but they never got off the ground for budget problems or casting problems. The thing is to just do the ones you really believe in."[50] "Never do a project you don't really want to do," he added, "because by the time it's over you've wasted two years of your life and you'll have nothing to show for it."[51]

He had a lot to show for *The Paper Chase,* particularly a clever (and largely un-noted) structure that maintained a rising line of dramatic tension despite the story being spread over a long academic year. Bridges' device was to shape each relationship like a contract: a promise for services (sometimes affection), negotiation, delivery, default, or abrogation. The film was a critical success and enough of a financial hit to be turned into a series for CBS television where it lasted a year, was rerun on PBS, and then was revived on Showtime for three seasons. Bridges had a hand in many of the episodes.

He took huge risks with his next film, the daring and disturbing *September 30, 1955* (a.k.a. *9/30/55*) starring Richard Thomas as a young man who is obsessed with James Dean and leads his friends on a rebellious spree on the day Dean dies. Not only was it an achievement for

---

50. Interview with the Author, October 28, 1978.
51. Conversation with the Author.

Thomas, hitherto the squeaky-clean star of television's *The Waltons*, it was that rare film that examines the impact of celebrities on the public that adores them. Semi-autobiographical as well, it was told by weaving visual and thematic references from Dean's signature films, *East of Eden* and *Rebel Without a Cause*, and even enlisted composer Leonard Rosenmann, who scored *Eden* and *Rebel*, to interpolate his music for those films into this haunting new work.

Despite the American film industry sliding toward mindless action movies in the late 70s, Bridges' next pictures were huge hits that focused on people over special effects. *The China Syndrome*, about a TV fluff reporter who becomes radicalized during a near-meltdown at a nuclear power plant, made headlines when its premiere coincided with a real-life near-meltdown at the Three Mile Island nuclear facility in Harrisburg, Pennsylvania on March 28, 1979.[52] Then he surpassed even that success when he paired John Travolta, fresh off *Saturday Night Fever*, with newcomer Debra Winger in *Urban Cowboy* (1980). Based on a magazine article by Aaron Latham, who co-wrote the script about Texas oil workers who drill all day but party at night at a honky-tonk called Gilley's, riding a mechanical bull instead of the real thing, it caused a sensation for its treatment of sex, sublimation, and the meaning of old-fashioned macho in a newfangled world.

Yet four years passed before Bridges could bring another project to the screen. *Mike's Murder* was ostensibly a mystery about a woman who tries to learn the truth behind her boyfriend's bloody death. But it fell into studio hands that cut back its treatment of violence and drugs, two of the reasons it had been green-lighted in the first place. It also had an undercurrent of bisexuality that made Warner Bros. uncomfortable, and they barely released it in 1984. Bridges bounced back the next year with *Perfect*, which starred John Travolta as a *Rolling Stone* reporter who romances fitness instructor Jamie Lee Curtis, ostensibly to do a story about the LA gym scene, but then betraying her by digging up a scandal from her past. Just as *The Paper Chase* was constructed like a contract, *Perfect* — which Bridges and Latham also co-wrote — took the form of a magazine with a main story, a sub-story, and numerous short takes along the way. Perhaps because *Perfect* attacked the media, the national press chose it as the film that they would vilify in 1985. It knocked Bridges out of the box for three years.

52. At the time the Author was working as a film critic for a TV station owned by Westinghouse, which had supplied materials to Three-Mile Island. He was prevented by station management from covering *The China Syndrome*.

Bright Lights, Big City wasn't even his idea. Jay McInerney's self-conscious second-person novel of 1984 about a would-be writer's descent into cocaine was originally a project that Robert Lawrence of Columbia Pictures bought and gave to producer Jerry Weintraub. He also asked Bridges to do the film with a pre-*Top Gun* Tom Cruise, but Bridges didn't want to work again with Jerry Weintraub (producer of *September 30, 1955*) so he declined. Weintraub then gave it to Joel Schumacher who worked with Cruise while McInerny wrote a first draft in 1986. Then Schumacher rewrote it. Their script reads like a cocaine binge, jumping from the protagonist's crumbling job, to party clubs, to his estranged wife, to his family, all of it set against the background of decaying New York City.

Meanwhile, Robert Lawrence moved from Columbia to United Artists, bought the project back from Weintraub, and brought in producers Sydney Pollack and Mark Rosenberg. Cruise and Schumacher left, Michael J. Fox was signed to star, and director Joyce Chopra and her writer-husband Tom Cole were hired. Fox suggested sending the script to Keifer Sutherland to play his sleazy enabler, Tad Allagash.

Chopra, who'd won awards for her independent films, started shooting in July of 1986. Reports differ on what she was aiming for but, as Pollack and Rosenberg watched her dailies, they felt she was off the mark. Lawrence asked Bridges to step in. Bridges said he wouldn't replace a director, but if UA closed down the picture he would take a look at the materials and then decide. They did, then he did, and his answer was "Yes."

By this time there were seven scripts, each of which got further from the novel as if succeeding executives had given notes, each more destructive than the ones before. Bridges ignored all of them. He came to New York, gave the cast copies of the book with instructions to read it until he had a script, locked himself inside the Sherry-Netherland Hotel, and started typing. With the film closed down for a week (with everybody kept on salary) the pressure was intense to get Fox back to his hit TV series, *Family Ties*. After all, $25 million was at stake.

To make it happen, Bridges laid down rules and Mike Ovitz at Creative Artists Agency got UA to agree to them: "What you're going to get is the novel; none of the executives will be allowed to see the script; and here are the locations we will need." Bridges delivered a final draft on June 29, 1987 and brought in director of photography Gordon Willis, hired actors John Houseman, Frances Sternhagen (replacing Shirley Knight), Charlie Schlatter, Swoozie Kurtz, and Jason Robards. He also wanted McInerny to be an advisor on the film because his novel was, after all, autobiographical. With Bridges at the helm, the production moved swiftly to completion. There was even applause in the screening room when dailies were shown.

Then the focus groups started.

Bright Lights, Big City is a story about a guy who does cocaine. From the git-go, the studio expected it to draw an "R" rating for drug use. But the focus groups were stacked, not with moviegoers, but with teenage girls who loved Michael J. Fox from *Back to the Future* and *Family Ties*. The results, unsurprisingly, showed that Fox's fans wanted to hear their idol speaking lines, not doing them. Bit by bit the cocaine scenes were cut until Bridges finally said "enough." The focus group kids also thought John Houseman looked old and ill (he was; he died of cancer seven months after the film was released) and should be "minimized." Bridges refused to "minimize" his mentor.

Then the sales people got involved. They learned that rival studio Warner Bros. had a turkey coming out at the end of March, and, if the release date of *Bright Lights, Big City* could be moved up a few weeks, it would have a clear shot at box office victory over it. UA did just that and found itself opening against the film that Warner Bros. insiders predicted would flop: *Beetlejuice*, which went through the proverbial roof.

For his efforts in saving the film, Bridges was in for a shock when it came to screen credits. Although it used his script alone, Bridges put McInerny's name on the title page in first position as a courtesy. Nevertheless, McInerny submitted notice of dispute to the Writers Guild, which ruled that McInerny, not Bridges, should receive sole writing credit. UA executives pleaded in Bridges' behalf but were rebuffed. When Bridges reminded the Guild that he was both writer and director, he was told that the Guild had to protect writers from writer-directors "like you."[53]

Bridges was working on his next film, *Desert Rose*, when the cancer struck. There were times when he was too ill from the regimen of radiation and chemotherapy that he was undergoing at UCLA Medical Center to attend production meetings. At first the disease responded to treatment. But then it returned with a mind of its own and, despite doctors' hollow assurances, he died on June 6, 1993.

Before he died, Bridges and his life partner, writer-actor Jack Larson, had set up the Bridges/Larson Foundation to help finance the master film theses of worthy UCLA students who had shown excellence in theatre. "Today's film schools aren't turning out directors," Bridges once said,

---

53. Author's interview with Jack Larson, associate producer, October 3, 2011.

"they're turning out second unit directors. They know all about what to do with the camera but nothing about what to do with the actors."[54]

On May 4, 2007 Jack Larson traveled to the University of Central Arkansas, Bridges' alma mater, to accept a posthumous doctorate in Bridges' name. The UCA Board of Trustees also renamed their James Bridges Theatre as the James Bridges-Jack Larson Theatre. The honor was seen as a repudiation of the 2004 decision by Arkansas voters to pass a state constitutional amendment that barred not only gay marriage but gay civil unions.

At Bridges' memorial service on June 16, 1993 Norman Lloyd described not only the man but the essential decency of his work. It stands as an epitaph to both:

> Jim was untouched by the least bit of snobbery. He was sensibly unpretentious, unaffected in manner, with no touch of malice in him. In Jim's presence one involuntarily felt in himself a desire to be simpler, more truthful, more oneself. Jim, it might be said, lived of his own soul; he was always himself.

---

54. Conversation with the author.

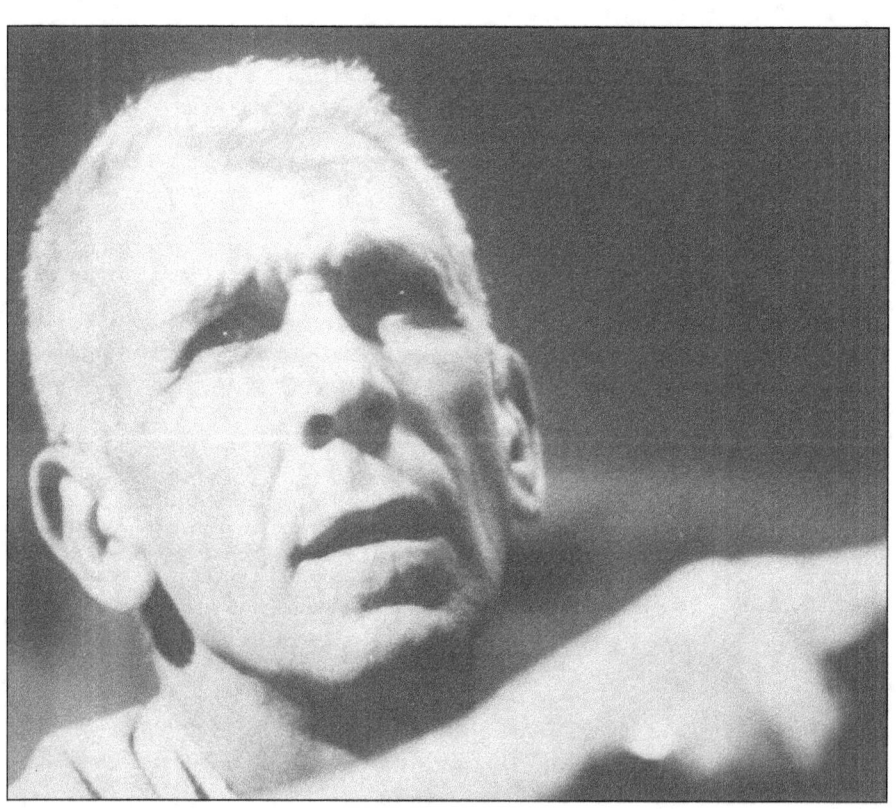
Richard Brooks.

RICHARD BROOKS
Raging Against the Machine

A dual personality was at work in the films of Richard Brooks, if not also within Brooks himself. One is the provocateur who probed explosive social issues such as school delinquency (*Blackboard Jungle*, 1955), the hypocrisy simmering within evangelical religion (*Elmer Gantry*, 1960), violence in a "safe" small town (*In Cold Blood*, 1967), the risk of anonymous sex (*Looking for Mr. Goodbar*, 1977), and checkbook journalism (*Wrong is Right*, 1982). Yet the Temple University-educated Brooks also adapted un-adaptable works of literature for the supposedly Philistine screen: *Lord Jim* (1965), *Sweet Bird of Youth* (1962), *Cat on a Hot Tin Roof*, and *The Brothers Karamazov* (both 1958). He even managed to slip a love story into his oeuvre: *The Happy Ending* (1969), starring his then-wife, Jean Simmons. Unlike his contemporary, Stanley Kramer, who sought to enlighten as well as entertain, Brooks was more like another of his contemporaries, Sam Fuller, who wanted to shake his audiences until they woke up to the world around them. He was, in the words of critic Scott Eyman, "fueled by raw ambition and a furious belief in the power of words."[55]

Born in Philadelphia in 1912 with the name Reuben Sax — he legally changed it in 1943 and seldom acknowledged his Russian-Jewish roots — Brooks was a sports reporter on the Philadelphia *Record* before moving to Los Angeles just prior to World War II. There he became a radio writer and veered into movies (those were the days when people who could write were scouted by studio story departments) carrying the leanness

---

55. *Wall Street Journal*, March 24, 2011.

and timeliness of journalism to a series of eclectic credits from the significant (*Brute Force*, 1947; *Key Largo*, 1948) to the ridiculous (*Cobra Woman*, 1944). He also wrote novels and, after the war, one of them, *The Brick Foxhole* (1945), was made into a hit (*Crossfire*, 1947) for RKO even though the studio changed it from the murder of a homosexual into the murder of a Jew. Nevertheless, the Adrian Scott production and the direction by Edward Dmytryk greased Brooks' ascension to his own director's chair in 1950 with *Crisis*, about a doctor in a foreign dictatorship forced to save the life of a despot whose people would be better off if he were dead.

His breakthrough was *Blackboard Jungle*, in which city teacher Glenn Ford was threatened by juvenile delinquents including Sidney Poitier, Vic Morrow, Jamie Farr, and Paul Mazursky. Adapted by Brooks from a novel by Evan Hunter (a.k.a. Ed McBain), who was himself a disillusioned teacher in the South Bronx, it was the first movie driven by a rock 'n' roll soundtrack (notably Bill Haley and the Comets' "Rock Around the Clock") and became a scandal as well as a sensation. It made Hollywood aware that there was a vast teenage market that wasn't being served by traditional pictures and it taught Brooks that there was gold in them thar social ills. He ventured into controversy again in 1957 with *Something of Value* about racial strife in Kenya; *Cat on a Hot Tin Roof* (1958), in which he had to change Brick Pollitt's homosexuality into a broken leg as the reason he couldn't couple with his wife, Maggie; and won an Oscar® for 1960's *Elmer Gantry* adapting Sinclair Lewis' scathing novel about a sinning faith healer exploiting a devout one.

In his later career, Brooks abandoned his social themes for high adventure. *The Professionals* (1966) became one of the screen's finest westerns pitting Burt Lancaster, Lee Marvin, Robert Ryan, and Woody Strode against the Mexican bandit Jack Palance who has kidnapped Claudia Cardinale, the bride of Ralph Bellamy, only to have the quartet learn at the end that Bellamy has tricked them into kidnapping Cardinale from Palance. It's played for humor, thrills, and resonances with Greek mythology (the kidnapping of Helen of Troy by Theseus), and it cleaned up at the box office. Brooks followed it with his bravura adaptation of Truman Capote's revolutionary non-fiction novel *In Cold Blood*. By the time he made his last film, *Fever Pitch*, he was on a roll that included the near-hit western *Bite the Bullet* (1975), the hauntingly brutal *Looking for Mr. Goodbar*, and the prescient but unsuccessful satire of TV news, *Wrong is Right*.

Fever Pitch (1985) poses Ryan O'Neal as a sports reporter who investigates the coyly named "gaming" industry while hiding the fact from his editors that he is the gambling-addicted "Mr. Green" who is the focus of his stories.[56] The device is clever but its reveal is not; rather than astonish the viewer at a dramatic moment, Brooks lets it drop like a banana peel that never gets stepped on. Maybe he wanted to make a gambling movie that's all bluff — O'Neal's lifeless performance suggests this — but it's a damn shame that the dynamic Brooks folded his cards with a disjointed, frantic polemic.

As Mae West once said, "I generally avoid temptation unless I can't resist it," and *Fever Pitch* is about exactly that. Temptation is the oldest story in the Bible, and the movies have used it (with varying degrees of sanctimony) since the first temperance play overacted its way onto the silent screen. As it happened, many early movies were moral tales aimed condescendingly at the great unwashed who had come to America at the dawn of the Twentieth Century — the carriage trade wouldn't be caught dead at a Nickelodeon — and there was general agreement among the first filmmakers that pictures should be uplifting.

A newspaperman never stops being a newspaperman, and Brooks knew that the thrill of chasing a story was often tempered with the danger of being drawn into it. *Fever Pitch* begins by having O'Neal do a series of interviews to bring himself up to speed on the size and threat of gambling in America. But Brooks falls into the expository trap of having characters tell each other things that they should already know just so the audience can eavesdrop. Among O'Neal's screen encounters (told while simultaneously writing his story and feeding his addiction) are a cocktail waitress/hooker (Catherine Hicks), a young athlete who owes money and whom he asks to throw a game (Tom Schanley), a suicidal soldier (Patrick Cassidy), and a high roller (Giancarlo Giannini). There is also an uncommonly helpful casino manager named Sweeney (Keith Hefner) who apparently just met O'Neal but spills secrets like an old friend. There is a good reason for this geniality: the film is an MGM release set in part at the MGM Grand Hotel in Las Vegas. Not surprisingly, Sweeney comes off as a kindly, protective mensch who helps O'Neal at every turn, even when he good-naturedly offers him a bribe to whitewash the gaming industry in his stories. People who don't work for MGM, however, are darker, such as "The Dutchman" (a highly effective Chad Everett) to

---

56. The device of using a fictitious figure to explore fact, for example, snared *Washington Post* reporter Janet Cooke in 1980 when she faked a series about a drug-addicted 8-year old in "Jimmy's World" and it won her the Pulitzer Prize. Although it was a throwback to the circulation-building "sob sister" reporting that went on in the tabloid press of the 1920s, the *Post* was not known for such gambits. Cooke resigned and returned her 1981 Pulitzer Prize.

whom O'Neal owes the money, and the Dutchman's menacing muscle, Panama Hat (William Smith), who becomes comic relief (it's unclear whether that was intended).

Brooks came to *Fever Pitch* through the side door. When *Wrong is Right* tanked, his *Looking for Mr. Goodbar* producer Freddie Fields, who had taken over MGM/UA, offered him *Road Show*, about a modern-day rancher who organizes his own cattle drive.[57] Jack Nicholson, Mary Steenburgen, and Jim Hutton had already been signed and the studio wanted Brooks to write as well as direct.[58] In July of 1983, however, Brooks was taken to Cedars Sinai hospital with a minor heart attack and was forced to drop out of the troubled project, which was never filmed.

While recovering, he became obsessed with the problem of gambling in America — a $200 billion industry, both legal and illegal, that involves a hundred million people, ten million of whom are addicts.[59] Brooks' research took him to casinos, private gambling clubs, Gamblers Anonymous meetings, and Alcoholics Anonymous meetings. He corresponded with an inmate at Danbury federal prison who told him that the thrill of stealing to find gambling money is the same as the thrill of gambling itself, and he hung with Los Angeles *Herald-Examiner* sports writer Allan Malamed to get the old journalism scent back. It wasn't until writer Hank Greenspan gave his nod, however, that doors truly opened to the writer-director.[60] It took Brooks two years to write, by which time the project was called *The Fever* and had moved to producer Dino DeLaurentiis. It would be a rare (for Brooks) original screenplay rather than an adaptation, and in February of 1984 he was holed up at the MGM Grand in Las Vegas finishing it. He desired Sam Shepard for the lead because "the press itself must believe that he is a writer," and Shepard was. He also wanted to avoid an "R" rating because, "wherever young people are, I want them to see it." Finally he said, defensively, "It's not an anti-Vegas story or a Mafia-linked story."[61] In the end, he lost his trifecta: instead of Shepard he got O'Neal, instead of a "PG" the film got an "R," and the moral vacuum of Vegas seeps through the green felt veneer.

---

57. The project had already had several directorial names attached including James Bridges and Martin Ritt. It also sounds suspiciously close to *The Cowboys* (Mark Rydell, 1972).
58. Douglass K. Daniel. *Tough as Nails: The Life and Films of Richard Brooks*. Madison, Wisconsin: Wisconsin University Press, 2011.
59. Statistics from presskit.
60. Arthur Knight, *Hollywood Reporter*, July 26, 1985.
61. Ray Lloynd. *Weekly Variety*. February 22, 1984.

By late 1984 DeLaurentiis was no longer connected with the project, which was finally called *Fever Pitch*. It began shooting in mid-October and wrapped at the end of January, 1985. Some fifty locations were involved from the MGM Grand, the Sahara, the Dunes, and Circus Circus casinos to the *Herald-Examiner*, Hollywood Park, and garages and back alleys in between.[62] The casino shooting had to be accomplished between 8 AM and 10 AM with actual patrons serving as extras.[63] Per his practice, Brooks wouldn't let anybody see a complete script. He also opted for realism in a scene in which O'Neal's character is thrown into the drunk tank at LA's Lincoln Heights jail. It happened to be the same jail where O'Neal had actually been tossed at age 18 for assault. For a scene in which O'Neal saves a suicidal soldier who has gambled away his grandfather's hospital money, Brooks needed actor Patrick Cassidy to cry, but the inexperienced young man couldn't summon the tears. Brooks apologized in advance for what he was about to do, rolled film, and then slapped Cassidy across the face. He got tears.

It took the director nine months to edit his film — unnamed studio executives defensively said he was just being meticulous — but when *Fever Pitch* was released in November of 1985 the results were not only disappointing, they were inexplicable. Not only does O'Neal have his debts miraculously erased by a *deus ex machina*, he leaves a Gamblers Anonymous meeting at the end and the first thing he does is drop money into a slot machine. And he wins. Some lesson.

Critics were not only flabbergasted, they were offended; Gene Siskel gave it zero stars.[64] Added *Newsweek*'s David Ansen, "Brooks writes dialogue as if he hadn't listened to a conversation in 30 years."[65] Everyone complained that scenes were not only confusing, they were randomly assembled, and the film was not just emotionally distant, it was downright incoherent. Its sole praise came from, not surprisingly, gaming magazines who lauded it for not portraying gamblers as losers, which is an interesting compliment because one of the most frequently heard comments on the Strip is, "These big casinos weren't built by winners."

Brooks wound down his career reluctantly. He lectured and gave interviews, formed a production company with actor-director Robert Culp to make TV docu-dramas, tried setting up an ambitious project at HBO dramatizing the Ten Commandments, and fought the colorizing of movies

---

62. Jane Galbraith, Daily Variety, October 30, 1985.
63. Army Archerd, *Daily Variety*, January 3, 1985.
64. Gene Siskel, *Chicago Tribune*, November 22, 1985.
65. David Ansen, *Newsweek*, November 25, 1985

by testifying at Congressional hearings in 1987. He died at his home of congestive heart failure on March 11, 1992.

"Richard Brooks is probably Hollywood's last angry man and certainly one of its last true idealists," wrote historian Arthur Knight, not as a memorial to Brooks, but in lament over *Fever Pitch* seven years earlier. "His best films are imbued with a bitter rage against social injustice, but also with an innate belief in the perfectibility of Man."[66]

---

66. Arthur Knight, *Hollywood Reporter*, November 20, 1985.

Frank Capra and his AFI Life Achievement Award.

FRANK CAPRA
Lost Horizons

The man who gave the movies their optimism made his last film under a cloud of his own pessimism. Frank Capra, who celebrated the basic goodness and resilience of the "little guy," found himself fighting not just big, egocentric guys but his own self doubts when he shot *Pocketful of Miracles*, his last feature film, in 1961. Like many aging masters[67] who had become unstuck in a changing Hollywood, he chose to remake one of his past successes, in this case the 1933 hit *Lady for a Day*. Both *Lady* and *Miracles* were based on the 1929 short story "Madame La Gimp" by Damon Runyon.

The original film was adapted for Capra by Robert Riskin, earned May Robson an Academy Award® nomination as Best Actress, and moved Poverty Row studio Columbia Pictures toward becoming a major player in Hollywood. In his autobiography, *The Name Above the Title*,[68] Capra writes that Columbia originally paid $1,500 to buy the rights from Runyon, but, when he wanted to remake it, his old studio charged him $225,000. It was only the first blow in a series of them that embittered Capra to what had become of the industry that he had helped build but that now was shoving him out to pasture. In the end he would lament, "The cause of [the film's] failure was not inept marketing, not inadequate advertising, not any commercial blunder. To me the real cause was deeply personal, deeply moral…*Pocketful of Miracles* was not the film I set out to make; it was the picture I chose to make for fear of losing a few bucks."[69]

---

67. Notably Leo McCarey (*An Affair to Remember*), Alfred Hitchcock (*The Man Who Knew Too Much*), Blake Edwards (*Pink Panther* sequels), Cecil B. DeMille (*The Ten Commandments*), and, to some degree, Howard Hawks (*Rio Lobo*).
68. New York: MacMillan and Company, 1971.
69. Capra, ibid.

Twenty-one years after Capra wrote those words in the hope of resurrecting his reputation, if not achieving apotheosis, writer Joseph McBride, who had come to know Capra when he wrote the American Film Institute's tribute to him in 1982, explored Capra's uncut manuscript and made some startling discoveries. Augmented by exhaustive research and published in 1992 as *Frank Capra: The Catastrophe of Success*,[70] McBride's book revealed that not only did Capra's love of the "little guy" run counter to the man's reactionary politics, it threw him into near paranoia in the 1940s when Red-baiters likened his populist sentiments to Communist propaganda. To Capra, a Sicilian immigrant who loved America and celebrated its opportunities, this was an outrage. Yet he took it not as a reason to repudiate the scoundrels who voiced it but to move closer to them in hopes of escaping their wrath. In other words, it might be said that when Capra wrote about the moral blunder of *Pocketful of Miracles* he was confessing his own hypocrisy.

In "Madame La Gimp," career gambler Dave the Dude decides to help Apple Annie out of a jam. In her vibrant youth she was the Toast of Broadway, a beautiful dancer who burned the candle at both ends. Eighteen years ago she had an illegitimate[71] daughter named Louise whom she sent away at the age of three to be educated among the best of Europe, supporting her from afar by depriving herself and convincing the girl that her absent mother was a society dame by writing to her on fancy hotel letterhead that she stole while cleaning rooms. Suddenly Louise announces that she's engaged to marry a Spanish nobleman's son and the family is coming to New York to meet Annie and her fellow nobs. To save Annie in Louise's eyes, Dave the Dude arranges for a fabricated husband and a coterie of "society" friends, summoning all of Broadway to make her look legit. Annie is scrubbed and decked out, and every gambler and swindler near Times Square is enlisted to pose as New York swells. Of course, as a Damon Runyon story, it involves a twist and a tear: when police show up to bust the gathering of criminals, they are so moved by the situation when it's explained to them that they join the charade. The happy couple gets married, the clueless parents return to Spain, Apple Annie marries the "judge" who posed as her husband, and Dave the Dude starts shaking down everybody for the loot they stole from the apartment where they staged the con.

The making of the first film adds resonance to the making of the second, which became Capra's last. In 1933 screenwriter Riskin and director

---

70. New York: Simon and Schuster, 1992.
71. This was before the Production Code started being enforced by Joe Breen in 1934.

Capra — whose legendary partnership would include *It Happened One Night* (1934), *Mr. Deeds Goes to Town* (1936), *Lost Horizon* (1937), *and Meet John Doe* (1941), among other classics — saw that they had a problem. A quick analysis of Runyon's story showed that Dave the Dude has no motivation for helping Apple Annie. When his wife, Billie, asks him what his stake is, he is baffled, offering, "Funny, I never thought about it. Guess I ain't got no stake, not that anybody can see." When he playfully adds, "You let that get out on the street and I'll cook you!" it hardly provides the fuel to drive a dramatic film. So Riskin, in his familiarity with the breed, made Dave superstitious, like all gamblers, to the point of needing to keep Annie alive and buy her apples as a good luck charm. Riskin turned it into a fairy tale by having the actual Mayor, Governor, and Police Chief crash Annie's party in the spirit of human kindness. He wrote four drafts between September of 1932 and May of 1933, finishing a polish on the second half of the script only three days before the start of filming. According to McBride, who tracked Capra's schedule during this time, Capra was working on another picture (*Soviet*, which was canceled) on loan-out to MGM and had little, if any, writing input into *Lady for a Day*.

Capra desperately wanted to borrow Marie Dressler and Robert Montgomery from MGM to play Annie and Dave but Harry Cohn, Capra's boss at Columbia, didn't want to owe any favors to MGM's Louis B. Mayer. Instead, he used 70-year-old Australian character actress May Robson and a serviceable contract player, Warren William. Capra was also unable to borrow W.C. Fields from Paramount to play the Judge, so he settled for Guy Kibbee. The rest of the roles were filled by durable character actors like Ned Sparks, Nat Pendleton, Halliwell Hobbes, Hobart Bosworth, Walter Connolly, and Ward Bond. Just before filming, Capra wrote, he took Cohn aside and confessed, "I want you to face the fact that you're spending three hundred thousand dollars on a picture in which the heroine is seventy years old." Responded Cohn, "All I know is the thing's got a wallop. Go ahead." It did; it did so well for Columbia that they produced a sequel of sorts the next year, sans Riskin and Capra, called *Lady by Choice*. Carole Lombard starred as a fan dancer who "adopts" an old lady (May Robson as Patricia "Patsy" Patterson) to convince the censors that she's respectable, but discovers that the old lady is as much of a scoundrel as she (Lombard) is.

The "wallop" is no doubt what Capra was trying to recreate when he told *The New York Times* on April 28, 1960 that he had three projects in mind: *The Best Man*, based on Gore Vidal's nasty and insightful stage play about a presidential convention (eventually made by Franklin Schaffner in 1964); Rebecca West's *The Meaning of Treason*, about Lord Haw-Haw, the Irish turncoat who propagandized for the Nazis; and a modern version of *Lady for a Day*. He said he was encouraged to make another "Capra-esque" film after *A Hole in the Head* (1959) did so well.[72]

In point of fact Columbia had been thinking of remaking *Lady for a Day* for several years. In 1957, independent producer Hal Wallis wanted to buy it as a vehicle for Shirley Booth, only to have Columbia's new management (Cohn had died in 1956) realize it was such a good idea that they asked Capra to do it. Capra toyed with updating it and injecting cold war politics, then lost interest.[73] When he was suddenly bankable again after *A Hole in the Head*, he changed his mind. But Riskin had died in 1955, so Capra hired Harry Tugend to rewrite the original, eventually bringing in Myles Connolly, Jimmy Cannon, and Hal Kanter. The credits went to Writers Guild arbitration, which decreed that only Tugend and Kanter would get their names on the screen.

It was United Artists that agreed to finance what became known as *Pocketful of Miracles* conditioned on Capra securing "a super nova or two prosaic novas to scintillate in the starring roles."[74] When Frank Sinatra, Dean Martin, and Jackie Gleason turned down Dave, he remembered Wallis' idea and approached Shirley Booth for Annie. Booth screened *Lady for a Day*, declared she couldn't do better than Robson, and said no. Capra then approached Helen Hayes, who accepted. He cast the role of Dave's no-nonsense wife, Queenie Martin, with Shirley Jones. Still needing a star for Dave, Capra asked the William Morris Agency, who represented nearly everyone who could "open" a picture, for help. They suggested Glenn Ford. UA and Capra agreed, but there were catches. One was that Ford wanted Jones fired and replaced by his friend Hope Lange. Capra argued that she was too young for the role, but the Agency took Ford's side. Further, they demanded Ford to be Capra's business partner, not just an actor.

What they were saying was that times had changed. Just as the industry smirked "the inmates are taking over the asylum" when actors Charles Chaplin, Douglas Fairbanks, and Mary Pickford formed United Artists, now UA was telling Capra that he could no longer be his own boss on his own picture. The casting required a rewrite and a change in shooting schedule, and suddenly Helen Hayes was out; she would be touring in a

72. *The Name Above the Title*, op. cit.
73. McBride, op. cit.
74. McBride, ibid.

play. Conferring with his associate producer Joe Sistrom, Capra sent the script to Bette Davis, who hadn't made a film in two years. When they met, Davis told Capra flat out that Hollywood hated her and she wouldn't even have considered the script if her daughter hadn't read it and told her to do it. Unlike Ford, Davis signed for straight salary.

That was the last cordial day, according to Capra. In his book he reported that Glenn Ford tied his guts into a knot "every time he bounced into a scene like a musical comedy funny-man" and, worse, insulted Bette Davis by claiming that he (Ford) rescued her from obscurity by giving her the lead in *his* starring film. Predictably, Davis responded by labeling Ford "that shitheel" among other sobriquets. Capra's sole praise is reserved for Peter Falk who was his "anchor to reality." It was Falk's first comic role.

But Capra told only part of the story, as *The Catastrophe of Success* later uncovered. What he removed from his autobiography was a confession that he used Ford as a scapegoat for his own diminished stature in the industry, notwithstanding — as supported by UA production executive Max Youngstein — that Ford was wrong for the part anyway but was "the only guy we could find." Capra was further inhibited during this period by the onset of "cluster" headaches.[75]

Principal photography took place from April 20 through mid-June of 1961 with a budget of $2.9 million, but it's deceptive because of the financial arrangements then associated with independent productions, deferrals, and personal service contracts. It was rushed into theaters for Christmas — it wasn't a Christmas picture *per se* although it was a feel-good movie — but Santa returned only $2.5 million in rentals. It was sold almost immediately to television in 1962.

Capra's decline (he was never able to get another project together, although he did TV specials including the Bell Science films) was countered in large measure by his presence on the lecture circuit where he showed his enduring classics and discussed them with a generation of eager young fans. The irony of his self-aggrandizing book is that, among scholars and his fellow filmmakers, he didn't need it. His reputation wasn't just secure, it was enshrined. He was an innovator. It was he who realized that an audience grasps things quicker collectively than individually, so he speeded up the playing of his scenes to meet their heightened attention. It was Capra (and Riskin) who, in *It Happened One Night*, virtually invented the modern romantic comedy by having the romantic leads also

---

75. Distinct from the more familiar migraine headaches, cluster headaches hit the sufferer with no onset and can last up to three hours. No relief for them is presently known.

be the comic leads rather than separating the laughter and the loving (*viz* any Marx Bros. film). He also perfected the device of cueing audience's response to a scene between two characters by cutting away to a third character's reaction. While filmmakers may have done this before, it was Capra who codified the devices. None of this has anything to do with the populism for which Capra was celebrated, and which ultimately embittered him, but it's worth appreciating.

In the end, *Pocketful of Miracles* is a film at odds with itself, just as its director was at odds with himself. When he died on September 3, 1991 at age 94, they said that Frank Capra, alluding to his most beloved film, had had "a wonderful life." They were wrong. Frank Capra gave *audiences* a wonderful life. The tragedy is that he was never really able to enjoy his own.

CHARLES CHAPLIN
Goodbye Charlie

No one will ever know for sure what compelled Charles Chaplin to make *A Countess From Hong Kong*. By all accounts, including his own, he lived happily in Vevey, Switzerland with his wife, Oona, their children, and enough money to assure not only their continued comfort but his cinematic legacy.[76] For the last decade he had been looking after the preservation of his work, which included some of the greatest motion pictures since the invention of the medium; had been composing musical scores for his silent releases; and was considering offers for the theatrical reissue of his collection in response to clamor from the entire world.

Perhaps he sought to give the public a new Chaplin film. Perhaps he wanted to address the tepid response to his 1964 autobiography with a celluloid addendum. Or perhaps he wanted to erase the reception of his 1957 *A King in New York*, a bitter satire that he had made in reaction to the 1953 confiscation of his passport by the U.S. State Department on charges that he was a Communist.[77] "I am the servant of the muses," he

---

76. Charles Chaplin. *My Autobiography*. New York: Simon & Schuster, 1964.

77. In his autobiography Chaplin notes that, while he was re-editing *Monsieur Verdoux* to meet the demands of Hollywood's Production Code, he was summoned by HUAC but that the Committee repeatedly postponed his appearance. After the third postponement he wired them, "For your convenience I will tell you what I think you want to know. I am not a Communist, neither have I ever joined any political party or organization in my life. I am what you call a 'peacemonger.' I hope this will not offend you. So please state definitely when I am to be subpoenaed to Washington. Yours truly, Charles Chaplin." He received a reply saying that the matter would be closed. As reference, here's the actual 1947 timeline: March-April, Chaplin edits *Verdoux*; May: HUAC holds preliminary hearings in Hollywood; July: HUAC Chairman J. Parnell Thomas announces he will call Chaplin; September: HUAC subpoenas Chaplin and then postpones his appearance three times; October: 19 "unfriendly" witnesses are called to Washington where only ten are called, refuse to testify, and become known as the Hollywood Ten.

said for publicity purposes. "When they say 'get back to work, you lazy bum' I go back."[78] But one thing is certain: when he sat down to write the script for a shipboard romance between a stuffy diplomat and the runaway Russian countess, he did not intend to star in it. Only once before — in 1923's *A Woman of Paris* — had he directed a film without appearing, and that was to give a career boost to his longtime silent co-star Edna Purviance. This time it would be different, but less out of generosity than pragmatism: Chaplin was 77, too old for slapstick, too grey for romantic leads, and too stocky to play his beloved tramp.

He took much of *A Countess From Hong Kong* from a script he had written in the early 1930s called *Stowaway* that he had intended as a vehicle for Gary Cooper and his (Chaplin's) then-wife, Paulette Goddard. The film was an outgrowth of his having met, while on a trip to the Far East, a number of émigré Russian nobles who had fled their country after the Bolshevik revolution with only their titles. As he reworked *Stowaway* into *Countess*, his producer, Jerry Epstein, set up the picture at Universal. Chaplin had partnered earlier with Epstein on the musical scoring and release of *The Chaplin Revue* (1959) combining three of his short films — *Shoulder Arms*, *A Dog's Life*, and *The Pilgrim* — into a single anthology feature. It was well received and began Chaplin's trick of scoring or re-releasing his classics whenever he needed to draw attention away from adverse publicity about his politics or personal life.[79] Epstein arranged a budget of $3.5 million from Universal marking the first time Chaplin had worked with studio money instead of his own since leaving First National in 1923. It bound him to a rigid shooting and completion schedule, something that threatened to cramp his creativity.

It also marked the first time he had to hire stars. First he sought Rex Harrison or Cary Grant to play Ogden Mears, the American Ambassador who finds a lovely stowaway in his stateroom headed from Hong Kong to the States. Instead, he cast the part with Marlon Brando who, although he could be wickedly funny in person, was not known as a comic actor.[80] For Natascha, the Russian countess who has been making ends meet by working in a dance hall, he chose Sophia Loren. Both Loren and Brando accepted without reading the script, with Brando announcing, "I would

78. Universal Pictures' production notes.
79. Eric L. Flom. *Chaplin in the Sound Era, an Analysis of the Seven Talkies*. Jefferson, North Carolina: McFarland, 1997.
80. As proved by the heavy-handed *Bedtime Story* (1964), remade more deftly in 1988 as *Dirty Rotten Scoundrels*.

have acted in the telephone book with him directing." (He was soon to discover that he'd dialed a wrong number). Tippi Hedren won the role of Mears' estranged wife, Martha, who shows up at the wrong time. Hudson, Mears' long-suffering butler who is ordered into an arranged marriage with Natascha to throw Martha off the scent, was Patrick Cargill. Chaplin had originally wanted Peter Sellers or Noel Coward until schedules and their salary demands persuaded him to go with the lesser-known Cargill (who wound up stealing the film). Lastly, Chaplin's son, Sydney, played Mears' assistant.

Irritating Chaplin even before production rolled, Brando insisted on top billing and warned that Loren's former husband, producer Carlo Ponti, would demand the same for her, only he would wait until negotiations were almost completed before bringing it up. Ponti indeed tried, but by then Brando had won, leaving Chaplin to wonder just whose film it was to be.[81]

Filming began January 25, 1966 at England's Pinewood Studio.[82] Or it should have, but Brando arrived three days late after reportedly partying so much in London that he had to get clean, forcing Chaplin to shoot around him. When he finally showed up, he had not lost weight as Chaplin had requested, and proceeded to alienate his co-star by telling her, as they prepared for a kissing scene, "Did you know that you have hair up your nostrils?" There were more interruptions: Brando had to be hospitalized in February with appendicitis (the press was also told "twisted intestine," but both excuses sound suspect); Chaplin for the flu in March; then Brando for the flu, shutting down production again; and finally on April 9 when Loren remarried Carlo Ponti four years after their first marriage had been annulled.

Both Brando and Loren reported that Chaplin's reputation intimidated them at first. Loren accommodated by mimicking her director's minute instructions, but Brando became increasingly resistant, saying later that he felt like a marionette. He also objected to the way Chaplin would browbeat his son, Syd, in front of cast and crew.[83] "There's too much noise, too much publicity, too much of everything," Chaplin said in a quote picked up by *Screen Stories*. He then shut the set to everybody, including the studio publicist.[84]

---

81. Jerry Epstein and Geoff Brown. *Remembering Charlie, a Pictorial Biography*. New York: Doubleday, 1989.
82. Flom, op. cit. *Screen Stories* says January 24, *Life* magazine says January 21.
83. Flom, ibid.
84. (unsigned). *Screen Stories*. New York: Dell, March 1967.

Something else, not played up at the time, is that scenes late in the film that take place in Hawaii were shot in the London studio using process photography. Because Chaplin's passport was still under official confiscation by the United States, he couldn't have gone to Hawaii to shoot it on location even if he had wanted to.

Production wrapped in May after fourteen weeks with the premiere scheduled for January 5, 1967 in London. Chaplin, working with an arranger, composed and conducted the waltz-heavy musical score, which included what became the film's break-out hit single, "This is My Song." His handwritten note for the music specified that its tone and speed should be based on the action, the comedy, and the romance and must reflect "the reality of life" as well as expression of "human reality."[85]

The London premiere was a disaster. The projectionist left the CinemaScope lens from the previous film on the projector when he rolled *Countess*, which was not CinemaScope, and the result was that the image was stretched across the screen. The film itself was misshapen in a different way. Chaplin was never known for visual inventiveness, and the flatly lit, eye-level photography, reminiscent of television, soon became monotonous. So did the largely unvarying camera angles. Where Chaplin may have wanted nothing to distract from the performances, the result was that *A Countess From Hong Kong* appears stagebound and heavy-handed. Other than Cargill, the only truly magical moments are Chaplin's brief cameo as an old steward who becomes seasick during rough seas.[86]

In both England and America the reviews read as though the critics felt betrayed that the Charlie Chaplin they adored had let them down. In reaction, Chaplin cut twelve minutes, including an end sequence where the old steward is seen mopping the ship's deck. Despite proclaiming that he felt that the shorter version was not really his film any more, he never restored it. Unlike his post 1917 pictures, whose copyrights he himself controlled, *Countess* belonged to Universal which, to date, has taken in only $2 million in rentals. The last word was Chaplin's who wrote, in his 1975 book *My Life in Pictures*, "Oona (his wife) was with me every day on the set. I needed her to be there." It is the only thing he has to say about the experience.

In 1971, however, Chaplin allowed the long-anticipated re-release of *The Gold Rush, Modern Times, City Lights, The Kid, The Great Dictator, Limelight, Monsieur Verdoux,* and *A King in New York.* (*The Circus* would

---

85. Undated note from Chaplin, Savoy Hotel, Charles Chaplin papers, AMPAS.
86. The seasick scene, in fact, is reminiscent of a similar one in Chaplin's 1917 two-reeler, *The Immigrant*.

follow years later). Their unexpected popularity inspired the Academy of Motion Picture Arts and Sciences to announce they would confer a special Academy Award® on Chaplin "for the incalculable effect he has had in making motion pictures the art form of this century" Returning to America for the first time since 1953, he accepted his statuette on April 10, 1972 at the Dorothy Chandler Pavilion. Visibly moved as well as clearly aging, Chaplin received a twelve-minute standing ovation, the longest in Oscar® history.

"My sister Josephine and I were very much against him going back to the United States," recalled his daughter, Geraldine. "We tried everything we could to make him not go back to the States. And he went. And we were so wrong. Because it gave him a new lease on life. When he did go back, they gave him a visa of only ten days! We thought, 'Oh this is disgusting! Oh, Daddy, how dare they?' He was thrilled. He said, 'They're still scared of me.'"[87]

Never having become an American citizen ("I consider myself a citizen of the world," he'd said on more than one occasion), and denied Swiss citizenship despite several applications, Chaplin was knighted Bachelor of the Order of the British Empire by Queen Elizabeth in her 1975 honors list. At the time, he was working on a script for *The Freak*, which he described as "an angel with wings." It was written for his youngest daughter, Victoria, but she left home before her increasingly infirm father could bring it about, both of them realizing, in all probability, that it would never be made.[88]

Charles Spencer Chaplin died in Switzerland on Christmas Day, 1977.

---

87. Beat Hirt & Felice Zenoni. *Charles Chaplin: The Forgotten Years*. Documentary. Zürich, Switzerland: Mesch & Ugge AG, 2002.
88. Ibid.

George Cukor flanked by Candace Bergen *(left)* and Jacqueline Bisset *(right)* in front of MGM's Thalberg Building.

GEORGE CUKOR
The Taste of Hollywood

They called George Cukor a "woman's director" because they couldn't call him a homosexual to his face, and that probably wasn't the word they used behind his back anyway. He was the most tasteful director in an era when taste was a dictate of the moguls who had none and, if he saved his vulgarity for his private parties, that was another example of the discretion by which he lived his double life.

"In his lifetime, there had been a lot of rumors about Cukor's lifestyle," his biographer, Patrick McGilligan, understated tactfully. "In recent years, especially after his death in 1983, some of that speculation had crept into print in various books."[89] Many of his films have been deconstructed in hindsight to reveal a gay subtext: the cross-dressing Katharine Hepburn opposite Cary Grant in *Sylvia Scarlett* (1935); directing Judy Garland, f'r'Chrissake, to her finest performance in *A Star is Born* (1954); being fired from *Gone with the Wind* (1939); wrangling the all-female cast of *The Women* (1939), probably by empathizing with them; and goading Maggie Smith over the top in *Travels with My Aunt* (1972). But it was his last film, *Rich and Famous* (1981), that called the question, offering a remake of 1943's *Old Acquaintance* that sparked Pauline Kael to label it a "homosexual fantasy" and bring the 81-year-old Cukor as close to the closet door as he had ever come. But Kael had it wrong; *Rich and Famous* was not a homosexual fantasy. It was, if anything, a blow for women's liberation struck by a man who, by virtue of his era, age, and stature, was denied a liberation of his own.

George Dewey Cukor was born on July 7, 1899 in New York City, the only child of Hungarian immigrant parents. He developed an early

---

89. Patrick McGilligan. *George Cukor: A Double Life*. New York: St. Martin's Press, 1991.

interest in theatre and won his first job moving scenery and playing small parts on stage when he was barely twenty. After directing several plays in New York (including the original 1926 Broadway production of *The Great Gatsby*), the advent of sound drafted him to Hollywood, along with many of his theatre peers, to guide fresh acting recruits similarly summoned to meet the challenge of talking pictures. First under contract to Paramount, he made himself *persona non grata* after suing the studio for removing him from *One Hour With You* (1932) and replacing him with Ernst Lubitsch when it looked like the picture was going to be a hit. That might have blackballed him as a troublemaker if his new friend, David O. Selznick, hadn't hired him at RKO. There Cukor came into his own, directing *What Price Hollywood* (1932; a "rough draft," if you will, of *A Star is Born*), *A Bill of Divorcement* (1932, for which he discovered Katharine Hepburn and tamed John Barrymore), *Little Women* (1933), and, on loan-out to Selznick's father-in-law Louis B. Mayer at MGM, *Dinner at Eight* (1933), *Manhattan Melodrama* (1934; John Dillinger's film fatale), and *David Copperfield* (1935). When the financial and critical disaster of *Sylvia Scarlett* soured RKO on him in 1935, Cukor followed Selznick to MGM and together they mounted such now-classics as *Romeo and Juliet* and *Camille*, both 1936. When Selznick left MGM to gear up for *Gone with the Wind*, he hired Cukor to direct it, then dismissed his friend three weeks into production under circumstances that have fueled gossip ever since (Cukor immediately returned to MGM where he made *The Women*).[90]

This resilience is significant; Cukor was a survivor, a skilled filmmaker, and a matchless director, not just of women, but of all actors, period. It was under his guidance that Cary Grant (in *Sylvia Scarlett*) attained what Richard Schickel called "his Cary Grant-ness;" that W. C. Fields in *David Copperfield* merged his comic genius with his definitive characterization; and that James Stewart, in *The Philadelphia Story*, became sophisticated. He also made Katharine Hepburn accessible in *Holiday*, Judy Holliday a star in *Adam's Rib*, and Rosalind Russell a comedienne in *The Women*.

Away from the studio, Cukor was known for hosting elegant Saturday dinners that cut across status and gender preference lines. "He reached out to gay men in every aspect of the business," *Los Angeles Times* film critic Kevin Thomas told author David Ehrenstein. "You would go to dinner at George's and meet a world-famous director or producer or an associate

---

90. Biographies differ on the firing. Some ascribe it to his increasing frustration at Selznick's micro-management of *GWTW*; some say Gable felt Cukor was favoring Vivien Leigh and Olivia DeHavilland; others claim that Gable thought Cukor believed he had turned tricks in his early Hollywood days.

producer or an editor or a set decorator, or Christopher Isherwood and Don Bachardy. As long as a person was presentable and could hold up a conversation, they were *in*."[91] "He made great friends because he really was interested in what you were up to," recalled Richard Stanley, who became close to the director during his final years. "If you had George Cukor as a friend, you really had a friend."[92]

Less well known were the Sunday afternoon pool parties he threw for his fellow gays and their current boyfriends, many of whom were trade. Before this kind of social/professional networking became known derisively as "Hollywood's gay mafia," Cukor was its Godfather, genuinely interested in furthering people's careers by connecting shakers with movers. Only someone who is secure professionally would, or could, do such a thing. "He became less and less concerned about being openly gay as he got older," said a friend. "In fact, he even gave an interview to *The Advocate*. He didn't care any more."

Cukor's inner circle was made of those men who had become closest to him over time, and they must have been stunned when the studio called him back after nine years to take over the loose reins of *Rich and Famous* in 1981. It must have seemed a perfect entry into the post-Women's Movement era of the 1980s when it was proposed by showman Allan Carr, who had clout after producing *Grease* (1978) before he lost it with *Can't Stop the Music* (1980).[93] Carr saw that women had risen (somewhat) from their usual roles in Hollywood — editor, casting, script supervisor (or "script girl"), costumes, tutor, and production secretary — to become executives, although only one, Sherry Lansing, then Fox's head of production, had any real power. MGM was still a men's club. Worse, the studio was headed by David Begelman, the convicted felon who had forged checks when he'd run Columbia Pictures in the mid-1970s. But he still had his friends, and they brought him over to MGM where he enticed Candace Bergen and Jacqueline Bisset to sign aboard Carr's updated version of the Bette Davis-Miriam Hopkins bitchfest *Old Acquaintance*.[94] Then, suddenly, Carr was no longer mentioned in connection with what was now called *Rich and Famous*. William Allyn was.[95]

91. David Ehrenstein. *Open Secret: Gay Hollywood 1928-1998*. New York: William Morrow & Co., 1998.
92. Author interview with Richard Stanley.
93. *Hollywood Reporter*, March 12, 1980.
94. Peter Bart. *Fade Out: The Calamitous Final Days of MGM*. New York: William Morrow & Co., 1990.
95. *Hollywood Reporter*, March 14, 1980.

The 1943 *Old Acquaintence*, written by Lenore Coffee from John van Druten's play, was a soap opera sporting dueling female leads: Bette Davis is a novelist whose books earn great reviews but no sales, so her fluttery, envious "old acquaintance," Miriam Hopkins, decides to try. She does, churning out a succession of trashy best-sellers. When Hopkins' husband, John Loder, tires of living in her shadow and leaves, she blames Davis, and pass the saucer of milk. The screen chemistry between Hopkins and Davis was more like friction; several years earlier, Davis had bedded Hopkins' then-husband, director Anatole Litvak, and their on-screen antipathy was palpable. Moreover, Davis let it be known that she'd wanted Norma Shearer as her co-star, not Hopkins. Miraculously, director Vincent Sherman pulled it off.

Rich and Famous (which everybody but Cukor insisted was not a remake) was written by Gerald Ayers, who had been commissioned by Universal, but the project died there. By chance Bisset saw the script on her agent's desk and brought it to Begelman at MGM promising to play the Davis role. Begelman was seeking ready-to-go projects and Ayer's script, plus Bisset's interest, kindled his green light. Begelman then signed Candace Bergen, who had just begun making a name for herself with *Starting Over* (1979), for the Hopkins role. The package was completed by adding Robert Mulligan as director.

Rehearsals began on July 7, 1980 and cameras rolled in New York on July 14.[96] The 61-day shoot (including holidays and travel) was scheduled for three weeks on the east coast, then to L.A. for the rest, with interiors at Metro.[97] On July 24, however, the Screen Actors Guild went on strike and *Rich and Famous* shut down. In the period that followed, Mulligan left the picture claiming that his next project could not be postponed.[98] Frantically, MGM and Allyn searched for a director capable of hitting the soundstage running. Someone suggested Cukor. If his age worried the studio's insurance underwriters, none of them said a word. Cukor was paid $300,000 for his work, the same fee he had extracted from Jack Warner for *My Fair Lady* in 1964.[99]

Cukor wasted no time. He asked screenwriter Ayers to come to his home to read the script out loud. He then screened Mulligan's footage and rejected it all, deciding to turn the film toward comedy and toning

---

96. *Hollywood Reporter* production chart, July 18, 1980. Also May 13, 1980 MGM schedule in William Allyn papers, AMPAS.
97. Teri Ritzler, *Hollywood Reporter*, June 26, 1980.
98. Jeff Silverman, *Los Angeles Herald-Examiner*, October 9, 1980.
99. McGilligan, op. cit.

down Bergen's histrionic performance. He also cast the sole remaining unfilled role: Matt Lattanzi as the darkly handsome young hustler whom Bisset picks up at Cartier's. When production resumed on November 10, 1980 on MGM Stage 28, the DGA's oldest working director was calling the shots.[100]

Cukor was both ready to work and easily tired. Co-workers reported that production stopped every afternoon for him to take a nap. He also apparently dozed during takes, although he claimed he was "just resting."[101] And yet he insisted on energy from others: "All right, ladies, at a brisk clip," he would say before a take, and if anyone overacted, he would say, "Do it again — less!"[102] *Village Voice* columnist Arthur Bell visited the set and quoted Bisset as saying that Cukor had his good and bad days but that "he's smart as a whip and more energetic than others I've worked with. He hates pauses and calls them 'McGreedys' [*sic*]."[103]

The struggles between Bisset's and Bergen's characters in the story were mirrored by Bisset and producer William Allyn, and there were rumors of discord. Cukor rode Bisset relentlessly, urging her into more accomplished and unguarded areas as an actress. The results are vastly entertaining and at times shocking. *Rich and Famous* is an old-fashioned drama told with new freedom, nostalgia dragged into the present, a brittle comic take on what would be low and broad were it not for Cukor's insistence on pace. It is an unexpected film that confounded expectations, particularly of those who were seeking a canvas for their own social politics upon its September 23, 1981 release.

Pauline Kael was the most reactionary, claiming in her *New Yorker* review that the Bisset and Bergen characters were "creepy" and that the film was "a homosexual fantasy." She held that Bisset's serial screen affairs had "masochistic overtones" and "don't seem like what a woman would get into. And Bergen is used almost as if she was a big, goosey female impersonator."[104] This caused gay critic Stuart Byron to chastise Kael in the *Village Voice* for the "tiredest homophobic myths" and to chart that whenever Kael disagreed with someone she accused the person of being gay and therefore emotionally arrested.[105] Critic-historian Vito Russo added that what seemed to bother Kael was that Bisset's character could

---

100. *Hollywood Reporter*, November 17, 1980.
101. Conversation with cast member, on background.
102. Richard Stanley, ibid.
103. Arthur Bell, *Village Voice*, February 14, 1981. No further definition of *McGreedy*.
104. Pauline Kael, *The New Yorker*, October 2, 1981.
105. Stuart Byron, *Village Voice*, November 11, 1981.

be as randy as men and just as desirous of one-night stands, something the critic couldn't comprehend, and therefore attacked.[106] Russo quoted Myron Meisel, writing in the *Los Angeles Reader*, who noted that the film was really about "the emotions associated with transient relationships, the role of friendships instead of family, sexual adventure, the privacy of intimate feelings, and even the allure of young sex objects."[107]

In the wake of the film's controversy — but not because of it — Cukor retreated to private life. He never made another movie, although he worked closely with historian/archivist Ron Haver to restore his 1954 masterwork, *A Star is Born*, which had been butchered by studio head Jack Warner. As Haver crawled through storerooms and met with shadowy collectors to track down footage thought long lost, Cukor began failing. Urgently, Haver, editor Gene Allen, and motion picture Academy President Fay Kanin set up a screening for Cukor at the Academy's Goldwyn Theatre for Tuesday, January 25, 1983 to show him their progress.[108]

He never saw it. On Monday, January 24, the director collapsed in his home while watching television. "I went over to see George around lunchtime" says Richard Stanley. "George, his male nurse (Robin Thorne), and I were in his bedroom. Ron Haver called while I was there to invite him to a screening of *A Star Is Born*. When I left, George and I kissed, as we always did, on the lips. George looked up at the nurse, wagged his finger, and said, 'OOOOhh!' — and we all laughed. That was the last time that I saw him alive. George Towers[109] called me first thing the next morning, maybe 7 o'clock, and said that he died overnight. There's always been a discussion that he died at the hospital. Probably he had an aneurism burst and died at home."[110]

The private screening of *A Star is Born* went on without its director just as Haver, Allen, and Kanin knew Cukor would have wanted, and the film's subsequent gala re-release brought him more acclaim than he had enjoyed in years.

Cukor was two of a kind. At work he was brittle, controlling, comforting, and decisive. At home he was brittle, controlling, decisive, and

---

106. Vito Russo. *The Celluloid Closet*. New York: Harper & Row, rev. 1987.
107. Vito Russo ibid.
108. Ron Haver. *A Star is Born: The Making of the 1954 Movie and Its 1983 Restoration*. New York: Alfred A. Knopf, 1988. Lost scenes were reconstructed from stills; some footage is still missing and rumored to exist in the hands of an elusive private collector.
109. Cukor's friend, lawyer, and executor.
110. Richard Stanley, op. cit.

himself. "Now, you couldn't get away with being as bitchy as George was," said Kevin Thomas. "You had to be careful not to emulate that too much. You couldn't be George Cukor, either."[111]

---

111. Ehrenstein, op. cit.

MICHAEL CURTIZ
Bring on the Empty Scrapbooks

"Before you ask," Michael Curtiz is supposed to have begun his interviews, "I don't know how *Casablanca* happened. It just did."[112] The quote isn't just apocryphal, it's patently false, because if Curtiz ever did give an interview, it's long disappeared. The Hungarian-born director of *Captain Blood, The Adventures of Robin Hood, Angels with Dirty Faces, Mildred Pierce* and, immortally, *Casablanca*, was better known for butchering English than speaking it to reporters. As his stalwart biographer, James C. Robertson, discovered after exhaustive research, he seems to have left no private correspondence and his record exists only in office paperwork and the colorful memories of those who survived working with him.[113]

Curtiz (born Mihali Kertesz in Hungary, probably in 1888) entered movies as an actor in Budapest with a degree from their Royal Academy of Theatre and Art. He began directing around 1912 at a time when Europe's film industry rivaled Hollywood's, if not in commerce, then in artistry. World War I put an end to that, and in 1919 when a Communist regime took over his country, Curtiz fled to Austria. His 1924 film, *Moon of Israel*, was seen there by Harry Warner who brought him to Hollywood in 1926. He hit his stride in 1929 when he directed the silent epic *Noah's Ark*, inspired more by the enormous commercial success of

---

112. Howard Hawks claimed that he was to direct *Casablanca* but swapped with Curtiz for *Sergeant York* (see Bogdanovich) but this cannot be confirmed. Producer Hal Wallis originally lobbied for William Wyler. (See Harmetz.)

113. James C. Robertson. *The Casablanca Man: The Cinema of Michael Curtiz*. London and New York: Routledge, 1993.

Cecil B. DeMille's *The Ten Commandments* (1923) than by any interest in the Old Testament. It was one of five pictures he made that year. The part-talkie (Warner Bros. had revolutionized movies with *The Jazz Singer* in 1927) went exponentially over budget until the studio quite literally pulled the plug: the climactic flood scene involved dumping the contents of huge water tanks on unwary extras. Many were injured and several drowned.[114]

The tragedy taught Curtiz a lesson: respect the budget. He did not, however, respect much else. When he was running out of script to shoot on the troubled *Casablanca*, he told co-writer Howard Koch "Don't worry what's logical. I make it go so fast no one notices."[115] He resisted *Mildred Pierce* with Joan Crawford saying, "Why should I waste time directing a has-been?" (Crawford won an Oscar®, is why.) On *Charge of the Light Brigade* he famously ordered "Bring on the empty horses" (meaning riderless) and yelled at Errol Flynn and David Niven for laughing at his comment, saying, "You think you know f**k everything and I know f**k nothing? Well let me tell you, I know f**k all!"[116]

Curtiz thrived at Warner Bros. for three decades, moving easily among genres. He was the compleat studio director for whom scripts, cast, and crews were laid out by others. It was not uncommon for him to wrap principal photography for one picture on a Saturday, have the script for his next film messengered to his home on Sunday, and show up on the set Monday morning ready to roll the new one. "If you gave Mike a decent script, he would do a good job staging it," said fellow director Vincent Sherman. "His whole life was his pictures. I never heard of Mike having any personal or social relationships outside that mattered."[117]

But Curtiz was far from a hack. He had the gift of knowing how to stage and shoot scenes, adding excitement to even the most mundane camera set-ups.[118] What he exuded was speed, not only by bringing in his pictures on schedule but in making them move; if his actors weren't doing something, his camera was. Few current directors know how to

---

114. Cass Warner Sperling, Cork Millner, Jack Warner, Jr. *Hollywood Be Thy Name*. Rocklin, California: Prima Publishing, 1994.
115. Howard Koch. *As Time Goes By: Memoirs of a Writer*. New York: Harcourt Brace Jovanovich, 1979.
116. David Niven. *Bring on the Empty Horses*. New York: G. P. Putnam's Sons, 1975.
117. Aljean Harmetz. *Round Up the Usual Suspects: The Making of Casablanca*. New York: Hyperion, 1972.
118. According to legend, his sole direction to Bogart in *Casablanca* about how to play scenes with Ingrid Bergman was "stand there and always let her come to you." The film bears this out.

block scenes as brilliantly (three who do are Steven Spielberg, Robert Zemeckis, and Martin Scorsese).

From 1947-1948 he set up Michael Curtiz Productions on the Warner Bros. lot. The four pictures he made under its banner (*The Unsuspected, Romance on the High Seas, My Dream is Yours, Flamingo Road*) suggest that some directors who chafe under the studio system actually benefit from its structure. Although Warners loaned him out to other companies while he was under contract to them, notably to Fox for *The Egyptian* and to Paramount for *White Christmas* (both 1954), he left for good in 1956 and continued his career as a freelancer.

1961's *The Comancheros*, made for Twentieth Century-Fox, would be his last. An enjoyable western that is very much a product of its time, right down to distinguishing between "wild" Indians and "tame" ones, it shot throughout the rocky parks and valleys of Utah earlier that year. James Edward Grand and Clair Huffaker adapted Paul Wellman's 1952 novel about Texas Ranger Jake Cutter (John Wayne) bringing accused killer Paul Regret (Stuart Whitman) to Louisiana to stand trial following Texas' independence from Mexico. The two are sidetracked into posing as gun runners to infiltrate a criminal gang called Comancheros who are selling weapons to the Indians (presumably the "wild" kind). A further relic of its less enlightened time is its use of the "magic bullet"[119] theory in which any white man or boy with a gun can kill multiple attacking Indians with unerring accuracy.

Wellman's novel was originally bought for the screen by George Stevens who intended to direct it after he finished *Giant* in 1956. By 1959 Stevens had become interested in *The Diary of Anne Frank* and sold *The Comancheros* to Fox for $300,000.[120] Clair Huffaker[121] was signed by the studio to adapt it for producer Charles Brackett (Billy Wilder's former writing partner) with an announcement that Gary Cooper would star as the first title in his three-picture deal with the studio.[122] The press release and the three-picture deal were probably more a kindness than a commitment, however, because by this time Cooper had already been diagnosed with the cancer that would take him in May of 1961. Meanwhile, at the

---

119. Devised in 1964 by Warren Commission investigator (and future U.S. Senator) Arlen Specter who explained how a single bullet from Lee Harvey Oswald's rifle shot both President John F. Kennedy and Governor John Connolly by veering left and right, doing a loop, and surviving practically intact.
120. *Daily Variety*, January 22, 1959
121. Philip K. Scheurer, *Los Angeles Times,* December 22, 1959.
122. *Hollywood Reporter* , December 16, 1960.

beginning of 1961, Douglas Heyes was announced to write and direct.[123] Four months later John Wayne and Charlton Heston were announced as stars, but three weeks later Heston exited and was replaced by Tom Tryon,[124] and Curtiz had replaced Heyes.[125] To make the project more attractive to Wayne, Fox had James Edward Grant rewrite Huffaker's script (Grant had just written *The Alamo* for Wayne).[126] By May tenth, the 150-person company was finally off to Moab, Utah to start their 41-day shoot.

It's tempting to say that the film takes on a number of styles because the story involves subterfuge and assumed identities, but that would be pushing it. It does, however, use two distinct types of dialogue. First there's the formal, courtly wording in scenes between Stuart Whitman, a Southern dandy, and Ina Balin as a temptress who lures him to her bed. The formality continues in Whitman's encounters with Balin's father, Nehemiah Persoff, as the wheelchair-bound philosopher who heads the violent, secretive Comancheros. It isn't quite Charles Portis (*True Grit*), but it's notable in that characters speak in complete sentences and seem to enjoy talking. The second style, by contrast, is found in John Wayne's scenes that give audiences what they expect from the Duke, such as, "He's just spittin' out words to see where they splatter" or "Don't say it too often, and once more will be too often." Wayne also needles Whitman by calling him "mon-sewer." Given Curtiz' love-hate affair with English, it's an open question whether this dichotomy mattered to him. Said his stepson, John Meredyth Lucas, "He spoke five languages, and I am told he spoke all of them equally bad."[127] The Elmer Bernstein score is a shameless copy of the one he wrote the year before for *The Magnificent Seven*, and at least two important action moments — Whitman hitting Wayne with a shovel and a peasant woman stabbing Persoff — are staged so off-handedly as to dull both their effect and their clarity.

But, by then, Curtiz was having his own troubles. It was on this film that he began showing the effects of the cancer that ended his life on April 10, 1962. When he was too weak to work, John Wayne took over the direction (and later refused credit). For some time it was believed

123. *Hollywood Reporter* and *Daily Variety*, April 4, 1961.
124. *Hollywood Reporter*, April 24, 1961.
125. *Hollywood Reporter*, May 10, 1961. Heyes wrote and directed features (*Ice Station Zebra*, the third *Beau Geste*) but became an enormously prolific episodic TV writer (*Cheyenne, Maverick*) and director (*Twilight Zone*).
126. Twentieth Century-Fox Production notes mention Grant but not Huffaker, suggesting that the shotgun collaboration went to Writers Guild arbitration that ordered both credits.
127. Harmetz, op. cit.

that Curtiz directed the interiors and Wayne or stuntman/second unit director Cliff Lyons handled the exteriors, but this is unclear. The film is a contest — *blend* would be the wrong word — of styles. Using the wide vistas of CinemaScope, Curtiz didn't have to move the camera with the fluidity that distinguished his earlier standard-width films. He and Director of Photography William Clothier were also reminding audiences that movies were grander than TV, so there are no tight close-ups, very few over-the-shoulder shots, a good amount of two-shots, and an enormous number of wide shots that are used for virtually all the action scenes (making it hard to tell, watching on video, who is attacking whom).

The Comancheros' strength is its colorful minor characters, a trick that Curtiz learned when he had the wealth of Warner Bros.' character players on his roster. Lee Marvin, as a drunken thug named Tully Crow, steals his few scenes from John Wayne, and would soon become one of the screen's most volatile stars. Nehemiah Persoff, well known from a myriad of television roles, channels Sidney Greenstreet as the witty yet perverse gang leader. Edgar Buchanan, best known as "Grandpa Joe" from TV's *Petticoat Junction*, has a playful cameo as a conniving judge. Jack Elam has little to do as a Comanchero henchman except, perhaps, bless the proceedings with his presence. There are other familiar faces, too (Bruce Cabot, Michael Ansara, Pat Wayne, etc.) and one gets the distinct impression that they were hired less for their acting chops than to fill out the "family" that could keep Wayne, Curtiz, and the crew occupied on location.

The fact that Curtiz, at 74, would consent to make an action film in the desert in the first place is proof of the sheer love of movies that he brought to everything he shot. Perhaps *The Comancheros* helped kill him. Or perhaps it helped him live a little longer. Even if Curtiz had explained it, in all probability nobody could have understood what he was saying.

Cecil B. DeMille *(left)* enlightens Yul Brynner *(right)* on The Word. Note matzo in foreground.

CECIL B. DEMILLE
Ready When You Are, C.B.

"Were you influenced by the early filmmakers?" a clueless reporter asks Cecil B. DeMille in a filmed interview promoting his 1956 remake of *The Ten Commandments*. DeMille looks momentarily surprised, then recovers, and, with graceful aplomb, responds, "The early filmmakers? Well, there really *were* no earlier filmmakers!"[128]

Before DeMille formed a partnership in 1913 with his friends Jesse Lasky and Samuel Goldfish (later Goldwyn) and left New York to find a place to shoot *The Squaw Man*, Hollywood was just a tiny community of unpaved streets and unsold lots. It had been incorporated in 1903 and the next year the city fathers voted to ban liquor sales as well as to give land to anybody who agreed to build a church. At first, municipal growth was stifled by a lack of water — the Los Angeles basin is a near-desert unable to sustain life (talk about metaphors) — but this was rectified in 1910 when Hollywood was annexed to Los Angeles and the water began to flow (see *Chinatown*). Soon, so did people. Most came for the sun and clean air, but a succession of motley movie companies was drawn there by the varied terrain, consistent good weather, and proximity to the Mexican border where they could escape enforcers for Thomas Edison's omnivorous Patents Trust. (The Patents Company monopoly was eventually busted in 1918.)

It was into this wilderness that Cecil B. (for Blount) DeMille ventured with his and his partners' life savings, rented a barn on the corner of Selma

---

128. *Cecil B. DeMille: American Epic*. Kevin Brownlow: Photoplay Films, 2004.TV.

and Vine Streets, and proceeded to direct what is arguably Hollywood's first feature film. At the time, DeMille enjoyed the enthusiasm of youth (he was 32) and the bliss of ignorance (it's doubtful he'd ever even seen a movie). He also had something else, something his partners lacked: Christianity.[129] It would shape his choices, both on screen and off, for the rest of his life.

The Squaw Man had been a successful stage play, in contrast with DeMille himself who had been an unsuccessful playwright and actor; he had tried both professions prior to turning to film. Born in Ashfield, Massachusetts in 1881 to a father who was an Episcopalian lay reader/part-time dramatist, and an actress mother, he was graduated from the Academy of Dramatic Arts in New York, where his father taught. He then rode the coattails of his more famous actor-writer brother William C. DeMille to land a position with David Belasco, the stage impresario known for flamboyance in his productions. Some scholars attribute DeMille's later penchant for over-the-top execution to Belasco's mentoring.

To cover himself while making *The Squaw Man*, DeMille hired Oscar Apfel, who was already established as a director of one and two reel shorts. Neither man took a directing credit, and it was a good thing too, for *The Squaw Man* almost ruined the young company. In order to evade the Patents Trust, DeMille had used bootleg equipment that was not compatible with the equipment that Lasky and Goldwyn owned back east. Thus, when he proudly sent his finished work to his partners, they were horrified when the film couldn't be projected because the sprocket holes had the wrong configuration. Fortunately, Goldwyn prevailed on producer Sigmund "Pop" Lubin who painstakingly re-perforated the negative. Not only was the company saved, *The Squaw Man*, released February 17, 1914, became a hit.[130] Within two years the Jesse L. Lasky Feature Film Company employed five directors, eighty performers, and turned out a stream of pictures, all of which were supervised by DeMille. In 1916, after a succession of mergers, the Lasky company joined Adolph Zukor's Famous Players company and became Paramount Pictures.

Although he entered films at about the same time as the other great pioneer, D. W. Griffith, DeMille was not so much an innovator as a showman who was more interested in commerce than art. He began with polished dramas of manners and morals that were considered

---

129. Technically, his mother, Beatrice Samuel, was a Jew who had converted in order to marry Henry Churchill DeMille.
130. Thomas R. Birchard. *Cecil B. DeMille's Hollywood*. Lexington, Kentucky: University Press of Kentucky, 2004.

groundbreaking, particularly in terms of their opulence and implied sexuality. *Male and Female* (1919), for example, plunged Gloria Swanson into a sunken bathtub with servants holding her robe "just so." Other titles such as *Don't Change Your Husband, Why Change Your Wife, Old Wives for New*, and *Changing Husbands* (all 1918-1920) are typical DeMille fare distinguished by stylish settings and what, at the time, was an alluring voyeurism tempered by a light touch. Rare for such stories, they looked at marital life rather than courtship. At the same time, he could also be a provocateur, such as with *The Little American* (1917), inspired by the sinking of the British ocean liner Lusitania by a German U-Boat, in which Mary Pickford not only chastised the Hun but called for United States entry into The Great War.

But it was films like *The Woman God Forgot* (1919) and *Manslaughter* (1922) that started what the world came to know as a "Cecil B. DeMille Production": a canny combination of the Bible, drama, and sex.[131] In *Manslaughter*, for example, which shows a socialite paying the penalty for killing a motorcycle policeman during a joyride, he used a biblical scene to demonstrate recklessness and sin through the ages. Likewise, in his original 1923 version of *The Ten Commandments*, he cited the biblical story of Exodus only as a prologue; the rest of the film had to do with a building contractor who cheats on construction costs. But it's the Moses footage that people remembered, and something DeMille never forgot. He also discovered that the censors were willing to forgive sex and violence as long as they came wrapped in sanctity; as the reasoning goes, if you're going to show redemption, you first need to show the temptation. So closely did audiences come to identify C.B. with the Bible that many are surprised to learn that, of his 80 films, only a handful have biblical themes: *The King of Kings* (1927), *The Sign of the Cross* (1932), *The Crusades* (1935), *Samson & Delilah* (1949) and two versions of *The Ten Commandments*. "Give me any two pages of the Bible," he often said, "and I'll give you a picture."

For all his screen piety, DeMille was a mass of private contradictions. A rabid anti-Communist, he nevertheless traveled to Russia in his younger years and marveled at how well Communism worked.[132] He supported the Hollywood Blacklist yet forgave individuals who were tainted by it.[133]

---

131. Joel Finler. *The Movie Directors Story*. New York: Crescent Books, 1985.
132. Brownlow, op. cit.
133. Edward G. Robinson credited DeMille with saving his career by casting him in *The Ten Commandments* after he was wrongly accused of being a Red. On the other hand, there is DeMille's ugly attempt to blackball director Joseph L. Mankiewicz, whose refusal to sign a loyalty oath caused a near-meltdown of the Directors Guild in 1950.

He respected the public, yet abandoned thirty million of them by quitting *The Lux Radio Theatre* over a one dollar union assessment. He was a stern taskmaster on the set but a loving father to his four children, three of whom were adopted.[134] Finally, a devout Catholic, he kept adulterous company with writer Jeannie MacPherson and actress Julia Faye while his wife, Constance, silently endured her husband's transgressions.

It may have been all of these issues, but most particularly his hatred of totalitarianism, that inspired him to re-tell "the story of freedom, the story of Moses"[135] and the giving of the Law. As he says in his on-screen prologue:

> "The theme of this picture is whether Man ought to be ruled by God's law or whether they are to be ruled by the whims of a dictator like Rameses. Are Men the property of the State or are they free souls under God?"

Acknowledging that little is known of the first thirty years of Moses' life from the time he was found in the bulrushes by Pharaoh's daughter at age three months "until he learned that he was Hebrew and killed the Egyptian,"[136] DeMille wasn't fazed. He had screenwriter Jesse L. Lasky, Jr. and three others write a 308-page script based on ancient works by Josephus and Philo as well as contemporary scholars and clergy. The history is questionable, but his intent was not.

He started work on *The Ten Commandments* as soon as *The Greatest Show on Earth* wrapped production in 1951 (released in 1952, it would win him his only Oscar®). Preparation was foremost for DeMille, including securing actual Middle Eastern locations. For that he ventured to Egypt to make a personal plea to the country's new president, General Gamal Abdel Nasser, and Hakim Amer, who headed the nation's military, for permission to shoot there. Nasser had already proven himself no friend of the West or of Israel, and DeMille chose his words carefully. Midway into his pitch meeting, he was surprised to see the men smiling. It was then explained to him that they had grown up watching his 1935 film *The Crusades* and were moved by the respect he had shown Arabs and their religion. Thence were all doors opened for him.[137]

---

134. Birchard, op. cit.
135. Cecil B. DeMille, prologue to *The Ten Commandments*, 1956.
136. DeMille, ibid.
137. Cecilia DeMille Presley. *The Ten Commandments* DVD special features.

Charlton Heston was cast as Moses not only because he and DeMille, both political conservatives, had gotten on so well during *Greatest Show*, but because DeMille had seen Michelangelo's statue of Moses in Italy and was taken by how much it looked like Heston. The 81-member Paramount crew then traveled to Egypt in June and shot from October 11 through December 3, 1954.[138] They were joined by another eighty Egyptian crew members to scout, build sets, and shoot in and around Cairo, the Valley of the Kings, and the Sinai Peninsula. They filmed on top of Mt. Sinai for two days and nights. It was there that Heston asked DeMille if, in addition to playing Moses, he might record the voice of God as it emanates from the burning bush. "It seems to me," Heston recalled telling his director, "that if you hear the voice of God you hear it inside yourself." DeMille said, "Well, Chuck, you've got a pretty good part as it is." Nevertheless, Heston's voice — slowed and reverberated — is what's on the track.[139] The actor also recalled that when his newborn son, Frazier, was three months old, DeMille arranged the shooting schedule so the infant could play the baby Moses.

Yul Brynner, who was causing a sensation in *The King and I* on Broadway, flew to Egypt for a single day of shooting before heading back for curtain. As he and Heston had several shirtless scenes together, both men made it a point to stay in shape lest one look hunkier than the other.

For the exodus itself, in which Moses leads the Hebrews out of bondage, DeMille had built hundred-foot tall towers of the gates of the Seti Rameses and found 20,000 extras, all of whom had to be costumed, made up, and fed. "We hired whole villages," said DeMille's daughter, Cecilia. "We hired men, their wives, their children, their families, their extended families, their animals. They were all tented outside the gates."[140] The people slept in the field the night before so they would be in place come sunrise. It was like moving an army.

All of Paramount marshaled behind DeMille. The film's budget was first announced as $10 million and 112 days not including the Egyptian shoot.[141] Adolph Zukor admitted that the studio had given DeMille an "unlimited budget." By the time of its release, the figure, reported in *Variety*,[142] had hit $13.5 million, making it the most expensive American motion picture to that time.

138. *Denver Post*, August 29, 1954.
139. DeMille biographer Charles Higham and *IMDb.com* say that the voice is that of Donald Hayne, who also edited DeMille's autobiography. Others insist it's DeMille himself.
140. Cecilia DeMille Presley, op cit.
141. *Los Angeles Times*, May 29, 1955.
142. *Variety*, October 10, 1956.

The production demanded a crushing amount of energy and DeMille, then seventy-seven, cut himself no slack. Finally it took its toll: while climbing a seventy-foot ladder to get an overview of a scene, he suffered a heart attack. His associate, Henry Wilcoxon, helped him down and DeMille's daughter Cecilia and his secretary Bernice Mosk placed him in a car. His doctor, Max Jacobson, was at hand, and took him back to his hotel. He forbade him to continue directing. DeMille refused the advice, prayed deeply for strength, and returned three days later (his wife had taken over in the meantime).[143] Principal photography moved to Paramount in Hollywood from March 28 through August 13, 1955 and then post production began, including the haunting visual effect of the final plague and the magnificent parting of the Red Sea.[144] Then he embarked on a nationwide publicity tour speaking with clergy, civic groups, and, of course, the press.

The Ten Commandments continued its crusade at the box office for the next two years. Undaunted by having to top himself, DeMille prepped other projects. But his strength began to wane. During January of 1959, he left his Paramount office in pain and headed home to bed. On January 20, he suffered a massive coronary and died the next morning. His long-suffering wife, Constance, had become senile by then and was not told of his death.[145]

It hardly matters that *The Ten Commandments* is an overlong film with stilted dialogue, vulgar excess, and stately pacing. It has become as much a part of cultural tradition as the story that inspired it, and remains an enduring legacy to inspiration, dedication, loyalty, and faith. Not necessarily to God, but to Cecil B. DeMille.

---

143. Charles Higham. *Cecil B. DeMille*. New York: Da Capo Press, 1980.
144. The effect was created by dumping water over a spillway and optically combining it with earlier shots of the Hebrews' exeunt. As many as six images were merged to show the walls of water stretching off into the distance. In subsequent years when he was asked, "How did they part the Red Sea?" Heston would playfully avoid revealing the trick by saying, "Well, I had this stick…"
145. Higham, ibid.

EDWARD DMYTRYK
Setting the Record Straight

When Edward Dmytryk died on July 1, 1999 the obituaries duly noted that he had been known as the "father of film noir" and had directed the groundbreaking *Hitler's Children* (1943), *Murder, My Sweet* (1944), and *Crossfire* (1947). But they also took pains to report that he was the only member of the Hollywood Ten — ten men who were jailed for contempt of Congress after refusing to testify before the House Un-American Activities Committee (HUAC) in 1947 — to later "name names" so he could resume his career. To those who were blacklisted, such a thing was unthinkable, and they shunned him. To those who hated Communism more than they loved the Constitution, he was a hero. To those who respected his talent, they were happy he cleared his name (a term used by those who did so) so they could safely hire him again. All three were true.

Scholars have scoured Dmytryk's films for themes that might illuminate his choices, including why he joined the Communist Party in the first place. But, like the man, his motives were complicated, frustrating, and inconsistent. His final film, the revenge-themed *The "Human" Factor* (not to be confused with Otto Preminger's last film, also called *The Human Factor*, sans quotes), may not display the complexity of Dmytryk the man, but it reflects his tenacity as a filmmaker.

The "Human" Factor is about revenge, plain and simple: when a NATO computer wonk's (George Kennedy) entire family is killed by terrorists, he goes after the murderers because the government won't. The 1975 film was little more than a programmer enlivened by some good casting, but it must have left a foul taste in its director's mouth because his 1978 autobiography doesn't mention it. After it was finished, so was Dmytryk's directing career. In 1976 he took a teaching post at the University of Texas in Austin and, in 1981, he moved back to Southern California to teach filmmaking for another 16 years at the University of Southern California's famed school of Cinema-Television.

Dmytryk was a man of his times. Born in Grand Forks, British Columbia, on December 4, 1908 to Ukrainian immigrants, his mother died when he was six and when he was fourteen he deemed his father's beatings to be, as he said in his autobiography, "counterproductive."[146] He ran away from what he could no longer call home and, when the authorities caught him, they agreed that he should be declared liberated. He found his way to Hollywood, rose through a succession of part-time jobs at the Famous Players-Lasky Studios (soon to be called Paramount), and tried to make himself indispensable by learning everyone's job. He did best in the editing room and, after attending Cal Tech and bouncing among studios, became an editor at RKO, then a director, then a hit.

That is when Dmytryk asserted himself. Admittedly combative (he once wrote that it must be because he didn't have enough vowels in his name), he brought his street smarts onto the studio floor. When RKO didn't have money for sets and lighting, he kept his actors in the dark, showing only highlights and proclaiming it *chiaroscuro*. This shadowy visual world perfectly matched the murky morality of the scripts they gave him to direct. Years later it would be named *film noir* and it first found a home in the Philip Marlowe mystery *Murder, My Sweet*; then in *Cornered* (1945); and in *Crossfire*. (Aside: Val Lewton also used *noir* techniques to create the atmospheric suspense films he produced at RKO such as *Cat People, Curse of the Cat People, I Walked with a Zombie*, etc., only nobody ever called it *noir*.)

Low budgets never seemed to bother the inventive Dmytryk who wrote, "It is my firm belief that affluence in art is debilitating and leads to the erosion of creativity…If you want to remain creative, stay poor — at all costs."[147] But he was keenly aware of money, particularly who had it and who didn't. It was his belief in equal opportunity and social justice that led him, as it did so many others in the 1930s, to join the American Communist Party, not because they wanted to overthrow the United

---

146. Edward Dmytryk. *It's a Hell of a Life But Not a Bad Living.* New York: Times Books, 1978.
147. Dmytryk, ibid.

States Government, but because the United States Government was not addressing the needs of its people.[148]

The House Un-American Activities Committee didn't see it this way and, in October of 1947, it subpoenaed Dmytryk and 18 other Hollywood writers, directors, and producers to Washington to probe their political beliefs and associations. Only ten were called before the hearings were suspended in disarray, but much has been written about the Ten's refusal to testify and their subsequent imprisonment for contempt of Congress. Like his colleagues, Dmytryk served his time — six months of a twelve-month sentence in Danbury Federal Prison in Connecticut — and was released. It was at that point (not before) that he signaled his willingness to testify. In his second memoir, *Odd Man Out*,[149] he stated that he stuck with the Ten throughout their ordeal as a matter of solidarity and honor even though he disliked their defense, the strategy, and some of the men themselves.[150]

"I backed out on the group," he added in a 1987 interview,[151] "but first I served my jail sentence. I wanted to separate myself from the Communist party and that was the only way to do it because I was inextricably tied with them unless I made a very strong move and it was the only way to get away." Many of his right-wing friends never forgave him (or his family) for what they saw as a betrayal when his past affiliations came out; many of his left-wing friends likewise never forgave him (or his family) when he recanted. He (and his family) had to rebuild their lives and friendships from scratch. Denied Hollywood work from his 1947 HUAC appearance on, he went to England, made *The Hidden Room* (1948) and *Give Us This Day* (a.k.a. *Christ in Concrete*) with fellow exile Ben Barzman (1949) and, after jail, shot the quickie *Mutiny* (1951) for the bottom feeding King Brothers. It was progressive producer Stanley Kramer who restarted

148. This is a crucial point that few people consider, particularly when discussing those who named names before House and Senate investigative committees or their numerous local offshoots. Just because someone named names didn't mean that he or she became an arch-conservative. Whatever can be said about people who turned against their friends in order to save themselves, in most cases they never abandoned their belief in the progressive ideals that drew fire from their persecutors. The real condemnation should be placed not on the souls of those who capitulated, but on those who forced them to do so, for they had neither morals nor souls in the first place.
149. Edward Dmytryk. *Odd Man Out: A Memoir of the Hollywood Ten*. Illinois: The Southern Illinois University Press, 1996.
150. It must also be noted that the Ten and their many supporters believed they would be exonerated on appeal. But, by the time their case reached the U.S. Supreme Court, two conservative justices had replaced two moderates and the Court refused to hear the Ten's petition, sending them to jail.
151. *Tales from Hollywood: The RKO Story*. Documentary. UK: BBC, 1987.

Dmytryk's career in 1951 by hiring him to direct the tense character study *The Sniper* followed by *Eight Iron Men* (also 1951), *The Juggler* (1952), and finally the widely heralded hit, *The Caine Mutiny* (1953).

Some film historians insist that Dmytryk's artistry changed after his HUAC compromise, that his widely diverse films of the 50s and 60s never recaptured the social concern or style of his work in the 40s. But a more accurate reading is that Hollywood itself lost its conscience after caving to the Red-baiters. Not until the influx of foreign language films in the 1950s and the rise of independent cinema in the 1960s did mainstream Hollywood respond by loosening its censorship and facing the fact that audiences wanted something more provocative. *Easy Rider, Bonnie and Clyde, The Wild Bunch, Putney Swope, Gimme Shelter, Darling, Alice's Restaurant, The Boys in the Band, Knife in the Water, Blow-Up, The Seventh Seal, If...*, and other revolutionary works followed.

During that period Dmytryk's two releases were the big-budget war drama *Anzio* (1967) and the western *Shalako* (1968), the latter distinguished by the presence of Sean Connery, Brigitte Bardot, Honor Blackman, Stephen Boyd, and Jack Hawkins. After making *Bluebeard* (1972) with Richard Burton as the ultimate misogynist, and then the quasi-religious *He is My Brother* (which Dmytryk also does not list among his credits), he was handed the straight-up action thriller *The "Human" Factor*.

Once his family is killed without apparent motive, John Kinsdale (George Kennedy), who works in computers for NATO, is frustrated by the Naples police's (Raf Vallone) inaction, so he uses subterfuge and his office contacts (John Mills, Rita Tushingham) to identify and pursue whoever did it. The culprits' reasons turn out to be human, all right, but not personal. They want political prisoners freed and they plan to kill Americans every three days until that happens.

The "Human" Factor is a film in conflict with itself: its capable, serious actors are looking for depth and motivations that just aren't there, nor are they required for the genre.[152] Dmytryk directs it in an eye-level manner as if he just wanted to tell the damn story and go home. On its release it was called a *Death Wish* rip-off, but only because of the killing, not the social overlay. What makes the film significant is its timing: it was released just as the film school generation was entering mainstream production and pumping up cinema's visual syntax. Against this, Dmytryk's devotion

---

152. The Author remembers a screenwriter saying how the head of a studio once rejected his action script by telling him, "Your characters are too complex for a budget this big."

to detail was of less interest to the growing audience with its shorter attention spans, less social sophistication, little life experience, and no inclination to correct any of it.

Dmytryk epitomized a particular kind of filmmaking that simply went out of style. It might thus be said, with sympathy, that, between 1975 and his death 24 years later, he found himself on another kind of list. Its color wasn't black. It was gray, as in his hair.

Blake Edwards.

BLAKE EDWARDS
Minky Business

Blake Edwards may be the most accomplished writer-director of comedies since Preston Sturges and, in the long run, was more dependable. Like Sturges,[153] he didn't make "just" comedies, he made films that stand as documents of the human condition displayed with all its wit, absurdity, and drama. Both men had a brilliant grasp of character, wrote dialogue so good you wished people spoke like that all the time, crafted gags that caught you edgewise, and could shift from laughter to tears and back again so fast it left skid marks on your heart.[154]

Born William Blake Crump, his grandfather was silent director J. Gordon Edwards, whom Kevin Brownlow regards highly despite none of his films having survived,[155] and his father the stage director Jack McEdward. He started as an actor but turned to writing, mostly frothy comedies for director Richard Quine. His directing career began in 1955 with the minor *Bring Your Smile Along*, but he soon began to specialize in witty star-driven romantic comedies with a tinge of sex like *The Perfect Furlough* (1958) and *Operation Petticoat* (1959), hitting his stride with 1961's *Breakfast at Tiffany's*. Then he switched gears to direct and

---

153. *The Great McGinty, Christmas in July, The Miracle of Morgan's Creek, Hail the Conquering Hero, Sullivan's Travels,* etc.
154. Aside: in *10* there's a scene where a minister (Max Showalter) is auditioning a song for Dudley Moore as Showalter's dog sleeps nearby. An elderly maid, Mrs. Kissell, enters with a tray of tea, shuffles slowly around the room, spilling everything and farting to beat the band. On her first bloozer, the dog flees. When (after Edwards milks the gag perilously) the old lady finally leaves, Showalter deadpans to Moore, "Every time Mrs. Kissell passes wind, we beat the dog." My fellow critic David Chute and I watched *10* alone in a screening room and couldn't stop laughing for the next ten minutes. Whenever one of us tried to stop, he set the other one off again.
155. Kevin Brownlow. *The Parade's Gone By....* New York: Alfred A. Knopf, 1968.

produce, creating the riveting *Experiment in Terror* and *Days of Wine and Roses* (both 1962). The rest of his career would include every other genre: westerns (*Sunset, The Wild Rovers*), musicals (*Victor/Victoria, Darling Lili*), satire (*S.O.B., What Did You Do in the War, Daddy?*), crime (*Gunn, The Carey Treatment*), drama (*That's Life, The Tamarind Seed*), and outright comedy (*10, The Party*). Yet even while working in a specific genre, his films contain asides, observations, and set pieces that expand upon their main narratives. You never quite knew where you were heading in a Blake Edwards film, but you knew you'd be in good hands.

Even the Pink Panther films didn't start off as the pure comedies that people misremember them to be. Peter Sellers' incompetent Inspector Jacques Clouseau didn't enter the original 1963 film until long after David Niven, Robert Wagner, and Capucine had already set the plot in motion. What it was — and what its sequels remained under Edwards' skill — was a well-plotted action crime drama with comic relief. Edwards revived the recipe in 1975 with *Return of the Pink Panther*, a surprise hit that resuscitated his flagging career. He returned to the well in 1993 for what became his last film: *Son of the Pink Panther*. By then, though, the ingredients were stale; although its concept was consistent within the Pink Panther universe, the performers were not. Peter Sellers had died in 1980 and was unavailable to play Clouseau. That detail hadn't bothered Edwards in 1982 when he and his producing partner Tony Adams made *The Trail of the Pink Panther* [156] or its sequel, *The Curse of the Pink Panther* (1983), shot in tandem. So what could prevent them from reviving the franchise a decade later? When they tried to clear the rights in 1991, however, they found them mired in a corporate battle within MGM/Pathé, which was trying to wrench itself free from the grasp of Italian media magnate/scoundrel Giancarlo Parretti, who had bought the company in 1990. Not until the beginning of 1992 did Edwards' and Adams' Geoffrey Productions reclaim their creation.[157]

Conceiving a new Clouseau was another matter. Finally Edwards realized that "you don't resurrect Sellers' Clouseau. You discover that he had an illegitimate son."[158] Thus does Gendarme Jacques Gambrelli appear as the bastard issue of late Inspector Jacques Clouseau and Maria Gambrelli. He becomes involved in finding a princess kidnapped by terrorists whose

---

156. Constructed of outtakes from Sellers' previous *Panthers* bridged by ingenious, if contrived, linking scenes with his surviving costars, *Trail* triggered a lawsuit by Sellers' widow against MGM/UA and Edwards for debasing her late husband's memory and reputation. She won.
157. *Daily Variety*, March 18, 1992.
158. *Hollywood Reporter*, April 7, 1992.

ransom demands include her family's abdication. Sort of. Gambrelli *fils'* existence is finally explained by Claudia Cardinale at the end of the second act to the long-suffering Commissioner Dreyfus (a returning Herbert Lom). It seems that, years ago, she and the original Clouseau were trapped in a cabin by a blizzard and the only way they could keep warm was to make love. The result was young Gambrelli, who has never been told who his father is. And of course he's a policeman.

Gambrelli is played by Roberto Begnini, the Italian actor and filmmaker who, in 1997, would win the Oscar® for his concentration camp comedy *Life is Beautiful*. Cardinale, who plays Maria, played Princess Dahla in the original *Pink Panther;* her part in *Son* was played by Elke Sommer in the second Pink Panther film, *A Shot in the Dark* (1964). Any questions? For *Son*, Burt Kwouk joined Lom in bravely rebounding as Clouseau's manservant and karate assailant, Cato, and Graham Stark also returned as Prof. Balls, the disguise expert.

Financing, which should have been a snap for a proven filmmaker like Edwards and a pre-sold property like a Pink Panther, was undone by MGM's chronic impoverishment even under its new president Alan Ladd, Jr., so the film's $28 million budget was assembled partly from Metro and then with $13.8 million from Aurielio DeLaurentiis' company, Filmauro.[159]

The picture started shooting on June 8, 1992 and wrapped fourteen weeks later. Based at England's famed Pinewood Studios, the company also shot in Jordan on the invitation of the royal family, who were fans of the Pink Panther. Production was stopped for five days when Begnini sprained his ankle, but, as they were five days ahead of schedule at the time, it all evened out. *Son of the Pink Panther* was released on August 27, 1993 in America and rolled out across the world over the next six months, going direct to video in the UK. Several sources give its domestic gross as less than $2.5 million, a disaster. What happened?

It takes a truly gifted filmmaker to get it all so staggeringly wrong. In this case, it's not matter of taking a risk and failing, it's from trying to *not* take a risk. For what may have been be the first time in his career, Edwards tried to play it safe. The film derails from its opening titles, a protracted $1 million[160] CGI indulgence in which Henry Mancini hands his baton to the Pink Panther himself, who then cues Bobby McFerrin, who begins an annoying vocal riff on Mancini's popular Pink Panther Theme. McFerrin performs it in scat, for which both definitions apply.

---

159. *Daily Variety*, October 22, 1992, although *Screen International* (June 5, 1002) says $6.5 million.
160. *Hollywood Reporter*, February 10, 1993.

The black hole is Begnini. In theory, Begnini's Jacques Gambrelli is just as inept as Sellers' Jacques Clouseau. In truth it is Begnini who is inept. In contrast with Sellers, whose comic characterization had a full spectrum, Begnini has two facial expressions: dumbstruck and stupid. His congenital butchering of language is compounded by the odd result that mispronounced French in his Italian accent just sounds mispronounced, whereas Sellers' mispronounced French managed to tweak France's linguistic chauvinism. Lom, Kwouk and Stark are troupers with Lom spending much of his time in a hospital bed after a bomb mishap that, atypically, was not Clouseau's/Gambrelli's fault. In general, everyone is just going through the motions, squeezing out one more movie.

Despite this, like all of Edwards' films, *Son of the Pink Panther* is gorgeously produced with the kind of visual polish that creates its own world (Edwards' son Geoffrey directed the second unit and, some sources insist, more). But the truly important ingredient is missing: those writers who created and developed the series with Edwards, Frank Waldman, Tom Waldman, and Maurice Richlin. It's hard to know who did what, but what's lacking is a diligence in story construction that provides a spine to hang the gags on. There is simply no discernable through-line, so the comic sequences all play like outtakes. *Son of the Pink Panther* is such an anomaly that it's best to dismiss it. But one cannot dismiss Edwards, whose brilliance in over a dozen gems guarantees him a place in film history. Unlike his grandfather, his work remains accessible.

In 1969, Edwards married Julie Andrews, with whom he had two children, and before that was married to Patricia Walker, with whom he also had two children. After a physical decline, he died of complications from pneumonia on December 15, 2008. In 2004, he had finally been given a special Oscar®, which he memorably accepted by snatching it from the presenter's hands while racing across the stage in a motorized wheelchair. As usual, his timing was perfect, but the gag didn't pay off because the TV camera was in the wrong place. It needed Blake Edwards directing it.

VICTOR FLEMING
The Man From Oz

Although he directed two of the most famous movies in Hollywood history, nobody places Victor Fleming in the pantheon of world filmmakers. Andrew Sarris files him under "Miscellany" in his auteurist taxonomy *The American Cinema*, dismissing his best work as "the law of accidents."[161] In a career that spanned over thirty years and all or part of fifty films, he developed a style that is best described as no style. And yet Fleming's movies, well, *move*. Whether cajoling Wallace Beery into sharing the screen with Jackie Cooper in *Treasure Island* (1934), suggesting that Clark Gable grow what became his trademark mustache for *The White Sister* (1933), or delicately handling Jean Harlow after the suicide of her husband during *Red Dust* (1932), Fleming is seldom given more than passing credit. He earned his invisibility because he not only thrived under the studio system, he exemplified it. Like his bosses at MGM, where he spent the bulk of his career, he lived by their credo, "Films aren't made, they're remade." He is listed as "uncredited" director on no fewer than six films, and the two for which he is best remembered, *Gone with the Wind* and *The Wizard of Oz*, were either begun, finished, or both, by others.[162]

If Metro-Goldwyn-Mayer was the Dream Factory, Victor Fleming was its sandman. Born in 1889 in the bedroom community of La Cañada, California, just outside wealthy Pasadena, Fleming had a mechanical aptitude that led him, first, into the U.S. Army's Signal Corps in World War I, and then to Hollywood as a cameraman for director Allan Dwan. Dwan was part of Douglas Fairbanks' creative retinue, and the

---

161. Andrew Sarris. *The American Cinema: Directors and Directions 1929-1968*. New York: E. P. Dutton & Co., 1968.
162. The Internet Movie Database *(IMDb.com)* and the American Film Institute listings are at odds over this.

athletic, energetic Fairbanks found a protégé in the outdoorsy young Fleming. Before long Fleming was directing, first for Fairbanks, then for Paramount, where he drew attention for guiding Emil Jannings in the silent *The Way of All Flesh* in 1927. The tear-jerker had more to do with Jannings' 1924 German triumph, *The Last Laugh*, than with its namesake in the Samuel Butler novel: a happily married bank teller descends to the gutter and ends up being shut out of his estranged son's violin recital. But it marked Fleming as a man who could handle sentiment without turning it into bathos. His first talkie, *The Virginian* (1929), was also his last for Paramount, and he moved to MGM in 1932 to prep *Treasure Island*. Apparently talkies — which doomed the careers of Jannings, Vilma Banky, and other European stars brought to Hollywood — didn't faze the adaptable Fleming. It was in these early years that he and Clark Gable developed a bond that would sustain them through numerous hunting trips, fishing trips, and five pictures. Their first, *Red Dust*, is a love triangle set in Indochina, in which plantation owner Gable is in love (but doesn't know it) with a prostitute (and she does know it) played by Jean Harlow. Their lusty byplay was refreshing in pre-Code Hollywood and the film became famous, if not notorious, for Harlow's nude shower in a rain barrel.[163] When John Ford remade *Red Dust* twenty-one years later as *Mogambo*, setting it in Africa and keeping Gable but replacing Harlow with Ava Gardner, everything was toned down, including Gable's interest in being in it.

The Fleming-Gable association flourished in *The White Sister* and *Test Pilot* (1938) and, later, *Adventure* (1945). But it was *Gone with the Wind* (1939) where it became a deal-breaker. It's now part of the legend of that film that Gable famously forced producer David O. Selznick to fire the original director, George Cukor, in favor of Fleming, with whom he felt more comfortable, particularly in scenes where his character, Rhett Butler, had to cry over the death of his daughter, Bonnie Blue. Scholars have politely explained the switch by saying that Gable felt Cukor was giving too much attention to Vivien Leigh and Olivia DeHavilland. Others have more directly opined that it was really because Gable felt uneasy with Cukor's discrete but well-known homosexuality. Whichever the reason, Fleming was pulled off of the film he was then directing at Metro, *The Wizard of Oz*,[164] which was running frightfully behind schedule, and

---

163. Supposedly, after a take, Harlow playfully stood up out of the barrel and flashed the camera, saying, "This is for the guys in the editing room." Fleming immediately took the film out of the camera and flashed it too, only with sunlight.

164. George Cukor, Richard Thorpe, and King Vidor also directed portions of *The Wizard of Oz*.

handed — with all the advance work having been done for him — *Gone with the Wind*.

GWTW almost killed him. Not only did he have to wrangle the cast, he had to placate Selznick, whose odd hours and endless memos drove everyone to distraction. Fleming simply ignored both and devoted all his energies to the film, backed by Selznick's nonpareil creative team and his own directorial efficiency. By April of 1939, however, he formally requested help, and Selznick — after mulling Jack Conway or William Wellman to assist — settled on Sam Wood. Only Fleming would be credited; he was particularly strident against giving Cukor any due despite Cukor's having spent two years prepping, testing, casting, and starting the job.[165] After the post-war *Adventure*, which was distinguished only by its sales slogan "Gable's Back and Garson's Got Him!," Fleming and MGM ended their association. It took him three years to make what would be his last film, *Joan of Arc*.

The project began years earlier in the mind of Ingrid Bergman who arrived in Hollywood in 1939 under contract from Selznick to appear in his American remake of *Intermezzo*, the original of which had given her success three years earlier in Sweden. One of her goals even then was to play the bedeviled fourteen year-old farm girl who, in 1429, believed she heard God ("voices") telling her to raise the defeated French army and lead them against the occupying British during the Hundred Years War.[166] She succeeds, returning Charles VII to the throne of France, only to have the weak-willed Charles sell her out to the rival Burgundians who hand her to the English. The English, in turn, relay her to the Church, which has always been impatient with outsiders favored by God, and they burn her as a heretic.

Fleming's *Joan* was not the first time the virgin of Lorraine had hit the screen. Several silent versions preceded it, including one in 1900 by George Méliès and, most prominently, Carl Theodor Dreyer's 1928 *The Passion of Joan of Arc*. In 1934 RKO production chief Pandro Berman had wanted George Cukor to direct Katharine Hepburn as Joan and asked Maxwell Anderson to write it. When Anderson declined (though he would soon write it on his own), Berman hired Thornton Wilder to do a treatment, and that's as far as it went. George Bernard Shaw, of course,

---

165. Rudy Behlmer, ed., *Memo From David O. Selznick*. New York: The Viking Press, 1972.
166. The Hundred Years War between the Valoises and Plantagenets for the throne of France lasted from 1337 to 1453. *Apropos* of absolutely nothing, Hollywood apocrypha notes a frustrated screenwriter who once devised a classically stupid line that fortunately never made it to the screen: As a serf leaves his home in 1337 he tells his wife, "So long, dear, I'm off to fight the Hundred Years War."

had already written his version of the story based on trial records in his 1924 play *Saint Joan*.[167] But it was Anderson's 1946 *Joan of Lorraine* that solidified Bergman's devotion to the role. Anderson constructed a play-within-a-play, in which a troupe of actors stages the trial of Jeanne D'Arc as a way of resolving the personal conflict between the actress playing Joan and her director, who becomes her inquisitor. Depending whose lore you buy, Victor Fleming either saw Bergman at the Alvin Theatre and was so moved by her performance that he decreed then and there to make the film, or he saw her there and became her lover, after which the film was assured.[168] Either way, Fleming and Bergman had a fling while shooting, though she was still married to Dr. Petter Lindstrom. When the actress won the 1947 Tony for her stage performance, Walter Wanger bought the film rights for his independent Sierra Pictures.[169] He expected MGM to distribute, but when that deal fell out he went to RKO.

The filmmakers early on abandoned Anderson's play-within-a-play conceit, a move that upset the playwright, who would later criticize them for it despite having failed at adapting his work to their specifications. Fleming brought in Lawrence Stallings, who had been Anderson's collaborator on the wildly successful 1924 play *What Price Glory?*, to help. Not only were the two men unable to resume their partnership, Anderson felt frustrated that Bergman was demanding more from the play than a movie could manage. In August of 1947 Anderson fled Hollywood and the producers engaged Andrew Solt to pick up the pieces. Even after Solt turned in his draft, Fleming and Wanger interpolated parts of the 1431 trial transcript. The delay cost the filmmakers precious pre-production time, and on September 16, 1947 — barely five months after Bergman closed in the play — *Joan of Arc*, budgeted at $4.65 million, began its 75-day shoot on five soundstages at MGM.

Everyone was excited with Bergman playing Joan of Arc, but none of them counted on her *becoming* Joan. She was single-minded in her portrayal, and Wanger — as he would later do with Elizabeth Taylor in *Cleopatra* — acceded to his star's every whim. At the same time, Bergman and Fleming shared a hotel room, and even a visit to the room by Lindstrom — who clearly knew of the affair — didn't stop them. Whether this was the reason, or it was just his manner, Fleming seemed

---

167. Filmed notably by Otto Preminger in 1957 after a nationwide casting search for "Joan" that began the haunted career of Jean Seberg.
168. Michael Sragow. *Victor Fleming: An American Movie Master*. New York: Pantheon Books, 2008.
169. She also reportedly received $129,000 salary during the November 18, 1946–May 10, 1947 run.

to have little interest in directing the actors, and he had them rehearse by themselves while he worked with the camera crew and, only afterward, viewed what his cast had managed on their own.[170]

Released on November 11, 1948, the film was not well-received by the critics or the public, although the motion picture Academy was impressed enough to give it seven Oscar® nominations, none of which was for Best Picture, causing a bitter Wanger to refuse the coveted Irving G. Thalberg Award that the Academy Board of Governors had voted to give him. Soon an ever-struggling RKO cut the picture by 45 minutes, recorded narration, and added Joan's hitherto-unheard "voices" to the soundtrack.[171]

Restored in 1998 by UCLA Film and Television Archive to its 145-minute running time, it is a work that is alternately moving and troublesome. Given that the Joan of Arc story itself is essentially about a schizophrenic girl who bewitches superstitious Catholics into following her into battle, wins by luck, and then threatens church hierarchy by her mere existence, the film treads on sensitive shoes. It carefully portrays the Church as first absolving Joan, then later accusing her of witchcraft, but hedges history by changing her inquisitor *Bishop* Pierre Cauchon into *Count* Bishop Cauchon to make him a politician instead of a cleric.[172] Of particular interest is Joan's last cry of "Jesus" as a crucifix is offered to her while she burns at the stake, notable in that, for a film about a Catholic saint, there is no other hint of the Holy Trinity.

The picture's aggressive piety is well embodied in Bergman's unflinching dignity, abetted by Hugo Friedhofer's exquisitely subtle musical score. Particularly illustrative is a near-silent sequence in which Joan miraculously finds the true dauphin Charles (Jose Ferrer in a complex portrayal) purposely hiding within his retinue in an attempt to mock her passion. The film suffers, however, from its use of soundstages for most of the action scenes; it's incongruous watching Joan lead her army through sets where one can see the seams in the painted cloud backdrops and hear dialogue echoing off the soundstage walls. As Joan's trial proceeds to its foregone conclusion, Fleming moves his camera into beatific close-ups, reflecting the influence of Dreyer's *Passion of Joan of Arc*. Fleming's own passion, however, is reserved; his film is serious, respectful, and reverent, even though it has a clever script and enjoys savvy casting.

170. Sragow, op. cit.
171. Wanger held Howard Hughes, who then owned RKO, personally responsible for not supporting the film.
172. Nevertheless, a Father W. J. Fallou wrote to the producers suggesting that they "kill the Vatican sequence." (Source: undated letter, AMPAS.)

Fleming had a heart attack and died on January 6, 1949, two months after *Joan of Arc*'s world premiere and a few weeks shy of his 60th birthday. That same year, Bergman was so impressed by the work of Roberto Rossellini that she wrote him in Italy asking to become involved in his next project, *Stromboli*. Not only that, she became involved with the director. She deserted the serially cuckolded Lindstrom and became pregnant by Rossellini; the scandal led to her denunciation on the floor of the United States Senate. Bergman was no stranger to controversy — while publicizing *Joan of Lorraine* during its Washington, DC tryout in 1946, she had criticized racial segregation in the Nation's Capitol — so she took the *Stromboli* affair with typical Swedish aplomb. "People saw me in *Joan of Arc* and declared me a saint," she told the press. "I'm not. I'm just a woman, another human being."[173]

As for Victor Fleming — direct, unpretentious, and cinematically conservative — he may not have been fancy enough for entry into Sarris' pantheon, but he certainly put a lot of rear ends into theater seats.

---

173. Quoted by Donald Spoto in: *Notorious: The Life of Ingrid Bergman*. New York: HarperCollins, 1997.

JOHN FORD
Fighting Irish

John Ford, the greatest poet the American movies have ever known, made two last pictures, only one of which he actually directed. The one he completed was *7 Women* (1966), but he also started *Young Cassidy* (1964) until illness made him withdraw and have his work finished by Jack Cardiff. It is still billed as "A John Ford Film" despite carrying only a few minutes of Ford's footage, though critics at the time made fools of themselves ascribing some of it to Cardiff and some of Cardiff's to Ford. Acknowledged Ford, "I only did a few days' work — some scenes between Julie [Christie] and Rod Taylor."[174] It was as though the critics respected "Pappy" so much, they *wanted* him to have made all the good parts.

It's hard to know how much of *Young Cassidy* besides the footage — that is, the sets, color palette, costumes, cast, and crew — is Ford's versus what was readied for him by his producers. For it was Robert Graff and Robert Ginna (a former *Life* magazine writer) who hired critic/essayist/playwright John Whiting to adapt Sean O'Casey's six-volume memoir *Mirror in My House*.[175] Whiting died in 1963 and it took the producers two years after that to raise production coin. Because O'Casey himself had approved the script, the question of a rewrite may have been moot.[176] Ford, passionate about both O'Casey and Ireland, agreed to direct what was sold to him as a low-budget film for $50,000 plus 5 percent of producers' profits, far below his usual fee. He may also have wanted to atone

---

174. Peter Bogdanovich. *John Ford*. California: University of California Press, 1968.
175. Specifically *I Knock at the Door, Pictures in the Hallway, Drums Under the Window, Inishfallen Fare Thee Well, Rose and Crown*, and *Sunset and Evening Star*, collectively *Mirror in My House*. Whiting also adapted *The Devils* from Aldous Huxley's *The Devils of Loudun*, scandalously filmed in 1971 by Ken Russell.
176. O'Casey died on September 18, 1964, four months after the film wrapped.

for giving O'Casey short shrift in *The Plough and the Stars* (1936). More likely, he wanted to make one last working trip to Ireland.[177]

Ford knew he was reaching the end of his trail. He was 69 at the time and exhausted from the just-wrapped, much-troubled *Cheyenne Autumn*. Moreover, he and his wife, Mary, were at odds over his desire to scale down his lifestyle, sell his beloved yacht the *Araner*, and make *Young Cassidy* his last film. Mary wanted to keep the *Araner* and berated her husband for turning down a big commercial paycheck in favor of yet another project on his beloved ould sod.[178]

Ford was a mass of contradictions, none of which bothered him as much as they did those who tried to figure him out. He was born in Maine (as Sean O'Fearna) yet felt a kinship with Ireland even though he made some of the most "American" movies that Hollywood ever knew. He was thought of as a conservative, yet his thinking (except about women) was surprisingly progressive. He created John Wayne as a star, yet gave him a hard time every chance he got. More than anything else, he had an eye for lighting and composition, a sense of mood and place, and a psychic's insight into human nature (both of his actors and his audiences), yet dismissed all these talents as merely what it took to get the job done.

These — let's call them *ironies* rather than *inconsistencies* — hit critical mass on *Young Cassidy*. With Ford off on *Cheyenne Autumn*, producers Ginna and Graff cast Sean Connery to play Johnny ("Johnny Cassidy" was just one of the names O'Casey used for himself in his memoir). But Connery was suddenly called away by *Goldfinger* and was replaced by Rod Taylor, who likely had more in common temperamentally with O'Casey than Connery did, although neither the Scottish Connery nor the Australian Taylor was Irish. They also cast Julie Christie (who had just caused a sensation in John Schlesinger's *Billy Liar*), Maggie Smith, and Flora Robson.

Taking a break before previewing his troubled *Cheyenne Autumn* in the States, Ford flew to Dublin for a week's location scouting. What the young *Cassidy* producers didn't know (few outside his circle did) was that Ford was a binge drinker, and he chose Pan American and Aer Lingus to careen off the wagon. Arriving in Ireland disheveled and too drunk to walk, he was taken off the plane in a wheelchair and in a foul mood. The location scout became combative; Ford had wanted to shoot in black & white and in Limerick, which looked more like O'Casey's slum youth;

177. Joseph McBride. *The Search for John Ford: A Life*. New York: St. Martin's Press, 2001.
178. Dan Ford. *Pappy: The Life of John Ford*. New Jersey: Prentice-Hall, 1979. Mary and John stayed married until his death in 1973.

the producers demanded color and to shoot in Dublin, which was then undergoing massive urban renewal and would need to be dressed to recreate the story's 1911-1926 period setting. In that case, Ford grumbled, why film it in Ireland at all?

Returning to America, Ford was crushed by a disastrous sneak preview of *Cheyenne Autumn*. He sulked back to Ireland and, on July 14, 1964, rolled *Young Cassidy*. After thirteen shooting days he contracted viral pneumonia and, by early August, was on his way back to Los Angeles under doctor's orders.[179] The film was shut down for four days and then finished by Jack Cardiff, the eminent cinematographer who had taken up directing five years earlier. It premiered in London in February of 1965 and in New York a month later.

By the end of 1964 Ford was physically and emotionally recovered from both films and signaled his interest to work again by agreeing to do a project brought to him by his business partner, producer Bernard Smith, and MGM. Set at the war-torn Chinese — Mongolian border in 1935, it was about seven missionary women caught between the warlords and their own personalities. The main character is Dr. D. R. Cartwright, a woman who is hardly anybody's idea of a missionary: she smokes, drinks, and has had sex. When the six other less worldly women are taken captive by warlord Tunga Khan (Mike Mazurky), Cartwright offers herself as his concubine in exchange for the others' freedom, then kills him with a final, heartfelt, "So long, ya bastard!" before taking her own life.[180]

A film about women in China hardly seemed like a John Ford production, but by the middle 1960s he was coming to the realization that much of what he had once believed no longer applied in a changing world, including his idea of womanhood. Previously, Ford's women had been sacred mothers, virgins, pioneers, or lusty bar girls (unlike his peer Howard Hawks who, for years, had deemed any woman to be the equal of a man if she was good at a man's job). What also might have sparked Pappy's interest in this tale was its $250,000 directing payout and 50 percent of net for himself and Smith.

Scripted by married screenwriters Janet Green and John McCormick from a story by historical fiction author Norah Lofts called *Chinese Finale*,

---

179. Dan Ford, (op. cit.) Lindsay Anderson (*About John Ford*. New York: McGraw-Hill, 1981) and Peter Bogdanovich (op. cit.) maintain that Ford quit out of frustration with the producers. Anderson also states that he, Anderson, was offered the project before Ford was.

180. The theme is similar to Guy de Maupassant's short story "Boule le Suif" which inspired "Stage to Lordsburg" by Ernest Haycox and which was turned into Ford's 1939 *Stagecoach* by screenwriter Dudley Nichols.

7 Women (Ford specified the numeral instead of the word *seven*) was cast with all the protocol of a prisoner exchange. Ford wanted Katharine Hepburn to play Cartwright, and possibly Ingrid Bergman, Jennifer Jones, or Maggie Smith (to whom he'd taken a liking during *Young Cassidy*). Rosalind Russell lobbied for the part. Eventually it went to Patricia Neal. For a supporting role, the studio wanted Sue Lyon, who had just played Lolita for Stanley Kubrick. Ford preferred Carol Lynley. In the end, Bernard Smith worked out a deal with MGM executive Red Silverstein wherein they would take Lyon but MGM would give them financing and *carte blanche* on all other casting.[181] The roster was then filled with Margaret Leighton, Mildred Dunnock, Flora Robson, Anne Lee, and Betty Field.

Ford took offices on the MGM lot in January of 1965 where many of the younger employees had to be told who he was. The studio celebrated his 70th birthday (he was actually 71) with a press party on February 1. Photography began on February 8. On February 17, Patricia Neal suffered a series of strokes that took her speech, sight, and much of her mobility, and Ford and Smith were forced to recast her part with Anne Bancroft. (Neal later made a miraculous recovery and returned to acting.)

The wordy script (the McCormicks previously wrote the socially themed pictures *Victim*, about homosexuality, and *Sapphire*, about race) was shot entirely on MGM's Stage 15 except for three days of exteriors at Glenmoor Ranch in Sutton Canyon near Chatsworth, California. According to Philip K. Scheuer, who landed a rare interview with Ford on the walled mission set, the director was uncommonly polite to his nearly all-female cast, being constitutionally unable to swear in their presence. Actress Jane Chang, who played a mission staffer in the film, reported that Ford was so kind that he even wiped her face with his handkerchief after a stressful take. Given that Ford had the nervous habit of sucking on his handkerchiefs, Chang had to go a long way to call it a compliment. The only person who caught hell from the director was Eddie Albert, playing a mission teacher, who realized early on that he would be Ford's scapegoat when things got dull on the set.[182] Also true to form, whenever anybody advised Ford that he was falling behind schedule, he would tear a few pages out of his script and announce, "Now we're back on schedule." In truth, he was tightening and rewriting as he went along, and he wrapped on April 12 with two days of pickups on April 20 and 21.

181. McBride, op. cit.
182. McBride, op. cit.

Only one retake was necessary to cover the Neal-Bancroft replacement, although the delay drove the picture six days over schedule and came in at just under $2,300,000.

Some reports say that Ford was not entirely happy with Bancroft's performance. Other reports say that Ford was pleased with Bancroft, who had just won an Academy Award® for *The Miracle Worker* and would continue to act on stage and screen for the next 39 years. If Ford had doubts about anything, it was himself, for he feared that the picture would end his directing career, which it effectively did. After Ford edited *7 Women*, MGM recut it, and to the end of his life the director claimed never to have seen the result. Showing similar disinterest, the studio released it in New York on the bottom half of a double bill with Burt Kennedy's *The Money Trap*. While Ford partisans like Andrew Sarris proclaimed the film's greatness, even he had to admit that the picture was "at once too profound for the art-film circuit, and too personal for the big, brassy Broadway houses…the beauties of *Seven* [sic] *Women* are for the ages, or at least for a later time when the personal poetry of film directors is better understood between the lines of genre conventions."[183]

There is conjecture that Ford began experiencing symptoms during *7 Women* of the cancer that began his long decline. Nevertheless, on April 23, 1973 he announced that he would go back to Monument Valley to make *Appointment with Precedence* about Josh Clayton, the first black graduate of West Point to lead a black cavalry regiment. It was written by Robert Johnson, who had acted for him in *Sergeant Ruttledge* in 1960, would co-star Woody Strode, who had played Ruttledge for him, with Fred Williamson starring as Clayton. Of course, it never happened.

John Ford, who always denied that he did anything more than just make westerns, died on August 31, 1973, not long after telling interviewers Joseph McBride and Michael Wilmington, "I'm just a hard-nosed, hard-working ex-director and I'm trying to retire gracefully."[184] As Ethan Edwards said, via John Wayne, in Ford's 1956 masterpiece *The Searchers*, "That'll be the day."

---

183. Andrew Sarris. *The John Ford Movie Mystery*. Bloomington, Indiana: Indiana University Press, 1975.
184. Joseph McBride and Michael Wilmington. *John Ford*. New York: DaCapo Press, 1975.

John Frankenheimer.

JOHN FRANKENHEIMER
Thirds

John Frankenheimer used to say that his 1966 film, *Seconds*, went from being a flop to being a classic without ever being a hit. In a similar twist of fate, his last film, *Reindeer Games* (2000), was turned from a possible success into a certain flop before it ever opened, and achieved prestige only after it was resurrected on DVD, but by then it was too late.

Born in 1930 in the upscale New York community of Malba, Queens, Frankenheimer wanted to be a professional tennis player until he attended Williams College, which he hated, and drifted toward acting, which he liked. His military commitment brought him into the Air Force's filmmaking unit in Los Angeles and it was there that he found his calling. When there was no work for him in California after discharge from the service, he used his mustering pay to travel to New York in 1953 where live television was just beginning and where he lucked into a job as an Associate Director at CBS under Sidney Lumet. Lumet and other tyros — Arthur Penn, Robert Mulligan, Delbert Mann, Arthur Hiller, Ralph Nelson — were literally inventing the medium as they went along, and by mid-decade the fearlessly inventive Frankenheimer had joined their ranks. He brought an angular, sometimes expressionistic camera and lighting style to the series *Danger*, *You Are There*, and — moving to Los Angeles — *Climax* and *Playhouse 90*. Like Mann, Penn, and other TV hotshots he was lured to motion pictures and in 1956 directed a feature-length expansion of his 1955 *Climax* episode, "Deal a Blow," as *The Young Stranger* (released in 1957). The experience was unpleasant; where he felt at ease in live TV, the demands of corporate studio movie production were, in his words, "constipated." He tried sticking with it and was set to direct *Breakfast at Tiffany's* with Marilyn Monroe, but when Monroe was replaced by Audrey Hepburn, and Hepburn and her husband, Mel Ferrer, had never heard of him, he was fired.

"I thought my life was over," he said. He was thirty, going through a divorce, had two kids, and eagerly took *The Young Savages* for producer Harold Hecht and star Burt Lancaster. He got the job, he said, "not because I was any good, but because I could do it in thirty-five days."[185] The picture, about a D.A. who prosecutes a racial murder by three teenagers, led him to a collaboration with Lancaster through four more pictures: *The Birdman of Alcatraz* (1962), *Seven Days in May* and *The Train* (both 1964), and *The Gypsy Moths* (1969). Despite this, Frankenheimer said of his benefactor, "We were never friends. We did five pictures but we were never friends."[186]

His Hollywood rise began in 1962 with an astonishing trio: *All Fall Down*, *The Birdman of Alcatraz*, and *The Manchurian Candidate*. *Candidate*, in particular, boasted an assertive visual style and a dramatic intensity on top of its explosive content. Adapted by George Axelrod from Richard Condon's conspiracy novel about a Korean War POW who was programmed to assassinate a presidential candidate at the covert behest of his super-patriot U.S. mother, it inspired a spate of paranoid political thrillers. But things changed two years later with his penultimate film with Lancaster, *The Train*. A taut World War II chase picture about the French Resistance hijacking a train full of art treasures seized by the Nazis, it was begun by Arthur Penn. After his first day, Lancaster had Penn fired and replaced by Frankenheimer, whom he had secretly called to location in France, having been released from post-producing *Seven Days in May* at Lancaster's request.[187] Although it emerged as a solid piece of work, *The Train* performed poorly at the box office. Frankenheimer followed it in 1966 with the racing picture *Grand Prix* and the moody, disturbing science fiction drama *Seconds*. The former featured the kind of technical challenge at which Frankenheimer excelled (Cinerama), and the latter — about a man who gets a reboot via a body transplant but screws up again — was the kind of stylized piece at which he was a past master. Both were box office disappointments and, following the bad karma of *The Train*, Frankenheimer plunged into a career slump.

185. Interviewed for the Archive of American Television by Michael Rosen, April 13, 2000 *(www.emmys.org)*.
186. Archive of American Television, ibid. Lancaster apparently felt the same way. When he had Arthur Penn fired from *The Train* and replaced with Frankenheimer, he told the film's screenwriter, Walter Bernstein, "Frankenheimer is a bit of a whore but he'll do what I want." (Source: Kate Buford. *Burt Lancaster: An American Life*. New York: Alfred A. Knopf, 2000.)
187. Penn said that Frankenheimer confessed to him years later that he "had been really pretty profoundly alcoholic during this period." He stopped drinking in 1980. (Penn interview with the author).

It got worse on June 5, 1968. He had become close friends with Robert F. Kennedy, traveled with the senator's presidential campaign for 102 days, and produced its film and television material. Kennedy stayed at Frankenheimer's Malibu Beach house while campaigning in the California primary, and, after winning it, was driven by Frankenheimer to his victory celebration at the Ambassador Hotel in downtown Los Angeles. There he was assassinated.

"If you want to date a moment that things started to turn," the director reflected years later, "it was after that night. I went through sheer hell. I went to Europe, and I just lost interest. I got burned out. I was really left very disillusioned and went through a period of deep depression. It took a long time to get it back."[188] He spent five years abroad, took cooking classes, and reassessed his life and career. Though he was never truly "between pictures" — whether it was *The Fixer* (1968), *The Gypsy Moths* (1969), *The Iceman Cometh* (1973), *The French Connection II* (1975), *Black Sunday* (1977), or *52 Pick-Up* (1986), he always delivered the goods — but by now the former wunderkind had become just another Hollywood director.

"I had gone through a relatively bad time in the 80s making some undistinguished movies," he admitted. "The phone literally didn't ring for a year and a half." When it finally did, it was an offer to go back to television. It was *Against the Wall* (1994) about New York's 1971 Attica prison uprising, and it both revived Frankenheimer's career and anointed HBO as a major industry player. It led him to *Andersonville* (1996), *George Wallace* (1997), and *Path to War* (2002), more Emmys, and revived respect (except for the bloated *The Island of Dr. Moreau* in 1996) from cineastes. The old Frankenheimer was back, and it was confirmed by his flawless blend of action and characterization in *Ronin* (1998). Lean and explosive, consistently captivating, and as stylish as Carol Reed's *The Third Man* (which was its director's intention), it was a perfect use of the medium for the then-68-year-old filmmaker.

Reindeer Games (2000) could have been of equal stature. Instead, it was hijacked by focus groups. Scripted by Ehren Kruger, it's a highly contrived yarn about a newly paroled convict (Ben Affleck) who takes on his dead cellmate's identity in order to romance Ashley (Charlize Theron) whom the cellmate knew only as a pen-pal. The plot thickens when Affleck is forced into committing an Indian casino robbery on Christmas Eve by Gabriel (Gary Sinise) who may be Ashley's brother.

188. Bernard Weinraub, *Los Angeles Times,* July 7, 2002.

To make the story work, Frankenheimer used every trick in his considerable catalog: Dutch angles (cocked framing), pre-lapped sound cuts, and screen composition with one character close and others distant. What's particularly savvy is the director's awareness of answering the audience's questions at exact moment they mentally ask them.

Dimension Films — a subsidiary set up by Miramax for their less sophisticated product — acquired Kruger's script in October of 1998 and put it on the fast track.[189] When Miramax attracted Frankenheimer two months later,[190] head honcho Harvey Weinstein enthused, "It's an honor to work with a guy like that. He's a legend and he's still cooking after all these years."[191] They even made it the first of a four-picture deal.[192] Production began on March 15, 1999 on a $40 million budget[193] in Prince George and Vancouver, British Columbia, Canada in order to catch the snow (some of which later had to be CGI'd when spring thaw arrived). It was scheduled for a Christmas release to capitalize on the title. Frankenheimer insisted on rehearsal and used the time to help the actors, particularly Sinise, shape their characters. Filming shut down for four days after Affleck was knocked unconscious when a bad-ass con played by San Francisco 49ers defensive tackle Dana Stubblefield accidentally fell on him during a prison riot scene. For a sequence in which Affleck and Theron fall through ice on a frozen lake, the ice was plastic and the close shots were done in a heated tank. Finding an Indian casino to rob was a matter of dressing the façade of a seedy lounge with "Tomahawk" signs and using clever staging to bridge the cut from exterior to a soundstage where the robbery and final shoot-out take place. Professional croupiers were hired for the tables.

The real drama of *Reindeer Games* didn't start until the film was finished and was shown to a test audience. Previews have become the bane of creativity ever since 1987 when the producers of *Fatal Attraction* famously changed the ending of their film after a handful of advance viewers said that they wanted to see the villainess (Glenn Close) dispatched by the wife (Anne Archer) instead of taking her own life in a way that would incriminate Archer's philandering husband (Michael Douglas). Never mind that nothing in the story or characterizations led up to it; pandering trumped story construction. Time and studio nervousness since then have only made matters worse.

189. Thom Geier, *Hollywood Reporter*, October 16, 1998.
190. Monica Roman, *Daily Variety*, January 11, 1999.
191. Kathleen Craughwell, *Los Angeles Times*, February 25, 2000.
192. *Daily Variety*, June 21, 1999.
193. *Daily Variety*, June 21, 1999.

In the case of *Reindeer Games*, the preview cards came in like those for Frankenheimer's previous film, *Ronin:* positive but not exuberant. That wasn't good enough for Dimension Films, who sided with the roughly twenty individuals who were selected for the after-screening focus group and whined that the picture started slowly. They were also disturbed by the movie's brutality, not just blood, but the personal violence visited upon the Affleck character. Frankenheimer countered that the Saturday night "date" mentality was "not the picture we set out to make,"[194] but it fell on deaf ears, so the film was shorn of much of its character detail. As commonly happens in such cases, this made it run shorter but feel longer. The focus group comments also triggered a major reshoot to answer the question, "why does Affleck go along with the robbery? Why doesn't he just leave or call the police?" The reshoots made *Reindeer Games* miss its timely Christmas release[195] and, when it finally came out in February of 2000, it was the version that had been contorted to feed the attention span of the focus group. On a budget of $34 million it grossed less than $24 million, meaning that film rental was roughly $12 million levied against costs for prints and advertising. Like *Seconds*, the public caught up with it on video where, with reconstruction to bring it back to the director's original plan, it now survives.

"Believe me, I was party to these changes," Frankenheimer admitted. "It's not like I was forced to make [them]. I willingly agreed to do it because I believed I could get the desired effect from a preview audience... [and] finally I got the movie that I want to be part of my work that people remember." But he added, "I wonder how a picture like *Casablanca* could ever have survived the preview process of today."[196]

As he prepped his next film, *Exorcist: The Beginning*, rumors began circulating that Frankenheimer was the biological father of filmmaker Michael Bay (*The Rock, Transformers, Pearl Harbor*, etc.). Although Frankenheimer admitted to having had a past relationship with Bay's birth mother, in May of 2001 he denied that he had fathered Michael and that "tests" had proved him truthful. Bay claimed otherwise, insisting that DNA tests at the time Frankenheimer had them were less sophisticated and were therefore unreliable. The matter blew back on Bay, who was accused of trying to raise his image by connecting himself with Frankenheimer.

194. These and other Frankenheimer remarks come from his commentary on the *Reindeer Games* DVD.
195. Having missed its Christmas release date, the film was momentarily retitled *Deception*. Kathleen Craughwell, *Los Angeles Times*, December 19, 1999.
196. Frankenheimer's DVD commentary.

On June 5, 2002 Frankenheimer announced that he was withdrawing from the *Exorcist* prequel over "health concerns" and checked into Cedars-Sinai Center for spinal surgery to relieve a chronically bad back.[197] Recuperating in the hospital, he had discussions with Gary Sinise about setting up a production company[198] and began rehab hoping to return to the director's chair and perhaps play tennis again. Instead, on July 6, he suffered a massive post-operative stroke and died at the age of 72.

"There's no happy ending for all of this," he had said in an archive interview for the Television Academy in the spring of 2000. "Nobody beats time, you know? I've reached a certain age where I have to start thinking that this is the last act. But I want it to be as good as it can right up until the end. I think that I'm capable of doing the best work in my life if I put it all together. I really love the process and I want to keep doing it as long as they'll let me do it."[199]

197. Army Archerd, *Variety*, May 21, 2002 and *Los Angeles Times,* June 5, 2002.
198. *TV Guide*, August 10, 2002.
199. Archive of American Television, op. cit.

SAMUEL FULLER
In a Word, Emotion

Once upon a time there was a cigar with a fire burning at one end and a filmmaker burning at the other. He was Samuel Fuller, a garrulous and totally committed force of life whether he was on a movie set or in combat (he said they were the same). In seminars, interviews, or working with his collaborators, he never wavered from his credo: "Film is a battleground: Love, hate, violence, action, death; in a word, emotion." That credo informs the first feature he directed in 1949, *I Shot Jesse James*, to his last completed American film, *White Dog*, released in 1982.[200]

Samuel Michael Fuller was the son of Jewish immigrants and he inherited the survival instinct that brought his father, Benjamin, and his mother, Rebecca, from Russia and Poland, respectively, to Worcester, Massachusetts, where he was born in 1912. As a youngster he hawked the *Worcester Telegram* on street corners to help support his family, which grew to seven children. When his father died in 1923, his mother moved the Fullers to New York City where Sam snared a job as copy boy on the *New York Journal*. In 1928 he moved to the *New York Graphic*, a scream sheet that confirmed his infatuation with newspapers, even though he languished in their morgue (archive). Soon he was made a reporter and assigned to the crime beat, which taught him how to find explosive subjects, write lurid leads, and compose lean narrative. "My love was the byline on a newspaper," he told writer Richard Schickel. "It was the biggest thrill I've ever had in my life."[201] It was a tradition that never left him, and he paid tribute to it in 1952 with *Park Row*.[202]

---

200. He adapted and directed *Les voleurs de la nuit* in France in 1984.
201. Interviewed by Schickel in *The Men Who Made the Movies*. Lorac Productions/TCM, 2002.
202. Fuller personally financed this legacy project set in the 1880s against the background of the invention of the linotype machine and lost his entire $200,000 investment when it tanked.

He had started writing for movies while he was covering crime — to Fuller, they weren't that far apart — and took his craft on the road when the Great Depression hobbled America, filing stories from the boxcars, truck stops, and dives he lived in as he headed west. He covered a Klan rally for the *San Francisco Chronicle* and a brutal labor strike for the *San Diego Sun*, finally settling in Southern California. He published his first novel in 1935 and continued writing for pulps, becoming a screenwriter in 1936 with *Hats Off, It Happened in Hollywood* (1937) and *Gangs of New York* (1938).

But it was World War II that shaped Fuller more profoundly than newspapers or Hollywood. Serving with the U.S. Army's First Infantry Division in North Africa, he was in the forefront of liberating Europe, and these experiences colored everything he wrote from then on, not only war stories but in a filmmaking style of immediacy and directness. When he got to direct his own script for *I Shot Jesse James*, he started right off breaking the roles. Fuller maintained that James was not a mythic western figure but "a lowlife thief, a pervert, and a sonofabitch."[203] "He and his brother, Frank James, the first job they had…they held up a hospital train, military train, killed the wounded and robbed them. That's number one. Number two, when he was sixteen he was a girl impersonator…He would dress as a girl, he would entice soldiers in there, and his brother Frank would kill them."[204] Fuller's film, although it contains the requisite western elements, also carries a subversive undercurrent. In the story, Robert Ford, who rides with James' gang but begins to feel trapped, deduces that the only way to free himself from James' thrall is by killing his notorious friend. While Ford's actions are explained by the plot device of an amnesty that's offered as the reward for killing James, the actual assassination is more like an exorcism, for Ford has clearly become sexually attracted to the outlaw in a way that westerns at that time — or, for that matter, the movies — never discussed.[205]

Fuller said that movies are like the bold headlines in a newspaper, and he talked that way, in large type with exclamation points. His interviews show him as crusty, opinionated, and cocksure but neither cruel nor arrogant, chiefly because his films delivered everything his personality promised. They reflect, for wont of a better word, a pragmatic avoidance

---

203. Samuel Fuller, Christa Fuller and Jerome Rhodes. *A Third Face: My Tale of Writing, Fighting, and Filmmaking*. Montclair, New Jersey: Hal Leonard Company, 2004.
204. Schickel, op. cit.
205. Similar themes were raised by Gore Vidal and subsequently by Leslie Stevens in Arthur Penn's 1957 film about Billy the Kid, *The Left Handed Gun*, until the Production Code ordered them dulled.

of romanticism. In *Forty Guns* (1957), for example, the only way for gunslinger Barry Sullivan to kill John Ericson, who has shielded himself by grabbing Barbara Stanwyck, is to shoot Stanwyck first. In *Pickup On South Street* (1953), pickpocket Richard Widmark is lectured by Feds that it's his patriotic duty to help their plan to close down a spy ring that he has unwittingly foiled by filching a purse containing evidence. Instead of having a moral epiphany like any other movie villain, Widmark sneers dismissively, "Are *you* waving the flag at *me*?" In *The Naked Kiss* (1964) a prostitute, Constance Towers, rolls her pimp for the money he owes her, but takes only what's rightly hers and tosses the change back in his face.

"Sammy's crime reporting and his experience in World War II taught him that we are predatory and we are animals and we're primitive," said Christa Lang-Fuller, Sam's widow.[206] Insisted Fuller himself, "Violence, to me, should be emotional. I like it [internalized], not a bar fight."[207] Nothing stated this more clearly than his 1951 Korean war film, *Steel Helmet*, in which Gene Evans as Sgt. Zack is blasé about the carnage going on around him until a little orphaned boy, rather than rampant death, causes him to let loose. "What Zack epitomized there was the symbol of a non-com," Fuller told Eric Sherman and Martin Rubin. "No emotion whatsoever. None! Because if you have emotions, you're not in war. There's no time for emotion. It becomes a job.... The only emotion you have inside of you is: 'When do I get out of here, and when does somebody replace me?'"[208] He updated that scene in *The Big Red One* (1980), his autobiographical magnum opus, in which Sgt. Lee Marvin tries to break through the emotional wall that a young concentration camp survivor has built around himself.[209] By controlling emotions on the screen, Fuller ignited them in his audiences.

Emotions for Fuller were seldom simply joy, fear, love, or tears, but those that were more complex: anger tempered with reason, frustration blended with irony, or — in the case of his last film — a tough combination of guilt, self-righteousness, pity, curiosity, and pride. As it turned out, those emotions nearly destroyed *White Dog*.

---

206. Where not otherwise credited, much of the information in this essay is drawn from the Criterion *White Dog* DVD special feature "Four-Legged Time Bomb" produced by Susan Arosteguy.
207. Schickel, op. cit.
208. Eric Sherman and Martin Rubin. *The Director's Event: Interviews with Five American Filmmakers*. New York: Atheneum, 1970.
209. *The Big Red One* was significantly cut upon its release in 1980 but was restored by Richard Schickel in 2004 based on the director's notes.

The story began with awful truth. When actress Jean Seberg and her then-husband Romain Gary were living in Hollywood in the 1960s, a beautiful white German shepherd stray entered their lives. A short time later they were shocked when the dog suddenly attacked and mauled their black gardener. After that, they confined it to their back yard, but twice it managed to get out and attack two more people, both black. It dawned on them that the animal had somehow been trained to go after non-whites. Gary wrote the incident as a short story for *Life* magazine in October of 1970, then expanded it into a semi-autobiographical novel titled *Chien blanc* that was published a month later.

For the book, the dog was named Batka and its previous ownership was traced to an Alabama police department. Given the history of Jim Crow racism in the South, it made dramatic sense that such a dog would exist, and, given Jean Seberg's well-known (and well-persecuted, by the FBI) history with the Black Panthers, Gary had a rich palette to work with. In the story, the dog is brought for deprogramming to a black dog trainer who then reprograms it, not to be docile, but to go after white people.

Despite the novel's explosive theme of White versus Black racism, Paramount Pictures' production head Robert Evans acquired it in 1975 and had Curtis Hanson adapt the book for Roman Polanski to direct. But when Polanski fled America in the wake of a statutory rape indictment, the project entered Development Hell. Writers Thomas Baum and Nicholas Kazan did versions for producers Edgar J. Scherick and Nicholas Vanoff when Tony Scott was scheduled to attempt making the film, and then it was shelved.[210] In 1979 Seberg died under circumstances that remain murky; and in 1980 Gary shot himself to death (they had divorced in 1970). In 1981, with a directors' and writers' strike looming, Paramount's new vice president of production Don Simpson and studio president Michael Eisner deemed *White Dog* to be far enough along in development to resuscitate. They brought Hanson back for another rewrite and handed it to producer Jon Davison. When Hanson couldn't get the studio to let him direct it (Hanson would later make *L.A. Confidential*) he suggested Sam Fuller. Fuller was 70 at the time.

"I don't think anybody at Paramount knew Sam Fuller or his work," said Davison. "They *did* know *The Big Red One*."[211] It was, to be sure, a daring choice; *The Big Red One* had suffered studio interference and had not performed well despite critical enthusiasm. But Hanson and Davison knew

210. *Daily Variety*, October 2, 1980.
211. Interviewed on Criterion DVD.

that Fuller had an affinity for the exploitation elements of *White Dog*, and he could also put on speed. For a rare time in his career he agreed to write with a collaborator — Hanson — and the two pounded away at dueling upright manual typewriters in Fuller's office for marathon stretches until the rewrite was completed in a record three weeks.

"I would type a draft of the scene and then I would give it to Sammy," Hanson recalled. "At a certain point he would go, 'My boy, come here' and I would get up and walk around his desk…and he would have a cigar and, if it wasn't lit, he'd light it, and he would then read me the rewrite of my scene — I should say the rewrite of *my* draft of *our* scene. I did my best to have absolutely no ego about it and enjoy the performance that Sammy did, and performance it was, as he read every part…I was there to serve Sam, and happily so."[212] Fuller later held that he promised to rewrite eighty-five percent of the script in ten days and finish the rest on the set.[213] True to his word, forty-three days after production started on April 21, he brought the film in.[214]

Meanwhile another drama was brewing in the Paramount suites. Almost as soon as *White Dog* was announced, the company defensively hired Willis Edwards of the NAACP and David L. Crippins of the local PBS station as paid consultants to examine script material and suggest how to keep from inflaming an already incendiary subject. Fuller didn't find out about this until Edwards showed up on the set one day to see if the director was "distorting the image of black people." Fuller was furious. "Why hadn't an organization as prestigious as the NAACP done their homework and checked out my record before sending a man to check on my work?"[215] When Fuller complained to Davison, Edwards was asked to leave but not go away, because, at a May 17 meeting among Davison, Edwards, Crippins, and actor Paul Winfield (who had been cast as Keys, the dog deprogrammer), the men agreed to delay release of the film until the Atlanta killer or killers had been apprehended;[216] to include Fuller's note that Nazis had used dogs to sniff out Englishmen in World War II; that it was troubling that Keys put down the dog only after it attacked a white person; and that Julie (the Jean Seberg character) should confront

---

212. Interviewed on Criterion DVD.
213. Roderick Mann, *Los Angeles Times*, June 29, 1981.
214. *Hollywood Reporter* production chart, April 24, 1981.
215. Fuller, Fuller, and Jerome Rhodes. *A Third Face: My Tale of Writing, Fighting, and Filmmaking*. Montclair, New Jersey: Hal Leonard Company, 2004.
216. Between 1979 and 1981, twenty-eight black children were murdered. In 1982 Wayne Williams was convicted of some, but not all, of the deaths.

Keys about his feelings toward racism.[217] In response to Davison's report of the meeting, Dom Simpson reminded all concerned that the dog must die at the end, not because of whom it attacks but because it has become unstable and to show that "racial hatred is not innate, but is taught." At the same time that Simpson deferred to his consultants, he also warned them that Paramount would make its own decisions and not listen to "a functioning actor on the set" (i.e., Winfield).[218] Production president Jeffrey Katzenberg tried to arbitrate the situation by telling Davison to include Crippins' and Edwards' concerns in the script while keeping it within Fuller's vision.[219] Remarkably, Fuller untangled the mixed signals and assured Davison, "I am in accord with their points, which have been incorporated in Scene 69, page 65."[220] The result reinforces the film's theme that hatred is taught: "He's not a monster," Keys tells Julie. "He was made into one by a two-legged racist." He then elaborates, "The owners had to sink low enough to find a black wino who desperately needed a drink or a black junkey [sic] who'd do *anything* for a fix — and paid them to beat your dog when he was a puppy."[221]

Fuller and Hanson did change Gary's ending so the trainer succeeded in deprogramming the dog but did not retrain him to go after whites. They took out Keys' Islamist politics and cast Carruthers, who believes the dog should be put down rather than retrained, with Burl Ives, although Fuller initially wanted Lee Marvin, Richard Widmark, or Burt Lancaster. Julie was played by Kristy McNichol after Jodie Foster and Kathleen Quinlan were unavailable. The dog was played by five separate canines trained by Karl Lewis Miller. At the core of the story was that if a dog could be taught to overcome racism, so could humans. In the end, however, as Hanson said, "this beautiful creature had been so polluted by the ugliness of racism that it had been driven insane."[222]

Sets were built at the Wild Life WayStation, an animal sanctuary that had been founded in the Angeles National Forest in 1975 by Martine Collette. The chief structure was a $750,000 gladiatorial cage in which Keys would try to change Batka. Paul Winfield gamely did his own stunt

217. May 18, 1981 memo from Davison to Jeffrey Katzenberg, Paramount President of Production. Jon Davison papers, AMPAS.
218. May 26, 1981 memo from Simpson to Katzenberg. Jon Davison papers, AMPAS. Winfield memorably played the father in *Sounder* and Rev. Martin Luther King, Jr. in the 1978 TV mini-series *King*.
219. June 5, 1981 memo from Katzenberg to Davison. Jon Davison papers, AMPAS.
220. June 6, 1981 memo from Fuller to Davison. Jon Davison papers, AMPAS.
221. Straw script pages (undated). Jon Davison papers, AMPAS.
222. Interviewed on Criterion DVD.

work, wearing body padding and battling the dog(s) himself despite an unusually hot Los Angeles summer.[223]

Paramount let Fuller finish his $6 million shoot, held a couple of sneak previews, allowed the picture to screen in festivals, and then quietly killed it.[224] Its latest reported gross is less than $100,000. Paramount then attempted to recoup some of its investment by selling the film to television in a trimmed, presumably less inflammatory, form. And that began another scandal. Originally sold to pay cable for $500,000, it drew such a large audience on its first run that NBC broadcast network agreed to pay $2.5 million if the studio would pull the film off cable so it could be scheduled during the network's important February ratings sweeps.[225] As soon as the deal was announced, the public firestorm resumed and NBC hurriedly cancelled plans to show the film, while never admitting that it had yielded to pressure.[226] Not until 2008 was *White Dog* restored to Fuller's cut and issued on Criterion DVD.[227]

The shelving and cutting angered Fuller who, unlike the entrenched studios, had a reputation for supporting integration. He had used stereotype-free casting all his career, and made a blazingly effective anti-racism subplot in *Shock Corridor* (1963) in which a black inmate in a mental hospital believes he's a Klansman and lays waste to the KKK's hate slogans. Were *White Dog* not based on a true story, nobody would believe it, although anyone who saw the newsreels of Civil Rights demonstrators being set upon by dogs in the South during the 1950s and 60s would have to watch the film with one eye on the screen and another on history. "In the fifties he could do much more controversial films than in 1982," said Christa Fuller. "That's strange."[228] "I was deeply hurt," Fuller wrote in his memoir. "The studio had used me as a scapegoat for their lack of determination and courage. *White Dog* was a thought-provoking movie exposing the stupidity and irrationality of racism in our society. Nothing more, nothing less."[229]

For the last fifteen years of his life, Fuller, like most of his generation of directors, was unable to raise financing for more projects, even from

223. Charles Taylor, *New York Times*, November 2, 2008.
224. Todd McCarthy, *Weekly Variety*, February 9, 1983.
225. Jefferson Graham, *Hollywood Reporter*, January 19, 1984.
226. *Hollywood Reporter*, January 16, 1984. On February 3, 1984 Christa Fuller wrote Rich Frank, who headed NBC-TV, thanking him for defending *White Dog* but adding a zinger that "maybe some other network will be more enlightened." Jon Davison papers, AMPAS.
227. Interviewed on Criterion DVD.
228. Interviewed on Criterion DVD.
229. Fuller et al., op. cit.

the executives who came to him for advice or asked him to act in their movies. In frustration he moved to Europe where he managed to adapt and direct *Les voleurs de la nuit (Thieves of the Night)* in 1984. He was at his most effective, though, in inspiring a new generation of directors and critics who saw in his no-frills pictures what his contemporary reviewers had missed or dismissed. A brilliant pitch-man — at 5'6" he may have been overcoming his height with personality — he relished playing the cantankerous, quotable *eminence grise* to interviewers, festival crowds, and young filmmakers. Those who admired him, like Curtis Hanson, Martin Scorsese, Jim Jarmusch, Jon Davison, Quentin Tarantino, and Tim Robbins, came away enriched. "He would grab your arm," Davison said, "just to make sure your attention wasn't drifting. He wanted to make sure you understood how much he cared."[230]

Fuller died on October 30, 1997 of natural causes.

---

230. Interviewed on Criterion DVD.

D.W. GRIFFITH
The Long Goodbye

There was something Messianic about D. W. Griffith. Like Moses, he posed as someone else while growing up (acting), then discovered his calling (directing) and led his people (nascent filmmakers) from the wilderness (nickelodeons) into a promised land (cinema). He gave them a codified law (screen syntax), only to see them worship idols (box office), and was then kept from enjoying the fruits of his achievement because of a past sin (*The Birth of a Nation*) and a capricious and vengeful god (the public).

Maybe that's pushing it a little, but it's indisputable that Griffith did more than anyone else to legitimize the art of film. In his choice of subjects, his development of young talent (who didn't have stage-taught habits to de-learn for movies), and by opening his bigger films in grand picture palaces instead of storefronts, he drew a higher class of patron, and favorable press attention followed. For all this, though, he died in relative obscurity eighteen years after his last picture, *The Struggle* (1931). True, the motion picture Academy recognized him with a special Oscar® in 1935. And producer Hal Roach hired him to advise his 1940 caveman picture *One Million B.C.* which, suggests Griffith biographer Richard Schickel, the clever Roach did as a compassionate handout as well as and to exploit Griffith's prestige.[231]

But by that time directing another picture was out of the question for Griffith, and as he entered his seventies the "father of film" occupied an apartment at the Hollywood Knickerbocker Hotel in a gin haze surrounded by the detritus of his life and career. This is where journalist

---

231. Richard Schickel. *D.W. Griffith: An American Life*. Milwaukee, Wisconsin: Hal Leonard Corp., 1996.

Ezra Goodman stumbled into what became Griffith's last interview, and even then the reporter had trouble selling it. For Griffith had drifted so far outside the recollection of mainstream editors that Goodman had to place the piece in Britain's *PM* magazine's March 28, 1948 Sunday edition. Four months later, on July 23, Griffith died of a cerebral hemorrhage. "The sacred cows of Hollywood gathered to pay him homage," Goodman wrote. "A week before that he probably could not have gotten any of them on the telephone."[232] When the Hollywood Masonic Temple, where the services were held, filled only halfway, its doors were opened to tourists. At the time of his death, Griffith had reportedly been working on a playscript called *The Treadmill* and had completed the first eighty or ninety pages of an autobiography he intended to call *D.W. Griffith and the Wolf*.

The wolf was poverty, which he knew growing up in rural Crestwood, Kentucky where he was born in 1875. It was there that young David Wark Griffith heard stories from his elders who had fought and lost the Civil War. "I suppose it began when I was a child," he told Walter Huston in a prelude to the 1930 reissue of *The Birth of a Nation*. "I used to get under the table and listen to my father and his friends talk about the battles they'd been through and their struggles. Those things impress you deeply." Years later he would weave their tales — and, more destructively, their racial attitude ("the Klan at that time was needed, it served a purpose."[233]) into *The Birth of a Nation* (1915), a film that made him a fortune, which he then sunk into the gargantuan *Intolerance* (1916) and lost. In those pre-tax days it was possible to go through one fortune after another, and since he had come to dominate the American film industry, Griffith saw no reason why he should not continue to do so. Even though subsequent films such as *True Heart Susie*, with his discovery, Lillian Gish, and, again, *Broken Blossoms* (both 1919), delivered cash, costs were rising and audiences — jaded by the hell of World War I — were changing. Griffith joined the newly formed United Artists that same year and built his own studio facility in Mamaroneck, New York, where he shot *Way Down East* in 1920. But even with the prestige of *America* (1921), *Orphans of the Storm*, and *Isn't Life Wonderful?* (both 1924) he was never to reclaim the success he had enjoyed during his steady climb to the top.

In his career he directed some 450 movies, most of them ten-minute one-reelers for Biograph Pictures in New York, one of the first companies

---

232. Ezra Goodman. *The Fifty-Year Decline and Fall of Hollywood*. New York: Simon & Schuster, 1961.
233. This and previous quote from the prelude to *The Birth of a Nation*, 1930 reissue.

to make product available to the burgeoning network of nickelodeons that opened up all across America in the early 1900s. Griffith came to the movies as an actor, appearing in, among other titles, *Rescued from an Eagle's Nest* (1907), for the Thomas Edison Company. When acting dried up at Edison, the aristocratic Griffith sold stories to, and became a director at, Biograph, using the wiles he had acquired in front of the Edison company's camera to inform what he commanded from behind it. His 1908 film *The Adventures of Dollie* was the first of his achievements there; he was soon grinding out two and three shorts a week. His output defines early film history: *The Lonedale Operator, The Musketeers of Pig Alley, A Girl and Her Trust, A Corner in Wheat, The New York Hat, An Unseen Enemy*, and scores more before 1915.

It is impossible to chart the advances that Griffith codified into the vocabulary of cinema. While he did not invent the close-up, dolly shot, cross-cutting, tracking shot, dissolve, or iris, he was the first to hone their use in storytelling and to combine them in ways that drew the viewer into what was happening on screen.

In December of 1930, his money waning, Griffith reissued a revised version of *The Birth of a Nation* with music, sound effects, and an introductory interview between himself and Walter Huston, who had starred for him in his first talkie, *Abraham Lincoln*, the preceding August. At about that same time, over dinner with Lillian and Dorothy Gish, he hinted that he was going to make a film about alcoholism. As Griffith was himself an alcoholic by this time, Lillian Gish assumed it was going to be autobiographical. Instead, the planned $300,000 picture was to be based in Zola's 1877 novel *The Drunkard (L'Assommoir)*, which he said he would finance with a 1929 tax refund[234] that had been fortuitously invested in stocks that did well despite the Depression, plus a loan from the Federation Trust Bank.[235] He arranged studio space at Paramount and hired a nurse to help him back on the wagon, but when word spread that he was drying out, Paramount reneged. So Griffith rented the Audio-Cinema Studios in the Bronx where he had made *Judith of Bethula* in 1913. Street scenes were shot there from July 6 to August 31, 1931 and on location in Springdale, Connecticut at a steel factory. He used the Westrex sound recording process and, when ambient noise interfered with dialogue, he worked with engineer Joe Kaufman to cover the microphone

---

234. Iris Barry. *D.W. Griffith: American Film Master*. New York: The Museum of Modern Art, 1940.
235. Lillian Gish and Ann Pinchot. *The Movies, Mr. Griffith, and Me*. Englewood Cliffs, New Jersey: Prentice-Hall, 1969.

with paper baffles that made it more directional. From reports, he was sober and attentive during the eight week shoot.[236]

The Struggle positions itself as an argument against bootleg liquor, not the Prohibition that created the market for it from 1920-1933. Griffith also preaches about the dangers of intoxication, making the obtuse point that hard liquor replaced beer, and therefore it was beer that was evil. In the story, Jimmy (Hal Skelly) swears off drink when he marries Florrie (Zita Johann) but resumes his habit when he consoles a fellow worker who has lost his job. It's on and off the wagon from there, and eventually it costs Jimmy his job, his wife, his daughter, and his happiness — until his daughter finds him and helps him dry out.

There are no surprises in the moralistic story. Iris Barry, who curated the first major Griffith retrospective at the Museum of Modern Art in 1940, wrote that the melodramatic dialogue in *The Struggle* "must have shocked audiences as much as the first florid love phrases that John Gilbert spoke aloud." She also cites the authenticity of the "everyday speech" that the stage-trained actors aren't up to delivering, blaming the problems on the limitations in early recording equipment.[237] Her judgment is not entirely fair. While the film is certainly labored in its conception and unmemorable in its content, the performers are encouraged to *behave* rather than *act*, often overlapping their dialogue in a realistic way. But compared with other films that same year (*The Public Enemy, Cimarron, Frankenstein, Dracula, Private Lives, A Free Soul*), *The Struggle* was an instant anachronism. Anita Loos, who wrote the script with her husband, John Emerson, had intended it to be a comedy, possibly starring the likes of Jimmy Durante. Instead, Griffith rewrote sections and shot it as straight drama. Audiences giggled at its premiere at New York's Rivoli on December 10, 1931.[238] Interestingly, that's where Joe Breen had to see it. Joseph I. Breen had just joined the Motion Picture Producers and Distributors of America, precursor to the MPAA, the lobbying organization that Hollywood set up under Will H. Hays to scrub its public image after a decade of scandals. Breen had been lobbying Hays for a job in public relations, but the Catholic Breen, with his garrulous manner and sharp mind, immediately became the bogeyman for studio moguls who had been treating the Code like so much

---

236. Robert M. Henderson. *D.W. Griffith: His Life and Work*. New York: Oxford University Press, 1972.
237. Barry, op. cit.
238. *Variety*, December 15, 1931.

smoke.²³⁹ It would take him until 1934 to make the Code stick, and would thereafter peruse scripts before they were shot and "suggest" cuts to finished films.²⁴⁰ On December 11, Breen wrote Griffith advising that some censor boards might delete the word *pansy* and, in some foreign English-speaking countries, they might delete the words *bum* or *bums*. But that was all he could do at the time.²⁴¹

The Film Daily deemed *The Struggle* "poor entertainment" and "old fashioned." One R. E. Plummer, who may have viewed the film for the MPPDA, called it 'an old-fashioned melo [melodrama], containing everything but an off-screen voice yodeling 'The Curse of an Aching Heart.'"²⁴² Other trade papers avoided reviewing it entirely, perhaps out of respect for its director. *The Struggle* played only one week (December 10-17, 1931) before UA pulled it. Its gross was less than $100,000.²⁴³

Griffith was so upset by the lack of support from his own company that he negotiated his separation in 1933 and used some of his buyout cash to pay down the film's debt. He was never able to get financing for another one. In 1935, United Artists considered re-releasing the picture and obediently submitted it to the Breen office for a Code Seal. Now Breen had his teeth in. He told UA's H. D. Buddy that he would have to eliminate "references to a baby" in the scene of a fat man rubbing his stomach (Breen couldn't bring himself to say, "pretending he's pregnant"); delete the scene of a girl throwing her leg over a man's knee; eliminate all references to the name "Jesus"; and eliminate the scene of the drunken father abusing and beating the child. In response, UA withdrew its request for a certificate, and a relieved Breen thanked them for their decision.²⁴⁴ Five years later, however, B. A. Mills of B&M Pictures acquired the rights and considered re-releasing it under the title *Ten Nights in a Barroom*.²⁴⁵

---

239. Leonard J. Leff & Jerold L. Simmons. *The Dame in the Kimono: Hollywood, Censorship, & The Production Code from the 1920s to the 1960s*. New York: Grove Weidenfeld, 1990.
240. Someone needs to say a kind word about Joe Breen. Although many over the years argue that the Code was regressive and stifled expression (which it did), even a cursory reading of Breen's correspondence shows a bright, worldly, literate man who deeply loved movies and respected the public.
241. Breen to Griffith, letter, December 11, 1931. MPPDA/MPAA papers, AMPAS. The noun *bum*, which means *vagrant* in America, refers to the buttocks in England.
242. Letter, December 15, 1931, MPPDA/MPAA files.
243. Ronald Bergan. *The United Artists Story*. New York: Crown Publishers, 1986.
244. Letters, Breen to UA August 31, 1935; Buddy to Breen, September 3, 1935. MPPDA/MPAA files, AMPAS.
245. Letter, F.S. Harmon to Mills, March 7, 1940, MPPDA/MPAA files, AMPAS. This title change has led some people to confuse the Griffith film with another 1931 film titled *Ten Nights in a Barroom* directed by William O'Connor and starring Dustin Farnum. O'Connor's film is based on Edwin Waugh's temperance play of the same name.

After he, too, asked the MPPDA for a Code seal and was informed of the Code cuts, he dropped the idea. By then Griffith had been dropped by the industry he helped found. Comfortable but not wealthy, in 1936 he had married Evelyn Baldwin, whom he had cast in a small role in *The Struggle;* she was 19, he was 55. They divorced in 1947.

"When D.W. Griffith stopped making movies, the purpose went out of his life," wrote Lillian Gish.[246] Added Iris Barry (rather callously) in her MoMA notes, published in 1940 while Griffith was still alive, "Ours is a very different world from the one he triumphed in; a simple story of right overcoming wrong at the last moment no longer serves as a scenario, and no one will ever create the art of the motion picture again. It is enough that Griffith did create it but — humanly — his story at this later stage has some bitterness in it."[247]

---

246. Gish, op. cit.
247. Barry, op. cit.

HOWARD HAWKS
It Takes a Pro

It took the French critics to discover that Howard Hawks made the same film every time, only differently. Whether it was a gangster picture like *Scarface* (1932), an action drama like *Only Angels Have Wings* (1939), a mystery like *The Big Sleep* (1946), a screwball comedy like *Bringing Up Baby* (1938), an adventure like *Hatari* (1962), a musical like *Gentlemen Prefer Blondes* (1953), a war picture like *Dawn Patrol* (1938), a western like *Rio Bravo* (1959), or whatever the hell *Land of the Pharaohs* was (1955), there were elements that recurred throughout Hawks' nearly fifty pictures. And all of them make an appearance in his last film, *Rio Lobo* (1970).

Hawks was a professional who respected professionalism. His men were pros at whatever they did, and the women who loved them had to step up to the man's plate. When there were love stories, Hawks realized it made "good scenes" (his term) for the woman to be the aggressor. He loved putting his heroes in tight spots, literally enclosed places like jailhouses, newsrooms, or isolated outposts, and had them use cunning to get themselves free.

In *Rio Lobo* he went to the well one last time, calling upon his decades-long friendship with John Wayne and a new production company called Cinema Center Films to get him there. It had been four years since he directed *El Dorado*, almost an exact remake of *Rio Bravo*, and, at age 74, he was still ready to work. Between 1966 and 1970 he toured Europe where he had been "recognized" by cineastes, whom he tolerated with patrician grace. He reserved his energy for Americans such as critics Peter Bogdanovich, Richard Schickel, and Todd McCarthy who venerated him. He also developed a friendship with young director William Friedkin (who was dating his daughter, Kitty), advising him to stay away from pictures like *The Boys in the Band* (1970), and supposedly, noodling with the script for Friedkin's as-yet-unshot *The French Connection* (1971).[248] "What you want to do is make some kind of adventure pictures," Friedkin recalled Hawks advising him, quoting him as saying, "Every time I made a film that went into some social problem or something else, it just fell right on its hind end. But when you make a film that's just an action picture that's exciting and has a lotta good guys against bad guys, it has a lotta success, if that matters to you."[249]

Rio Bravo follows that dictum. John Wayne is a Yankee colonel during the Civil War who loses a shipment of gold to Jorge Rivera and his Confederate marauders because a traitor in Wayne's regiment sold them intelligence. After the war Wayne joins with Rivera, explaining, "what you did was an act of war, what [the turncoat] did was an act of treason" and together the men free the town of Rio Lobo from a corrupt sheriff and landowner, who happens to be the traitor. Screenwriter Burton Wohl's plot probably made sense before longtime Hawks collaborator Leigh Brackett did her rewrite, but there are "good scenes" along the way (including some sassy moments that feel as though they were made up on the spot) to meet Hawks' formula.

All the Hawksian elements are present. Wayne's and Rivera's mutual respect, of course, unites them. Christopher Mitchum is the "kid" — the James Caan/Ricky Nelson character — to Wayne's seasoned pro. Jack Elam plays the Walter Brennan role of the wizened coot who's sharper than he looks. And Jennifer O'Neill is the last in a long line of forward, self-reliant Hawks "girls" that includes Angie Dickinson, Joanne Dru, Jean Arthur, and Ann Sheridan. The evil enemy is Victor French, and his puppet is Sheriff Mike Henry, who's also good at his job, but not good enough. Naturally the heroes are holed up in the town jail in the third act and use ingenuity as well as guns to vanquish the villains.

When he directed the film, Hawks was secure to the point of being blasé. Peter Bogdanovich, who had just started directing pictures himself (*Targets*, 1968), visited the set of *Rio Lobo* in Old Tucson, Arizona and reported that it was John Wayne and not Hawks who was telling Chris Mitchum how to play the scene: "I asked Hawks if he didn't mind Wayne's directing the actors like that. 'Oh, no,' he said definitely, 'Duke and I have done so many pictures together, he knows what I want. It saves my breath.'"[250] He was less generous toward former model Jennifer O'Neil, whose hiring was decided by the film company. Hawks claimed

---

248. *IMDb.com;* not confirmed elsewhere.
249. Interview with the author. *Hurricane Billy.* New York: William Morrow and Company, 1990.
250. Peter Bogdanovich. *Who the Devil Made It.* New York: Alfred A. Knopf, 1997.

that the picture slowed down when she appeared ("She started out great and then she was busy being a star"[251]). He preferred a young actress he cast in the subplot of a girl whose face is sliced by the villains for helping the heroes: Sherry Lansing, whom he immediately tried to mold. "He had a very fixed image of what a woman should be," Lansing said. "Tall, long hair, long legs, big eyes — a very specific type. Basically she had to be Lauren Bacall." Noting a "lack of self-examination" and impersonality about Hawks that "sounds cool when you read it but is terrible in real life," Lansing soon gave up acting to become an executive and eventually headed production at Paramount pictures.[252]

With a budget of $5 million, Hawks intended to shoot in Durango, Mexico, until British director Michael Winner locked up the facilities at that location for his film, *Lawman*, forcing Hawks and Cinema Center to spend an extra $1 million setting up for two weeks in Cuernavaca followed by twenty-five days in Old Tucson, a week in Nogales, and twenty-two days at Cinema Center's facilities outside of Los Angeles. The start date for the sixty-five-day shoot was March 16, 1970 aiming at a December 18, 1970 release. The schedule was efficient but tough. Wayne was showing his age (sixty-three) and relied on his long-time stand-in/double Chuck Roberson for the long shots. Although famed stuntman/second unit director Yakima Canutt staged the spectacular train robbery that begins the film (greased rails, ropes strung across the tracks), Hawks was present to supervise. The director was seriously injured when he was thrown off a rail car into a camera platform and tore open his leg, sending him to the hospital. Production was later shut down again for a week when the seventy-three-year-old Hawks re-injured the leg racing dirt bikes on his weekend off.[253]

Even though he had a Brackett script to work with, Hawks constantly rewrote dialogue and seldom gave his actors pages, preferring to tell them what to do on the set, explaining to a visitor, "I don't change dialogue, I 'word' it how I think it should be read."[254] That he had to do it to such an extent was required not only by O'Neill's limited acting experience but by Rivera's inability to speak English and a shortage of competent supporting players resulting from Cinema Center's parsimony. At times

---

251. Bogdanovich, ibid.
252. Todd McCarthy. *Howard Hawks: The Grey Fox of Hollywood*. New York: Grove Press, 2000. Lansing married William Friedkin in 1991. Friedkin also noted Hawks' distant personality (see Segaloff, op. cit.).
253. McCarthy, op. cit.
254. McCarthy, ibid.

Wayne himself seems impatient with the lack of energy and resorts to interrupting his fellow performers (to fine effect, it should be added). "There wasn't anything you could do," Hawks later admitted. "The scenes didn't come off at all; you couldn't build on them. If you got *passable* scenes, you were awfully glad."[255]

Even though *Rio Lobo* trods a well-worn directorial trail, it contains pleasures for Hawks fans, but there weren't enough of them to bring in any more than $4.25 million in rentals. If anything, the picture is "comfortable," a word used by several throughout the story to describe Wayne's character. Jerry Goldsmith's score is fitting and contained, William Clothier's photography — mostly long shots and eye-level two-shots in the Hawks style — is functional if not as grand as, say, Lucien Ballard's images in *True Grit*, which Wayne made three films prior to *Rio Lobo*. And *True Grit* was on everybody's mind when Wayne flew from Old Tucson to Los Angeles on April 7, 1970 to attend the Academy Awards® where he was nominated for Best Actor as the one-eyed Rooster Cogburn. He left location armed with Hawks' orders, "Don't come back without it." He came back, Oscar® in hand, to find the entire *Rio Lobo* company with their backs toward him. All at once they turned around and everybody — including Wayne's horse — was wearing an eye patch.[256]

Howard Hawks never enjoyed the same recognition from Academy voters even though he had entertained them all their lives; it took the Academy's Board of Governors to confer a special Oscar® in 1975 which Wayne presented. But maybe that was as it should have been because, for Hawks, a "professional" was something that you're *supposed* to be, and you shouldn't need to be honored for it.

Hawks was hospitalized in early December, 1977 following a fall at home — he tripped over his dog and hit his head on the stone floor — but demanded quite lucidly to be taken home at mid-month. On Christmas night he lost consciousness and died on December 26 of a stroke brought on by heart disease. Even in death, it seems, Hawks was denied his due; Charles Chaplin died the day before and the Tramp's coverage pushed the Grey Fox into second place. It's only over the years that Hawks has become venerated as one of, if not *the*, most successful and versatile directors in American film.

In other words, he was a professional.

---

255. Bogdanovich, op. cit.
256. McCarthy, op. cit.

ALFRED HITCHCOCK
A Piece of Cake

When challenged by interviewers for his darkly comic approach to the macabre, Alfred Hitchcock would coyly counter, "For me, the cinema is not a slice of life, but a piece of cake." While the celebrated Master of Suspense never shied from gruesome subjects, he was usually oblique in presenting them. *Psycho* (1960), for example, which became known for its violence, actually contained only the *suggestion* of violence; what audiences reacted to was Hitchcock's skill in making them *think* they saw it. Even *The Birds* (1963), in which avians attack humans, was, on inspection, the result of dynamic editing and a smidgeon of stage blood. Not until *Torn Curtain* (1966) did Hitchcock yield to his (considerable) dark side by showing, as he stated at the time, just how hard it is to physically kill a man when he had Paul Newman strangle and gas Wolfgang Kieling in a grueling and nearly silent fight scene. So when it came to *Frenzy* (1972), about a sexual deviate who strangles women with designer neckties, Hitch reveled in the freedom granted by Hollywood's newly liberalized production code. It's his first film to include nudity, bones snapping on the soundtrack, a graphic strangulation, and the strong suggestion of male orgasm. *Frenzy* was a hit ($6.3 million returns on a $2 million cost) and received the best reviews Hitch had earned in years.[257]

By 1976, however, Hitchcock had become a prisoner of his own reputation. Where he had earlier pretended that his work was all in fun, now others were taking it seriously. Those "pieces of cake" he was so fond of baking now weighed him down. He wanted to do a different kind of film

257. Although this may be disingenuous because the 1966 publication of Francois Truffaut's Hitchcock interviews, plus auteurist essays by Andrew Sarris and populist writings of Peter Bogdanovich, triggered a reappraisal of the director's work that compelled up-and-coming American critics to take him more seriously than had their predecessors.

but his studio, Universal (where he was a major stockholder), leaned on him to stick to his genre, if only to erase the commercial blots of *Torn Curtain* and its even more unfortunate 1969 successor, the hopelessly muddled spy picture *Topaz*.[258] He had purchased — on recommendation of his tireless assistant, Peggy Robertson — Victor Canning's novel *The Rainbird Pattern* prior to its 1972 publication while he was in Europe publicizing *Frenzy*. Canning was primarily a television writer, mostly semi-mysteries like *Mannix, Curtain of Fear*, and *Breaking Point*, although he had done one called *Disappearing Trick* for Hitch's anthology TV series in 1958. *Rainbird*, which would be Canning's last novel (he died in 1986), is about a swindle involving a fake psychic who might, it seems, be a real psychic. Hitchcock contacted Anthony Shaffer, who had scripted *Frenzy*, and asked him to perform the same duties here. Shaffer recalled that the director wanted to make a light-hearted romp whereas he found the notion of psychic duality more intriguing.[259] Shaffer was eager to work again with Hitchcock, but his London and Los Angeles agents couldn't agree on how to negotiate a fee and, before it could be resolved, Hitch decided on Ernest Lehman, with whom he had created the classic *North by Northwest* (1959).[260]

In the intervening years Lehman had flourished as an adapter/producer: *West Side Story, The Sound of Music, Hello Dolly*, etc. Although he agreed in October of 1973 to write once more for Hitchcock, the men quickly discovered that their roles had become reversed: Lehman was now the powerhouse while Hitch was fading. Nevertheless, protocol had to be observed; at each work session the two men would gossip, neither wishing to raise the issue of the work-at-hand. "How much more pleasurable," Lehman recalled, "this sharing of the problems of others, than to have to sit there, sometimes in terribly long silences, trying to devise Hitchcockian methods of extricating fictional characters from the corners into which you painted them the day before."[261]

Progress was slow except for the first decision to throw out Canning's plot, which Hitchcock didn't care for, and start from scratch with Canning's characters, whom he liked. By mid-April, 1974, Lehman had crafted a first draft, called *Deception*, and gave it to Hitchcock who, one week later, responded with brilliantly detailed notes. Hitchcock was back.

---

258. Donald Spoto. *The Dark Side of Genius*. Boston, Massachusetts: Little-Brown, 1983.
259. Spoto, ibid.
260. Hitchcock cable to Shaffer September 26, 1973. Alfred Hitchcock papers, AMPAS.
261. Ernest Lehman, *American Film* magazine, May, 1978, quoted by Patrick McGilligan in: *Alfred Hitchcock: A Life in Darkness and Light*. New York: Regan Books, 2003.

But not for long. Because rather than start shooting *Missing Heir, Deceit, One Plus One Equals One* and *Deception* — all four of which were used at various times as titles — Hitchcock inexplicably began stalling again. First he surprised Lehman by asking him to prepare a prose treatment of their already finished script, then had him do a second draft of it. Then he had a pacemaker installed (possibly after a small heart attack), then passed a kidney stone. Then he equivocated about casting, preferring to hire lesser known actors than to throw large salary at stars. In a way, he was playing with the film the way he had been playing with his audiences for the last fifty years.

Family Plot is two parallel stories that become one. The first involves a fake psychic (Blanche) and her taxi driver boyfriend (George) who are bent on swindling an aging widow (Julia Rainbird) who wants to find her long-lost illegitimate nephew/heir. It falls to George, serving as Blanche's legman, to track down the now-grown heir and get the $10,000 reward. The second story is a kidnapper (Adamson) who demands that his ransoms be paid in jewels, and his girlfriend (Frances) who is his mule. When Adamson realizes that the person he has kidnapped is being sought by George, he decides he has to kill George and Blanche. Naturally, there is a neat and ironic ending.

Perhaps Hitchcock's and Lehman's biggest modification is, in fact, the ending. In the Canning novel, which is set in England, the main characters die horribly. In *Family Plot* (the new title was suggested by a studio employee toward the end of July) the characters not only survive but have futures, however unpleasant.

For Blanche, the faux psychic, Hitchcock became enamored of Barbara Harris. The studio had urged him to choose Liza Minnelli but her salary quotes were too high (Harris got $50,000). He made Bruce Dern, whom he'd once cast as a bit in *Marnie* in 1964 as George (Dern got $75,000). He acceded to Universal's wishes to use Roy Thinnes as Adamson ($25,000), and engaged Karen Black as Frances (for $150,000 plus $50,000 deferred). He saved the part of the elderly Ms. Rainbird for Cathleen Nesbitt, whom he had once seen on the London stage, despite Lillian Gish lobbying him for it in a touching personal letter.[262]

As always, Hitchcock was meticulous in his preparations. He dispatched location scouts to find and photograph possible sites with the instructions, relayed by his longtime assistant, Peggy Robertson, "as you know, Mr. Hitchcock's name should not be used in any connection with

---

262. Budget and March 28, 1975 letter from Gish to Hitchcock, Alfred Hitchcock papers, AMPAS.

the project." Bradner Petersen of the studio legal department pored through the script to clear names, places, and products. His biggest concern was that the film's proposed shooting in a real cemetery "keep actual headstones in the background, or illegible." adding that there is no privacy for dead persons, but don't linger on any in order "to avoid complaints."[263]

Principal photography began on May 12, 1976 in Los Angeles, although no specific city is identified as the film's setting. The budget was set at $4,490,375 and was monitored on a daily basis by Universal's fiscal watchdog, Marshall Green. Hitchcock also shot in San Francisco at the Fairmont Hotel and Grace Cathedral, and at Sierra Madre's Pioneer Cemetery. By the time cameras rolled, however, Hitch had barred Lehman from the set because the writer had become argumentative. Then, within two weeks, the director replaced Thinnes with William Devane and reshot Thinnes' scenes at an additional cost of $69,375, which covered Devane's salary of $50,000 plus retakes. Where Thinnes appeared in extreme long shots but couldn't be recognized, that footage remains in the film. There is no indication why Thinnes was replaced, although Hitchcock's files contain a letter from him suggesting ideas, just the actorly sort of thing that Hitchcock loathed discussing. On the other hand, he allowed Barbara Harris and Bruce Dern to improvise, including Harris' enigmatic final close-up in which she winks at the camera, clouding whether she really is a psychic or was just pretending to be one. Devane and Black, however, were held more tightly to the script. Devane, who would ask for insights into his motivation, was frozen out by the filmmaker, and Black, dressed in a blonde fright wig and trench coat to suggest Patty Hearst (who was in the news during production), was told to stop trying to make herself look attractive.

Hitchcock, seventy-six and more overweight than usual, varied in his attention span while directing this, his fifty-third film. At times he would seem to doze off, yet awaken in time to say "cut" and make minute adjustments that nobody else would have noticed. Other times Bruce Dern would have to engage him in conversation to keep his interest from flagging. For a man who so often told interviewers that once a film was written and storyboarded he found the actual shooting a bore, he seemed bent on playfully veering from his plans throughout production. Nevertheless, he wrapped at fifty-four days, including retakes, two days ahead of schedule.[264]

263. August 21, 1975 memo, revised September 4, 1975. Alfred Hitchcock papers, AMPAS.
264. Schedules and budgets from Alfred Hitchcock papers, AMPAS. One unusual scheduling note: instead of using the term "magic hour" to indicate the cinematic time between sunset and darkness, Hitchcock's schedule used the term "witching hour."

Reviewers, perhaps having long since realized that any criticism of a Hitchcock film was pointless, praised it politely on its April 9, 1976 opening. It was highly publicized (major reporters were invited to interview the director in a cemetery where their names had all been written on tombstones) and retuned over $6.5 million in film rentals.[265] Buoyed by its reception by press and public alike, Hitchcock announced that he would make a fifty-fourth film. Not long after *Plot* was released, however, Mrs. Hitchcock, Alma Reville, suffered a massive stroke and spent the rest of her days confined to their house on Bellagio Road in Los Angeles' exclusive Bel Air section. Begrudgingly accepting his beloved Alma's diminished capacity, and crowded by her caregivers, Hitchcock allowed himself to be talked into going to the office and planning that other film.

The studio had bought Ronald Kirkbride's 1968 novel *The Short Night* for him when it was published. The story of a double agent who works in Britain's Foreign Office, it was a throwback to such classic Hitchcockian spy stories as *Foreign Correspondent* and *The Saboteur* (as well as, unavoidably, *Topaz* and *Torn Curtain*). He went through several writers — James Costigan, Ernest Lehman, Norman Lloyd — before settling on David Freeman, a playwright and beginning screenwriter with two previous films, *Heroes* and *First Love* (both 1977), only the latter of which carried his screen credit. Starting on what could have been taken as a symbolic date — December 7, 1978 — the two worked together until it was clear that the Master of Suspense was physically, intellectually, and emotionally unable to continue.[266]

Hitchcock died on April 29, 1980. Alma attended his funeral in a wheelchair at the Church of the Good Shepherd in Beverly Hills. By some accounts, she did not know whose service it was. She died on July 6, 1982.

A few years earlier Norman Lloyd — who used to produce the Hitchcock TV series and, before that, acted in several of his films — was writing *The Short Night* with him before Freeman was bought in. Lloyd was surprised when, out of nowhere, Hitch blurted, "You know, Norm, we're not ever going to make this picture." Lloyd was stunned and reminded him that he already had a crew working on it and asked, "Why do you say that?"

"Because," Hitch declared, "it's not *necessary*."[267]

---

265. *IMDb.com*
266. Freeman put his recollections into a compassionate but distressing memoir, *The Last Days of Alfred Hitchcock*. Woodstock, New York: The Overlook Press, 1984.
267. McGilligan, op. cit.

John Huston.

JOHN HUSTON
The Last Lion

John Huston's *The Dead* (1987) was adapted for the screen by Huston and his older son, Tony, from James Joyce's novella of the same name that concludes Joyce's 1912-1914 compendium, *Dubliners*. Its evocative narrative begins at a dinner party in a private home in Dublin on the night of the Epiphany and soon focuses on the lives of Gretta and Gabriel, a middle-aged couple who long ago accepted their unvarying marriage. On this night, a quiet snow falls and Gretta recalls, in her thoughts, a boy in her youth named Michael Furey, whom she once loved and who loved her, and who died for his love, and the memory of this tragedy continues to haunt her. *The Dead* is considered one of the most beautifully written pieces in English literature, and the responsibility of translating it to motion pictures weighed heavily upon all who worked on it. The fact that Huston died after the film was finished, but before it was released, adds to its legacy.

"Dad first thought of *The Dead* as a viable project back when he was making *Moby Dick*," recalled Tony Huston. "I remember when I was 17 or 18 and I was enamored of Joyce and *Dubliners* in particular, talking about *The Dead* which is, of course, the outstanding story in that collection, and asking him about making it into a film, and even talking with people we knew and how they might have played various characters."[268] The project eventually came together while John was directing *Under the Volcano*, financed by Chris Sievernich and Weiland Schulz-Keil, who would later produce *The Dead* after they purchased its screen rights from the Joyce estate for $60,000, then raised another $3.5 million to make the movie.[269]

---

268. Interview with the author during filming of *The Dead* in 1987.
269. Lawrence Grobel. *The Hustons*. New York: Charles Scribner's Sons, 1989.

"They were talking about how few films existed which actually discuss the interior life of marriage," Tony continued. "There were lots of films which were about the breakups or falling in love or that side, but relatively little that had to do with what actually went on when two people were committed to one another. And somehow *The Dead* came up. Dad always collaborates with somebody, and he didn't have anybody on hand at that time, and he said, 'Tony, how'd you like to collaborate with me?' knowing that I was a struggling writer. It's been the greatest pleasure of my adult life."[270]

The elder Huston was enjoying a professional renaissance when he began shooting *The Dead* in a warehouse in Valencia, California in January of 1987. His immediately preceding films, *Under the Volcano* (1984) and *Prizzi's Honor* (1985), had restored a directorial reputation that had been severely tarnished, if not thought irretrievable, by his previous flops *Annie* (1982), *Victory* (1981), *Phobia* (1980), and *Love and Bullets, Charlie* (1979, on which he had been replaced by Stuart Rosenberg). And yet, before those disappointments, he had made the remarkable *Wise Blood* (1979) and *The Man Who Would Be King* (1975). To say the least, Huston's screen work was as unpredictable as the man himself, who was eighty when he said "action" on *The Dead* on January 19 and wrapped it a tight thirty-three days later.

His was, in retrospect, a turbulent life. John Marcellus Huston went through five wives, four countries, several avocations (including prize fighter, big game hunter, art collector/smuggler, reporter, and actor), and forty-one feature films as director, only thirty-six of which carry his screen credit. He was a good friend to some, an annoyance to others, and a cantankerous trickster to those who didn't qualify as one or the other. He came by his talent by dint of being his father's son, his father being Walter Huston, the respected stage and screen star whose experiences ranged from introducing the enduring "September Song" in Kurt Weill's *Knickerbocker Holiday* on Broadway in 1938 and winning an Oscar® under his son's direction in *The Treasure of the Sierra Madre*. He was also a scalawag, a trait John shamelessly inherited and polished to perfection.

Even as John Huston wrapped *The Dead* in February of 1987 he was at work with writer Janet Roach on an adaptation of Thornton Wilder's 1973 novel *Theophilous North* for his younger son, Danny, to direct that summer in Newport, Rhode Island, the former playground of America's Gilded Age rich. Retitled *Mr. North*,[271] it was the gentle, even magical, tale

---

270. Tony Huston interview, op. cit
271. James Costigan is also credited as writer.

of a young teacher (Anthony Edwards) who brings life to an assortment of Newport denizens including Mr. Bosworth, a housebound invalid who Huston intended to play. Ever the manipulator, Huston brought many of his *The Dead* crew with him to *Mr. North*. These included film editor Roberto Silvi, script supervisor Karen Golden, second assistant director Joe Brooks, soundmen Bill Randall Jr. and Sr., personal publicist Ernie Anderson, and his indomitable production manager, Tommy Shaw, who'd served him on nearly every picture since *The Unforgiven* in 1960.

During *The Dead* it had become painfully clear that Huston's emphysema was worsening. Sitting in a wheelchair, tethered to an oxygen tank from which he was increasingly unable to stray, he would ruin take after take with his coughing. When it came time for him to shoot the landscapes that would create the mood for his cinematic chamber piece, he dictated a list of locations — sometimes right down to specific road intersections — for cinematographer Fred Murphy and his second unit crew to shoot in Galway as his proxies. He also had to face the challenge of directing his older daughter, Anjelica. Her role of Gretta Conroy posed an immense challenge, for it had to be played both with dialogue and against her reactions to voice-over playback.

Despite her image as a secure, even regal, actress, the real Anjelica Huston (who had just won an Oscar® for her father's *Prizzi's Honor*) was anything but. It took legendary acting teacher Peggy Furey to convince her she could act. "Peggy Furey was a most validating teacher," Anjelica stated. "I think you're either born with it or you're not, but…someone who is insecure, as I was at a certain point, can be helped by going to acting class, and, particularly, by a teacher who is as reassuring as she was. I think there's a level of insecurity that's a constant, but I don't think it has any place in front of a camera unless that's what you're playing. I would say I'm a lot more secure now than I was before I went to Peggy, because I didn't know if I was any good or not." Once she earned Furey's approbation, she found her father "very inspirational. "I could look at him and tell exactly what it was he wanted, and, if I was hard pressed to find something, I could look to him and find it."[272] The combination led her to devise a trick that helped her assimilate Gretta. "There was very little about it that didn't strike home," she revealed. "I didn't know a Michael Furey, but I knew a Martin Furey and I knew Peggy Furey. I knew those walks in the rain and I knew Galway and there was a lot to identify in it. I knew women like Gretta. There's that kind of style and the essence of that time that

---

272. Interview with the author, 1987.

haven't gone out of Ireland; it still exists: gentility, decency, dignity, and conversation, all of those things, and there are times that I miss radically. So there's very little that doesn't strike me about the book."[273]

With *The Dead* awaiting theatrical release, John Huston took up residence in a house in Newport (actually Middletown), Rhode Island to act in *Mr. North*. When it became clear that he was too weak to come to the set on July 26, 1987, the first day of shooting, an old friend stepped in: Robert Mitchum. Huston had secretly asked Mitchum to take over his role while *The Dead* was still in post-production in California. Moreover, he knew that headlines about Mitchum's last-minute "rescue" would benefit the film and Danny. During production he occasionally looked at dailies, advised Danny, and gathered his friends and family 'round: Tony and daughter Allegra from England; actors Lauren Bacall, Harry Dean Stanton, Tammy Grimes; ex-wife (Danny's mother) Zoë Sallis; and producers Michael Fitzgerald and Steven Haft.

On Friday, August 28 at 2 AM, without ever coming to the set, John Huston died.

Most of the press initially reported that he passed in his sleep.[274] This was not the case, as Anjelica later set straight at her father's memorial service at the Directors Guild of America. "On that last night, I think he knew pretty well where he was going — or maybe not *where* he was going, but *that* he was going," she said. Asking that his family not see him in his final hours, he requested that only his companion Maricela Hernandez be with him. As he lay dying, he assumed the part of a cavalry officer, perhaps like José Olimbrada, the Colonel under whom he had once studied dressage when he had joined the Mexican army in his twenties:

"How many express rifles do we have?" he asked Maricela.

"Thirty, John," she answered.

"How 'bout ammunition, baby?"

"Oh, we got plenty of ammunition."

Then he held her hand aloft the way a victorious prize fighter would do — another of his youthful adventures — and said:

"Then give 'em hell."

He died in her arms.

Hollywood was not surprised at Huston's passing, only that it came in such a mundane locale as a rental house in Rhode Island. After all, he had slipped through Death's hands so many times before in the Congo,

---

273. Ibid.

274. The author covered the filming for the *Boston Herald* and broke the stories of Huston's death, including his last words, which the paper's editors initially disbelieved and refused to run.

Morocco, Yugoslavia, Mexico, Finland, or any of the hostile locations where he had made his eclectic movies. This was, after all, the man who had once had a loaded pistol held to his head by a marauder who then pulled the trigger, only to have it jam. He was a man who suffered respiratory collapse, heart disease, and once bragged about having smoked cigars while he'd had pneumonia. A man who outlasted a youthful boxing career, filmed World War Two documentaries on the front line (in which soldiers were seen killed on screen), and survived attacks from Mexican banditos, a meal of "long pig" while shooting *The African Queen* (later discovered to have been human flesh), and who got the better of producer-moguls Jack L. Warner, Ray Stark, and his fifth wife, whom he referred to as "the crocodile."

Ironically, Huston had planned to return to California that day anyway. He was hoping to get another picture together for January but, because he carried a canister of pressurized oxygen, the commercial airlines would not board him, so he and the producers chartered a private plane for the trip back to the coast. John Huston, a meticulous filmmaker who never overlooked any useful detail, did not let the plane go to waste.

That December *The Dead* was released theatrically. It garnered better box office revenues and more appreciative reviews than any of his films in the previous ten years. As the opening titles end — following the credit "Directed by John Huston" — comes the dedication: "for Maricela."

ELIA KAZAN
The Fabulous Fink

When the Academy of Motion Picture Arts and Sciences announced that Elia Kazan would receive an honorary award during their 1999 ceremony, all hell broke loose in Hollywood. While everyone acknowledged Kazan's brilliance as a director who changed the style of screen acting with such films as *Splendor in the Grass, East of Eden, On the Waterfront,* and *A Streetcar Named Desire*, many others remembered that, in 1952, he had been an informant before the House Un-American Activities Committee. Although the Committee was dredging for Communists, their actual intent was to crush freedom of thought in America, and Kazan testified before them knowing full well that those he named would be blacklisted. If anybody could have stopped the Committee, opponents said, it was Kazan, who was at the height of his prestige and could have, should have, exposed the Committee for the bullies they were.[275] Some even accused him of swapping his testimony for a long-term Fox contract. This was not true — the dates don't jibe — but studio heads Darryl F. Zanuck and Spyros Skouras did let Kazan know, in no uncertain terms, that he wouldn't work any more if he didn't sing. So he testified, and the eight people he smeared as Reds were through.

As ever in such things, the deed wasn't clear-cut. While, to some, Kazan was a patriot, he was also an egotist (he took out an ad in *The New York Times* to brag about what he'd done), and others, including those who shared his hatred of Communism, remembered that those he named were those whom he himself had recruited into the Party in the late 1930s.

Two years after his HUAC appearance, Kazan directed — and won the Oscar© for — *On the Waterfront*, a riveting drama of a New York

---

275. It frustrates those who even now support HUAC that Communism was and is legal in America.

dock worker, Marlon Brando, who bucks the Mob, even at the cost of his brother's (Rod Steiger) life, to bring down a corrupt union boss, Lee J. Cobb. The film has long been considered Kazan's expiation for his Committee appearance, particularly since as it was written by another informant, Budd Schulberg, and co-starred a third, Cobb. But Kazan maintained that what drew him to the material was the Brando character being shunned by his friends for speaking out against corruption, not for the socially contemptible act of informing.[276]

Elia Kazan was one of the most talented, innovative, and complex directors of the twentieth century. His place in history is assured by his nurturing of such explosive talents as Brando, Tennessee Williams, Arthur Miller, Kim Stanley, James Dean, Julie Harris, Rip Torn, and Geraldine Page. A Yale drama school graduate who joined the Left-leaning Group Theatre in 1932 and then co-founded The Actors Studio in 1947, Kazan utilized The Method of Constantin Stanislavski to bring unprecedented emotional realism to American theatre. Along the way he acquired the nickname "Gadge."[277] When he began making motion pictures in 1945 with *A Tree Grows in Brooklyn,* he brought these abilities to the screen, changing the "indicated" acting style that had dominated Hollywood into one in which the actors actually *felt* their characters' emotions and, by training, conveyed this to the viewer. Honored with Academy Awards® for *Gentleman's Agreement* in 1947 and again for *Waterfront,* he also made such diverse and edgy films as *Baby Doll, Viva Zapata!, Pinky,* and *Panic in the Streets.* Like many in Hollywood who were later accused of Communist sympathies, Kazan was originally led to the Party because it promised human rights that American society lacked. Later, of course, this was shown to be a lie. But so fervent was Kazan's embracing of the Party, and so persuasive was he as a man, that he enticed many of his peers to enlist with him.

A disillusioned Kazan left the Party less than two years after he had joined when Party leaders summoned him to a purge at Lee and Paula Strasberg's studio and attacked him for refusing to submit to their artistic dictates. Thus Gadge's grudge wasn't only philosophical, it was personal, and testifying was his revenge. "I've never denied that there was a personal element in it," he confirmed in 1974, "which is that I was very angry,

---

276. As proof, the year before, Kazan and Arthur Miller tried to set up *The Hook,* Miller's script about Mob influence on the Brooklyn docks. Every studio rejected it unless Miller changed the villains to Communists. Miller refused because his research showed that Reds had no waterfront presence.

277. Supposedly because he was so handy with mechanics that he could fix any gadget.

humiliated and disturbed — furious, I guess — at the way they booted me out of the Party."[278] In his 1988 autobiography he added, "Do I now feel ashamed of what I did? The truth is that within a year I stopped feeling guilty or even embarrassed...Reader, I don't seek your favor, but if you expect an apology now because I...name[d] names to the House Committee, you've misjudged my character."[279]

While some named names so they could work again or had differences with the Party (see Edward Dmytryk), Kazan's selfishness was, many noted, consistent with his creative ethos. Could he have neutered the Committee by refusing? No one can say. Even if he was blacklisted in Hollywood, he could still rule Broadway. But he wanted both.

"Kazan was a big feather in [HUAC's] cap," said blacklisted writer Walter Bernstein. "He was that important because what the Committee was after wasn't any names...they had all the names. They wanted *your* name."[280]

Communism figures into Kazan's final film, *The Last Tycoon*, the novel that F. Scott Fitzgerald was writing when he died in 1940 after finishing only a few chapters and leaving fractured notes for the rest. Ironically, "unfinished" is a theme of both the book and the film: unfinished lives, unfinished loves, unfinished careers, and an unfinished beach house, take your pick. Its central character, Monroe Stahr (Robert DeNiro), is based on the sickly but brilliant "boy genius" Irving Thalberg who headed production at MGM during its golden age in the late 1920s until his death in 1936 at age thirty-seven. Set vaguely against the background of the forming of the Writers Guild in 1933 and an internecine power struggle between Stahr and studio head Pat Brady (Robert Mitchum), the story has Stahr in a teasing romance with moon-faced Kathleen Moore (Ingrid Boulting) while the boss' daughter, Cecilia (Theresa Russell), hovers. Stahr's downfall comes when he transfers his frustration over losing Kathleen into fisticuffs with union organizer named Brimmer (Jack Nicholson). In actuality, Thalberg was forced out by MGM boss Louis B. Mayer after he'd had one heart crisis too many.[281]

Interestingly, where Hollywood is usually criticized for changing books when they film them, the makers of *The Last Tycoon* respected the source

278. Michel Ciment, ed. *Kazan on Kazan*. New York: The Viking Press, 1974.
279. Elia Kazan. *A Life*. New York: Alfred A. Knopf, 1988.
280. Interviewed on *None Without Sin: Kazan, Miller, and the Blacklist*. TV. PBS/American Masters, 2003.
281. Mayer, whose competition with Thalberg was no secret, supposedly said, on learning of Thalberg's death, "God has been good to me."

so highly that they failed to add what the book desperately needed: a plot. After Fitzgerald died, his friend Edmund Wilson cobbled together the manuscript from notes, which included an ending in which Stahr dies in a plane crash (the film has him walking off disconsolately into the darkness of a soundstage). There are other significant changes from page to screen, most of them serving to simplify Stahr's character, failing to set him apart from his milieu, and removing his inner monologue about an actress named Kathleen (which was supposed to drive the love story).[282] To be sure, there are remnants: Stahr works too hard; he broods over a woman who teases and rejects him; he knows everything about movies except how to make one himself; and he stays aloof while his fellow moguls grouse about Communists and "fairies."[283]

Tycoon was made for Kazan. In some ways, he and Thalberg were alike. Both were hailed as geniuses, both were skilled at their craft, both were utterly ruthless in waging it, and both were so seductive that they made their victims feel as though surrender was voluntary. Producer Sam Spiegel, for whom Kazan made *Waterfront*, was setting up *The Last Tycoon* at Paramount after being cut loose from Columbia following the big-budget disappointment of his bloated 1971 Czarist epic, *Nicholas and Alexandra*. He engaged Harold Pinter to write the screenplay feeling that, because Pinter knew little of Hollywood, he would be faithful to Fitzgerald rather than to his notions of the movie capitol.[284] He first sought Kazan to direct but was dissuaded by the knowledge that, at the time, Kazan was happily retired and writing novels (plus his last films had not performed well).[285] So Spiegel engaged Mike Nichols, who had come off a flop in 1973's *The Day of the Dolphin*. While Pinter stayed in Spiegel's Grosvenor Square flat in London getting through a divorce from actress Vivien Merchant, Nichols consulted with both him and Spiegel

---

282. Sheilah Graham, *New York Times*, November 14, 1976. Graham and Fitzgerald lived together from 1939 until his death.

283. In point of fact, Thalberg was just as intolerant of communists as Mayer, only he was craftier in fighting them. For it was Thalberg who quietly backed the 1934 media smear against novelist Upton Sinclair, who was running for governor of California on the EPIC (End Poverty in California) ticket of Socialist reform. Thalberg was so opposed to Sinclair's policies (even though he employed him at the studio) that he had the MGM short subject unit produce fake newsreels in which actors, dressed as reprobates, enthused over Sinclair, leaving viewers no doubt that California could be saved from a Bolshevik takeover by voting for Sinclair's opponent, Frank Merriam (see also Greg Mitchell). *The Campaign of the Century*. New York: Random House, 1992).

284. Andrew Sinclair. *Spiegel: The Man Behind the Pictures*. Boston, Massachusetts: Little, Brown and Company, 1987.

285. *America, America* (1963), *The Arrangement* (1969), *The Visitors* (1972).

for the better part of a year until it was clear that Pinter was making scant headway extracting a dramatic throughline from Fitzgerald's manuscript. Meanwhile, Nichols had wanted to cast Dustin Hoffman, with whom he had worked in *The Graduate*, as Monroe Stahr. Spiegel disagreed, preferring Jack Nicholson. When Spiegel refused to delay the project a year until Nichols could finish editing *The Fortune* (1975), Nichols departed,[286] although rumors persisted that his real reason was frustration at Spiegel's micro-managing.

At this point Spiegel approached Kazan, who was in a twofold personal crisis with a terminally ill mother and a dysfunctional marriage to his second wife, Barbara Loden. The director's solution was, first, to cheat on Loden and, second, to accept *The Last Tycoon*. Whether Kazan manipulated Spiegel or Spiegel manipulated Kazan is academic; each probably believed he controlled the other. Kazan recommended Robert DeNiro for the Stahr role and suggested Ingrid Boulting for Kathleen Moore. Spiegel wanted newcomer Theresa Russell to play Cecilia Brady, although Kazan noted that the role the randy Spiegel really wanted for Russell was as his mistress. Kazan wrote that Spiegel managed to dodge culpability for his decisions by maneuvering other people into making them, and he kept Spiegel from interfering with him by throwing occasional tantrums to scare him off.[287]

Inspired by DeNiro's dedication (among other things, he starved himself down to 128 pounds to look sickly), Kazan, Russell, and Boulting took to rehearsing on Sundays in addition to the rest of the week prior to production. Principal photography began on October 25, 1975 on a sixty-five day schedule[288] and a $5.5 million budget. Kazan seethed throughout shooting at Spiegel's insistence that he observe every word and nuance of Pinter's script, including the writer's celebrated pauses. The pauses bleed the film of what little energy it has, what with the laconic Mitchum and the introspective DeNiro. Add to that that Boulting has neither presence, chemistry, nor acting ability, and it was a formula for disaster.[289] Kazan's hands were further tied by Pinter's failing to add sufficient material for the film to make dramatic sense. The chief problem is the central love story between Stahr and Kathleen that is so passionless as to stall the picture whenever they appear together. Perhaps this can be attributed to

286. Stephen Farber, *New York Times*, March 21, 1976.
287. Kazan, op. cit.
288. Call sheet from production file.
289. Oddly, or perhaps not, in a movie about an industry that was founded and run by Jews, none of the actors playing studio personnel is Jewish.

the fact that both Pinter's and Kazan's marriages were coming apart. In any event, Kazan confessed, "I shut off my objections, dived in, and did the best I could."[290] His diaries reveal that, even before shooting started, Spiegel thought DeNiro was "common," not on the basis of his acting (a streetwise Italian trying to play a bookish Jew), but from his petty discussions about salary and reimbursements. His opinion didn't change when he saw the first rushes; Spiegel continued to regard his star as having a "petty larceny look." Kazan agreed: "Bobby has never played an executive, he's never played an intellectual, he's never played a lover. I had to find that side of him. It was unexplored territory."[291]

Kazan's frank but emotionless diaries portray a director losing interest in his own craft. Nevertheless, he writes on February 3, 1976, after production wrapped, that he and Spiegel felt they had something good. He and editor Richard Marks had a rough cut ready by March 1 that pleased Spiegel, and when Pinter screened it on April 27 the writer agreed. On June 1, Spiegel showed it to Barry Diller, the head of Paramount, as much to keep him excited about *The Last Tycoon* as to reassure him about DeNiro who, he felt, had just given a poor performance in Bertolucci's film *1900*.[292]

Reactions from the Hollywood crowd were less coded variations on "failure." Some notables who saw early screenings praised supporting players but not the leads; others were silent; still others bemoaned a lack of conflict. When Spiegel took the film to Europe in mid-July to generate enthusiasm, there was none to be had. "Long before this," Kazan wrote in *A Life*, "I'd made up my mind never to work in films again, that *The Last Tycoon* would be it." As he cleaned out his office at Paramount and went home, he thought, "It was all over, and I knew it."

Opening on November 17, 1976, the picture got soft reviews and earned a reported gross of only just over $1,800,000 despite its prestige, powerful starring cast, and Paramount's considerable publicity machine. The reviews said the same thing about the film that had troubled Kazan throughout and that also flawed Fitzgerald's novel: it had good scenes but no impact. Kazan apparently never attempted to direct another.

If an artist creates his own moral universe, Gadge was God. His films contain some of the most shattering moments of truth in American cinema: Stanley carrying Stella up the staircase to their bed in *Streetcar*; James Dean alone with his invalid father at the end of *East of Eden*;

290. Kazan, op. cit.
291. Farber, op. cit.
292. Kazan, op. cit.

Stavros and his fellow immigrants kissing the ground of *America, America*; and, of course, Steiger and Brando in the back of the taxi in *Waterfront*. His credo was that the production comes first, and he focused his energies on that even to the point of setting actor against actor to achieve his desired result.

Thalberg shared that philosophy but had the charm to be forgiven for it. Kazan did not. At the end of *The Last Tycoon*, Stahr has been fired. In his darkened office he looks into the camera and says, "I don't want to lose you." A cutaway to Kathleen suggests he's thinking about her. But he could also be thinking about his power. Or the magic of the movies. Or perhaps his respect. And in that concern there was really nothing inconsistent with Elia Kazan sacrificing his friends. The ends justified the means, whether on the stage, screen, or in the theatre of American politics.

Stanley Kramer.

STANLEY KRAMER
Hollywood's Conscience

The moment is pure Stanley Kramer: He is in a Los Angeles television studio on satellite hookup with a New York TV interview. It's 1989 and it's the seventy-fifth anniversary of the Scopes "Monkey Trial" that pitted evolution against religious ignorance. Kramer directed and produced *Inherit the Wind*, the 1960 film adaptation that dramatized the trial, and he was tolerating the host's questions. As they wrapped the live conversation, the host thanked him. "You're welcome," said Kramer, then seventy-six, and added, "Maybe next time we can talk about something that *I'd* like to talk about."[293]

Kramer was a filmmaker who was fiercely independent in best sense of both words. As an example of the first, at a college seminar in October of 1971, promoting his animal rights film *Bless the Beasts & Children*, he parried a student's presumption of his wealth by snapping, "What do you people do here, go into my financial records?" As to the second, he corrected another student's exaltation of independent, rather than studio, production by saying, "All my career I've been independent. I may release through studios, but I've always been an independent."[294]

In an industry where few dare express belief in anything, Stanley Kramer believed in a great deal. His views were complex, so much so that, throughout his career, which included thirty-four theatrical films (fifteen of them as director), he was variously embraced and criticized by Conservatives as well as Liberals, sometimes both at the same time. He even rankled reviewers who felt pressured that, because his films spoke truth, they should be cut some artistic slack.[295] Although Kramer denied

---

293. ABC-TV's *Day's End*, on which the author was a staff writer.
294. The author was Kramer's co-publicist for this appearance at Boston University.
295. Saul Austerlitz. "Rethinking Stanley Kramer." Museum of the Moving Image. August 25, 2010.

that he made "message" pictures, he did, in the final analysis, achieve more than mere entertainment.

"Why do I keep directing?" he told interviewer Walter Wagner. "That's an easy question to answer. Because you once heard Spencer Tracy say in that extraordinary speech he gave in [*Judgment at*] *Nuremberg* when he sentenced the four Nazi judges to life imprisonment: 'Before the whole world let it be known that this then is what we stand for: truth, justice, and the value of the individual human being.'"[296]

Tracy made his last four films for Kramer, who adored him and who, because of his craggy face and grey, brush cut hair, was sometimes mistaken for him. Their last collaboration was *Guess Who's Coming to Dinner* (1967) which was, Kramer maintained, "a fairy tale" in its drama of how two traditional white parents (Tracy and Katharine Hepburn) come to terms with their daughter, Katharine Houghton, marrying a black man, Sidney Poitier. Kramer tirelessly explained that he and screenwriter William Rose purposely made Poitier's character so perfect that, "if you didn't want her to marry him the only reason had to be racism."[297] Ironically, the film was attacked by both blacks and whites for this contrivance. It also earned a fortune.[298]

Stanley Earl Kramer was supposed to be a lawyer; that's what his parents wished for him when he was born in New York in 1913. Despite his infatuation with FDR and Clarence Darrow, he was in his final year in a business degree at New York University when he was recruited by Twentieth Century-Fox to come to Hollywood and be a writer. It turned out to be a whore's promise and he was let go after three months but, lacking the fare to return to New York, he stuck around and got odd jobs crewing for film companies. After Signal Corps service during World War II he returned to LA and formed a company with four men, one of whom was young screenwriter Carl Foreman. He conned a friend out of $7,500, bought two Ring Lardner stories, and made the first one into a movie called *So This is New York* in 1948. It flopped. He did better with the second one: *Champion* (1949), which made Kirk Douglas a major star, Mark Robson a major director, and Kramer a major producer. Over the next thirty years be produced — and, with *Not as a Stranger* (1955), also directed — a remarkable run of films that courted controversy, both for their content and, sometimes, for the people with whom he made them. In addition to the themes above he took on racism in *Home of the Brave*

---

296. Walter Wagner. *You Must Remember This*. New York: G.P, Putnam's Sons, 1975.
297. Conversation with the Author.
298. $25.5 million in rentals on a $4 million budget (don't tell those B.U. students).

(1949), *The Defiant Ones* (1958), and *Pressure Point* (1962); the emotional and physical residue of World War II in *The Men* (1949), *The Juggler* (1953), and *Judgment at Nuremberg* (1961); atomic apocalypse in *On the Beach* (1959); campus upheavals in *R.P.M.** (1970); and the attitudes that led to the Holocaust in *Ship of Fools* (1965).

At the same time, his Liberal credentials were challenged — or perhaps displayed — when he hired Edward Dmytryk to direct *The Sniper* (1952), *Eight Iron Men* (1952), *The Juggler* (1953), and *The Caine Mutiny* (1954). Dmytryk, one of the Hollywood Ten, had refused to cooperate with HUAC's 1947 hearings and went to prison for his beliefs, but then agreed to testify when he emerged so he could work again. Not only did Kramer hire Dmytryk, he also hired blacklisted writers Nedrick Young, Harold Jacob Smith, Michael Blankfort, and Ben Maddow for various projects, even if they had to use pseudonyms.

But the chief fly in the Kramer ointment is *High Noon*, the western he produced in 1952, in which Marshall Will Kane (Gary Cooper) is abandoned by his town and must face an avenging group of outlaws alone. Adapted from John W. Cunningham's magazine story "The Tin Star," it has long been interpreted as its blacklisted writer-producer Carl Foreman's challenge for people to stand up to the ongoing McCarthy and HUAC inquisitions. Just before it was released, Kramer yielded to pressure from distributor United Artists (who were afraid that the American Legion would picket the picture) and deleted Foreman's producer credit. The Writers Guild, however, stood behind Foreman, who later said, "So the picture was only half-tainted...I was only the writer and didn't matter."[299] With that, the Kramer-Foreman friendship was destroyed.[300]

By 1978 Kramer, at sixty-five, had hit a career snag. His 1977 release, *The Domino Principle*, had fared poorly and talks broke down with its producer, Lew Grade, to next direct Grade's big-budget *Raise the Titanic*. Kramer also shelved his own project, *The Sheiks of Araby*.[301] So when *The Runner Stumbles* was offered to him, Kramer — always looking for Big

---

299. Jeremy Byman. *Showdown at High Noon: Witch-hunts, Critics, and the End of the Western.* Lanham, Maryland: Scarecrow Press, Inc., 2004.
300. The matter was rekindled in Lionel Chetwynd's 2002 documentary *Darkness at High Noon: The Carl Foreman Papers*. Chetwynd, a protégé of Foreman, accused Kramer of selling Foreman out, a position with which Foreman's son, Jonathan, concurs. Kramer's widow, Karen, felt that the documentary unfairly attacked Kramer who, after all, hired blacklisted writers. Source: Victor Navasky. *Naming Names: Afterword.* New York: MacMillan and Company, 2003.
301. Gregg Kilday, *Los Angeles Times*, May 13, 1978.

Themes — was intrigued.[302] "I think this is a love story," he said. "That it happens to be a love story between a Catholic priest and a nun makes it a special love story...It's a story about values, about what you believe in and how much you're willing to back those beliefs."[303]

Milan Stitt, who wrote the source play, had studied for the priesthood before switching to the drama program at Yale. Born in Detroit, he was in John Gassner's drama class whose course assignment was to write a play. His marriage was dissolving but his future ex-wife told him about an incident that had happened in her Isodore, Michigan home town years earlier. In 1906 Sister Mary Janina arrived at a convent school in that town that housed two older nuns and a priest, Father Andrew Bieniawski. When fire destroyed the rectory, Bieniawski moved into the convent, which was against Church rules. Then Sister Mary disappeared. Bieniawski organized search parties but she was never found. Ten years later Janina's bones were discovered buried in the basement of the rectory; she had been pregnant. In 1919 the housekeeper was tried for her murder.[304]

The writing of the play did not go smoothly. Starting in 1965 and continuing through numerous drafts over ten years, Stitt tried making it variously a courtroom drama, a thriller, and a theological play. He changed the priest moving into the convent into the young nun moving into the rectory. In 1971 it debuted at Boston University's Playwrights Project; in 1974, after more rewriting, Austin Pendleton directed it for the Manhattan Theatre Club.[305] A subsequent successful run in Stamford, Connecticut's Hartman Theatre Company was followed by a less-well-received opening on Broadway in 1976.[306] The critics were split but the producers kept it going until the audience caught on, and it ran 396 performances. The cast included Nancy Donohue, Stephen Joyce, Craig Richard Nelson, and Katina Commings.

In his autobiography, Kramer writes that he had wanted Oskar Werner, whom he had used in *Ship of Fools*, to play the troubled priest, now called Father Rivard, but that Werner was dead (perhaps Kramer was being metaphoric; the prickly Austrian actor was alive at the time). Instead, he made the unusual choice of Dick van Dyke, better known as a light comic actor. He cast Kathleen Quinlan, who had recently distinguished

---

302. *Hollywood Reporter*, May 8, 1978.
303. Presskit.
304. Mardi Link. *Isadore's Secret: Sin, Murder, and Confession in a Northern Michigan Town*. Ann Arbor, Michigan: University of Michigan Press, 2009.
305. Curt Davis, *Horizon Magazine*, Cleveland, Ohio, October, 1979.
306. Program Notes, New York: The Actors Company Theatre, 2007.

herself in *I Never Promised You a Rose Garden*, as the nun, now called Sister Rita, with the venerable Maureen Stapleton as Mrs. Shandig, the troubled housekeeper. In his last screen role, Ray Bolger played Monsignor Nicholson, the unyielding prelate.

The picture unfolds in multiple flashbacks: first, as Father Rivard relates his story to his defense lawyer Beau Bridges; second, as Rivard privately recalls the events; and third at the trial itself. The tangled narrative follows events leading up to the crime: upon her arrival, Sister Rita's optimism shakes Father Rivard from his depression over having been exiled to the small town of Solon because he was too "radical" (we never learn how). When the two older nuns are diagnosed with consumption, Rivard moves Rita into the rectory against Msgr. Nicholson's orders; Rita lies to Nicholson about it, alerting Rivard that she is corruptible; and Mrs. Shandig, who converted to Catholicism because she trusted Rivard, is offended by the duplicity. When a fire breaks out in the convent it kindles the one between Rivard and Rita. Not long after, Rita is found murdered and Rivard is charged. At trial, Shandig confesses that she murdered Rita because the nun had corrupted Rivard (something that may be her perception, not fact).

Filming went smoothly. Kramer and Stitt moved the period to 1927 and shot in the small town of Roslyn, Washington, doubling for Solon, Michigan. Kramer and his family had recently relocated to nearby Seattle.[307] After two weeks' rehearsal, shooting started on July 6, 1978. Two months earlier, production designer Al Sweeney and his crew had taken over Roslyn to remove billboards, paint out highway lines, and build a jail in the basement of The Brick Tavern. A warehouse in Ellenberg owned by Central Washington University served as production office and soundstage, and townspeople were asked to lend Kramer their old furniture to make the rectory set look authentic. When the metal roof of the warehouse noisily heaved in the heat of the sun, water hoses were carried up to wet it down. Between takes, Ray Bolger and Dick van Dyke entertained the crew with song-and-dance routines. Cast and crew enjoyed a weekend raft trip; there was a memorable cookout at which Hungarian-born cinematographer Laszlo Kovacs served spiced cabbage rolls he made from an old family recipe; and at the wrap celebration Kramer handed out his traditional gift — engraved silver goblets — to those who had helped him make his film.[308]

---

307. Tom Buckley, *New York Times*, November 24, 1978.
308. Presskit.

The Runner Stumbles had been financed independently by Melvin Simon, a shopping center magnate who dabbled in motion pictures. On its completion, Simon prevailed on Twentieth Century-Fox, with whom he had an overall deal, to distribute. When Fox hesitated, Simon bankrolled a test run in five cities in September and October of 1978.[309] After that, Fox took over and the film opened on November 17, 1979.[310]

To put it mildly, the film was not well-received. David Ehrenstein in the *Los Angeles Herald-Examiner* called it "a shotgun wedding of *Going My Way* and *The Children's Hour*." In *The New York Times*, Janet Maslin likened it to "an office romance" and said Kramer treated the film's serious religious questions as afterthoughts. And *The New Yorker*'s Renata Adler deemed Quinlan's nun "uncontagiously perky." All found fault with van Dyke's overwrought Father Rivard, many of them noting that the cheery entertainer lacked the gravitas that the role demanded.

Kramer knew his film was in trouble even before it opened. "I feel today that I really don't understand everything that's going on," he lamented. "I don't know what I believed. I don't know what Milan wrote about the play, but my doubts were beginning to be expressed on the clothesline that he had."[311] "The script had not been well-constructed," he added 18 years later in his autobiography, "and that was not the fault of the writer, either. He wrote it the way I wanted, but what I wanted turned out to be a total miss."[312] He was right; by corrupting the linear flow of story he breached the emotional arc so essential to holding audience empathy. There is also not enough incident to make a plot: the love between Rivard and Rita blooms with no emotional obstacles, only the smoky ethics of the Church. One also senses that the budget wasn't sufficient to afford the number of set-ups needed to tell the story effectively; Kramer and Kovacs knew cinema too well to leave out so many camera moves and cutaways.

The Runner Stumbles is the least "messagy" of Kramer's avowed social issue films. As always, his heart was in the right place as he challenged long-held views of love, celibacy, religious doctrine, and the drama of human desire versus ethics. If his last shot misfired, he'd already earned a dozen bull's-eyes to secure his position as Hollywood's conscience. "After all these years of making a lot of movies, I don't believe I could

---

309. *Weekly Variety*, June 20, 1979.
310. *Daily Variety*, September 4, 1979.
311. Davis, op. cit.
312. Stanley Kramer with Thomas M. Coffey. *Mad Mad Mad Mad World: A Life in Hollywood*. New York: Harcourt, Brace and Company, 1997.

revolutionize the world, nor do I want to," he summarized. "Nor do I believe I could change anybody's mind…I don't think it's required that you provide answers. But I certainly do think you're obligated creatively to ask the questions."[313]

Stanley Kramer died on February 19, 2001 of pneumonia.

---

313. Davis, op. cit.

Stanley Kubrick.

STANLEY KUBRICK
The Uncanny Valley

Stanley Kubrick was the most publicly secretive filmmaker of all time. No one since Chaplin, who self-financed his productions, had as much control over every aspect of his work or as much influence in its marketing. When Kubrick finally released *Eyes Wide Shut* (1999), his first film in twelve years — "finally" because it had been in development for eighteen years, in production for 400 days, and in post-production for nearly as long — it was received as had most of his previous work: discussed, debated, understood, misunderstood, loved, and hated. But not ignored.

Like his movies, Kubrick was an enigma, except, apparently, to those who knew him. Despite the coldness of his films, he was reported as warm and genial to family, friends, and co-workers. Not that Kubrick was the guy who put the lampshade on his head at parties, but he was hardly the stuffy academic that outsiders imagined.

"[He] was a very interesting intellect," recalls Douglas Trumbull, who got his start with visual effects for *2001: A Space Odyssey* (1968). "I think he put a lot of people off, but he didn't me at all. I had an incredibly good, supportive, and positive relationship with Stanley because I really admired that he was trying to break new ground and do something new."[314] But his hermitic image was strong enough that, in the early 1990s, imposter Alan Conway successfully passed himself off as the long-unseen Kubrick until he was unmasked.[315]

---

314. Susan King, *Los Angeles Times*, February 6, 2012.
315. Kubrick's associate Anthony Frewin unmasked Conway, who died in 1998, and then dramatized the events by writing the film *Colour Me Kubrick: A Tru…ish Story* (2006) starring John Malkovich and directed by another Kubrick acolyte, Brian W. Cook.

Eyes Wide Shut is about the need to escape the ordinariness of life and relationships; about a marriage whose partners cheat with their minds but not with their bodies; and about the danger of average people flirting with non-average situations. The fact that it starred Tom Cruise and Nicole Kidman, two of the least average people in the world, posed a conundrum that may have vexed Kubrick and certainly baffled audiences on its July 13, 1999 release.

The screenplay by Kubrick and Frederic Raphael (*Darling, Two for the Road*) was inspired by the 1926 novelette *Traumnovelle* (*Dream Story*) by Arthur Schnitzler, a prolific German novelist, playwright, and short-story writer who died in 1931. Filmed for German television in 1969, its feature rights were acquired by Kubrick in 1971 and he scheduled it for filming that fall.[316] Considered shocking in its day, the novel follows Fridolin, a young doctor, and his wife, Albertine, over a two-day period starting with Albertine's confession to Fridolin that she has had sexual fantasies about a soldier she met on vacation the year before. This inspires Fridolin to confess that he was attracted to a woman during that same holiday. He then embarks on an odyssey involving a patient's daughter who makes a pass at him; a prostitute; an old friend who tells him about a sex orgy; crashing the sex orgy and being saved from danger by a woman who sacrifices her life for his; and his eventual return to his wife, to whom he confesses everything. She says that they both should be grateful for surviving their recent travails.

The film keeps the theme intact but changes certain details in the transition from the novel, which is interior, to the exterior medium of cinema. The German-Jewish Fridolin and Albertine became Midwestern Protestants Bill (Tom Cruise) and Alice Harford (Nicole Kidman). As Cruise and Kidman were married at the time, their real-life relationship added resonance to their portrayal of a fictitious couple facing bedroom ennui.[317] Finding external metaphors was more challenging. The haunted nighttown that Fridolin traverses becomes, on screen, the glittery, abnormally clean, geographically fake Greenwich Village fabricated at England's Pinewood Studios. Because Kubrick loathed traveling, he dispatched a second unit to shoot footage of Manhattan that he combined with his actors via process projection. He and Raphael added the character of Victor Zeigler (Sydney Pollack), a rich friend of the Harfords, who explains plot points that would otherwise have remained locked in prose.

---

316. *Hollywood Reporter*, April 21, 1971 described *Traumnovelle* as "a psychologically dramatic story of a doctor and his wife whose love is threatened by the revelation of their dreams."
317. …which acquired added resonance when they divorced in 2001.

Typically, the project began with vagueness wrapped in secrecy. When the then-married Cruise and Kidman were announced in 1995 to star in the film following two weeks of negotiations, *Eyes Wide Shut* was described curtly as "a sophisticated drama based on a novel." (Official capsule summaries would change over time.) It was slated to go into production that July.[318] Harvey Keitel was cast as Zeigler and Jennifer Jason-Leigh was requested by Kubrick to play a woman mysteriously involved with him. To no one's surprise and everyone's anticipation, production stretched on. Cruise and Kidman had put all other projects on hold. Julian Senior, Warner Bros.' London-based executive, deflected press inquiries by saying, "It's a modern-day story and it's called *Eyes Wide Shut* — we know that much."[319] Filming finally started at England's Pinewood Studios on November 4, 1996 and wrapped, more or less, in December of 1997.[320]

The first ripples surfaced a year later when *The Observer* reported that Harvey Keitel had walked out "in protest at the conditions under which Kubrick was expecting him to work." He was replaced by director-actor Sydney Pollack. The change would necessitate re-shooting scenes that Jason-Leigh had performed with Keitel, but, when they were scheduled for March of 1998, she was unavailable, so Kubrick was forced to cut her from the film and recast her role with Marie Richardson.[321] Locations included Madam JoJo's, described as "a Soho transvestite club," which was booked for one week of shooting but required three weeks to finish; the Lanesborough Hotel; and the Luton Hoo mansion which was used once for Keitel's scenes and, again, three months later for the reshoot with Pollack.[322] Although the official wrap date was in September of 1997, filming continued until January 31, 1998,[323] Cruise was called back for retakes in February[324] and May.[325] The changes forced Warner Bros. to reschedule the premiere from Christmas of 1998 to late in 1999.

318. Anita Busch, *Daily Variety*, December 15, 1995. Cruise had to fly to Kubrick's 172-acre Childwickbury estate to read the script and "decide then and there if he wanted to commit." (Joanna Blonska, *People* magazine, January 27, 1997.)
319. David Gritten, *Los Angeles Times*, April 21, 1996.
320. Claudia Eller, *Los Angeles Times,* September 29, 1998.
321. Richard Brooks, *The Observer*, October 4, 1998.
322. John Harlow and Nicholas Hellen, *Sunday Times* (London), December 21, 1997.
323. Stephen Galloway, *Hollywood Reporter*, April 29, 1998.
324. Army Archerd, *Variety*, February 4, 1998.
325. *People* magazine, May 18, 1998. During this time Cruise was needed to promote his previous film, *Jerry Maguire*, so that film's distributor, Tri-Star, paid *Eyes Wide Shut* a week's expenses to release Cruise. (*People*, March 24, 1997.)

Despite his long production schedule and perfectionism — one scene supposedly ran to ninety-three takes[326] — Kubrick was considered an efficient, even frugal, filmmaker. For *Eyes Wide Shut* he received $8 million against ten percent of the gross and he gave Cruise $15 million against fifteen percent of gross. At a time when feature films cost $80,000 to $100,000 a day to shoot, Kubrick used a small, minimally paid crew and racked up only $12,000 a day.

Despite all the efforts, *Eyes Wide Shut* emerged as an unsatisfying work, which may be its whole point, but it's hard to be sure. Originally touted (incorrectly, as it turned out) as an erotic film, it disabuses that notion in its first ten seconds as Kidman perfunctorily shucks her clothes while dressing to go out with her husband, and moments later she is seen sitting on the toilet. At the party, she rebuffs a comically lubricious lothario Sandor Szavost (Sky Dumont), who is so über-Continental that he could give Pepé Le Pew a run for his stripe. Likewise, Cruise refutes his action hero genes and becomes awkward in sexual situations, first with flirty girls at the party, and later with a prostitute. Finally, the film's celebrated orgy — in which a group of masked, well-heeled observers watch masked, g-stringed women having simulated fornication with masked, dispassionate men — is presented so mechanically that, if it's supposed to be Bill's dream, how sad that he couldn't think of anything more interesting, and if it's real, how sad that Kubrick couldn't.[327] As people said at the time, *Eyes Wide Shut* was made by someone who doesn't get out much.

Kubrick was the ultimate autodidact. When he picked a subject, he mastered it obsessively, phoning sources at all hours to debrief them. In each of his movies he gained the reputation for not only capturing a genre but transcending it: caper films in *The Killing* (1956), literate epics in *Spartacus* (1960), the sex farce in *Lolita* (1962), black comedy in *Dr. Strangelove* (1964), exploitation films in *A Clockwork Orange* (1971), costume dramas in *Barry Lyndon* (1975), gothic horror in *The Shining* (1980), the Vietnam war in *Full Metal Jacket* (1987), and, most famously, the "really good science fiction movie" in *2001: A Space Odyssey* (1968).[328]

But there were limitations: *Spartacus* was begun by Anthony Mann, who was fired by producer-star Kirk Douglas, and was completed by Kubrick to Douglas' specifications. *Lolita* was gutted by censorship. *Barry*

---

326. Liz Smith, *Los Angeles Times*, April 30, 1997.
327. The theatrical release won its R rating by adding CGI figures that blocked the "naughty bits." The unblocked version was released on home video. Kubrick had approved of both before his death.
328. Arthur C. Clarke's oft-repeated description of Kubrick's enticing pitch.

Lyndon, for all its beauty, suffered from acting that was less expressive than required. *The Shining* was intellectual where it should have been visceral[329] and *Full Metal Jacket*, though its first half was mesmerizing, came out too late to say anything about the military that *M*A*S*H* hadn't covered eighteen years earlier.

2001 may be Kubrick's finest film, not just from its perfect blend of specificity and obscurity, but for being that rare example of pure cinema. Scholars have pointed out that anything of narrative importance in the film is conveyed by images, movement, and juxtaposition, not the purposely banal dialogue. Critic Stuart Byron went further by noting that *2001* marked the demarcation between young and old critics: the older ones, raised on books, were baffled when the film failed to make literal sense to them, whereas younger critics, raised on television and comics, understood what was being conveyed. This explained why Pauline Kael and Andrew Sarris could have called the film "monumentally unimaginative" and "boring," respectively, while Byron and his peers recognized it as "the ultimate trip."[330]

It may be that *Eyes Wide Shut* demanded the next stage of film criticism, although it fared badly, though by no means exclusively, across the critical realm. It contained all the Kubrick trademarks: wide angle lenses, symmetrical composition, tracking shots, a studied lack of spontaneity, and enough symbols and homages to keep trivia hunters busy for years. It also grossed in excess of $161 million worldwide, presumably enough to pay off its $65 million negative cost, plus prints and advertising.

Stanley Kubrick died on March 7, 1999, four days after screening his finished film for Cruise, Kidman, and the Warner Bros. executives who had supported him for the years it had taken to make it, as well as previous films throughout his highly touted relationship with the studio. Is the released version truly Kubrick's locked cut? Had he lived longer, would he have continued to play with the editing as he did on other films? Who knows? Observers at the time noted its uncharacteristically uplifting — for Kubrick — final moments, in which Alice assures Bill, "I think we should be grateful, grateful that we've managed to survive through all of our adventures, whether they were real or only a dream." But others cite

---

329. The author of the book *The Shining*, Stephen King, loudly disliked the film. "I got hold of some Valium just in case I got scared watching it," he told the Author in a 1985 conversation. "And I didn't need it." Nevertheless, a *Shining* cult has grown; culminating in a 2012 documentary by Rodney Ascher titled *Room 237*.

330. It was the *Christian Science Monitor* that called *2001* "the ultimate trip," ironic given that Christian Science eschews drugs.

their next exchange as being closer to the filmmaker's attitude: "There is something very important that we need to do as soon as possible," Alice says. "What's that?" Bill asks her. She responds, "f*ck."

So much for directorial inscrutability.

David Lean.

DAVID LEAN
A Passage to Costaguana

After he directed *Doctor Zhivago* in 1965, David Lean swore he would never make another film. At $11 million and three years of his life, he was stunned when the critics deemed it a trivialization of the Russian revolution, a coffee table movie, and too stately for its own good. Within weeks of its December release, however, audience word-of-mouth repudiated the critics and, to date, *Doctor Zhivago* has returned over $60 million to become one of MGM's, and certainly Lean's, most financially successful films. So he reconsidered and made *Ryan's Daughter* (1970).

The critical assault on *Ryan's Daughter* was also vicious and it got personal. The venom spewed at the dinner meeting of the National Society of Film Critics at the Algonquin Hotel and the inquisition was led by *The New Yorker*'s Pauline Kael, who tore Lean and his new film to shreds for turning a small love story into a bloated epic. When it was over, Lean managed to respond, "You won't be content until you've reduced me to making a film in black and white on 16mm" to which Kael, with the lack of humor that characterized her writing, shot back, "We'll give you color."[331]

"They just took me to bits," Lean later told interviewer Melvyn Bragg. "If you get, as I had on *Zhivago* and on *Ryan's Daughter*, particularly, the sort of notices I had, you begin to think that maybe they're right. One's awfully easily shaken, you know."[332] This, despite a track record that included two Oscars® (*Lawrence of Arabia*, 1962; *The Bridge On the River Kwai*, 1957), *Summertime* (1955), *Hobson's Choice* (1954), *Oliver Twist* (1948), *Great Expectations* (1946), and other successes. Lean's funk lasted

---
331. Kevin Brownlow. *David Lean, a Biography.* New York: St. Martin's Press, 1996.
332. Melvyn Bragg. *David Lean: A Life in Film.* London Weekend Television. South Bank Show, 1985.

fourteen years[333] and made him skip the 1984 New York premiere of *A Passage to India* because he was still smarting from the critical brickbats. When many of those same critics lauded him *in absentia,* however (Kael still equivocated), it became the triumphant climax to a remarkable career which had begun as a messenger at Gaumont British studio.

E. M. (Edward Morgan) Forster's 1924 novel reflected its author's contempt for the British he met while working in India in the early 1920s. An impressionable young woman, Adela Quested, sails to India with an older companion, Mrs. Moore, and happens to meets a young Indian doctor named Aziz at the home of an English schoolmaster named Fielding. Aziz generously (if ill-advisedly) invites Miss Quested to tour the fabled Marabar caves. There the high-strung young woman is either molested or imagines that she was molested, and Aziz is tried for the assault. When she withdraws her charges, Aziz is exonerated and Quested sails blithely back to England, but the ordeal has fractured the friendship between Aziz and Fielding, symbolizing the tensions between India and Britain's occupying Raj.

A Passage to India was financed by EMI Films and HBO (Home Box Office) the then-new cable TV network that was establishing itself as an oasis of programming for more selective audiences. With a budget of $16 million it was low for a feature but monumental for a young cable company. Good call; the film brought in $26 million and boosted the network's upscale subscriber base. But it was not an easy birth. Although Forster had allowed BBC TV's *Play of the Month* to adapt some of his writing in the middle sixties, he resisted selling anything to the movies and, even after his death in 1970, his estate continued to respect those wishes. It was only when King's College, to whom Forster had bequeathed his rights, appointed a new head, Bernard Williams, that Forster's properties were licensed, mostly to James Ivory and Ismail Merchant, but also, in this one case, to David Lean.

Lean's biographer, Kevin Brownlow, charted the process by which the filmmaker discovered how to tell the elusive story within *Passage.* It focused on the question, "What happened in the caves?" "Our audience is tough and emancipated," Lean wrote Santha Rama Rau, a writer who held sway with Forster's estate. "Unless we play our cards true and right,

---

333. This is by no means to suggest that Lean was meek. While shooting *Ryan's Daughter* in Ireland in 1969, James Aubrey, the Philistine new head of MGM, flew there to force Lean to cut his $9 million budget. Aubrey failed and, in revenge, put the projects of fifteen other people on MGM's chopping block (see Bart, *Fade Out*). When Aubrey died in 1994 he was remembered as one of the most destructive and despised executives in Hollywood history.

they'll be only too ready to laugh at Miss Quested having a self-imposed fit of the sexual horrors of a dark cave."[334] To some audiences the matter would remain maddeningly unresolved; perhaps to encourage this, Lean repeats the incident several times without showing specifics. Of course, he wants the viewer to identify with Miss Quested's (actress Judy Davis) uncertainty, and the enigma drives the rest of the film. Rather than pursue the matter with Rama Rau, who had once adapted portions of the book for the stage with Forster's permission, Lean decided to have a go at writing the screenplay himself — notably without involving his *Lawrence, Zhivago,* and *Ryan* collaborator, Robert Bolt, with whom he had had a falling out. In 1979 Bolt had suffered a heart attack and a stroke that some quarters accused Lean for bringing on. "I wrote the others with Robert Bolt," Lean told producer John Brabourne, "I never got any credit for it. Why shouldn't I get credit on this one?"[335]

As Lean wrote his script, he added a scene in which Miss Quested bicycles into the woods and encounters an ancient temple with suggestive sculptures, the sensuousness of the location kindling her sexual yearnings. He also reduced Forster's criticism of the Raj. In so doing, the social distinctions between "natives" and British remain rigid, but now the Brits are less twittish. What Lean hadn't counted on was having to defend his adaptation to the King's College dons. When they complained about his changes, he told them forthrightly that the novel would live forever but that his movie would be forgotten in five or ten years. They swallowed it.

Scouting locations in India proved both liberating and frustrating. Because of the threat of sabotage, the Indian government forbade the photographing of certain bridges and public buildings, but Lean, his wife Sandy, and his friend/production manager Eddie Fowlie and Fowlie's wife, Kathleen, managed to do so surreptitiously. The biggest challenge was finding suitable Marabar caves. Fowlie came through by locating a sheer rock cliff at Savandurga for the exteriors. Except there were no caves in it. So the company blasted openings, upsetting the locals who voiced their displeasure to the *Sunday Times*. Additional locations were found at Bangalore and Kashmir, and the exterior sets for Forster's fictitious city of Chandrapore were built on a private estate. The latter was particularly important not just for artistic freedom but also for crowd control.

And it was control, or lack of it, that began to produce tension on the set. Lean was used to having his way, but in the years since he had last

---

334. Brownlow, op. cit. The biography contains a meticulous history of the making of *A Passage to India*, which the Author hereby acknowledges.

335. Brownlow, op. cit.

been behind the camera the bean-counters had completely taken over the film business. Where Lean had always enjoyed a certain extravagance because he made prestigious, reserved seat attractions that invariably won Oscars®, on *A Passage to India* he had to shoot in the more confined TV aspect ratio, had to hold to a schedule (no more waiting for clouds to form and flowers to bloom), and was denied his preference to shoot in continuity. Watching the intimate documentary footage, one sees the normally confident Lean checking with his team for approval, watching him grow tense over delays, being unusually specific with Ernie Day, his cameraman, and standing out as a reluctant sage among a young crew.[336] Said one young crew member to Kevin Brownlow, "David committed the crime of getting old."[337] Lean fought back by printing the first take of the first shot of the film; he wanted everyone to know that he was in charge. Unfortunately, no one told that to Judy Davis or Victor Banerjee, playing Miss Quested and Dr. Aziz, respectively. Banerjee complained that Lean wanted him to play a stereotypical, obsequious Indian complete with lilting speech. It wasn't until midway through the shoot that he grasped that he was to have lost the accent as he went along to show he was becoming more at ease with English society.

As for the argumentative Davis, she saw her character as Forster did: a frumpy spinster. Lean wanted her to be more a more stylish, yet repressed, woman on the brink of a sexual awakening. Although she had lobbied for the role, Davis apparently possessed little knowledge of Lean's body of work. The two tangled during production but made rapprochement toward the end. A more long-held tussle was the one between Lean and Alec Guinness as the mystic Godbole who appears throughout the story at important moments. Though the two had made numerous unforgettable films together from *Great Expectations* on, each was a contest over how Guinness should portray his various characters. His acting technique included minute research and preparation, and Sir Alec was irritated by Lean's last-minute adjustments. Even Dame Peggy Ashcroft seemed unable to grasp the technical requirements of cinema versus stage and ignored Lean when he tried to guide her. Concluded the director when it was all finished, "I enjoyed doing this last picture, but I didn't have any fun."[338]

All of that was a forgotten when *A Passage to India* premiered to praise, even glory, for its master craftsman. Buoyed by the reaction, Lean began

336. Bragg, op. cit.
337. Brownlow, op. cit.
338. Brownlow, op. cit.

work on Joseph Conrad's *Nostromo*, a complex story of greed, corruption, and obsession among three men over a cache of silver in the fictional mining town of Costaguana. In early 1986 Lean, still on the outs with Bolt, approached playwright Christopher Hampton to write the script, and the two Englishmen began work. They wrote together for over a year until, one day, Hampton phoned Lean and asked the director, "Is this a bad time to talk to you?" Responded Lean with cold matter-of-factness, "I'm here with Robert," ending the Lean-Hampton collaboration.

In 1989 Lean, by then Sir David, received renewed international acclaim when his 1962 masterpiece, *Lawrence of Arabia*, was restored and theatrically reissued. He'd hoped that this renaissance, added to the success of *A Passage to India*, would attract financing for *Nostromo*, and, when Steven Spielberg came aboard as Executive Producer, there was momentary hope.[339] But by then Lean had begun failing physically past the point of being able to direct, and on April 16, 1991, he died at the age of eighty-three.

In 1996 a television adaptation of *Nostromo* directed by Alistair Reid and scripted by John Hale, aired on the BBC. Lean's proposed version remains unshot.

---

339. At age eighty Lean was considered uninsurable, so Arthur Penn, then fifty-seven, was engaged as standby director. Penn recalled that the insurance company demanded that he be not just on call but actually on the set with Lean. Penn reported that he told them, "Are you kidding? I have to sit here and wait for this man to drop dead or get sick? Absolutely not!"

Sidney Lumet.

SIDNEY LUMET
Everybody Loves Sidney

Sidney Lumet wrote two books on directing: the one in print was called *Making Movies* and the other was his entire body of work.[340] His last entry in the latter, *Before the Devil Knows You're Dead* (2007), was every bit as good as his first, fifty years earlier, *Twelve Angry Men* (1957),[341] and, even if there were a few misfires among the forty-two that came between, the astonishing fact is that he was able to keep working at a pace that left his contemporaries — and even most of his successors — in the dust. There probably has not been a director since the heyday of the studio system who was as prolific as Lumet.

"If you didn't know him [to be] eighty, you'd figure a thirty-year-old man made this movie," said Phillip Seymour Hoffman during *Devil*. "It doesn't smack of an older man trying to make it...really, this movie is so infused with such youthful vigor."[342]

Lumet was like that his whole career, which began as a child actor. Born in 1924 to Baruch Lumet and Eugenia Wermus, the family moved from Philadelphia to New York so they could perform in the Yiddish Art Theatre.[343] At the age of four Sidney started acting on radio, then began a stage career. "I gotta tell you," he said, "I loved it. It kept me off the streets. I loved the exposure to the whole world."[344] He was in Sidney Kingsley's memorable 1935 stage play about New York's slums, *Dead End* (the one

340. Sidney Lumet. *Making Movies*. New York: Alfred P. Knopf, 1995.
341. It may be significant to note that *Twelve Angry Men* was, for a time, the most popular teaching film with motivational speaking consultants because it showed how one man can change the opinions of eleven others by logic and persuasion (Author's conversation with Don Krim, United Artists, later Kino International).
342. DVD interview comments, *Before the Devil Knows You're Dead*.
343. Philip French, *The Guardian*, April 9, 2011.
344. Lumet, DVD commentary, op. cit.

that spawned the Dead End Kids from its 1937 movie adaptation), and appeared consistently in Broadway and off-Broadway productions during his youth. He attended the Professional Children's School and Columbia University.

Lumet served in the Far East in the Army Signal Corps during World War II and returned to an American theatre in transition, entering television in New York in 1950 as director of live dramas such as *Danger* and *You Are There*. Not only was television challenging motion pictures as mass entertainment, but the introduction of Method acting was creating new stars and a new performance aesthetic. As a young actor turned director, Lumet was uniquely able to understand these sensibilities and apply them to his work.

It was also a time of political repression, primarily the Blacklist, and Lumet was brave enough to flaunt pressure groups by hiring writers (often under pseudonyms) who were under fire for their beliefs. When television drama blossomed with such Golden Age anthology series as *U.S. Steel Hour*, *Goodyear Playhouse*, *Alcoa Hour*, *Kraft Theatre*, and *Playhouse 90*, Lumet directed episodes for all of them. He became known for his speed, facility, and firm control without being domineering.

It was Reginald Rose's 1954 *Twelve Angry Men* for *Studio One* that brought him to feature films. The original broadcast had been directed by Franklin J. Schaffner, but when United Artists asked Henry Fonda to produce as well as star in the film adaptation, Fonda asked Lumet to take the reins. Lumet insisted on two weeks' rehearsal, which later allowed him to shoot the whole film in an astonishing twenty-one days. He did so with an unobtrusive but effective visual style that conveyed the rising drama by starting with wide angle lenses that distanced the jurors from each other deciding a murder case, then moved closer as the tension rose. It was an auspicious debut.

Unlike many of his contemporaries who "went Hollywood," Lumet was a passionate, proselytizing New York filmmaker. His most memorable films are set in the city and exude its ambience, from the screwy adventures of mourners heading to a funeral in *Bye Bye Braverman* (1968) to the discomfiting tour of the Apple's underbelly in *Prince of the City* (1981) with 130 locations. He even led the campaign in the 1970s to revive the classic Kaufman-Astoria, Long Island studios where so many early talkies had been shot.

Lumet may be America's least celebrated great director. The omission is as glaring as that of John Ford, Howard Hawks, Alfred Hitchcock, and other notable filmmakers who were ignored at home until they were "discovered" by the *nouvelle vague* in Europe and by such visionary American critics as Peter Bogdanovich, Todd McCarthy, Joseph McBride, Stuart Byron, and Andrew Sarris. Yet even Sarris dismissed Lumet as "efficiently vehicular."[345] Nevertheless, it took the motion picture Academy's Board of Governors to finally recognize him with a special Oscar® in 2005 after five unfulfilled nominations. Perhaps this was because he was remarkably devoid of ego; indeed, the first comprehensive book about him took until 1991,[346] and it wasn't until 2006 that a collection of his interviews appeared.[347]

Known for being inordinately well-prepared, shooting his movies quickly, and bringing them in under budget, he was a producer's dream as well as an actor's protector. He planned his films scrupulously and always knew what he wanted and how to get it. And even though he claimed to have the right of final cut[348] since *Murder on the Orient Express* (1974), he eschewed the "a film by" possessive credit. He knew better. "I'm dependent on weather, budget, what the leading lady had for breakfast, who the leading man is in love with," he said pragmatically, if not modestly. "Like all bosses — and on set, I'm the boss — I'm the boss only up to a point."[349]

Lumet was celebrated for adapting plays to the screen, but they were seldom his most interesting work. Marlon Brando may shine in *The Fugitive Kind* (adapted from Tennessee Williams' *Orpheus Descending*); Katharine Hepburn may distinguish Eugene O'Neill's *Long Day's Journey Into Night*;[350] Sean Connery, Ian Bannen, and Harry Andrews may sizzle in the unrelenting *The Hill*; and Michael Caine may bring Christopher Reeve up to his level in *Death Trap*. But *Child's Play*, *Equus*, and *The Wiz* capture none of their stage magic. When he had original screenplays set in small spaces, however, such as courtrooms, Lumet achieved what can only be called liberation within confinement: *Twelve Angry Men*, *Fail-Safe*, *Murder on the Orient Express*, *The Verdict*, *Network*, *Q&A*, *Guilty as Sin*, and *Find Me Guilty*. *Find Me Guilty* alone can serve as a textbook on how to keep a film moving. While star Vin Diesel doesn't score as a mobster caught in a bizarre but true court case, Lumet is dazzling in keeping its courtroom scenes visually alive without showing off.

345. Andrew Sarris. *The American Cinema*. New York: E.P. Dutton, 1968.
346. Frank R. Cunningham. *Sidney Lumet: Film and Literacy Vision*. Lexington, Kentucky: University Press of Kentucky, 1991.
347. Sidney Lumet and Joanna E. Rapf. *Interviews*. Jackson, Mississippi: University Press of Mississippi, 2006.
348. Lumet, *Making Movies*, op. cit.
349. Lumet, *Making Movies*, ibid. Also in conversation with the Author, 1983.
350. Always frank, Lumet said he didn't understand the theme of the film but he "let the play tell me." Clearly he listened. Source: *Making Movies* (ibid).

And then there were the pictures that used the power of film to tell socially relevant stories: Al Pacino's clenched brilliance as the honest cop crossing the thin blue line in *Serpico*; the operatically tragic bank robbery of *Dog Day Afternoon* with, again, a fearless Pacino; the anguish of families torn apart by history in both *Daniel* and *Running on Empty*; and, of course, the pitch-perfect writing, casting, cinematography, editing, tone, and prescience of *Network*.

All of which lead up to *Before the Devil Knows You're Dead*. It began with an original screenplay by Kelly Masterson, a former Franciscan brother who gave up his calling when he heard a clearer voice: theatre.[351] Although a produced playwright, his spec screenplay about two friends who conspire to rob a jewelry store to bail each of them out of debt hit home with Lumet eight years after it was written. It was Lumet who suggested changing the two friends to two brothers. He cast the physically mismatched Philip Seymour Hoffman and Ethan Hawke who arrange for a third party to rob their parents' mall jewelry store, in the course of which both the thief-for-hire and their mother, Rosemary Murphy, are killed. While their father, Albert Finney, grieves, the guilty siblings — Hoffman has embezzled from his firm and Hawke owes loan sharks — melt down. The film's mood is one of increasing doom and yet the storytelling and the performances are so compelling that it's impossible to look away from the screen.

The $18 million film[352] was not shot on film. It was shot on Panavision Genesis high-def digital video cameras, often two at a time to cover both sides of a conversation, allowing the actors to be more spontaneous and to overlap their dialogue as in real life.

"There are so many advantages to HD I can't begin to enumerate them," Lumet said, "not the least of which is I can use a multi-camera technique which takes me back to my live television days. So I feel there are things that we got in this from a performance point of view that I never would have been able to get with a single camera technique. But there's such a prejudice among older film people about high def, so, often, they go for it for the wrong reasons: 'oh it's so much cheaper,' 'I won't need as much light,' 'I won't need anything.' That's not true. You need everything that you normally need, except less of it."[353]

Lumet rolled on July 10 in New York's unbearably hot summer of 2006.[354] The jewelry store was in a shopping mall in Bayside, Queens

---

351. Official biography on *IMDb.com*.
352. *IMDb.com* estimate.
353. Lumet, DVD commentary, op. cit.
354. *Hollywood Reporter*, July 18, 2006.

and the home where Finney and Murphy lived was also in Queens (the community of Douglaston). St. Agnes Hospital in White Plains was where the family gathered and grieved. Hell Gate Studios in the Astoria complex was the anchor studio, and various apartments and storefronts were secured by location manager Alvaro Donado (who had worked with Lumet on the 2002 A&E TV series he created, *100 Centre Street)*. He purposely had production designer Christopher Nowak and set decorator Diane Lederman make the sets look as ordinary as possible. Casting director Ellen Lewis, who had peopled practically every other New York-based film but had never before had the chance to work with Lumet, did so here for the first time.

As usual, Lumet was prepared in the extreme, recognizing that it's the director's job to chart the emotions in each scene and remind the actors where they are in the flow. He insisted on a two-week rehearsal so that, even if the scenes were shot a month later, the material would steep in their psyches. This enabled him to work fast; a ten-page exchange between Hawke and Hoffman took only seven hours to complete (most features shoot only three to five pages a day). For a nude scene between Hawke and Marisa Tomei, before both actors bared everything for their art, Hawke told the crew, "Oh, by the way, you guys standing around, if you want to stay you've gotta take your clothes off." Those who did, did. When any of the actors needed thespic help, Lumet would give them something that was, in Hoffman's words, specific and active. "I learned that from Sandy Meisner," Lumet said. "He was a great action teacher that way because he kept saying, 'verbs, verbs, verbs.'"[355]

After festival screenings, *Before the Devil Knows You're Dead* was released on October 26, 2007 and became a sleeper that woke up among the cognoscenti and then on home video, accruing a worldwide gross in excess of $25 million. As it did, Lumet was already planning his next films. He announced a two picture deal with the Buddha Group with an option on a third. His first would be *Getting Out*, a prison break picture from his original script. "I forget I'm an old man," he said. He was then eighty-two.

But at eighty-six he was dead from lymphoma.

"Melodrama is reality pushed to where it's improbable but still possible," he was fond of saying. The idea of a five-foot-five dynamo turning out film after film for fifty years, as regular as Manhattan traffic and as vital as the city itself, is equally improbable, but Sidney Lumet made it all happen.

355. DVD commentary, ibid. Lumet studied with Sanford Meisner at the Neighborhood Playhouse after World War II.

Rouben Mamoulian.

ROUBEN MAMOULIAN
"Stockings" Stuffer

Rouben Mamoulian is one of only four directors in this book — Orson Welles, Elia Kazan, Arthur Penn and himself — who had Broadway success before coming to Hollywood, and only he, Penn, and Kazan returned to the boards with any regularity to refresh the muse. Some, such as Vincente Minnelli, Otto Preminger, and George Cukor started in theatre but left for Hollywood, and a few, such as Robert Altman and Blake Edwards, made forays to the stage between movie assignments. But Mamoulian was equal parts klieg lights and footlights, and his best films combine the intimacy of movies with a sense of the live theatrical experience. In this regard, his last film — his last completed film, that is — *Silk Stockings*, is a perfect example of both disciplines.

Born in 1898 in Tiflis, Georgia, Russia and trained at the Moscow Art Theatre, Mamoulian worked his way to New York in the 1920s where he joined the Theatre Guild. He staged the original *Porgy* under their aegis in 1927 that brought him to the attention of Paramount Pictures who were, like the rest of panicked Hollywood, speeding the conversion to sound. It was for them in 1929 that he directed his first picture, *Applause*, at the company's Astoria, New York studios, a convenient commute from Broadway for theatre actors who could shoot by day and still make their evening curtains. *Applause* made new rules by breaking old ones. A stock story of a self-sacrificing chorus girl who tries to keep her pure daughter from entering the acting trade, it was distinguished not only by a touching performance by torch singer Helen Morgan but by innovative visual storytelling. Rather than submit to confining the noisy early sound camera to its bulky soundproof isolation booth, Mamoulian liberated it and, like DeMille was doing in California, muffled its racket with crude padding. Unlike other early sound films, which forsook the eloquence of silent cinema for the bland novelty of talk, *Applause* is a fully realized *moving picture*. He also experimented with off-screen sounds while Morgan was playing her final scene, bringing in traffic and people chattering happily against the mood of the on-screen tragedy. "I don't know whether you noticed it," Mamoulian told Fellows at the American Film Institute in his later years, "[but] there's no relationship to the scene at all. So you say, 'Why have it, then?' Because that happiness of someone else makes her misery ten times worse."[356]

Two years later, in 1931, he made *City Streets*, a gangster saga in which Gary Cooper sacrifices his honor for Sylvia Sidney, and it's remarkable not only for its fluidity in storytelling but because, between it and *Applause*, Mamoulian returned to New York and directed at least four plays on Broadway.[357] Although he would later enjoy twin triumphs on stage with *Porgy and Bess* (1935) and American theatre's revolutionary *Oklahoma!* (1943), he continued to distinguish himself in Hollywood. His *Dr. Jekyll and Mr. Hyde* (1931) is memorable not only for its opening sequence shot from Jekyll's point of view but for its dark tone and brave performance by Fredric March.[358] It was also celebrated for March's transformation from doctor to brute which was achieved on camera without lab tricks.[359] The next year *Love Me Tonight* was supposed to be a throwaway musical done as a favor for the studio, but Mamoulian turned it into a charming Maurice Chevalier-Jeanette MacDonald romance. *Queen Christina* contains one of Garbo's finest performances, helped immeasurably by the camera, and *Becky Sharp* — though best known as the first three-strip Technicolor feature — actually toned down two elements that might have become irritating: the palette and Miriam Hopkins.

Despite his track record, Mamoulian was neither a tyrant nor a pushover. What he was, was curious about his ever-changing medium. "Experimentation is a very silly occupation, unless it has a purpose," he said. "You experiment when you say, 'the conventional way isn't strong enough, isn't beautiful enough, isn't elegant enough. How can I do better?

---

356. Eric Sherman. *Directing the Film: Film Directors on Their Art*. Boston, Massachusetts: Little, Brown, 1976.
357. *Wings Over Europe, The Game of Love and Death, Marco Millions, A Month in the Country*, and a revival of *Porgy*.
358. Considering that a fully-loaded blimped 35mm camera weighed several hundred pounds and had to be rolled on a dolly that weighed several hundred more pounds, this scene is breathtaking.
359. The process used successive colored filters to reveal various layers of make-up. Since the film was in black and white, the effect was a blotching of March's skin and the emergence of grotesque facial features.

What if I do this? Ah, let's experiment.'"360 This was not always appreciated. Fresh from his triumphant staging of Broadway's revolutionary *Oklahoma!* in 1943 he was sent the screenplay for *Laura* by Fox's chief Darryl F. Zanuck. He may not have known that other directors such as Lewis Milestone and Walter Lang had already passed on it, deeming it a mere potboiler. The only person who fought to direct it was Otto Preminger, but Zanuck resolutely refused, demanding he remain a producer. Perhaps because of this, Preminger and Mamoulian had instant enmity. As Preminger told his biographer, Gerald Pratley, "From the moment he got the script [he] treated it like dirt, and me too. Whatever I said about the story, he didn't listen."361 The chill continued when Preminger contrived to hire Clifton Webb to play what became his defining role, Waldo Lydecker. Mamoulian disliked Webb and, according to Zanuck biographer Leonard Mosley, took it out on the picture. When Zanuck, who viewed all the studio's rushes, saw how sluggish Mamoulian's footage was, he fired him and installed Preminger, who eagerly reshot every frame.362

Unfazed by the firing, Mamoulian returned to Broadway where he adapted and directed *Sadie Thompson* from W. Somerset Maugham's *Rain*; directed Rodgers and Hammerstein's *Carousel*; directed and supervised *Lost in the Stars* (Maxwell Anderson and Kurt Weill's adaptation of Alan Paton's *Cry the Beloved Country*), three other plays, and two revivals of *Oklahoma!*, managing to fit in a small film, *Summer Holiday*, for MGM in 1948. After that he waited until 1956 to give Hollywood another try with *Silk Stockings*.

Silk Stockings was a reworking of the 1939 Ernst Lubitsch *Ninotchka*, in which Greta Garbo starred as a Russian bureaucrat sent to Paris to learn why three earlier emissaries had not completed their mission of obtaining and selling Grand Duchess Swana's jewels. The Duchess' friend, Melvyn Douglas, tries to placate Ninotchka and she is soon seduced not only by him but by Capitalism. The original story was by Melchior Lengyel, a Hungarian playwright who had achieved success in Hollywood.363 It was adapted for Lubitsch and MGM by Billy Wilder, Charles Bracket and Walter Reisch, but by the time it was licensed as a Broadway musical by

---

360. Sherman, op. cit.
361. Gerald Pratley. *The Cinema of Otto Preminger.* New York: Castle Books, 1971.
362. Leonard Mosley. *Zanuck: The Rise and Fall of Hollywood's Last Tycoon.* Boston, Massachusetts: Little, Brown Company, 1984.
363. Lengyel — who also wrote the story for Lubitsch's classic *To Be or Not to Be* (1942) — moved back to Europe in 1960 and died in Budapest in 1974.

Cy Feuer and Ernest Martin in 1954 the Red Scare was in full swing and Communism was thorny territory. George S. Kaufman and his wife, Leueen MacGrath, adapted the book, which Kaufman intended to direct until he had a falling out with the producers and Feuer took over (with uncredited assist from Jerome Robbins). Abe Burrows rewrote the Kaufmans' book, and the only person who seems to have stayed above the fray was composer-lyricist Cole Porter.

By the time *Silk Stockings* opened on February 24, 1955, the movie's Duchess with the jewels had become a male composer with a score, and Melvyn Douglas had become a movie producer who wanted to keep Ninotchka from bringing said composer back to Moscow. The title comes from the hosiery that Ninotchka first deems decadent, then buys for herself. Even though *Silk Stockings* had one of Porter's less interesting scores, it ran 478 performances. MGM immediately locked up the screen rights[364] — not a problem inasmuch as *Ninotchka* was already theirs — for $300,000 (the show had been capitalized at $375,000) and Arthur Freed came in to produce.[365] Freed assigned two Leonards — Gershe and Spigelgass — to adapt the adaptation of the adaptation.

Dance rehearsals began on September 18, 1956 and went on for thirty-one grueling days with Eugene Loring (who had choreographed the Broadway show) guiding the chorus and Janis Page, with Hermes Pan, as usual, working with in seclusion with Fred Astaire. On October 22 the principal personnel went for wardrobe, makeup, and hair tests. During the month-long pre-production schedule people were called as needed to pre-record their vocals. Astaire and anybody appearing with Astaire rehearsed with Pan whenever they were freed from other duties.

Cyd Charise's "Silk Stockings" solo number raised the eyebrows of the Production Code censor who was on the set. Performed in lingerie, it was an imaginative fantasy number. The censor complained and MGM compromised by letting Charise dance in lingerie but having her do it behind a stuffed chair. She always claimed that it made it seem more alluring.[366] MGM hired accent expert Zoia Karabanova to coach Chase on what would pass for Russian-accented English, and had André Previn conduct Conrad Salinger's remarkable arrangements. The first day's shoot, which passed with no incident on Stage 15, started with simple shots of people arriving in the hotel, then moved on to shoot the "Too Bad" number in the afternoon. The entire schedule interlaced dramatic scenes with dance

364. *Daily Variety*, March 24, 1955.
365. John L. Scott, *Los Angeles Times*, January 13, 1957.
366. Cyd Charise, *Silk Stockings* DVD special features.

numbers, deemed the best way to preserve everybody's stamina, especially the ageless fifty-seven-year-old Astaire.

There were offscreen dramas, too. Astaire, who had been widowed when his wife, Phyllis, died in September of 1954, found himself attracted to a young dancer in the chorus, Barrie Chase. They started seeing each other, and he asked her to co-star with him on the television special *An Evening with Fred Astaire* that aired on NBC on October 17, 1958.

By day forty-two (January 8, 1957) the company was ready to shoot the "Ritz Roll and Rock" number in which Cole Porter, via Astaire, satirized the emergence of rock 'n' roll. Formal wrap was January 31, 1957 on schedule and under budget. It opened July 18 of that year to rave reviews and solid business.

The film is a study in contradictions. It's Mamoulian's first in the unwieldy CinemaScope process, yet he and director of photography Robert Bronner[367] surmounted challenges in composition by shooting in extended takes that reposition the frame as people change places. There are few close-ups or over-the-shoulder shots (such was the style before TV changed the movies' syntax), but this is one of those cases where the performances and craft dominate. Eugene Loring staged the chorus numbers, and when it came to Astaire's weightless dances the filmmakers were hamstrung by Astaire's demand, in effect since his RKO days, that he be photographed at full length. 'Scope being what it is (Joseph L. Mankiewicz once said it the perfect aspect ratio to show snakes f**king), the framing often left Astaire looking like a zucchini standing on a dashboard. Hugh Hunt's and Edwin B. Willis' subtle but appropriate sets filled in the rest of the frame.

Cyd Charise (vocals dubbed by Carol Richards) is no Garbo but her performance — intentionally humorless and innately sensuous — becomes breathtaking when she dances. Astaire is his normal fluttery self and was still dancing like, well, Fred Astaire. Peter Lorre commits grand theft on the few scenes he is a part of as one of the commissars, and Janis Page channels Carol Channing in a rosy turn as Astaire's Esther Williams-type musical star. Her winning comic persona is the hit of the picture. Plus she has the best line when she can't quite place the author of *War and Peace*: "Oh, *that* Tolstoy."

Silk Stockings returned $4,417,753 on a negative cost of $1,853,463 but the results gave Mamoulian little clout. In 1958 he began directing

367. Bronner would next shoot the Elvis Presley vehicle *Jailhouse Rock*. His work for Mamoulian comes in the middle of numerous exploitation-type films, none of which matches his work in *Silk Stockings*.

the film version of *Porgy and Bess* for producer Samuel Goldwyn but left the project over creative differences. Once again he was replaced by his *bête noir* Otto Preminger. Mamoulian had hoped to bring to the screen the theatrical excitement he had created when he staged the original Gershwin-Heyward opera in 1935. Instead, the film reflects Preminger's vision which so disappointed the Gershwin estate that half a century has not softened their refusal to allow its re-release.[368]

Soon thereafter, Mamoulian was asked by producer Walter Wanger to direct what was then going to be a low-rent production of *The Life and Times of Cleopatra* for Fox based on Carlo Mario Franzero's potboiler about the Egyptian Queen. Although the studio leaned toward Dana Wynter, Mamoulian pushed for Elizabeth Taylor and for a more meaningful screenplay. The rest is history, but Mamoulian wasn't to be a part of it. Over his objections, and yielding to Taylor's tax demands, Fox decided to make the picture in London. London's predictable bad weather made it impossible to shoot "Roman" exteriors and led to Taylor's well-covered near-death bout with pneumonia. Little, if any, usable footage was shot by then, so, with $7 million down the Thames and nothing to show for it, Mamoulian departed on January 3, 1961.[369] He was replaced by Joseph L. Mankiewicz, but that's quite another story. Mamoulian never directed another picture. He spent the next 26 years in reluctant retirement, giving occasional seminars on directing but being largely ignored by both Hollywood and Broadway, two institutions that he had revolutionized while he was their artist in residence. He died on December 4, 1987 at the age of ninety.

---

368. For the record, the Author has seen it and agrees with the Gershwin estate opinion but not their decision.
369. Stephen M. Silverman. *The Fox That Got Away*. Secaucus, New Jersey: Lyle Stuart, Inc., 1988.

Joseph L. Mankiewicz.

JOSEPH L. MANKIEWICZ
Talking With Style

He did *The New York Times* Sunday crossword puzzles in ink. He wrote, directed, and produced the classic bitch-fest, *All About Eve*. He introduced Spencer Tracy to Katharine Hepburn. And he went out with an Oscar®-nominated triumph yet spent the next twenty-one years looking for another picture. Joseph L. Mankiewicz was lured into the studio system in the 1930s by his older brother, Herman, who was promising his friends riches everywhere and only idiots for competition. He became house producer and phantom script doctor at MGM but wanted to direct, only to be told by the studio's head, Louis B. Mayer, that he had to crawl before he could walk, "which," Mankiewicz later said, "was about the best definition of a producer I ever heard."[370]

At sixty-three when he directed *Sleuth* (1972) he was still in his prime. The dialogue-rich, character-driven stage hit by Anthony Shaffer was the kind of project that fascinated the urbane filmmaker. As the title of his biography suggests (*Pictures Will Talk* by Kenneth L. Geist (New York: Charles Scribner's Sons, 1978), Mankiewicz had a near-fetish for overwriting, even pontificating. But so did Oscar Wilde. Yet he was above one-liners (with the notable exception of *All About Eve*'s "Fasten your seat belts, it's going to be a bumpy night"); his was a fascination with language itself, its rhythm, its precision, and its sophistication.

He also functioned on multiple levels. For example, his 1951 *People Will Talk*, which is ostensibly about a surgeon who is persecuted for his unorthodox practices, is not only a debate about the danger of being a visionary, it's Mankiewicz's rebuke to the right-wing political forces who

---

370. Joseph L. Mankiewicz. *More About All About Eve: A Colloquy with Gary Carey*. New York: Random House, 1972.

tried to blackball him from the Directors Guild during the HUAC-McCarthy witch hunts. *The Honey Pot* is his cheeky reinterpretation of Ben Jonson's *Volpone* which, before reaching its muddled climax, offers a spirited defense of venality. And *Cleopatra*, which is far better than its reputation, is a remarkable essay on how history is shaped in bedrooms as well as on battlefields.[371]

Mankiewicz came to *Sleuth* after the disappointment of his 1970 *There Was a Crooked Man*, in which screenwriters Robert Benton and David Newman tried to infuse modern attitudes into westerns the way they brought sex to crime films three years earlier in *Bonnie and Clyde*. Unlike the latter's director, Arthur Penn, who embraced new cinematic styles, Mankiewicz was too much of a traditionalist, and *Crooked Man* suffered from a conflict between old form and new content. The director was also briefly involved in remaking the classic newspaper picture, *The Front Page*, but left the project.[372]

The Tony award-winning *Sleuth* offered the wily Mankiewicz a verbal playground. A fertility dance that becomes a deadly contest, Shaffer's skillful drama is a one-set play that asks the audience to help solve a crime that may not have taken place. Mystery writer Andrew Wyke (Laurence Olivier) invites Cockney hairdresser Milo Tindle (Michael Caine) to his country estate knowing that Milo is having an affair with his wife, Marguerite. Instead of revenge, Wyke seeks a gentlemen's deal: he will help Milo rob his home, run off with Marguerite, and fence her jewels so that they can collect the insurance money. That way he, Wyke, will be relieved of alimony and live happily ever after with his mistress, Téa. The two men merrily conspire until Milo attempts to leave the Wyke home laden with booty, at which time Wyke pulls a gun, pronounces Milo a fool for setting himself up to be justifiably killed, and shoots him dead. That's only the end of the first act but it was so intense that Alan Bates, viewing the play to consider playing Tindle, walked out of the theatre wrongly thinking that his character didn't survive the interval.

Act two brings Inspector Doppler to Wyke's home acting on reports of gunshots. Wyke explains that he was playing a game with Milo, who fainted when blanks were fired at him, then recovered and cheerfully departed in full health. Doppler faults Wyke's story for its cruelty and proceeds to uncover evidence that Wyke did, indeed, murder Milo. At first Wyke is amused but, as Doppler persists, he begins to worry. When Wyke

371. Trimmed drastically after its release, it was restored to its four-hour original length for home video.
372. Billy Wilder made it in 1974, proving Mankiewicz' trepidations correct.

finally reaches his wit's end, Doppler takes off a heavy disguise to reveal himself as Milo. Wyke congratulates Milo on his cleverness but Milo will have none of it. He announces that he has killed Téa and left clues around the room that will incriminate Wyke. He has also called the police, giving Wyke only a few moments to destroy the clues, which are hidden in plain sight but can only be found by solving riddles. Milo toys with Wyke (and the audience) until all the evidence is addressed, then reveals that he and Téa, who is still alive, have conspired to humiliate Wyke, whom they both detest for his sadism. Milo leaves with Marguerite's possessions after all, but Wyke, believing that Milo is bluffing again, shoots him for real — as police sirens and lights approach.

Sleuth is a brilliantly constructed two-hander that was so involving that audiences and critics gleefully kept its secret that it was, well, a two-hander. As with the play, three non-existent supporting actors were credited with Olivier and Caine, including Marguerite, played by "Eve Channing" and represented by a painting of Mankiewicz's friend, Joanne Woodward. Publicity was careful to allude only to the first act (although the distributor clumsily released a film clip from the second act until Caine himself told them to withdraw it).

Andrew Wyke is a toy and games enthusiast, a trait that Shaffer admits he gleaned from visiting Stephen Sondheim's home, and which production designer Ken Adam utilized for the film. "No one, to my knowledge," Shaffer revealed shortly before his death in 2001, "had ever done a play about a character [who] is pathologically concerned with gamesmanship and one-upmanship. It was not the life of Stephen Sondheim, I insist on that, but [it has] the characteristics of a man *like* that."[373]

Production memos and blueprints reveal meticulous planning of hundreds of set design elements from the kind of games in Wyke's house to the color of wall paintings to the layout of the maze of shrubvery at Athelhampton where the opening was shot. "The whole film is to be treated like a game," Mankiewicz told Adam, adding that the overall look of Wyke's world should have "a feeling of the 1930s."[374]

Shaffer's Wyke is a grandly theatrical character whose allegiance is to a more genteel (read: WASP) era before immigrants like Milo Tindle (*nee*: Tindolini) sullied England. Olivier, whose acting experience ranged from Shakespeare and Restoration to O'Neill and Osborne, was the perfect embodiment of Wyke, even though Anthony Quayle had played

373. Interview included on *Sleuth* DVD.
374. Joseph L. Mankiewicz papers, AMPAS.

him in both the original West End and Broadway productions. Michael Caine reported that he was at first intimidated at appearing opposite the English theatre's greatest living actor. The story goes that, on their first day of rehearsal on April 3, 1972, he asked, "How should I address you?" and Olivier replied, "Well I am the Lord Olivier and you are Mr. Michael Caine. Of course that's only for the first time you address me. After that I am *Larry* and you are *Mike*." A few days later, according to Shaffer, Olivier allowed that, at first, he thought of Caine as his assistant but quickly came to regard him as his collaborator.[375] That didn't quell their playful upstaging, however. Several days into their Pinewood Studios shooting (scheduled from April 17 through June 19), Mankiewicz became aware that Olivier would shift his weight or move his hands as he threw Caine his dialogue cue. This meant that, to keep editorial continuity, Mankiewicz would have to favor Olivier in the cutting. Soon Caine caught on and started pulling the same trick. Eventually Mankiewicz had to remind them both that he, not they, was the director.[376]

Production ran over schedule. Kenneth Geist, who spent time on the set for his book, reports that Olivier had trouble remembering Shaffer's precise dialogue. He also noted that Mankiewicz, who already had back problems, tore open his thigh when he fell onto a piece of camera equipment. He tried directing from a wheelchair but soon had to be taken to the hospital, shutting down production.[377]

Additionally, Olivier, who had been plagued by a decade of health problems, suffered an injury during a one-time take that was so complex that it had to be kept in the finished film: When Wyke helps Milo sack the house to make it look as though there has been a struggle, Olivier pulls out a drawer of trinkets, flings them in the air, holds it above his head to shield himself from the falling debris, and then crosses to the mantel to sweep a row of glass figurines onto the floor. As he slides his hand across the surface, the broken glass cuts open his palm. Wincing but keeping his presence of mind — and unnoticed by Caine at the time — Olivier blots his bleeding hand on the unseen upstage side of an upholstered chair and jams it into his trouser pocket. As soon as the "cut" came he announced that he was bleeding and asked to be taken to hospital.[378]

Mankiewicz and Shaffer, well matched in intellect and ambition, developed a rivalry as their collaboration progressed. Not only had they

---

375. Author conversation with Michael Caine, January, 1973.
376. Author conversation with Caine.
377. Kenneth L. Geist. *Pictures Will Talk*. New York: Scribner's, 1978.
378. Author conversation with Caine. The shot appears in the film.

both won an Edgar[379] award from the Mystery Writers of America, they shared a more personal bond: each had a brother with whom he was in competition, openly or not; Joseph with the elder Herman, who co-wrote *Citizen Kane* and was a talented, garrulous Hollywood drunk; and Anthony with Peter, author of *Equus* and *Amadeus*, among other hits.

On its December 10, 1972 New York release, the critics (with the exception of Andrew Sarris, Pauline Kael, and a few others) applauded the results, as did audiences, although, with its literary appeal and character-driven drama, *Sleuth* was not destined to become a crossover smash.

Defensively, producer Edgar J. Scherick and Palomar Pictures International sought changes prior to the film's wider national release in mid-January of 1973. In two detailed memos, Scherick first demanded that an intermission be added and that cuts be made, particularly of an elaborately designed credit sequence which, he insisted, made the film appear stage-bound.[380] Then, on January 12, 1973, Daniel H. Blatt of Palomar notified Mankiewicz that he wanted the director to make certain cuts or else "we shall have no further obligation to you with regard to the cutting and editing of the film."[381] A furious Mankiewicz let his agent, Robby Lantz, reply to Blatt by reminding him that the matters had been settled long ago by Mankiewicz and Palomar's rep Steven Bach, that most of them would be expensive to make at this late stage, that "a suspense story requires certain foundations," and that they would only shorten the film by three and a half to four minutes anyway. "Against this background of fact and experience," Lantz stated, "Mr. Mankiewicz has given due consideration to the seven specific suggestions…none of which are new, all of which have been fully ventilated and explained, and all of which he regretfully advises you he rejects." In case Blatt decided to pursue the matter, Lantz reminded him that Mankiewicz, as an artist, would speak out fully and openly."[382] The matter subsided, but not entirely, because some cutting — specifically the intermission — had already been attempted, resulting in damage to the original negative that would, in later years, need to be addressed.

Then the MPAA got into act. When Palomar submitted *Sleuth* for a Code rating, Albert E. Van Schmus of the trade organization sent a list of words and phrases (*orgasm*, O*lympic sexual athlete*, etc.) that would earn

379. The forlorn ceramic Edgar statuette seen in the film is Anthony Shaffer's for his play *Sleuth*.
380. October 19, 1972 memos from Scherick to Mankiewicz.
381. Memo from Blatt to Mankiewicz, Joseph L. Mankiewicz papers, AMPAS.
382. January 16, 1973 letter from Lantz to Blatt, Joseph L. Mankiewicz papers, AMPAS.

the picture a PG (Parental Guidance) rating. But he also said that even if the words were taken out, the very nature of the story would keep it from getting a G (General audiences).[383] Thus even four years after the Code was liberated a vestige of its Puritanism remained. *Sleuth* went out with a PG and returned $5.6 million in rentals on an estimated $3.5 million budget — respectable but not a smash.

What hurts the film, if anything does, is not its thespic roots or verbiage but that, when Michael Caine returns in act two as Inspector Doppler, he still looks, sounds, and moves like Michael Caine. Even viewers who are unaware of the ruse must sense a familiarity; after all, this is what makes Caine a star. In live theatre, Doppler's distance from the audience eliminates the problem; movies, however, are like an X-ray. Scherick raised this matter with Mankiewicz by noting that his wife "recognized Michael Caine when Laurence Olivier first opened the door. He was all in the darkness of the backyard except for his eyes, and his, Michael Caine's eyes, are unique."[384] No written response is on file.

When *Sleuth* was needlessly remade in 2007 by Kenneth Branaugh with Caine inheriting the role of Wyke, Jude Law as Milo, and a reworked script by Harold Pinter, it was a disaster. Trimmed to 86 minutes, dumbed down, and with gay plot points intrusively included, it grossed less than $1 million worldwide and made Caine vow, "No more remakes!" By then both Anthony Shaffer and Joseph L. Mankiewicz were long dead — Shaffer in 2001 and Mankiewicz in 1993.

Despite the *success d'estime* of his film, Mankiewicz never directed again. "Supposedly you're as good as your last picture," he said a decade after *Sleuth*. "My last one was nominated for Best Picture. I was nominated, and it was the only time in the history of the Academy that the entire cast of the picture was nominated. I haven't worked since."[385] He tried to bring Dee Wells' novel *Jane* to the screen, and famously fantasized about pairing Marlon Brando and Maggie Smith in *Macbeth*, but neither came even close to being green-lighted. In a film industry that was increasingly taking its cues from the youth market, a classicist like Joseph L. Mankiewicz was an anachronism. "Steven Spielberg directed a rubber shark in *Jaws* and 165 special effects in *Close Encounters*," he said bitterly in 1978. "When's he going to direct *people*?"[386]

383. March 21, 1972 letter from Van Schmus to David Weitzner, Palomar Pictures International. Joseph L. Mankiewicz papers, AMPAS.
384. October 19, 1972 memo from Scherick to Mankiewicz, Joseph L. Mankiewicz papers, AMPAS.
385. Stephen M. Silverman. *The Fox That Got Away*. Secaucus, New Jersey: Lyle Stuart, Inc., 1988.
386. Author conversation with Mankiewicz, October 3, 1977.

He received an even deeper blow when a moving van containing a great portion of his life's work crashed and burned *en route* from California to the New York town where he and his third wife, Rosemary, had moved to escape the philistines of Hollywood. The remainder of his archive is now housed (in fireproof storage) at the motion picture Academy in Beverly Hills.

Mankiewicz once declared, "I think it can be said fairly that I've been in on the beginning, rise, peak, collapse, and end of the talking picture." What he modestly omitted was that the movies' rise and peak came about largely because of him.

LEO MCCAREY
Going His Way

Leo McCarey's last film is a sad example of what happens when one of the movies' most gifted directors sends a message that his artistry cannot support. Usually it's the Liberals who are criticized by Conservatives for promoting a progressive agenda on screen, but at least their attempts are usually entertaining (see Stanley Kramer). In *Satan Never Sleeps* (1962) it's the arch-Conservative, rabidly anti-Communist McCarey who sullies decades of genius with one hysterical diatribe. Following his even more frantic picture of ten years earlier, *My Son John*, the home stretch of McCarey's brilliant filmography raises questions that are not easy to answer. This is, after all, the man whose keen insight into the human condition led to such achievements as *Love Affair, Once Upon a Honeymoon, Ruggles of Red Gap, Going My Way, Duck Soup*, and some of Laurel and Hardy's best comedies. Of McCarey's *Make Way for Tomorrow*, a rare Hollywood movie about the elderly, Orson Welles said admiringly, "It would make a stone cry." *An Affair to Remember* may well be the greatest "chick flick" of all time, and *The Awful Truth* one of the movies' most joyously subversive comedies. Actors who worked with McCarey invariably said they never felt him directing them — some swore they never even saw a script — and yet his best pictures are timeless.

Satan Never Sleeps, starting with its title, is so arch it practically fulminates. Set in November of 1949 as the Chinese Communist revolution of October has overthrown the government and installed Mao's repressive regime, it brings Father O'Banion (William Holden) to relieve Father Bovard (Clifton Webb) at the Church's mission in the southwest Yiwang province. O'Banion was delayed on his journey by a flood, during which he has rescued Siu Lan (France Nuyen), a young woman who has become attached to him despite his priestly resistance. O'Banion's tardiness has kept Bovard at the mission long enough for it to be overrun by Communist forces led by Ho San (Weaver Lee) whom Bovard had raised as a Christian, but who is now a fervent and humorless Red. Ho San becomes attracted to Siu Lan but O'Banion protects her, placing all their lives in jeopardy. Separately Bovard presses O'Banion to examine whether he was saving the girl *from* Ho San or *for* himself in violation of his vows. When Ho San rapes Siu Lan, she becomes pregnant and delivers a son whose birth inspires Ho San to switch back to Christianity. When the regime orders all foreigners to leave or face execution, Bovard sacrifices himself so O'Banion, Siu Lan, and the newly re-re-converted Ho San escape to free Hong Kong and to live happily ever after. What brought McCarey — whom Jean Renoir notably said, "is one of the few directors in Hollywood who understands human beings" — to have made *Satan Never Sleeps*?

He was born in Los Angeles in 1898 into an Irish-American family and the poetry of that heritage runs through his work. His father was a Los Angeles boxing promoter and Leo himself tried a career in the ring before taking up mining in Utah and then going to USC law school to become an attorney. He was a failure at all three ("A discouraging factor in my legal career is that I lost every case," he admitted cheerfully).[387] Asking favors from friends who had "in"s in the movie business, in 1918 he became an assistant to Tod Browning at Universal Pictures, directed a little, got fired, then cashed in a chit from producer Hal Roach, whom he'd met on the handball court. McCarey started for Roach as a gag man on the *Our Gang* shorts, directed pictures with comedian Charlie Chase, and, in 1927, influenced Hal Roach in pairing Stan Laurel and Oliver Hardy — who had appeared separately in Roach films — and making them an official comedy team with *Putting Pants on Phillip*.

It was the Laurel & Hardy comedies that enabled McCarey to discover that less was more. Unlike Mack Sennett, whose philosophy was to cram as many gags into each film as possible, McCarey stressed character and built gags upon each other. The team's emblematic early films — *Battle of the Century, Two Tars, From Soup to Nuts, Wrong Again*, etc. — owe their stylistic unity, even if they had separate directors, to McCarey's supervision. By 1930, however, he had left Roach, eager to get into features.

387. Much information about McCarey comes from Peter Bogdanovich's heartbreaking interview in *Pieces of Time* (New York: Arbor House/Esquire, 1973; reprinted from the February, 1972 *Esquire*), transcribed and expanded in *Who The Devil Made It*, op. cit.

"He was a dazzling little man," praised actor Ralph Bellamy, who worked with him in *The Awful Truth*, and others agreed that he could have been a star himself. Instead, his films did the dazzling. The best of them offer a mercurial blend of character, wit, warmth, and drama, which is not to say that they are treacly or contrived. Somehow he managed to create complex emotional situations that defied screen conventions of good and evil. In *Love Affair* (1939), for example, Irene Dunne is attracted to Charles Boyer despite both of them being engaged to others and he being a lothario. When they fall in love, they change, and then tragedy strikes. (When McCarey remade it in 1957 as the slower-paced *An Affair to Remember*, he took out much of the texture and went straight for bathos.) With *Going My Way* he practically made a recruitment film for the priesthood as Father Bing Crosby not only saves Father Barry Fitzgerald's parish, he reunites the elder priest with his aged mother from the old country while "Too-ra-loo-ra-loo-ra" plays in the background. It's absolutely shameless, and it absolutely works. And in *The Awful Truth* he has Cary Grant divorcing Irene Dunne and then spending the entire film wooing her back, consummating their love (and this is the subversive part that the Production Code missed) moments *after* their divorce becomes final.

All of which made McCarey's films hard to pigeonhole and McCarey himself impossible to predict. According to legend he would show up on the set, noodle around on the piano for a little while, and then take out scraps of brown wrapping paper on which he'd scribbled ideas for the day's scene.[388] "At the end of the [first] day nobody knew where we were going," recalled Bellamy, who played the Ralph Bellamy role in *The Awful Truth*. "We all tried to get out of it....But we realized after two or three days that he knew what he was gonna do. There was never a script. They recorded what we got, which turned out to be the script, and it turned out to be a very successful picture."[389]

McCarey used episodes from his own life in his films, not necessarily whole plots, but quirks he collected. Barry Fitzgerald's Father Fitzgibbon in *Going My Way*, which won an Oscar® for Best Picture and McCarey's second as Best Director, was inspired by Los Angeles Monsignor Nicholas Conneally, a charming conniver. Hauled into traffic court for failing to signal a turn, Conneally — who was constantly begging for money for the church building fund — was released by the judge, who said, "Come to think of it, it's the first time you were caught *without* your hand out."[390]

388. McCarey is credited as writer on most of his films, and even those of others.
389. Interviewed by John A. Gallagher and archived at TVDays.com (Ira H. Gallen Video Resources)
390. Bogdanovich, op. cit.

He hit upon the comic device of escalating destruction in Laurel and Hardy's *Two Tars* and *Big Business* when he was at a formal party and guests playfully started untying each other's bow ties.

There was always an underlying sophistication in McCarey's films no matter how low the humor was ("Excuse me," said Cary Grant in *The Awful Truth*, "you're sitting on my prospectus"). But even though he outwitted the censors, he couldn't escape the politicians. In 1947 the House Un-American Activities Committee garnered headlines by looking for Reds in Hollywood. McCarey testified as a friendly witness. Several of his writers, such as Donald Ogden Stewart, had been named as Soviet sympathizers, and he lost no time distancing himself from them. In 1952 he directed and co-wrote *My Son John*, one of the more bizarre anti-Communist movies, in which Helen Hayes demands that her son, Robert Walker, whom she grows to believe is both a Red and an atheist, swear to her on the family bible that he is neither. The scene ignores the simple fact that, if he is, indeed, an atheist, swearing on the bible means nothing to him.

McCarey returned to that reactionary well in 1962 with *Satan Never Sleeps*. Based on an original script titled *China Story* that famed China scholar Pearl S. Buck sold to Twentieth Century-Fox, the project had a history before McCarey took it over. *China Story* was originally acquired in 1950 by producer Hal Wallis who gave it to writer John Meredyth Lucas to adapt.[391] Ten years later it had switched to McCarey who announced he was completing the screenplay himself.[392] At the time, the story called for Father O'Banion to die, not Father Bovard. McCarey had wanted O'Banion tested by his love for Siu Lan, not that he would ever break his vows, but that, as McCarey put it, "He asked God for help to solve what, to mortal man, was unsolvable. He prayed to God for a solution to his predicament, and God gave him the answer. The solution was that he gave his own life. Instead of the old priest — Clifton Webb — Holden sacrificed himself."[393] But Holden refused to die on screen, so McCarey and newly named co-writer Claude Binyon changed it to satisfy their star, grumbling all the way.[394]

Satan was shot in England and Wales doubling for southwest China (both the U.S. and McCarey being *de facto non-grata* in the People's

---

391. *Hollywood Reporter*, November 13, 1950. No studio is identified but Wallis was set up at Paramount at the time.
392. *Hollywood Reporter*, September 27, 1960.
393. Bogdanovich, op. cit.
394. Wes D. Gehring. *Leo McCarey: From Marx to McCarthy*. Lanham, Maryland: Scarecrow Press, 2005.

Republic). On the eve of production, Herbert Aller, business representative for International Photographers Local 659 of the IATSE, groused to Spyros Skouras, head of Fox, about the picture being shot in England instead of the U.S.[395] Skouras left it to McCarey to respond through the trade press that the reason he was going to England was because that's what William Holden wanted.[396] This admission was emblematic of the duality McCarey felt for his star, whom he resented for both usurping his power and for being the reason he got funding in the first place. Moreover, production was slow because Holden, who had become disillusioned with the acting profession since *The Bridge On the River Kwai* (1957), had started drinking.[397] The tension mounted and McCarey walked off his own picture five days before the end of principal photography, leaving it to his assistant to finish.[398]

Nobody knew what to make of the results. The McCarey blend of gentle humor within a dramatic context misfires. The loving byplay between young and old priests that worked in *Going My Way* is charmless here because the begrudging affection between O'Banion and Bovard never rings true and comes off as a frivolous compared with the world collapsing around them. As expected, critics likened it to *Going My Way* but questioned whether McCarey's humor was appropriate to the solemn story. The exhibitor-oriented trade magazine *Boxoffice* was adrift when they advised theatres to use the catchlines "A New Kind of Comedy That Everybody Will Be Talking About" and the even more grotesque "Big Laugh-Devastating Drama" as marketing handles.[399] Shortly after the film's February 25, 1962 release, producer Gene Schwartz sued McCarey, Binyon, and Fox for plagiarism charging that their film was copied from two story treatments he had submitted to the studio in 1955 for the novel *No Secret is Safe* by Father Mark Tennian. Schwartz demanded $150,000 actual damages and $50,000 punitive damages.[400] But the death blow was struck symbolically by Pearl S. Buck herself who, when asked to novelize the screenplay, did so, but refused to allow it to be published in hardcover,

---

395. *Hollywood Reporter*, April 12, 1961.
396. *Daily Variety*, June 13, 1961.
397. Michelangelo Capua. *William Holden: A Biography*. Jefferson, North Carolina: McFarland & Company, 2009.
398. This cannot be confirmed. David Orton is listed as First Assistant Director on the studio's abbreviated credits, but an Assistant Director isn't the same thing as an assistant *to* a director, and there is no listing for that position.
399. *Boxoffice*, March 5, 1962.
400. *Hollywood Reporter*, March 23, 1962.

so only a paperback was issued.[401] It may be the only subtle thing about the picture.

Satan Never Sleeps was the end of an otherwise remarkable career. Leo McCarey lived another seven years and died a prolonged death from emphysema at age seventy-two on July 5, 1969. Nobody since then has matched the ineffable combination of laughter, sophistication, and tears that he conjured so effortlessly. Come to think of it, nobody before him did, either.

---

401. Several sources say that the film was based on Buck's novel. The reverse is true. Gary Giddens. *Natural Selection: Gary Giddins on Comedy, Film, Music, and Books.* New York: Oxford University Press, 2006.

Vincente and Liza Minnelli.

VINCENTE MINNELLI
Passing Time

Although he directed some of Hollywood's best musicals during MGM's golden age, Vincente Minnelli was at home in just about any genre the studio handed him. His last picture, however, was for a bare-bones company that was hoping to build prestige by giving the man who made *The Bandwagon* a chance to create a picture for them. What happened, unfortunately, took them all down.

A Matter of Time was Minnelli's dream project, for it gave him the chance to direct his daughter, Liza, just as he had often directed her mother/his wife, Judy Garland, in *Meet Me in St. Louis, The Pirate, Babes on Broadway, Strike Up the Band*, and *Till the Clouds Roll By* (the last three uncredited). What he didn't count on was that, while he would be guiding Liza, nobody would be guiding him. Minnelli was one of the factory artists whose originality flourished under the studio system but who couldn't function away from it.

A Matter of Time is drawn from Maurice Druon's 1954 novel *The Film of Memory*, in which an aging Contessa who has known romance, riches, and intrigue recounts her tales to an entranced chambermaid in the seedy hotel where she is forced to live in her declining years. Druon based his Contessa Sanziani on the Marchesa Luisa Casati, whom he had known when both she and World War II were winding down. In 1965 his book was adapted for the stage by Paul Osborne and titled *La Contessa*. It starred Vivien Leigh who was, herself, nearing the end of a fabled career. Minnelli read the book in 1966 but only in 1973 was he able to get the film rights. By then the old-line studios were dead, so he approached philanthropist and sometime-producer Jack Skirball. At first Frederic Raphael (*Two for the Road*) was announced to write the script,[402] but three

---

402. *Daily Variety,* January 2, 1973.

months later Raphael was out and Terrence Rattigan (*Separate Tables*) had been approached with an eye toward a September start date and Katharine Hepburn to essay the Contessa.[403] Rattigan was soon replaced by John Gay (*Sometimes a Great Notion*), and when Gay turned in his adaptation, Minnelli saw it as a chance to work with his daughter, who had just won the Oscar® for *Cabaret* and would, he and Skirball logically believed, easily attract financing. When she did not, they attached Ingrid Bergman and Charles Boyer — who forsook retirement for his old friend — to make the package more attractive. Skirball shopped the $5 million project all over Hollywood and was again surprised when nobody bit. Perhaps the chill came from the fact that Minnelli had just managed to flop with *On a Clear Day You Can See Forever* in 1970 despite having Barbra Streisand. Or it might have been that the director, then in his seventies, was developing the uncertainty about his craft that would later become Alzheimer's disease.

At last Samuel Z. Arkoff of the low-rent but ambitious American International Pictures stepped in with an offer of distribution and co-financing with Italian producer Giulio Sbarigia. The picture was shot over fourteen weeks beginning in February, 1975 in Rome and Venice, variously titled *Carmela, Carmilla. Nina, Nina and the Countess, Film of Memory*, and *Search for Beauty* before settling on *A Matter of Time*. Minnelli quickly fell behind schedule, hampered not only by language differences between the American and the Italian crews but by three Italian unions' daily two-hour strike against the production company. At one point an electrical shortage in the film lab ruined six days' work; insurance covered the $250,000 reshoots. When production began to stretch to twenty weeks, AIP announced that their investment was limited and Sbarigia would be stuck with the overage.

Arkoff visited Minnelli in Rome to assess the situation, but all the director talked about were the sets and costumes, not the performances. John Gideon Bachmann, reporting for *The Guardian*, wrote that, after almost every take, Liza would ask, "Was I all right, daddy, or should I do the scene again?" (Vincente later said that, "When I directed her, I treated her just like I treated her mother, as a fine actress, a marvelous comedian, and a great tragedian.")[404] There was no indication of trouble. Press visitors were proudly shown an assembly of scenes before they spoke to the filmmakers, and they took note that Liza was accompanied by her pack

---

403. *Weekly Variety*, April 11, 1973.
404. Emanuel Levy. *Vincente Minnelli: Hollywood's Dark Dreamer*. MacMillan, 2009.

of toy mongrel dogs. What they didn't know was that the 29-year-old star had secretly arranged for her father and herself to be protected by round-the-clock bodyguards following a wave of European kidnappings.

Something had never been settled in the script, and soon it loomed large. Minnelli wanted the ending to be a guessing game: would Nina, having absorbed the Contessa's stories, become a movie star or would she pursue a libertine life as the Contessa had done? "We end the picture in such a way that we leave it to the audience to decide which way the girl goes," the director originally announced. "It's an intriguing situation, one, I think, [that] will have people talking and arguing like mad."[405] Arkoff felt differently; Minnelli biographer Emanuel Levy writes that the studio chief demanded an emotionally fulfilling action climax in which the chambermaid would become a film star, and Minnelli shot such a scene, believing he could excise it later, only to discover that AIP had final cut.[406] "Over the years," Arkoff wrote in his memoirs with a touch of disappointment, "Vincente Minnelli had become one of Hollywood's most respected directors. By the time he directed *A Matter of Time* in 1976 he was past his prime and, as a result, I think the picture suffered."[407] Arkoff further reported that friends had warned him before production started that Minnelli had always depended upon MGM's highly skilled personnel to bring his vision to the screen. "All of them knew what the pictures needed without even asking him," he said.[408]

Minnelli returned to Rome in April of 1975 for what *Weekly Variety* called "finishing touches," then delivered a three-hour first cut to Arkoff. Arkoff was appalled. To him, the story, with its multiple flashback fantasies in which Nina relives the Contessa's escapades, didn't make sense. Two songs ("A Matter of Time" and "The Me I Haven't Met Yet") by John Kander and Fred Ebb were added, but they were too modern for the style of the film and, moreover, weren't production numbers, only voice-overs.

Arkoff asserted his right of final cut. He also prevailed on Liza to ask her then-husband, Jack Haley, Jr., to see what he could do in the editing room. It was a painful compromise; ever since she was a child she had

---

405. AIP presskit.
406. Levy, op. cit.
407. Samuel Z. Arkoff with Richard Trubo. *Flying Through Hollywood By the Seat of My Pants*. New York: Carol Publishing Group, 1982.
408. Moreover, MGM and producer Arthur Freed were so protective of Minnelli that, when portions of *Gigi* (1958) weren't working, they sent him off to Europe to scout locations for a film they knew would never be produced and had director Charles Walters quietly redo several scenes to "save" what became Minnelli's Academy Award®-winning film. Sources: Turner Classic Movies website plus Author's conversation with Assistant Director Hank Moonjean.

wanted her father to direct her in a film, and now that he had, it was turning to dust in their hands. Haley's re-cut trimmed the three hours to its 97-minute release length but it had already acquired the odor of failure. Between Haley's and AIP's changes the picture opened on October 7, 1976 at the Radio City Music Hall and pleased no one. Both Minnellis disavowed the finished product. Filmmakers rallied to the director's support. Martin Scorsese — who, after *New York, New York* would direct Liza on Broadway in Kander and Ebb's *The Act* (calling upon Gower Champion for last-minute help) — had been given a career-building chance by Arkoff in 1972 to direct *Boxcar Bertha*. Now he circulated a petition among fellow directors to decry his benefactor's handling of *A Matter of Time*.

The press was wedged between straining to appreciate the remnants of an old master's work and wondering what it might have looked like had it been left in his hands. Vincent Canby of *The New York Times* took the former stance, Pauline Kael of *The New Yorker* the latter. Canby lamented that it "has moments of real visual beauty, but because what the characters say to each other is mostly dumb, it may be a film to attend while wearing your earplugs." Kael: "From what is being shown, it is almost impossible to judge what the tone of the film was, or whether it would have worked at any level. But even if his own version was less than a triumph, that was the film that I wanted to see, not this chopped-up shambles."

Kael's generous appraisal is apt. After a perfunctory framing device — a press conference where clips from Nina's new film are somehow shown without a screen or even the room being darkened — the story unfolds of a gamine (Liza) from the provinces trekking to Rome for no apparent reason to share a room with her cousin (Tina Aumont), who is also a chambermaid but who augments her salary by turning tricks. When she brings Nina to the fabled Borghese Park to start her at the trade, the newcomer freaks out. Gone. So are the fantasy sequences in which Nina acts out the adventures that the Contessa (Bergman) describes to her. Snippets of them appear as the prologue, which was supposed to be the epilogue. Through a series of lucky meetings in the hotel where she works, Nina gets a screen test for a movie that just happens to be shooting in town. By then she has been remade by the eccentric Contessa and gives two emotional — and, it must be said, beautifully performed — outbursts about self-respect that so impress the filmmaker that he hires her for the lead. It's cheese, and if Minnelli had been making it for MGM it would have been sharp cheese. But shooting on location, with the palazzo rooms (sets?) lacking character, and with lazy zoom shots and wide angle lenses erasing Minnelli's legacy of elegant camera moves, the results look tawdry.[409] The supporting players' dialogue is dubbed by announcers rather than actors, further alienating the viewer despite the obvious passion and love that everybody brings to the project.

"I just lost all interest in the picture," Minnelli diplomatically told Gregg Kilday of *The Los Angeles Times* a week after his film opened and failed. "It really was a beautiful picture, but when you have an American producer and an Italian producer, well, things get mixed up. AIP was really charming about it all."[410]

Minnelli died on July 25, 1983. Ironically, in 1979 American International Pictures had been purchased by Filmways and in 1982 was merged into Orion Pictures, whose titles are now held by MGM, so, in the end, *A Matter of Time* became an MGM movie after all. But it has never received wide distribution on video. Very few people, therefore, have seen it, so Vincente Minnelli's reputation rests solidly and fortunately on a folio of movies that includes *Meet Me in St. Louis, Lust for Life, The Clock, The Bad and the Beautiful, Father of the Bride, An American in Paris*, and a dozen others, rather than the one he did for love.

---

409. The cinematographer was Geoffrey Unsworth who had glowingly photographed *Cabaret*.
410. October 16, 1976.

Sam Peckinpah.

SAM PECKINPAH
The Peckinpah Weak End

Cineastes wonder how the man who directed *The Wild Bunch* could have made *The Osterman Weekend*. Others question how the man who made *The Osterman Weekend* could have made *The Wild Bunch*. This is the riddle of Sam Peckinpah, a director who seduced critics, shocked audiences, and frustrated executives ever since his breakthrough 1962 feature, *Ride the High Country*. That revisionist western established him as a bold new voice in an old genre, but after that he dropped the ball more often that he scored with it, infusing his films with personal touches, none of which included consistency. This defines the legend of "Bloody Sam," the screen's most prolific — though far from its most effective — purveyor of movie violence.

Peckinpah's reputation is built as much on what he represents as by the films he made. He is seen as a rebel who functioned within the studio system; as a stylist who pushed the envelope cinematically as well as morally; and as a poet who used blood instead of ink to show how Man's civility diminishes as he approaches his limits. In person, Peckinpah drank too much (even while on the job), did drugs, abused some collaborators, and was fiercely loved by others. He married and divorced three women (marrying his second wife twice), had at least six pictures tampered with, and is celebrated in spite of his achievements as well as because of them.

Born to an old and well-connected California family in 1925, Peckinpah was raised on ranches and was sent to military academy when public schools would no longer tolerate his outbursts. As a Marine at the end of World War II he was stationed in China where the defeated Japanese were being mustered out and, he claimed, where he was shot during an altercation between Chinese and Japanese soldiers he was supposed to be supervising. After the war he attended college where he met his first wife and, through her, became interested in drama. A job at a Los Angeles TV station led to others, and eventually to an assistantship with director Don Siegel. He began writing for television, mostly westerns, and created two popular series: *The Rifleman* (1958) and *The Westerner* (1960). Friendship with Brian Keith on the latter enabled him to direct his first feature, 1961's *The Deadly Companions,* but differences with the producer turned it into a formless debut. He did far better with his second film, *Ride the High Country* (1962).

Ride the High Country, which Peckinpah rewrote (as he would all his films, credited or not, authorized or not), articulates themes he would revisit throughout his career. Joel McCrea and Randolph Scott are old buddies hired to guard a gold shipment. As they travel, Scott tries to talk McCrea into helping him steal it. When they are confronted by actual thieves whom they vanquish in a final shootout, McCrea is mortally wounded. The two old friends bid goodbye and Scott rides off to let McCrea die with dignity. The film was more than a valediction to two stalwart western stars, it was a re-imagining of the genre itself, showing how its heroes could be not only past their time but what happens to them at that point. With *The Wild Bunch* (1969) — which begins with a bank robbery in a frontier town as a motor car passes through the frame — Peckinpah's entire oeuvre falls into place. Modernity has hit America. The old morality, and even the old immorality, is dead.

Between these two westerns came *Major Dundee* (1965), a rusty Civil War saga in which Charlton Heston leads soldiers into Mexico to stop a band of looting Apaches. The picture went into production without a finished script and unraveled from there. Even Heston, whose diplomacy was legendary, threatened to run Peckinpah through with his cavalry sword for mistreating the extras. Nevertheless, he and his fellow actors — L.Q. Jones, James Coburn, Richard Harris, and others — stood by their director when a Columbia Pictures functionary showed up on location to fire him. In the end, the film ran vastly over budget and was heavily cut by the studio anyway.

But all was forgiven with *The Wild Bunch*. Peckinpah stunned moviegoers with his lyrical violence as William Holden, Ernest Borgnine, and their gang try to pull off one last bank robbery but are pursued by Robert Ryan, who used to ride with Holden. An elegiac end-of-an-era tale, it speaks to loyalty, friendship, situational ethics, and a touch of geopolitics during the Mexican revolution. It was also cut prior to its release, though it has since been restored.[411] *The Wild Bunch* renewed public discussion of violence in American film, coming, as it did, during anti-Vietnam war protests and just after the MPAA rewrote its Production Code into the more modern, but still controversial, Rating System. It wasn't just *The Wild Bunch*'s blood (enabled by the development of special effects explosive squib) that drew scrutiny but the fact that it spurted in slow motion.

Even though Peckinpah was not the first director to use graphic violence — Arthur Penn (*Bonnie and Clyde*, 1967) and Peter Yates (*Bullitt*, 1968) beat him to the draw — but where they used it for dramatic purposes, Peckinpah used it, or said he did, as social commentary. "Slow motion sequences work for me," he maintained. "I was shot once and I noticed time slowed down, so I started making pictures where I slowed down time — because that's the way it is."[412] Nevertheless, Howard Hawks had little use for Peckinpah and famously said, "I can kill four men, take 'em to the morgue, and bury 'em before he gets one down to the ground in slow motion."[413]

The slow-mo may not even have been Peckinpah's original idea. Walon Green, who wrote *The Wild Bunch* with Roy N. Sickner, says it was already in the script. "I put the slow motion in because, when I wrote it, I had just seen *The Seven Samurai* (1954), which had the first use of slow motion in an action scene that I'd ever seen. [Kurosawa] uses it two or three times. And I thought, 'Wow, that's great! How would it be to see a whole action sequence in slow motion?' So I wrote all the slow motion into the sequence and they shot it and cut it like that. Luckily they had covered it both ways; when they shot it and cut it together it was a disaster because the sequence was fifteen minutes long in slow motion. They were gonna ditch it and go with normal speed. It was Lou Lombardo [the film's editor] who came up with the idea of just cutting to that moment of action in slow motion, and he re-shaped the sequence."[414] But it became Peckinpah's trademark.

Fourteen years passed between *The Wild Bunch* and *The Osterman Weekend*. They included the critically hailed *Ballad of Cable Hogue* (1970), *Straw Dogs* (1971), and *Junior Bonner* (1972); the box office smash *The*

---

411. Interesting problem: the cut scene is a flashback that explains Holden's and Ryan's characters. It's important for the story but is so clumsily shot that it stops the film dead. What would you do?
412. *The Osterman Weekend* presskit.
413. Todd McCarthy. *Howard Hawks: The Grey Fox of Hollywood*. New York: Grove Press, 1997.
414. An examination of Warner Bros.' 114 page "Estimating (budgeting) Script" dated 10/26/67 and the 128 page "Final" script dated 2/12/68 have no written notation for slow motion, although the specific descriptions of action could have dictated its use. Lou Lombardo separately told the Author about the editorial changes in a 1973 conversation.

Getaway (1972), the heavily cut *Pat Garrett & Billy the Kid* (1973), and the self-indulgent *Bring Me the Head of Alfredo Garcia* (1974). By the time of *The Killer Elite* (1975), Peckinpah had become his own parody.

"[He] was into the Scotch malts at the time," recalled Stirling Silliphant, who rewrote Marc Norman's script for *The Killer Elite* and nearly came to blows with Peckinpah during a pre-production confab. After that, Silliphant said, "I refused to come on the set, and there was no need for either of us to be too polite to each other nor for me...to be even courteous." Studio (United Artists) insiders reported Peckinpah's drinking and abuse of personnel on the picture.[415] Nevertheless, they hired him again three years later to direct the trendy trucker film *Convoy* (1978). Even though it turned a profit, its director was finished. It took his old mentor, Don Siegel, to rehabilitate him in Hollywood's eyes by hiring him as second-unit director on *Jinxed* (1982).

And that led him into the convoluted gambit of *Osterman*, which had been in progress since 1972 when Robert Ludlum's thriller was purchased by producers William Castle and Walter Seltzer. Castle, better known as the master of exploitation films (*The Tingler, Macabre, House on Haunted Hill*, etc.), had just gained respectability by producing *Rosemary's Baby* in 1968.[416] He and Seltzer set up the project at Warner Bros. and hired Dalton Trumbo, who was an expert at translating long and involved novels (*Spartacus, Exodus*), to tackle *Osterman*.[417]

While not as Byzantine as Ludlum's other books, few of which have been tamed for movies, *Osterman* was actually more muddled than complex, but at least it was linear: an investigative TV reporter named Tanner (Rutger Hauer) is recruited by CIA operative Fassett (John Hurt) to help "turn" three Soviet spies (Craig T. Nelson, Chris Sarandon, and Dennis Hopper) who also happen to be old friends of his, at the guys' annual get-together. For unclear reasons, the reunions are named Osterman weekends after the Nelson character. In point of fact, none of the men is really a spy; Fassett is manipulating them all to get revenge on his boss (Burt Lancaster) for ordering the assassination of his wife and doesn't care how many civilians and CIA agents must die to achieve it.

The story may have been linear but its production was not. By 1979 Trumbo had left the project, which had not moved forward in development. At the beginning of the year Paul Aaron (*Deadly Force, Maxie*) was

---

415. A vivid report to the Author from an observer had Peckinpah standing behind his editor and signaling him to roll the film forward or back by cuffing his corresponding ear.
416. *Entertainment World*, March 31, 1972.
417. *Hollywood Reporter*, April 3, 1972.

announced as director and Alan Trustman (*Bullitt, The Thomas Crown Affair*) would write. The next year Aaron was out and Lewis Gilbert (*Alfie, The Spy Who Loved Me, Educating Rita*), was in. But not for long, because in 1981 William Panzer and Peter Davis of American Cinema Group picked up the property, assembled the $10 million budget from international investors, and hired Alan Sharp (*Ulzana's Raid, Night Moves*) to wrestle the plot into script form.[418] They also announced Peckinpah to direct and Twentieth Century-Fox to distribute in the U.S.[419] with a collection of international distributors to cover the rest of the world. Shooting would take place over sixty-one days from October 14, 1982 to January 16, 1983.[420]

"The script never worked," Sharp admitted. "I never anticipated from the script I wrote that they'd ever get it made. Ludlum leaves a lot to be revealed later and you find yourself saying, 'How could that happen?'" When Peckinpah astutely brought this little plotting wrinkle to the producers' attention in May of 1982, they didn't respond, perhaps because they were too eager to ride his coat-tails into big-time Hollywood status, as he would later charge.[421]

Yet they let Peckinpah take a pass at rewriting, only to reject it, engendering a snit over whether the producers ever read the pages he submitted.[422] Although Davis/Panzer's Osterman Weekend Productions and producer Michael Murphy agreed to a $450,000 fee and $150,000 in expenses, they alienated the director by refusing to hire his core crew and by negotiating with actors Tommy Lee Jones and Nick Nolte without his input.[423] Perhaps they were being cautious about letting Peckinpah take too much control; Panzer reported driving with him through Malibu on a location scout and having to pull off the road to let him vomit. Subsequently, a representative from the insurance company would monitor

---

418. *Weekly Variety* retrospective item, October 14, 1982.
419. *Hollywood Reporter*, July 20, 1982.
420. At the end of 1981 American Cinema Releasing and Motion Picture Investment Fund sued their own subsidiary American Cinema Group for $1,668,778 for costs accrued to that point without having rolled production (*Weekly Variety*, December 30, 1981).
421. May 10, 1982 memo from Peckinpah to his agents Marty Baum and Hal Friedman. On August 9, 1982 he wrote Davis/Panzer to stop using his name in connection with their fundraising for the film. Sam Peckinpah papers, AMPAS.
422. August 29, 1982 letter from Peckinpah to David/Panzer that the August 23 script is not acceptable, that it was "patchwork," and that he still doesn't have a deal with them. Sam Peckinpah papers, AMPAS.
423. April 30, 1982 letter from Peckinpah to producer Michael Murphy. Sam Peckinpah papers, AMPAS.

the set.[424] This may stem from the producers' insistence that Peckinpah was uninsurable because of past budget overruns.[425] Peckinpah also filed no fewer than five OSHA claims between October, 1982 and December, 1983 for injuries sustained during and after production, from tripping over cables to a crushed finger.[426]

Despite that, the film wrapped on schedule and, after seven months of editing, on July 22, 1983, the producers screened *Osterman* for an invited audience from the National Research Group. NRG's Joseph Farrell deemed the picture "unplayable,"[427] and Peckinpah angrily responded that the test screening was a violation of his DGA contract, which specified a preview to a "paid audience," not a papered crowd. This sent the picture into a nasty arbitration during which Davis made the point that it had to be delivered to international distributors in order to collect fees, and he faulted Peckinpah for delays in editing. The director argued that the producers had failed to respond to his notes, that his directorial rights were being violated, and his reputation for making "a Sam Peckinpah film" was at stake.[428] The arbitration process also revealed that Davis and Panzer had issued numerous salary and expense checks throughout production that had bounced.[429] Regardless of Peckinpah and the DGA, it was the producers' cut that was released by Twentieth Century-Fox on October 14, 1983, one year to the day after cameras rolled.

While playing "what if" is a dangerous game, a comparison between the Fox theatrical release and the director's workprint that was issued on home video by Anchor Bay shows that both were lost causes. The failure lies in the concept and in the playing of the scenes themselves, not their sequence. "We made the story more of a satire on the media," says Sharp, whose sophisticated action scripts belie a wicked sense of humor. Yet Sam Peckinpah is the last person in whose heavy hands satire plays. Despite the inherent absurdity of the story, Peckinpah has the actors behaving so self-seriously that the laughs are on them. As a newscaster, Hauer comes off as badly as all actors who play newscasters (if a news twinkie can read a Teleprompter, why can't a trained movie actor do the same thing?), and

424. Marshall Fine. *Bloody Sam*. New York: Donald I. Fine, Inc., 1991.
425. June 25, 1982 letter. Davis says all bonding companies but Taft Broadcasting refuse to cover Sam or want to hold his $450,000 fee in escrow. Sam Peckinpah papers, AMPAS.
426. Sam Peckinpah papers, AMPAS.
427. July 28, 1983 response from Peter Davis to Scott Roth of the GRA as a precursor to arbitration. Peckinpah papers, AMPAS.
428. Davis, ibid.
429. August 22, 1983 statement from Bonnie Engels, Diversified Skills (Peckinpah's assistant) offered at arbitration.

only Hurt, Nelson, and Meg Foster, as Tanner's excluded wife, have any clue what they're doing.

A film can survive one or two absurdities, but not the legion that surface in *Osterman*. In order to ply his scheme, Fassett installs video cameras throughout Tanner's home (in *one* day; does Comcast know about this?) and somehow the fixed surveillance cameras have the miraculous ability to tilt and pan to follow the action. A chase near the beginning involves a helicopter, a station wagon, a truck, and a taxi cab, the latter of whose sole function is to get impaled by a construction pipe in slow motion. That the one person who has nothing to do with the plot — the cab driver — is the one who is placed in the most jeopardy suggests strongly that the director was keener on creating a "Sam Peckinpah scene" than in contributing to the narrative. But by this time his slow-motion-from-multiple-angles trademark had become its own satire. Not parody, satire. In the end *The Osterman Weekend* brands Sam Peckinpah as the movies' most celebrated second unit director. If the film had simply been a disappointment, that would be merely unfortunate; that it was made by a man who had created his own genre is a true tragedy.

Sam Peckinpah died of a stroke on December 28, 1984 at the age of 59. What killed him wasn't the years, it was the mileage.

ARTHUR PENN
A Quiet Revolutionary[430]

By 1988 the man who fired the first shot in Hollywood's film revolution could no longer get ammunition. Arthur Penn, who, in 1967, knocked the staid studio system on its rear with *Bonnie and Clyde*, had ushered in a new generation of savvy, movie-literate, rule-breaking filmmakers. Within a handful of years his work would influence an emerging cadre of film school graduates twenty-five years his junior. His editor Dede Allen's cutting style would bring European syntax to American cinema; his use of violence would be usurped and exceeded by Sam Peckinpah; his cinematographer Burnett Guffey's evocative imagery would be developed by Terrence Malick and Roman Polanski; and his writers Robert Benton, David Newman, and an uncredited Robert Towne would redefine romantic anti-heroes as the symbol of American hypocrisy.

The major movie studios, crushed by dwindling box office receipts and mired in outdated musicals like *Star, Darling Lili, On a Clear Day You Can See Forever*, and *Doctor Doolittle*, turned in panic to young Turks like Francis Coppola, George Lucas, Steven Spielberg, John Milius, Martin Scorsese, Walter Hill, and Paul Schrader when the graying moguls no longer had the slightest idea who or where the audience was.

Penn was at the nexus of this upheaval, yet found a home in neither camp. Raised in circumstances of Dickensian deprivation and tempered by the successive crucibles of World War II, early live television, and the emergence of Method acting, he was brighter and more articulate than the old guard who clung to the calcified studio system (he once overheard his cameraman disparage him to a colleague as "one-a them TV guys").

---

430. Material drawn from Author's book *Arthur Penn: American Director*. Lexington, Kentucky: The University Press of Kentucky, 2011, interviews with Penn Jillette and Teller, and countless conversations with Arthur Penn.

Even when he made *Bonnie and Clyde* he was, at forty-five, a father's age to the film school tyros he inspired. They may have been thrilled by what he had accomplished, but their sensibilities increasingly revolved more around show *business* than show *art*.

Fortunately, Penn had other avenues of expression. He taught directing at Yale, maintained a presence at the Actors Studio, and nurtured countless projects from established filmmakers as well as upstart newcomers (he said he kept his phone number listed so people would at least call first instead of just showing up at his door asking him to look at their work). He joined playwright William Gibson, director George Tabori, and actress Viveca Lindfors in the Berkshire Theatre Festival, developed the *Volpone*-inspired stage comedy *Sly Fox* with playwright Larry Gelbart, and directed *Golda, A Partial Portrait*, by Gibson, with whom he had previously won Broadway plaudits for *Two for the Seesaw* and *The Miracle Worker*.

Two difficult film projects wove in and around his stage work in the 1970s: *The Highest*, a segment from producer David L. Wolper's anthology documentary *Visions of 8* about the 1976 Munich Olympics, and *The Missouri Breaks*, an ill-conceived western starring Marlon Brando and Jack Nicholson. *The Highest*, which explored the sport of pole vaulting using the intimacy of extreme slow motion photography, was overshadowed by Black September's terrorist murder of eleven Israeli athletes while he was shooting it. And *The Missouri Breaks* owed more to producer Elliott Kastner's contrived tax shelter packaging than its ambivalent writing by novelist Thomas McGuane that even Robert Towne's location doctoring couldn't save. Working under huge financial and professional deadlines, Penn wrestled the star package into a shape that never quite jelled and, on its 1976 release, *The Missouri Breaks*, while engagingly eccentric, disappointed those who were expecting more after the challenging *Night Moves* the year before.

Between directing *Four Friends* (1981), which paid homage to his and writer Steve Tesich's immigrant backgrounds, and the action-thriller *Target* (1985), Penn grew more involved with the Actors Studio and a writing group in which he, Elia Kazan, and Joseph L. Mankiewicz mentored established novelists who wanted to become screenwriters ("the writing was not all that good," he recalled, "but the criticism was superb"). In 1986 he was lured into saving a gothic horror film that he had agreed to executive produce as a favor to two young filmmakers. When they fell behind schedule, the financing company, MGM, called in Penn's chit and he took over the helm of *Dead of Winter*. He couldn't save it entirely, but he had too much class to reveal what had happened behind the scenes.

It was about this time that Penn accompanied his son Matthew to a studio sneak of an unreleased blockbuster (see Introduction), after which the audience was asked how to "improve" the filmmaker's work. It was a disheartening hint that the age of the auteur was over and henceforth it would be filmmaking by consensus. Not until 1989 would Penn have another chance to make a film of his own, and it turned out to be his last.

Penn & Teller Get Killed was born in 1987 in the playful minds of Penn Fraser Jillette and Raymond Joseph Teller, the team professionally known as Penn & Teller. They had just ended their off-Broadway illusion show after nearly two years and were urged by their manager, Bernie Brillstein, to try writing a movie. They did, they called it *Dead Funny*, and Warner Bros. bought it, thereafter sending Penn and Teller an endless stream of hip young directors to gain their approval. None proved worthy.

"They would just be parroting what the studio said about 'What The Film Should Be,'" recalled Teller, adding that they turned them all down because none of them "got" the joke. In desperation, their agent, Sam Cohn (Brillstein was their manager), suggested they speak with another of his clients, Arthur Penn.

"The three of us met and started talking," Arthur Penn said, "and I realized that they were serious guys, but that the people they had been talking to had been treating them like comedians. So I said, 'Tell me the story,' and it was the story of Penn and Teller getting killed. I said, 'It's operatic.' And Teller said, 'My God, that's it!' That was the beginning."

The story is as perverse as Penn & Teller's stage humor: Appearing on a TV talk show, Jillette foolishly says that life would be more exciting if somebody were really trying to kill him. A deranged fan takes him up on his dare and succeeds, but not before the viewer has been served a series of practical jokes, stage illusions, and red herrings, all of which are an effort on the part of Teller and the boys' manager, Carlotta (Caitlin Clarke) to teach Jillette the folly of his arrogance. By the end of the story, however, it backfires and P&T have, indeed, been killed.

Placed in the uncomfortable position of having to approve a filmmaker from whom they themselves sought approval, Jillette recalled conspiring: "He came in and said, 'I really want to do your movie.' We said, 'Are you Arthur Penn?' He said, 'Yes.' We said, 'Done.'" But that didn't mean that Arthur Penn would be a hireling; he saw problems in the script. "It's funny until right up to about fifteen minutes from the end," he told them. "Let me see what we can do before that to make it work." What he did, says Jillette, was create a scene earlier in the picture that established the team as compulsive practical jokers. "It's something called 'exposition,'" Jillette adds wryly.

"We started shooting on April 19, 1988," Teller recalls. "We started that day by filming the sequence in which we toss coins into the toll booth along the Garden State [New Jersey] Parkway. It was raining. Arthur shot insanely fast because, as he later told me, 'At the beginning, always shoot something easy and unimportant and shoot it so fast you leave the heads of the crew spinning. You need to inculcate in the crew a certain degree of recklessness.'"

Locations included the Atlantic City, New Jersey casino and theatre of Trump Plaza, and at assorted other locations there and in neighboring Ocean City. Interior sets were built in an abandoned New Jersey meat-packing plant. After eight weeks, the company pulled two days of shooting in New York at JFK airport and a 42nd Street studio.

During production, the working title *Dead Funny* was changed to the more utilitarian *The Penn & Teller Film*. Meanwhile the publicity-conscious magicians were working on advertising slogans. "I had gotten obsessed with the slogan, 'Sequels be damned: Penn & Teller Get Killed,'" Jillette confessed. "And because Arthur and Teller thought I was the best salesman, I called up people along this long ladder of studio authority and said we had a slogan we really liked and wanted to bounce it off you: 'Sequels de damned.' And he laughed and said, 'Yeah, five guys in Hollywood will laugh at it. It's an 'in' joke. Americans don't know what sequels are. If they did, they wouldn't be eating this shit we're feeding them.' How do you argue with that? I just hung up the phone."

The resulting film, which director Penn deemed "the first comedy for the assassination generation," slyly pushes the cinematic envelope. For most of it, Penn and Teller play increasingly dark practical jokes on each other, culminating in a moment in which Jillette is shot by a sniper. At first he ascribes it to one of Teller's jokes gone awry, but the viewer knows it's real and the film crosses over into a new universe where the medium is no longer the message, it's a lie. In so doing, *Penn & Teller Get Killed* becomes one of the very few American movies to examine the phenomenon of celebrity as well as to posit whether film is a reliable medium for telling truth.

"We didn't do any magic in the movie for that reason," Jillette said. "You can't compete with the real magic that's going on, like being able to change from one scene to another. We were trying to avoid it altogether, but Arthur didn't want it; in the movie, he wanted people to see what we did for a living. So we created a bit that is, indeed, impossible: the drill table.[431] Then to take the curse off it, we said we would never knowingly expose a trick, and then do so. Of course, the trick we expose could never work, but it looks like it *kinda* would work, but look at the movie and go out and try to build it."

The most inventive gag, and yet the one that doesn't look like one, is the end sequence in which the obsessed fan kills the boys. It is staged so that he videotapes the event (adding more texture) by aiming the camera directly at its own monitor. It looks unremarkable until one realizes that it isn't pre-taped and that the film crew ought to be seen photographing themselves. But they're not. The trick? The camera was hidden under a raised set and shot through a periscope. "You get the choice of watching the reality or the television screen," said Teller. "Arthur says that making a movie is making a deal with the Devil: when you get something, you always have to pay for it." In a weird way it's reminiscent of Jean-Luc Godard's oft-quoted pronouncement, "Film is truth twenty-four times a second."

Proving (or perhaps because of) the studio's lack of faith in it, *Penn & Teller Get Killed* was given only limited release in late 1989. As Arthur Penn's last film (he made two TV movies in the next seven years, then nothing else before his death in 2010) it remains just as experimental as *Bonnie and Clyde* was twenty-two years earlier. In a way, it's even more profound, for, instead of exploring how criminals become legends, it ponders how Truth becomes Lies, and vice-versa.

Arthur Penn never settled down in any one medium; he was equally at home on the stage, in live television, and on a movie set. Rather than seek success in any of them — through he once said he would have been happy staying in TV until the point at which it changed once sponsors took over program content — he simply picked the best of whatever was offered to him at any given time. This caused his lifelong friend and collaborator, playwright William Gibson (*The Miracle Worker*), to suggest that Penn had had "an accidental life." That life ended on September 28, 2010, the day after his 88th birthday. The cause was given as acute respiratory collapse, but it might also be said that the movie business collapsed first. Wrote Patrick Goldstein in *The Los Angeles Times*, "It's hard to think of a director who changed the course of Hollywood films as much with one movie [*Bonnie and Clyde*] as Arthur Penn."[432]

---

431. Teller is impaled by descending power drills as volunteer audience "assistants" stand watching helplessly, and then are berated afterward by Jillette for doing nothing.
432. Patrick Goldstein, *Los Angeles Times*, September 30, 2010.

MICHAEL POWELL
Master Archer

Michael Powell is one of a handful of filmmakers whose influence on modern directors is profound, yet whose films general audiences may be hard-pressed to name. This may be because his work is so resoundingly British that they turned up in U.S. "art" houses more frequently than in mainstream theaters. He was driven into obscurity following the scandal of his 1959 film, the deeply disturbing *Peeping Tom*, and was rediscovered largely through the efforts of the British scholar Ian Christie and American filmmaker Martin Scorsese.

Although Powell, born in 1905 in Canterbury, England, had been in films since 1925, it was his eighteen-year association with Hungarian-born Emeric Pressburger that created a staggering number of original works that, as a whole, form their own genre. Working in total collaboration as writers, producers and directors, they made their films magical yet not fantastic, stylized without being self-conscious, and had them radiate a consistent outlook no matter how varied their stories were. Watching their use of color, sound, editing, camera movement, sets, costumes and, of course, acting is to see the entire vocabulary of motion pictures. *The Thief of Bagdad*, *The 49th. Parallel*, *One of Our Aircraft is Missing*, *The Life and Death of Colonel Blimp*, *A Canterbury Tale*, *I Know Where I'm Going!*, *Stairway to Heaven*, *Black Narcissus*, *The Red Shoes*, *The Fighting Pimpernel*, and *The Pursuit of the Graf Spee*, among others, are captivating as stories while keeping the viewer aware that he's watching a movie.

Powell came to films from an introverted childhood buried in literature and photography. After assorted studio jobs as grip, stills photographer, assistant director, and sometimes-actor on British silent and early sound films, he co-wrote *Blackmail* without credit for another young British filmmaker, Alfred Hitchcock, in 1929. Its success propelled him to the director's chair on a stultifying number of British "quota quickies" churned out for £1/foot for tax and tariff purposes rather than art. He made the leap to pictures he wanted to do with *Edge of the World* (1937), a drama about the aging population of the Shetland island of Foula in the Outer Hebrides.[433] Powell would return to the area in 1945 to make *I Know Where I'm Going!*. Producer Alexander Korda was so impressed with *Edge of the World* that he hired Powell to make *The Spy in Black*. It was in pre-production on that film in 1939 that Korda introduced him to a fellow Hungarian who had just turned the script inside-out, improving it immeasurably: Emeric Pressburger.

Powell and Pressburger formed a company called The Archers and worked together as one, but by the 1950s Pressburger sought to devote more time to writing novels and Powell moved on. Unfortunately, it was a time when the studio system that had nurtured him was evaporating. In 1959 he directed *Honeymoon*, an uneasy blend of travelogue and ballet that was not well received. But it was his next effort, also in 1959, that drew the critics' wrath. *Peeping Tom* was a story about a young man (Carl Boehm) who takes home movies of women as he stabs them to death to record their look of fear. Perverse in conception and graphic for its day, it made its director an instant pariah.

"They yanked the film out of the Plaza [Cinema]," Powell wrote in his memoir, "they canceled the British distribution, and they sold the negative as soon as they could to an obscure black marketeer of films who tried to forget it, and forgotten it was, along with its director, for twenty years."[434] "I was no longer bankable. I was too independent. I wanted my own way. I'd grown up. Audiences had grown up. Films had stayed in the nursery."[435]

Seen today when slasher movies have become a lucrative sub-industry, *Peeping Tom* is still unsettling. Not only is it an ugly film to watch, with contrasty colors, stark lighting, and Spartan sets, but its main character is so deeply etched and his background so believably explained that one develops an understanding of him, and thus a sense of betrayal. Certainly the British Board of Film Censors felt something close to this because they ordered *Peeping Tom* heavily cut before its April 7, 1960 London premiere. Despite restoration in ensuing years, some of the deleted footage remains lost.

433. The story is actually about the forced relocation of the residents of St. Kilda but Powell was denied access to their island, so he set his film on Foula.
434. Michael Powell. *Million Dollar Movie*. New York: Random House, 1992.
435. *Michael Powell: A Life in Movies*. London Weekend Television: The South Bank Show, October 26, 1986.

Powell was able to find work in the early 1960s directing episodes of television's *Espionage* and *The Defenders*, but his bravura was too large for TV. When he landed financing from Australian sources he made *They're a Weird Mob* in 1966 about an Italian immigrant who arrives in Australia to find that the job he was promised is gone and the money he was given to get there has become a debt, so he goes into construction and begins wooing the boss' daughter. Powell became as astute about the Australian mindset as he had been about the British and, while the film does not travel well, it was a huge success Down Under and made it possible for him to direct *Age of Consent*.

Age of Consent was a 1935 novel by Australian writer-sculptor-illustrator Norman Lindsay that was banned in his country until 1962. Lindsay is also known for having written and drawn the 1918 children's book, *The Magic Pudding*, which Powell had long sought to direct as an animated film. *Consent* came to him by a circuitous route. It was originally announced by producer Oscar Nichols who wanted Dan O'Herlihy and Glynis Johns, who had just appeared in the remake of *Cabinet of Dr. Caligari*,[436] to head a cast that would include Barbara Eden.[437] It's unclear whether Nichols actually had the rights at the time because actor-producer Michael Pate was reportedly in negotiations with author Lindsay for them, an acquisition that was complicated by the book's being banned in Australia. Despite this, at the beginning of 1962 Pate took over the project and brought in Fred Jordan, head of Producers Studio, who announced he would produce it independently the next year.[438]

Here the chronology bifurcates. In one thread, Pate brings it to Michael Powell via another Aussie actor, Chips Rafferty. Powell was then in talks to direct *The Bone is Pointed*, a mystery written by Arthur Upfield for producer John McCallum. Instead, he favored *Age of Consent*, perhaps seeing in it his primary theme of the artists' compulsion to create.[439] In another version of the odyssey, James Mason and his producing partner Pat B. Rooney found Eady Plan[440] money to make the film in Australia with Mason directing and starring opposite Susannah York.[441] Either way, by 1967 *Age of Consent* had come to Michael Powell. With James Mason

---

436. *Daily Variety*, November 22, 1961.
437. *Hollywood Reporter*, November 28, 1961.
438. *Weekly Variety*, September 5, 1962.
439. *Weekly Variety*, August 23, 1967.
440. An un-annotated budget in the files of the Motion Picture Academy shows $263,000 which includes $44,500 in deferments. Powell received $10,000, the writer $15,000, and the four principal cast members an undifferentiated $60,000. These are apparently U.S. Dollars.
441. *Hollywood Reporter*, May 7, 1964.

offered to co-produce as well as star (abandoning directing), finances presented themselves (see below).

Consent's autobiographical premise has a painter, Brad Morahan (James Mason), moving from New York City's trendy gallery society to an Australian island. There he finds a young girl named Cora Ryan (Helen Mirren) who becomes his model but not, contrary to audience expectations, his lover. This is misunderstood by Cora's alcoholic grandmother (Neva Carr-Glynn) as well as his annoying leech of a friend, Nat Kelly, played by Jack MacGowran. In the course of his spiritual reawakening, Brad paints his beach shack with colors more vibrant than those he had used in New York and the film comes alive before Brad realizes that he has been reborn, too, thanks to Cora.

The script was adapted by Peter Yeldham and the shoot ran from April through June, 1968. Eight weeks of exteriors were filmed on Dunk Island and the Great Barrier Reef in Queensland, Australia; a few days at Albion Race Parkway; and the rest at the Ajax Film Center in Sydney. There were some delays on Dunk when the fall weather, scouted by Powell for its photogenic cloud formations, poured down rain and the company was stuck with no cover sets. In the end, Brad's shack had to be struck and reassembled in Sydney where facilities (and the weather) were better.

By coincidence, the director's son, Kevin Powell, was hired as the film's unit manager — "coincidence" in that apparently Michael knew nothing about it until he was told by Michael Pate. Powell also decreed that editor Anthony Buckley and composer Peter Sculthorpe should be on location to inspire their work. According to Kevin Powell, his father was a generous director but also a clever one; during production he would publicly compliment one department for a job well done on a given day, then a different one on another day. "It made a bit of competition with the crew," the son said, "but it also made the crew feel that they were really appreciated."[442]

Helen Mirren, then twenty-three, had just signed a multi-year contract with the Royal Shakespeare Company when Powell chose her for Cora. For a while it was at issue whether they would let her go to make her first film. "Finally," Powell wrote, "it occurred to somebody that if a girl they already had under contract was going to play opposite James Mason in a film, there might be something in it for Stratford."[443] Mirren showed her mettle early on by doing her own underwater scenes in the Great Barrier

---

442. Kevin Powell's comments on the *Age of Consent* DVD.
443. Kevin Powell, op. cit.

Reef, a well-known cruising area for great white sharks. The footage was shot by Ron and Valerie Taylor, the team who won international praise in 1975 for capturing real shark footage there for *Jaws*.

Another notable moment occurred when Powell threw James Mason in bed with Clarissa Kaye for a scene between Brad and a local "bird." Perhaps it was Powell's direction or the South Sea air, but Mason and Kaye became attached during the filming and got married in August, 1971. "The James Mason I met was a very lonely man," recalled Mirren. "He'd had this difficult marriage [to Pamela Ostrer Kellino] that was long gone and had emotionally destroyed him. He met Clarissa *on Age of Consent* and proceeded to marry her and be very happy the rest of his life."[444]

The film was financed in part by Columbia Pictures. In 1968, Columbia was flush with money from recent hits *Oliver!* and *Guess Who's Coming to Dinner*, but they had also expanded too quickly for their assets and were fast approaching their credit limit from the First National Bank of Boston. (By 1970 they were nearly bankrupt and were forced to sell their Gower Street studios as well as write off millions.) In short, by the time Powell delivered *Age of Consent* to Columbia, they were in no position to handle it properly. This did not prevent their British production head Max Setton from making demands. He objected to the film's nudity even though it was "model nudity" as opposed to sexual, claiming they would face censorship problems and be denied a television sale. The company also inexplicably replaced Peter Sculthorpe's complex, sensual score with one by Stanley Myers (*Dreamchild, The Deerhunter, My Beautiful Laundrette*) whom they deemed more commercial. The studio even reshot the main titles which contained witty paintings by Paul Delprat, whose artwork stands in for Brad's throughout the film, because it contained a nude Helen Mirren as the Columbia lady. (Both Sculthorpe's and Delprat's work were restored for the DVD release.)[445]

"Between *Peeping Tom* and *Age of Consent* there was the Diaspora when there was no way to get a picture made," said Martin Scorsese, who became Powell's great friend and, in some ways, his protégé. "So it did turn out, not by choice, that *Age of Consent* was the last feature, and he had to find a way to make it sort of off the beaten path, so to speak, out of the industry, in Australia. I think that the greater challenge was trying for so many years to make so many more films and finally coming to realize, at

---

444. Mirren's comments on the *Age of Consent* DVD.
445. Observers will note that superimposed beneath the Columbia lady logo is the misspelled text *Columbia Picture* [sic] *Corporation*. The restored film's DVD running time is 106 minutes vs. 98 minutes as listed on *IMDb.com*.

a certain point, that this one was going to be the last. It was very painful for him, because I saw him go through it, but he never gave up hope.... He would have gone on making them right to the end of his life if the money had been there."[446]

After *Age of Consent* Powell and Mason tried to finance a film of Shakespeare's *The Tempest* (which *Age of Consent* in many ways references) but *Consent*'s poor returns outside of Australia rendered their efforts unsuccessful. Powell and Pressburger reunited for the short children's film *The Boy Who Turned Yellow* in 1972 and in 1978 he directed the documentary *Return to the Edge of the World* (1978, in which he revisited the land he had memorialized on film in 1937. Also in the 1970s Scorsese, who had been shaped watching Powell's films on New York television, sought him out and became his great champion. In 1980 Powell lectured at Dartmouth College in New Hampshire through the patronage of critic/admirer David Thomson, and in 1981 Francis Ford Coppola made him Director-in-Residence at Zoëtrope Studios. Neither Coppola nor Scorsese was ever able to raise money for him to direct again, even though he kept active preparing projects and writing his memoirs. In 1984 he married Scorsese's editor, Thelma Schoonmaker, and, until his death in 1990, they enjoyed the acclaim that came with the restoration of his films and his rediscovery as one of the most creative filmmakers the medium had ever known.

---

446. Scorsese's comments on the *Age of Consent* DVD.

Otto Preminger.

OTTO PREMINGER
The Man You Hate to Love

With the convenience of hindsight it has become clear that Otto Preminger was a producer first and a director second, though his supporters see the two roles reversed. In practice they were intertwined and, when combined with Preminger's flamboyant public persona, made him a triple threat in the executive suite, on the set, and in the media. Whether this yielded memorable films or just famous ones is something cineastes continue to debate.

His personality was its own contradiction. In his private life he was an art collector, a charming companion, a discrete lover, and a fearless supporter of progressive causes. When he was with cast and crew, however, he could be monomaniacal, creatively rigid, and thoughtlessly cruel (he fired actor Tom Tryon from the lead of *The Cardinal* while Tryon's parents were visiting the set, and he browbeat Liza Minnelli to tears on *Tell Me That You Love Me Junie Moon*). Love him or hate him, you couldn't ignore him, and that was the whole point.

"I passed Otto Preminger's house last night," writer-director Burt Kennedy once needled, making fun of the possessive credit Preminger used on his movies, "or was it 'A House by Otto Preminger'?" And fellow Austrian Billy Wilder, who directed Preminger in *Stalag 17*, once jabbed, "I have to be nice to Otto; I may still have family in Germany."[447] Mort Sahl, bored at a screening of Preminger's overlong 1960 epic about Israel's 1948 independence, *Exodus*, reportedly shouted out, "Otto! Let my people go!"

---

447. The comment is grotesque; Wilder's mother and grandmother died in the Holocaust.

Born in 1905 in a region that was then Austria-Hungary but is now Ukraine, Otto Ludwig Preminger was raised to follow his father, a prosecutor, into the practice of law, but he veered into theater when he fell under the tutelage of impresario Max Reinhardt in Vienna in 1933. There he became an actor and producer, venturing to Broadway in 1935 to direct *Libel*. Notoriety summoned him to Twentieth Century-Fox to learn film and to direct whatever script Darryl F. Zanuck handed him. Predictably, Preminger balked at being told what to do, and was fired. He returned to Broadway and starred in *Margin for Error*, playing a Nazi. Despite being Jewish, the characterization stuck (the accent, bearing, and shaved head helped) and he made his way back to Fox to play a Nazi in *The Pied Piper*, after which Zanuck decreed him a producer and left to wage World War II. While Zanuck was away, Preminger promoted himself to director and took over *Laura* (1944), firing director Rouben Mamoulian and reshooting his footage. A scandal was averted when *Laura* became a hit and Zanuck forgave him, after which Preminger's film career ascended.

Although he functioned reasonably well at Fox (*Forever Amber*, *Daisy Kenyon*, *River of No Return*, etc.), his greatest work was made for United Artists, the independent company that gave its directors almost total freedom. Preminger's films for UA include *The Moon is Blue* (1953) which challenged the sexual inhibitions of Hollywood's censorious Production Code; *The Man with the Golden Arm* (1955) which did the same for the Code's drug prohibition; and *Exodus* (1960) for which he hired blacklisted screenwriter Dalton Trumbo, helping to end the industry's political witch hunt.[448] Even at this stage, however, it's not clear whether Preminger hired Trumbo solely for his talent (any number of other blacklisted writers including Michael Wilson, Ian McLellan Hunter, Carl Foreman, and Ring Lardner, Jr. were just as skilled) or because Trumbo was the most famous blacklistee, feeding Preminger's penchant for publicity.

It also explains why he pursued, for the rest of his career, the practice of adapting best-selling books to the screen, particularly those that threw off a whiff of scandal. *Anatomy of a Murder* (1959) featured a lurid courtroom scene using the words *bitch, contraceptive, panties, penetration, rape,*

---

448. There is debate over whether it was Preminger or Kirk Douglas who broke the Blacklist by giving screen credit to Trumbo, who had hitherto been working anonymously through fronts. By Preminger publicly crediting Trumbo for *Exodus* and Douglas for *Spartacus*, both men showed courage. Chris Trumbo (Dalton's and Cleo's son) advised the Author that it was Preminger who first told the heads of United Artists that he would credit Trumbo on *Exodus*. After that hit the trades, but before the film was released, Universal Pictures production chief Ed Muhl okayed Douglas to credit Trumbo on *Spartacus*.

slut and *sperm*; *Advise and Consent* (1962) had a homosexual subplot; *The Cardinal* (1963), although it was supported by the Vatican, had incendiary content; and *Hurry Sundown* (1967) was a steamy tale of Southern sex and intrigue. Criticized for changing the books when he made them into movies, Preminger would unashamedly reply, "When I buy a book I can do anything I want with it. It's mine."[449]

What he meant was that he could tell his *writers* to do anything he wanted, for Preminger's resume includes no writing credits. Even his thin autobiography, published by Doubleday in 1977, was done by ghostwriter June Callwood. Still, he hired the best. Besides Trumbo, his scripters included Tom Stoppard (*The Human Factor*), Horton Foote (*Hurry Sundown*), Wendell Mayes (*In Harm's Way* and *Anatomy of a Murder*), Elaine May (writing as Esther Dale for *Such Good Friends*), Arthur Laurents (*Bonjour Tristesse*), and Graham Greene (*Saint Joan*).

For *The Human Factor* (1979), which became his last picture, he engaged Stoppard to adapt Graham Greene's 1978 spy novel when Greene declined to do so himself even after Preminger paid him six figures for the book rights. Greene wove a low-key but tight story about a mid-level British Intelligence worker who does a favor for a South African Communist who wants to keep his wife out of prison, and it blows back upon him. Rare for a spy novel, the motivation was not money, ideology, or patriotism but, literally, the human factor, love. When both Richard Burton and Michael Caine turned down the lead (Caine no doubt remembering *Hurry Sundown*), Nicol Williamson was signed. He joined a cast that included Richard Attenborough, John Gielgud, Derek Jacobi, Ann Todd, Robert Morley, and model-turned actress Iman.

With the end of his lucrative Paramount deal in the 1960s,[450] Preminger had to raise his own production money by selling off the film's rights in various territories until the promissory notes underwrote his $5.5 million budget. The British and several international rights went to Rank and the U.S. and Canadian rights were presold to MGM. Production manager Val Robins led him to financier Paul Crosfield to provide the liquid production coin. Stoppard turned in a first draft on August 1, 1978 and a revision on August 24, and said afterward that he was pleased and amazed that Preminger shot it as written.

449. Conversation with the Author.
450. Although Paramount's sales VP George Weltner was enamored of Preminger, the studio's production chief at the time, Marty Rackin, detested him. The internecine struggle blew back on Rackin, who was fired. (Rackin is interviewed memorably by Walter Wagner in *You Must Remember This*. New York: G. P. Putnam's Sons, 1975.)

Production began May 30, 1979 in Kenya, doubling for the story's South African setting. Almost immediately tension developed between Williamson and Preminger, who berated him in public whenever he fouled his lines. Cinematographer Mike Molloy recalled that his hands were creatively tied by the director's demand for high key lighting and straightforward camerawork. Preminger shot so fast and with so little coverage that, said Robert Morley, "He is the only director who tires of the scene before the actor does."[451] Throughout the African shoot Preminger would fire crew members, yell at the actors, and act as though he was shelling out his own money. By July, he was. Eager to get rolling, Preminger had advanced his own cash on Crosfield's promise that reimbursement would be forthcoming. When the backer's checks started bouncing, it became clear that it would not. By the end of the month Preminger had put up $1 million and hurried out of Africa for England, where he intended to finish. There he convened a press conference in his penthouse apartment and announced to reporters that he owed his crew $500,000 and estimated that he would have to dig into his pockets to raise as much as $2,500,000 of the film's budget. He named three financiers who, he said, had been contracted to pay $7.5 million by March 30 and displayed a signed copy of the contract.[452] In late October he sold pieces of his art collection, including two Matisses, and a house in the south of France. It still wasn't enough to meet his obligations.

Midway through December, British Actors Equity agreed to a settlement by which their performers, including Morley and Attenborough, would receive their fees from first monies. The debt was announced at £150,000. In January of 1984 the press reported that various creditors still hadn't been paid and they sued Preminger's company, Sigma, and Preminger personally for £500,000.

The Human Factor was released in Los Angeles in mid-December of 1979 for an Oscar® qualifying run and rolled out to limited playdates in early 1980. Although the reviews were cordial, business was not. One wag within MGM went so far as to explain the failure by saying, "Otto Preminger's *The Human Factor* is obviously not autobiographical."

It is also not a fully realized work. Preminger was seldom a visually inventive director, but *The Human Factor* is downright spare; most scenes are played in unbroken master shots with little movement by either actors or camera. This is particularly disappointing because Stoppard's

---

451. Chris Fujiwara, *The World and Its Double: The Life and Work of Otto Preminger.* New York: Faber & Faber, 2008.
452. *Daily Variety*, August 20, 1979.

adaptation is so lean, his dialogue so precise, and the acting so finely tuned (with the blatant exception of Iman)[453] that one wishes Preminger had been more interested in what he was doing. Although some of the older critics, many of whom had known him over the years, praised the film for its professionalism, others considered it sluggish. The rejection, combined with the debt (which he settled on his own, according to MGM[454]), shocked Preminger into retreat.

In December of 1971 he had married Hope Bryce, who had been his costume coordinator since 1958, when he was married to Mary Gardner, whom he divorced in 1959. Preminger and Bryce had two children. In 1944 he had also been romantically involved with famed ecdysiast Gypsy Rose Lee and sired a son, Erik Lee, who used the name Erik Kirkland until Lee died in 1970, after which he publicly took his father's surname.

Preminger, trying to get another project together after *The Human Factor*, wanted to film *Open Secret*, the story of executed atomic spies Julius and Ethel Rosenberg.[455] Unable to do so, he remained a public figure doing talk shows, documentaries, and being a man-about-town. He was invariably charming, if opinionated, and made people wonder why he was known behind his back as "Otto the Ogre." By 1980 it was apparent that he was having memory lapses, which the family at first denied. He died on April 23, 1986 at age 80 of lung cancer complicated by Alzheimer's disease.

As a pure entertainer, Preminger's reputation is secure. He challenged himself, his audience, and convention with nearly every film. Whether he challenged the art of cinema remains an open question.

---

453. Nevertheless, Preminger was so taken with Iman that he lobbied the distributor to support her for a Best Actress Oscar® nomination.
454. *Daily Variety*, November 15, 1979.
455. Peter Bogdanovich. *Who the Devil Made It*. New York: Alfred P. Knopf, 1997.

NICHOLAS RAY
A Stranger in Peking

Reputable critics and film historians find fascinating meanings, struggles, and themes running through the films of Nicholas Ray and an equal number of them in the man himself. In 1959 Jean-Luc Godard said, "the cinema is Nicholas Ray." Ephraim Katz gives him a generous three-quarter page in his *Film Encyclopedia* and notes, "his heroes are frequently anguished social rebels who consume themselves in the quest for love or in fast and furious living," adding that, "his work is characterized by tense and restless camera movement that matches the turbulence of the action on the screen."[456]

Even by this generous measure, *55 Days at Peking* is not "a Nicholas Ray film." It would certainly apply to Ray's earlier works — i.e., those before marriages, alcohol, and auteurism set in — like *They Live by Night*, *Knock on Any Door*, *Johnny Guitar*, *Bigger than Life*, and the iconographic *Rebel Without a Cause*. But *55 Days at Peking* (1963) is the last time he worked within the mainstream system that had sustained him. Technically, it's not really his last film; that slot is held by *We Can't Go Home Again* (1975), a feature he directed between 1971 and 1974 with his students at SUNY Binghamton where he was filmmaker in residence at Harpur College. (Its production, and a great deal else about Ray, is covered in the passionate 1975 documentary *I'm a Stranger Here Myself*.)[457]

"Nick was very sensitive," notes critic Myron Meisel, who wrote *Stranger*. "He had a very strong power of conveying his identification, not just with actors, but with everybody. It was partly an act, partly something he couldn't help, and partly a talent. But nevertheless it worked and he

---

456. Ephraim Katz. *The Film Encyclopedia* (second edition). New York: Harper Perennial, 1994.
457. Per screen credits: Directed by David Helpern, produced by James C. Gutman, and written by Meisel, Gutman, and Helpern.

was aware of it. Everything that had to do with the actor came first and everything else would be incidentally supportive. Everything was about the truth of the performance in the moment, and anything else was subsidiary. How much of that ability to communicate with actors mattered to *55 Days at Peking*, I have my doubts."[458]

55 Days at Peking was not a Hollywood movie *per se*, which makes the story of its production unusual. It was produced by Samuel Bronston, a somewhat mysterious independent showman who cobbled together financing from various international sources before farming out distribution to a succession of companies. Bronston hired the prolific and controversial Philip Yordan to write a script about the Boxer Rebellion. Like Bronston, Yordan was a mercurial a presence, a man whose writing credit appears on films his collaborators frequently insist he never wrote (see below).[459]

The film's setting is remarkably accurate even if the plot is not. In 1898 a Chinese nationalist army, whom the British called "Boxers" but who called themselves the "Righteous Harmony Society," arose to expel Christian missionaries and other foreign interests from China. Eight nations claimed a share at the time: the United States, Britain, France, Germany, Italy, Russia, Japan, and Spain. In June of 1900, when the film starts, the Boxers attack Peking (Beijing) in a fifty-five day siege against 1,000 people who had retreated to the legation compound for protection. The Chinese Imperial Court of the dowager empress Cixi (Ts'u-hsi) vacillated between supporting the Boxers and offering peace, and as the Court became mired in competing intrigues, the eight occupying nations managed to gather 20,000 soldiers to defeat the Chinese armies and capture all of Beijing.

For *55 Days at Peking* Charlton Heston is the American major whose brashness first provokes, then outwits, the "natives"; David Niven is the British diplomat whose decision to remain in Peking despite an eviction order dooms everyone to the attack; Ava Gardner is the Baroness who abandons her haughtiness to become a nurse; John Ireland is the sergeant who becomes Heston's conscience; Robert Helpmann is the prince who tries to play both sides of the street; and Flora Robson is the dowager empress who must face the fact that her dynasty is finished. Thousands of Chinese extras were recruited from restaurants and laundries throughout Europe, according to the film's production notes.

458. Interview with Author, April 7, 2012.
459. Yordan's legend has him hurriedly departing for Spain after delivering scripts to Darryl F. Zanuck at Fox and Milton Sperling at Warner Bros., each of whom thought he had Yordan under exclusive contract. They learned otherwise when Yordan mistakenly gave each the other's script.

Ray had previously directed *King of Kings* for Bronston, a meat-and-potatoes retelling of the Christ myth that MGM released as a roadshow attraction in 1961, and which, because hunky Jeffrey Hunter played the title role, was somewhat unfairly nicknamed *I Was a Teenage Jesus*. Like that film, *55 Days* would be shot in Spain where Bronston had facilities; for reasons dating back to the opium wars, China was closed to the West. The sprawling embassy and legation set was erected on 250 acres at Marques de Villabragima, sixteen miles outside of Madrid. They were created by production designers Veniero Colasanti and John Moore, both of whom had just finished *El Cid* for Bronston. This was notable in that Ray had studied architecture under Frank Lloyd Wright at Taliesin and was more than capable of designing them himself.[460]

Meanwhile, the script was being written by Bernard Gordon, which leads to another adventure. Although Philip Yordan would take shared credit for it (during production, additional writing is said to have been done by Arnaud D'Usseau, Robert Hamer, Ben Barzman, and Ray's then-wife Betty Utey), in 2000 the Writers Guild issued a formal correction giving the then-blacklisted Gordon full credit.[461] "During the years I worked with him I saw very, very little of his own writing efforts," Gordon insisted. "I just don't recall any instances of him doing that. As to what went on before I started to work with him, I just can't say."[462] It is worth noting that, like Gordon, D'Usseau and Barzman were also blacklisted at the time and were originally denied screen credit. Speaking years later at Oklahoma University after a screening of *55 Days*, Gordon said, "they had a woman there who was a specialist, a historian, about the Far East, and she gave a long talk about what the Boxer Rebellion was all about. When she got through I said, 'If I'd known as much about the Boxer Rebellion then as you said now, I never would have been able to write the script.' They asked me what I was thinking about when I had to do the script and they expected some kind of profound cultural response. I said I was thinking about how to keep my job."[463]

Production began on June 20, 1962, sixty-two years to the day that the actual siege took place. Shooting ended on October 31. Some sources indicate a July 2 start, which is the day that the filmmakers blew up the Boxers' arsenal in a spectacular nighttime fireball.

460. Katz, op. cit.
461. David Robb, *Hollywood Reporter*, August 4-6, 2000.
462. Patrick McGilligan, ed., *Backstory 2*. Berkeley and Los Angeles: University of California Press, 1991 and in conversations with the Author.
463. Unpublished interview Ed Rampell and the Author, August 4, 2004.

There was another fireball brewing behind the camera: *55 Days* would mark the breakdown of Ava Gardner and the collapse of both Nicholas Ray and his career. At the time, Ray was among Hollywood's most highly paid directors, earning upwards of $75,000, although it could also be said that he was considered unemployable in Hollywood. Bronston ignored that and offered him *55 Days*. Alas, Ray's days would number less than fifty-five.

So would Gardner's. On June 28, 1962 in Madrid, she hosted a cocktail party for selected cast and crew. Someone took her aside and told her such interesting information about Empress Ts'u-hsi that she wanted to forsake her starring role as Baroness Natalie Ivanov, the expatriate Russian aristocrat, and play the Empress. Bronston wouldn't hear of it, but the thought incubated in the troubled star's mind. Two days later at a script reading at Ray's villa the actress, approaching 40, sat curled up drinking vodka and tonic, and suddenly let loose a stream of profanity about the script. Charlton Heston simply left the house ("a macabre evening" he wrote in his diary) but Ray sat and tolerated it.[464]

Shooting only worsened Gardner's drinking. Wrote Heston in his diaries, "Today marked the worst behavior I've yet seen from that curious breed I make my living opposite. Ava showed up for a late call, did one shot (with the usual incredible delay in coming to the set), and then walked off just before lunch when some Chinese extra took a still of her. She came back after a painful three hour lunch break only to walk off, for the same reason."[465] Ray catered to Gardner's behavior because he had become smitten with her, something that strained his marriage to Betty Utey, who was with him in Spain and surely must have noticed. But he was also prone to moods of his own. "Nick didn't hardly say anything," Philip Yordan recalled. "In fact, he would sit with his back to you when you talked to him. Look out a window, even if it's night. And I would say something and wait fifteen minutes, then Nick would turn around and he still wouldn't say anything."[466]

The crisis for both of them came with Gardner's death scene at the end of September. "She was drinking all the time," recalled Gordon. "You heard a lot of stories about her in Madrid, how she was kicked out of the Ritz Hotel and all of that. I had the impression that she was a lonely woman. I know that one time on the set she spoke to Paul Lukas,

---

464. Lee Server. *Ava Gardner: Love is Nothing*. New York: MacMillan, 2007 (reprint).
465. Charlton Heston; Hollis Alpert, ed. *The Actor's Life: Journals 1956-1976*. New York: Dutton Books, 1976.
466. McGilligan, op. cit.

who was playing the doctor in the thing, and asked him if he knew how they could make their scene play better, and Lukas looked at her and said, 'Yes, it would help if you stop drinking before noon every morning.'"[467] When she refused to show up for reverse angles, Yordan (or possibly Ray) gave her lines to Lukas and he played them to a stand-in. The existing scene in the finished film is cobbled together from whatever footage was usable.

The next day it was Ray's turn to play a death scene, only nearly for real. Depending on the source, he was either taken directly from his villa to the hospital with tachycardia; or he had a gastro-intestinal problem; or he collapsed on the set with a heart attack and was taken to the hospital in an ambulance; or he had a "warning" heart attack and was driven to the hospital in someone's car.[468] In any event, he was off the picture, which might have been his plan all along because only the previous week Bronston had hired Andrew Marton, a skilled second unit director, to take over action scenes.[469] Once Ray was gone, director Guy Green took charge of the dramatic scenes. Whether Ray actually had a heart attack or the ambulance was summoned to cover his firing (a similar face-saving courtesy had been used when he was removed from *Wind Across the Everglades* four years earlier), is unclear. But Marton efficiently directed sixty-five percent of the finished film, mostly its first half, and petitioned for co-directing credit, which the DGA in those days did not offer. Ray fought Marton's petition. At a rough cut screening arranged for him by Bronston in November, 1962, Ray was so abusive of what he was watching that the producer stopped the projector after the first hour and never showed the rest. To mollify Marton, Bronston gave him money and a cryptic "Second Unit Operations" credit.[470]

Shot and presented in the unwieldy Super Technirama 70 process that rendered sweeping camera movements as graceful as aiming a truck at a knothole, *55 Days at Peking* is composed for the large screen yet works better in its dramatic scenes, a Ray specialty. Ray's use of wide screen was renowned (*Rebel without a Cause*, for example, approaches surrealism), but here the massive screen hamstrung his sense of space.

Given what China has become in the world economy, it's hard not to watch the film through revisionist eyes. It is a mixture of cynicism and

---

467. McGilligan, ibid.
468. *Variety* (September 14, 1962) went with gastro-intestinal.
469. *Variety*, September 6, 1962.
470. Patrick McGilligan: *Nicholas Ray: The Glorious Failure of an American Director*. New York: HarperCollins, 2011.

jingoism, which ought not to surprise anyone who notes the politics of its writers, whether credited or uncredited. It displays the pig-headedness of the occupying nations in overstaying what was never their welcome anyway, yet urges the audience to cheer for the triumph of white men over the yellow peril. Throughout the entire film, which encompasses numerous battles and untold explosions, not one single Chinese casualty is accorded a close-up, whereas even minor Western characters are given honorable, if sometimes fleeting, deaths. Then there is Charlton Heston as the stolid military man and putative love interest, although the latter plotline never works emotionally. Heston is grand at nobility but when it comes to quiet moments that require sensitivity he was always aloof; he needs to *react* rather than *act*, as his best directors, William Wyler and Tom Gries, saw and exploited.

"Why did he get discouraged?" producer John Houseman — who worked with Ray early on — asked rhetorically. "This is the terrible evil of the Hollywood system. Because you do get screwed occasionally by the studios. I think Nick…almost anticipated the screwings before they actually occurred. It is not rare, but it affected Nick more than other people."[471] And *55 Days at Peking* was his last chance. As his widow, Susan, acknowledged, "Nicholas Ray's career within the legitimate film industry had come to an end in September 1962, on a set near Madrid."[472] Physically, Ray died June 16, 1979, of lung cancer.

---

471. Houseman, *I'm a Stranger Here Myself,* op. cit.
472. Nicholas and Susan Ray. *I Was Interrupted: Nicholas Ray on Making Movies.* Berkeley and Los Angeles, California: University of California Press, 1995.

Michael Ritchie.

MICHAEL RITCHIE
Competitive Edge

After he had directed his first few features in the late 1970s, Michael Ritchie became pegged as a man who made films about competition. While *Downhill Racer* (skiing), *The Candidate* (politics), *The Bad News Bears* (Little League), *Semi-Tough* (pro football) and *Smile* (teen beauty pageants) were unquestionably about contests, they were also about the toll that winning and losing take on those who win or lose, particularly in America where winning is everything.

But after those initial successes his muse seemed to wander: a rote sequel, *The Bad News Bears Go to Japan*, Peter Benchley's pulpy *The Island*, Bette Midler's concert film *Divine Madness*, and the uneven Robin Williams comedy *The Survivors*, not to mention *Student Bodies*, which he directed surreptitiously during the 1981 writers' strike and from which he removed his name. Although he was never at a loss for work, the demarcation between early Ritchie and middle Ritchie could not have been more stark. He was the first to acknowledge this when he was asked why he switched focus and he replied matter-of-factly, "Because they don't make my kind of movie any more." Then he would add, "I never made the cataloguing, never believed in pigeon holes. I've always tried to do new and different things for me, whatever the risks, and I've tried to avoid safe choices."[473] At that point he still had ten theatrical films and twenty years left until he was taken by prostate cancer in 2001. His last released picture, *A Simple Wish* (1997), neither summarizes his work nor adds to it, yet it reflects the tension between his talent and how the system allowed him to practice it.

Ritchie was nothing if not adaptable. Born in Waukeesha, Wisconsin, he moved to Berkeley, California when his father became professor of

---

473. September 22, 1980 conversation and interview with the Author.

Experimental Psychology at the college and his mother an art and music librarian for the city. He started directing while a Harvard student and gained notoriety when he staged his classmate Arthur Kopit's surrealistic black comedy *Oh Dad, Poor Dad, Mamma's Hung You in the Closet and I'm Feeling So Sad* at Adams House in 1960. Ritchie did publicity for it, too, cajoling the Boston critics for reviews and attracting the attention of TV producer Robert Saudek. Saudek tapped the young man to direct an episode of his *Omnibus* public affairs show, then kept him on to direct two *Profiles in Courage* episodes for the prestigious series based on the book credited to President John F. Kennedy. Thus anointed, Ritchie went back to California and started directing episodics like *The Man From U.N.C.L.E., The Big Valley, Run for Your Life, Felony Squad,* and a few TV movies. This drew the interest of Robert Redford in 1968 just when he reached stardom with *Butch Cassidy and the Sundance Kid*. Redford tapped Ritchie to direct *Downhill Racer* (1969), a quietly clenched examination of a champion skier (Redford, of course) who takes his talent for granted. Further distinguished by a signal performance by Gene Hackman as his coach, the picture drew fine reviews and led Redford to work with Ritchie again on *The Candidate* (1972). Written by Jeremy Larner and augmented by input from professional political consultants, *The Candidate* showed how a young progressive (Redford) is slowly but surely corrupted by the mechanics of the electoral system, personified by campaign manager Peter Boyle. At the very end he recaptures his ideals but is stymied figuring out how to implement them. The best political movie since Gore Vidal's *The Best Man, The Candidate* is satiric, funny, angry, clever, and idealistic all at once, and its semi-documentary style was the perfect articulation of Ritchie's talent.

"The early seventies was quite an amazing period for Hollywood film," Ritchie recalled. "Anything that appeared to be anti-Hollywood, or opposite the Hollywood formulas, was sought after and easily financed. Not only films like *The Candidate* or *Smile* but *Midnight Cowboy* [and others]. You don't imagine anyone green-lighting those films any more." Ritchie blames *Rocky* (1976). "People think today that *Rocky* won his first fight. He didn't, he went the distance and he lost. The misinterpretation of the end of *Rocky* was that Hollywood wants happy endings. The studios got the message that audiences wanted victory, and not only victory, but humiliation of your opponent."[474]

An imposing figure at six foot seven inches, the gaunt Ritchie had a playful, almost conspiratorial air about him, which was the sensibility

---

474. January 13, 1988 interview with the Author.

that he brought to his best movies. Not only do the characters in Michael Ritchie films live within the confines of their story, they carry an observer's awareness of the absurdity of it all. This is the mood expressed in *Smile* (1975), about a teenage beauty pageant, whose humor is surreal, if not seditious to Main Street values, and frequently crosses over into being downright nasty. That attitude was also on fine display in 1985 when he directed *Fletch* from Andrew Bergman's adaptation of Gregory Mcdonald's mystery novel about an investigative reporter who solves murders off the record. It was the perfect match: Ritchie's style, Mcdonald's dry wit, and Chevy Chase's condescending humor. Unfortunately, a sequel, *Fletch Lives* (1989), written by Paul Mazursky's frequent collaborator Leon Capitanos, failed, largely because it had nothing to do with any of Mcdonald's *Fletch* books. Between *Fletches*, Ritchie directed *The Golden Child* (1986) starring Eddie Murphy as a specialist in finding lost children and whose particular quest sucks him into the realm of supernatural evil. The result was a $149 million gross on a $25 million budget and a career boost for both men.

A Simple Wish (1997) returns to the family market of *The Golden Child* and is interesting for the performances of its supporting players rather than its leads. The script by Jeff Rothberg must have been sold on a one-line pitch but has nothing to back it up: a misfit male fairy godmother (Martin Short) who must make good comes up against evil queen Claudia (Kathleen Turner) who is bent on destroying all fairy godmothers, of which she used to be one. When Short is assigned to eight-year-old Anabel, played by Mara Wilson, whose "simple wish" is for her father, Robert Pastorelli, to be a Broadway success in a musical adaptation of *A Tale of Two Cities*,[475] Claudia stands mightily in the way for reasons having nothing to do with Anabel.

The uneventful shoot started on July 22, 1996 in Toronto as *The Fairy Godmother*, changed to *A Simple Wish* by the time the company moved to New York, and was called *The Godmother Project* until publicity concerns brought it back to *A Simple Wish*.[476]

Films that place magic within a realistic setting depend on the viewer's willing suspension of disbelief. *A Simple Wish* forsakes it from its very first scene by having Martin Short flub his final exam at fairy godmother school yet somehow win his wand. (What didn't survive the cutting room was the explanation that he was there through affirmative action.) But by

---

475. With songs by Ritchie and Lucy Simon that out-Miz *Les Miz*.
476. *The Hollywood Reporter*, September 3, 1996.

then the film is off balance and stays that way. Short's character, though earnest, predictably botches a number of spells until, when curse comes to shove, he vanquishes Claudia and saves the day. The third act climax, which is a wand-power showdown set against a ticking clock, is so protracted that it looks like a demo reel for a CGI company. That's one part of the movie.

The other is a showcase for the supporting performers who, even though they don't mesh as a cast, have their moments, particularly Pastorelli, Teri Garr, Miss Wilson, Ruby Dee, and Francis Capra as Wilson's know-it-all brother, Charlie. Their dialogue is full of asides, homages, wisecracks, and genuinely charming moments that add an adult layer to a routine kiddie movie. As for Martin Short, he shamelessly channels Jerry Lewis right down to the stammers, the stumbles, the rambling, and the gurns that Lewis brought to his beloved "kid" character. Taken as two mismatched halves of a bent coin, *A Simple Wish* is the old Michael Ritchie back in form, the one who coached natural performances out of actors and made his films seem as if they were happening for real. Then there's the Michael Ritchie who wanted to make a family film with wit and sophistication (his words from the presskit) but was sabotaged by a poorly structured script and an overkill of visual effects.

When Ritchie died of complications from prostate cancer in 2001 at age sixty-two he was just regaining his stride. And so was Hollywood with a generation of edgy young actors who wouldn't have been afraid to stretch if they'd had a director like Michael Ritchie to let them. "Film has become more of a ritual experience," Ritchie once noted, "and must meet expectations. Not everything has to be *The Candidate* or as dark as *Smile*. I've had films that didn't get off the ground and meanwhile I've had great fun doing entertainments."[477]

---

477. Interview with the Author, January 13, 1988.

Martin Ritt.

MARTIN RITT
The Real Thing

Marty Ritt — nobody who knew him ever called him "Martin" — tried to pretend that the failure of *Casey's Shadow* in 1978 didn't matter. "I did all these films about important causes and nobody came to see them," he sighed. "So I figured this time I'd do one that everybody would have to like. And they still stayed away."[478]

But of course it mattered. Everything mattered to Ritt, even an apparently lightweight story about a boy and his racehorse. Because it was also about how a motherless family is held together through hard times by merging their dreams, and thereby finding hope. Ritt made *Casey's Shadow* between two other projects that define his oeuvre: *The Front*, a biting comedy about the Blacklist, and *Norma Rae*, one of a minuscule number of studio pictures about labor unions. Seen in the context of his lifelong legacy of socially conscious movies such as *The Great White Hope*, *The Molly Maguires*, *Sounder*, *Conrack*, and nineteen others going back to his directorial debut in 1957 with *Edge of the City*, *Casey's Shadow* is, at its heart, about the restorative power of family values. Not the arrogant "family values" that would soon be exploited in Ronald Reagan's America, but the kind that met challenges with love, respect, and tolerance. (It also didn't hurt that producer Ray Stark lured gamblers Ritt and star Water Matthau to the project with the promise of their getting to hang around race tracks.)

So when, in 1989, he was offered another family drama, *Union Street*, Ritt took it knowing that it would allow him to explore his core theme, one that critic Carrie Rickey astutely saw as "marginal characters who care more about getting recognized as humans than they do about beating the system."[479]

---

478. Conversation with the Author in 1985.
479. Carrie Rickey, *Philadelphia Inquirer*, February 9, 1990.

Lumpy and avuncular, with a fireplug frame and face like a back door (legend has it that Paddy Chayefsky named his title character in *Marty* after Ritt, with whom he'd worked in early television), Ritt used his gruff exterior to mask an exquisitely sensitive soul. His preference for jumpsuits, even on dressy occasions, was legendary, as was his reputation for over thirty years as Hollywood's progressive voice. Ritt came by his beliefs through hardscrabble experience. Born in New York in 1914 and educated at PS 64 and DeWitt Clinton High School, he was raised Jewish in a neighborhood that felt more Eastern European than American. He went to Elon College in North Carolina where he played on the football team, the Fighting Christians. After Elon he returned to New York and enrolled at St. John's University with aspirations to be a lawyer. Instead, he found himself drawn to acting and, thanks to the WPA, found a home at the Left-leaning Group Theatre. Soon he added directing to his skills and, when live television came along in the 1950s, he migrated there.

Then came the Blacklist. Because of his involvement with the Group Theatre, Theatre of Action, and other activities of the WPA's Federal Theatre Project, and had given money to a front organization for Communist China, his name was circulated by the FBI as, if not exactly a Red, then a Red sympathizer. He was never called to testify before HUAC but was told that he could take a newspaper advertisement admitting he was "misled" that would allow him to work again. He refused, and his TV career was over. For upwards of five years he supported himself and his wife, Adele, by acting, dancing, and teaching at the then-new Actors Studio. He also taught himself to become an expert poker player and racetrack handicapper. When the Blacklist finally lifted he was able to direct his first film, *Edge of the City* (a.k.a. *A Man is Ten Feet Tall*), a story of an inter-racial friendship between John Cassavetes and Sidney Poitier set on New York's docks.

It started Ritt's career-long examination of race relations in America, a journey he had begun in North Carolina in the full flower of Jim Crow. "I like to set my stories in the south," he recalled later, "because the essence of drama is change, and that section of the country has undergone more change than any other section. There were so many violations of the human spirit that existed there. They exist all over the country, of course, but there they seem exacerbated. You've got your Carson McCulleres and Faulkners and Tennessee Williamses, and you've got your fat sheriffs. It's a very complicated and dense psychological forum. I went to school down there and it stuck with me: this massive contradiction, day by day.

I still feel it's a place where extraordinary American films can be made. Also, the country itself is pretty. It has a lot going for it. It's not the best place in the world to live, but, to work, it's interesting."[480]

Ritt's passionate concern for racial equality sometimes drew criticism from African-Americans who wanted a black director instead of a white one to tell their stories. Ritt had little patience for them. "I said, 'Fellas, make your own God damn pictures; get off my back. I've spent a lifetime believing in integration. You want to make another film, make it. Why do I have to deliver a film that you approve of?"[481]

It was not a story of racism but of devotion that became the setting for *Stanley & Iris*, which became Ritt's last film. It began as *Union Street*, the title of Pat Barker's 1982 novel on which it was based, and lived for a while as *Letters*. Although Barker's novel was set in England, married screenwriters Irving Ravetch and Harriet Frank, Jr., who had been shown the book by producers Alex Winetsky and Arlene Sellers, easily relocated it to a struggling New England industrial town they named Laurel. The novel tells the story of seven women whose lives intersect as they try to survive; in reality, said Barker, "My seven women are in fact one woman. They have the same memories."[482] But it still posed a problem because, as Frank explained, "There was no love story in the novel." She and her husband solved it by focusing on a woman named Iris King, the town's earth mother, and discovered a nugget that was only a throwaway in the novel: her husband couldn't read. They named him Stanley, made both him and Iris single, fashioned a love story between them, and approached their friend and frequent collaborator Martin Ritt with the idea.[483]

To many observers, *Stanley & Iris* became a story about adult illiteracy, but that's a misreading. It is actually a story about how knowledge (literacy) is a liberating force, especially when Stanley — played by Robert De Niro — comes to care about Iris, who is a new widow as the film begins, and she, in their sharing, finds release from her past. Iris is one of those people of whom others take advantage: she has a pregnant daughter, a homeless sister and brother-in-law, misguided fellow factory workers who think pregnancy is their way out, and just surviving day-to-day on a single income.

---

480. Interview with the Author, December 6, 1985.
481. Interview with the Author, February, 1979.
482. *London Times*, February 26, 1989.
483. The Ravetches previously collaborated with Ritt on *The Long Hot Summer* (1958), *The Sound and the Fury* (1959), *Hombre* (1967), *Conrack* (1974), *Norma Rae* (1979), *Murphy's Romance* (1985), and the groundbreaking *Hud* (1962).

When Jane Fonda was cast as Iris, an old specter arose. Some veterans' groups still held a grudge against her for visiting North Vietnam in July of 1972 and appearing in a photograph aiming an anti-aircraft gun at the sky.[484] Although the war had been over for thirteen years, protests against her were not. In fact, three New England towns either passed alderman measures or conducted straw polls opposing her, and one activist, Gaetano "Guy" Russo of the self-proclaimed "American Coalition Against Hanoi Jane," announced he would picket the film and any theater playing it. Other veterans' groups, however, opposed such proposals. In December, Ritt told Fonda, "I decided that we should go to Waterbury [Connecticut] regardless of what opposition exists." And go they did, rolling film on August 1, 1988.[485]

"We've had trouble from some right-wing people about Jane," Ritt countered at the time. "I guess nobody had heard from [the groups] in a while and they've had no moment in the sun."[486] To test the depth of anti-Fonda sentiment, the producers hired the polling firm of Fairbank, Bregman & Maullin. They found that fifty-eight percent of the local residents favored her and eighty percent said it was time to move on.[487] Fonda appeared at local fundraising events for veterans' and anti-illiteracy groups, and during one outdoor shoot five pickets against her were outnumbered by 400 supporting her. Nevertheless, after two weeks in a stifling heat wave, the company relocated to Toronto to finish principal photography. The film wrapped on October 22, 1988 on a budget of $21,008,975, of which Fonda and DeNiro each received $3.5 million, Ritt $1,650,000, and the Ravetches $500,000.[488]

In February of 1989 Ritt did what some consider an unusual thing — not for him, but for Hollywood. He wrote to the performers who had appeared in a subplot involving two women, Bertha and Elaine, one black, one white, to advise them "ahead of seeing the film" that their scenes had been trimmed for reasons of length and because the Stanley/Iris plot had become dominant.[489]

484. In 1988 she apologized for her actions but not her anti-war stance.
485. Ritt to Fonda, letter, December 17, 1987, AMPAS files.
486. My conversation with Ritt did not end there. He continued: "And all through this discussion with Jane nobody has even mentioned that she was right about the war." I put his whole quote in my interview, which I wrote on assignment for *The Boston Herald*. When the piece appeared in print it was the only line that my editor had deleted. "I'm not surprised," Ritt said when he saw the tearsheet. "What surprises me is that *you're* surprised."
487. Wolf Schneider, *The Hollywood Reporter*, February 9, 1988.
488. July 30, 1988 MGM budget estimate.
489. February 16, 1989 letters from Ritt to Julie Garfield, Karen Ludwig, Loretta Devine, Mary Testa, Kathy Kinney, Laurel Lyle, Katherine Cortez, and Zohra Lampert.

Stanley & Iris emerged as a strong film but it drew odd criticism. Some reviews felt that Fonda was simply too innately regal to be effective as Iris despite her acting chops (many had said the same thing about her star-making 1969 performance in *They Shoot Horses, Don't They?*). De Niro, of course, was completely at home in a blue collar role, and his emotional pain and embarrassment are palpable when he loses his job at a drug store because he can't tell aspirin from poison. Cinematographer Don McAlpine, production designer Joel Schiller, and costume designer Theoni V. Aldridge evoked the omnipresent decay of a failing industrial locale, and Ritt deftly kept the characters from being swamped by their settings. There was, to be sure, a certain amount of fantasy at work, and it drew comment as well: it turns out that Stanley is a latent genius who has covered up his inability to read by memorizing a world of information that he has heard throughout his life.[490] And Fonda's character, as in *Coming Home* (1978), finds liberation in service to, and love of, someone else.

Stanley & Iris was released in New York and Los Angeles on December 22, 1989 to qualify for Oscars® and hit its general release on February 9, 1990. In the meantime Ritt spent time at his Pacific Palisades home with his wife, Adele, who was a guiding force in his life, considering new projects. Already weakened by diabetes, he succumbed to heart disease and died of complications from both on December 8, 1990. With him pretty much died mainstream Hollywood's interest in movies about the human condition, a note of defeat that would never have crept into a Martin Ritt film.

It's hard to overstate the importance of Ritt's body of work. His films are about serious themes, but they're not all serious; they're character-driven and the characterizations are rich and deep. They aren't flashy, but they illuminate their subject. More importantly, like the man himself, they are about taking responsibility for one's actions. "I always choose to do realistic films," he said. "I've only made two overtly political films, *The Front* and *The Molly Maguires*. The rest of the films have all been social films dealing with the human condition."[491] As Carrie Rickey wrote, a Martin Ritt happy ending "isn't that a poor *person* becomes rich, it is that poor *people* become *enriched.*"[492]

---

490. Ritt and the Ravetches had different notions about this. The writers wanted him to be smart but "not a nuclear physicist." Source: Irving Ravetch letter to Ritt, May 27, 1987, Martin Ritt papers, AMPAS.
491. Interview with the Author.
492. Rickey, op. cit.

John Schlesinger.

JOHN SCHLESINGER
Everybody's Talking

British director John Schlesinger made a movie about New York in 1969 and it won the Academy Award® even though it was rated X. It was *Midnight Cowboy*, and people ascribed its acute portrait of a decaying America to the fact that it was directed by an outsider from Britain and, because Schlesinger had started off in documentaries, why, of course, that explained its gritty look. But that was too facile. Because for a decade Schlesinger had been making films in his native England that saw that country just as clearly, and nobody there called him an outsider. What he was, was a sensitive, keenly observant filmmaker who could be objective without being removed, involving without being manipulative, and intimate without being invasive. He was as gentle as they come (although his humor could be piercing) and yet he made at least two films, *Marathon Man* and *The Believers,* that contained unbearable violence. He was openly, even jubilantly gay, yet went both ways in his ability to make richly romantic films (*Far From the Madding Crowd, Darling, Sunday Bloody Sunday*). Best of all, he loved actors and had the ability to convey dry humor without belittling people, notably in *Cold Comfort Farm*. Even the profound 1981 financial debacle of *Honky Tonk Freeway*, which Schlesinger playfully called "Wanky-Wank Freeway" (cost: $24 million; returns: $500,000), has remarkable moments as it targets examples of American excess — the film itself being one of them.

The Next Best Thing in 2000 brought Schlesinger back to the territory he had cruised casually in *Darling* and more profoundly in *Midnight Cowboy*, only this was positioned as a romantic comedy wrinkled by homosexuality. In *Darling,* homosexuality was just another component of the jet set, nothing more than passing glances and glancing passes. In *Midnight Cowboy* it darkened into a tale of a straight Texan, Joe Buck, who lit out for New York to become a paid stud for lovelorn women. Instead, he becomes a gay hustler in order to survive. When he forms a friendship with a dying derelict, Enrico "Ratso" Rizzo, a symbiosis develops partly out of mutual exploitation but primarily out of desperate loneliness. Its frankness tempered with sensitivity earned it one of the first "X" ratings (before "X" meant pornography) as well as an Academy Award®. It was a groundbreaking film, not just for its style (like *Darling* it was more "observed" than "staged"), but for its non-sensationalized portrayal of friendship between two people whom most of the audience wouldn't want to spend time with. Its release a few weeks before the June, 1969 Stonewall riots in New York City, where the gay rights movement began, didn't hurt either.

"I didn't say, 'I'm going to make a landmark film.'" Schlesinger chided modestly. "I've always been conscious that the kind of subjects that I like are not mainstream. I've usually had to struggle to get them off the ground. I'm not used to playing to the youth-orientated audience. I'm just interested in taking the widest possible audience through an experience, and if they go, it's wonderful, and if they don't, it's not very joyful."[493]

There's a direct line between *Midnight Cowboy* and Schlesinger's last film, *The Next Best Thing*. For one, they both deal with homosexuality, a subject with which, over the intervening 31 years, Hollywood had become comfortable, although not exactly ecstatic. Perhaps more importantly, the years saw a schism between the general public's attitude toward gays and their rights under the law. The AIDS crisis brought this most sharply into focus, but for a while it seemed that the only way for filmmakers to make a movie about gay life was to make it about AIDS (*Longtime Companion*, 1989; *Philadelphia*, 1993). Eventually the subject of gay marriage was introduced (*The Kids Are All Right*, 2010). Somewhere in the middle falls *The Next Best Thing*.

Its story begins simply and ties itself in moral, legal, and emotional knots: a straight woman, Abbie (Madonna), and her gay best friend, Robert (Rupert Everett), get drunk, have sex, and have a child. They live together in Los Angeles and raise little Sam in a loving home, except they never get married. So when Abbie becomes engaged to Ben (Benjamin Bratt) and wants to move with Sam to New York, a custody battle ensues during which Robert, although he's the father, learns that he has no rights.

The Next Best Thing began as an original screenplay by Thomas Ropelewski titled *The Red Curtain*, which he intended to direct and which

---

493. Interview with the Author, December, 1984.

his wife, Leslie Dixon, would produce. Originally a United Artists project with Richard Dreyfuss attached, it was put into turnaround in February of 1995.[494] By October of 1996 Dixon had set it up at the independent Lakeshore Entertainment which had received $75 million financing from Banque Paribas to produce it and four other films. By February of 1997 Dreyfuss was no longer mentioned as star, but Helen Hunt was, at a $5 million salary. Hunt was replaced by Madonna in May, 1998, Rupert Everett was brought in, and Schlesinger joined the project a month later. Paramount Pictures stepped in as co-producer and distributor.

This became an unexpected obstacle, as Schlesinger quickly discovered. Although he had directed the blockbuster *Marathon Man* for Paramount in 1976, times and studio regimes had changed. "Now everything is subject to greater control," he told Manohla Dargis of *The New York Times* during production. "It's become irritating when you've got three producers with earphones looking at your every move on the set."[495]

Under this scrutiny, Schlesinger shot on locations throughout Los Angeles between April 23 and June 30, 1999. The crowded, classic communities of Silverlake and Los Feliz were used as well as the varied neighborhoods around the Mid-Wilshire district, Inglewood Cemetery, Venice Beach, the Cat & Fiddle Pub, and Los Angeles Airport to lend their flavor to the tale, which was pitched as "a *Kramer vs. Kramer* story," only gay. And that became a problem: specifically, nudity. In this case it was a momentary glimpse of Everett's rear end as he climbs out of the bed he shares with a male partner. Although Hollywood's closet had long been an open secret, Paramount kept watering down the gay elements in its story about a gay man. "It was much freer thirty years ago," noted the director of *Midnight Cowboy*. "There were many problems early on getting this off the ground. Disagreements about the script. It wasn't that the producers resisted, but they wanted it told sort of in a different way. [The Everett character] was always gay. Perhaps it was a question of how much to show of that. I think it's quite discrete but also quite clear."[496]

Seen with the perspective of time and the continuing battle over gay rights in America, *The Next Best Thing* settles in as a polemic whose heart is in the right place(s). And that's its problem. The film shows its battle scars. Its catalyst — that all you need to do to turn a gay man straight is get him drunk — perpetuates the "lifestyle choice" myth even though

---

494. In turnaround a company allows the producer to set up the project elsewhere upon repayment of its development costs to date.
495. March 5, 2000.
496. Victoria Price, *The Advocate,* March 28, 2000.

there are several contorted attempts in succeeding scenes to explain it.[497] But the real problem is Madonna. She is simply an unlikable screen presence so that, even though Abbie's actions are clearly motivated, having Madonna in the role is self-defeating. Indeed, on the film's release on March 3, 2000, she once again proved to be a box office Jonah and it was dismissed by audiences and critics alike, often with notices so nasty it seemed as if the reviewer had been personally assaulted. Some (such as the ever-observant Roger Ebert)[498] complained that the film's failing was that it tried to show all sides of a problem, some of which were extraneous to the plot. Not only were there no "bad guys," but even the antagonist, Bratt, was portrayed so understandably that you had to agree with him. In addition, the soundtrack was so laced with popular songs, including Madonna's cover of Don McLean's hackneyed "American Pie," that even the picture's marketing came under attack.

These were all smart people. What happened?

Leslie Dixon shed light in a letter she wrote to *The Los Angeles Times* in response to their critic Kenneth Turan's pan. "*The Next Best Thing* was a highly regarded script that several studios wanted to buy," she explained. "However, the version that John Schlesinger signed to direct was not the version that made it to the screen. Although uncredited, Rupert Everett was allowed to rewrite the screenplay, bragging loudly to any journalist that would listen that he had 'improved' it. I think the result speaks for itself."[499] Additionally, Ryan Murphy (*Glee*) claimed in an *Advocate* article (April 11, 2000) that *he* rewrote Ropelewski first and then Everett rewrote *him*.

Faced with poor reviews and poorer business, Paramount abandoned the picture in the marketplace. Schlesinger accepted its fate with pragmatism. "However much we may work on something, the distributors have decided their pattern of release and how much they're going to spend promoting something," he once said. "You know early on. It's one of the fights — there are many, but it's one of the chief fights — and it makes me very despondent at this stage of the game when you know that the distributors are not behind the film that you worked so lovingly and carefully on. We're all going to have flops. It's not comfortable, and we all want to be loved. I like stirring it up every now and again, [and] I'm

---

497. There was a similar film in 1978 called *A Different Story*, in which a gay man and woman get married for immigration purposes but then fall in love. It was a lovely picture even as it fed the "gays can go straight" lie.
498. Review, *Chicago Sun-Times*, March 3, 2000.
499. April 16, 2000.

sick and tired of just entertainment. You go out and have a good time and leave — that's all right — but I don't want to spend two years of my life doing it."[500]

Schlesinger never made another movie. The December after *The Next Best Thing* was released he suffered a debilitating stroke and retired to Palm Springs with his partner of 30 years, photographer Michael Childers. By the spring of 2003 his condition worsened and he descended into coma until July 24, 2003 when he was removed from life support and allowed to die the next day.

Schlesinger is something of an anomaly, not because he and many of his pictures were openly gay, but for his larger, related theme of people who struggle to survive within systems constructed to oppress them. Ratso (Dustin Hoffman) and Joe (Jon Voight) in *Midnight Cowboy* live on the outermost fringes of a society that doesn't even know they exist. Babe (Hoffman) in *Marathon Man* is damn near killed in the crossfire between a Nazi (Laurence Olivier) and Uncle Sam's turncoat (Roy Scheider). Diana Scott (Julie Christie) in *Darling* is trapped in the glamorous jet set. Tod Hackett (William Atherton) in *Day of the Locust* faces Hollywood apocalypse. Bathsheba Everdine (*Far from the Madding Crowd*) is a passionate woman in a passionless age. Daulton Lee (Sean Penn) and Christopher Boyce (Tim Hutton) become mired in a world of espionage they thought they could weather in *The Falcon and the Snowman*. Likewise, Schlesinger was the artist who struggled to keep his integrity within an art form that is also a business, and a business that resists being an art form.

500. Conversation with the Author.

Donald Siegel.

DONALD SIEGEL
Efficiency Expert

At a time when American directors were lapping up the critical adoration they were finally receiving in 1970s, Don Siegel was still largely in the shadows. Oh, the auterists noticed him, chiefly because of *The Big Steal* (1949), *Riot in Cell Block 11* (1954) and *Invasion of the Body Snatchers* (1956). But the general public never heard of him even as they flocked to see his movies. Perhaps it's because he was never terribly interested in giving interviews.[501] More likely it was the unpretentiousness of his movies. Indeed, one is hard pressed to think of a Siegel film that studies its own navel. Instead, they're marked by clear narratives, strong characters, and precise motives that collide with stunning insight, and, sometimes, violence. There are no wasted shots of flowers or sunsets. In other words, Siegel knew how to spice up meat and potatoes when they wouldn't give him a budget for dessert.

In fact, until about the last ten years of his career, Siegel seldom had enough money at his disposal, so he compensated with ingenuity. His storytelling is lean and dynamic, an economy learned during his servitude in the Warner Bros. montage department from 1939 to 1948. He often spoke of how he would shoot inserts of, say, Bette Davis walking into a house, on the pretext of saving time for the film's official director but, in reality, learning how to direct on the studio's dime.[502] Little good did it do him; Jack L. Warner knew the value of keeping where he was, and, when Siegel refused to sign a contract extension unless he could direct, Warner suspended him. When he was summoned back, the mogul punished him

---

501. For example, when I needed to talk to him about his 1974 film *The Black Windmill* , I phoned the studio expecting to be rebuffed or put on hold forever. Instead, Siegel picked up the phone himself and we had a lovely chat. I had the same experience with Robert Wise. This says a lot about both men's approach to their craft and their honor as people.
502. Peter Bogdanovich. *Who the Devil Made It*. New York: Alfred A. Knopf, 1997.

by making him direct short subjects. This was akin to B'rer Fox tossing B'rer Rabbit into the briar patch; Siegel made two shorts in 1945: *Star in the Night*, about the birth of Christ, and *Hitler Lives*, about the Nazis' continuing influence, both of which won Academy Awards®. Only when Peter Lorre and Sidney Greenstreet, whom Siegel had directed in second unit shots, pleaded his case to Warner was he was finally given a feature — with them in it. It turned out to be a complex murder mystery called *The Verdict* (1946) and it became a hit.

For the next 22 years Siegel's work was both eclectic and electric. From the horribly miscast *Night Unto Night* (1949) with Ronald Reagan, Broderick Crawford, and Viveca Lindfors (whom he married), he drifted into a western, *Duel at Silver Creek* (1952), and other programmers until producer Walter Wanger handed him for *Riot in Cell Block 11* (1954). Shot in Folsom Prison, the picture showed a warden who was not corrupt but swamped and, thanks to Richard Collins' complex, thoughtful script, was provocative without becoming preachy. It was *Invasion of the Body Snatchers* in 1956 that brought Siegel acclaim that several remakes (including a fine one by Phil Kaufman in 1978) have not obscured. Based on Jack Finney's serialized sf novel about humans taken over by emotionless alien pods, it was widely interpreted as being about repression under both Communism *and* McCarthyism. Allied Artists, who financed the $400,000 picture, feared it was the latter, and ordered a prologue and epilogue intended to mitigate the message. Despite this, *Invasion* stands as one of the most paranoid pictures ever made.

Unlike most of his peers, Siegel was unafraid to divert his talents to television. He directed pilots and episodics for *Man from Blackhawk, Alcoa Theatre, Bus Stop,* and *The Line-Up* (which, despite having the same title, had nothing to do with his 1958 feature). This made him attractive to Universal Pictures which, in 1964, was experimenting with feature films for television and engaged him to helm *The Killers*, a color remake of Robert Siodmak's 1946 drama about guilt coming home to roost. But when NBC, which had contracted in advance to show the production, got a look at how powerfully Siegel had done his job, they deemed it too violent to air and it went to theatres instead.[503] This made Siegel a hero at Universal, who gave him *Madigan* (1968), a particularly well executed

---

503. *The Killers* is also known as Ronald Reagan's last film before entering politics. Based on a Hemingway short story and scripted by Siegel (uncredited) and Gene L. Coon, it opens with a memorably brutal sequence, in which hit men Clu Gulager and Lee Marvin enter a school for the blind, terrorize the blind receptionist, and assassinate teacher John Cassavetes, who accepts death without resisting. This intrigues the hit men who are compelled to find out why.

policier that spun off into a TV series, and *Coogan's Bluff* (1968) that also became a series (*McCloud*). *Coogan* marked the first time Siegel worked with Clint Eastwood and the two would encore in *Two Mules for Sister Sarah* (1970) and *The Beguiled* (1971). In between there was *Death of a Gunfighter* (1969) which is noteworthy only because Siegel took over for Robert Totten during production and the studio recut it so heavily that both men demanded their names be removed, marking the first use of the DGA pseudonym "Alan Smithee."

But it was Siegel's 1971 return to Warners that made history, not just for him but for Eastwood. *Dirty Harry* had begun at Universal, but the studio dropped the project and it was picked up by Warners as a vehicle for Frank Sinatra. A hand injury gave Sinatra trouble holding Harry's trademark .44 magnum, so he left. Eastwood was not the studio's first choice — Warners wanted Steve McQueen or Paul Newman — but when Eastwood was cast he loyally asked that Siegel replace Irvin Kirchner as director. The script by R. M. Fink and Harry Julian Fink was rewritten by Dean Riesner, polished by Terrence Malick, and burnished by John Milius, who contributed the "I know what you're thinking" speech.[504] The film's $18 million in rentals on a $4 million outlay not only solidified Eastwood's stardom and triggered a franchise, it made Siegel attractive again to Universal where he was brought back, only to misfire in two highly competent but doomed thrillers: *Charley Varrick* (1973), whose star, Walter Matthau, was too laconic for the job, and *The Black Windmill* (1974), which was forced into production one rewrite too soon during a writers strike.[505] It still has some remarkable moments, such as a car chase in which Michael Caine nearly wipes out on a confined city street, and a perverse performance by John Vernon as the kidnapper of Caine's son.

The Shootist, which Siegel made with John Wayne in 1976, was an "end of an era" western about a dying gunfighter, John Books, who outlives the public's tolerance of his profession. It opens with an enormously inventive montage (Siegel's Warner Bros. training paying off) showing Books drawing his gun over the decades as he grows older in quick shots taken from Wayne's *Red River, Hondo, Rio Bravo, and El Dorado*. Though Wayne and Siegel didn't get along while making it, it stands out among the best work of each.

504. Recalled Milius, "Clint Eastwood said — and he's right — 'I'm good at grunting and squinting and shooting people, mostly squinting. I don't do words, I do squinting.'" (Interview with Author, *Backstory 4*, California: University of California Press, 2006.)
505. Conversation with the Author, May, 1974. It was invigorating that a director of Siegel's stature willingly acknowledged the importance of writing.

As time went on, Siegel never recaptured the success he enjoyed in the 1970s. Although he and Eastwood teamed for the sure-handed *Escape from Alcatraz* (1979), his nadir was *Rough Cut* (1980), in which he replaced Blake Edwards only to be himself replaced by Peter R. Hunt, then to be hired back a week later by mercurial producer David Merrick. Just when it seemed he could sink no lower, along came *Jinxed!* (1982).

The dust-up over *Jinxed!* has entered Hollywood lore. It began as a 1980 novel called *The Edge* by Frank D. Gilroy, the Pulitzer Prize-winning playwright of *The Subject Was Roses*. Gilroy intended to direct it himself, and under those conditions it was bought by the Ladd Company at Warner Bros.[506] Almost immediately, Ladd sold it to producer Herb Jaffe who took it to United Artists, got them to pay Ladd $300,000, hired David Newman (*Bonnie and Clyde*) to rewrite it, and called it *Jackpot*.[507] It was also announced that Don Siegel would direct and that Sam Peckinpah would handle second unit.[508]

Siegel's attachment was doubly unusual. As critic David Ehrenstein has noted, he was not a director known for comedy, nor had his films featured women, and *The Edge* / *Jackpot* demanded both.[509] It centers on Bonita Friml, a mediocre Nevada lounge singer who is browbeaten by her gambling common law husband, Harold Benson, into following him from casino to casino in search of a blackjack dealer named Willie Brodax who, it seems, is jinxed into eternally dealing Harold winning hands. In order to break the curse, Willie needs to possess something of Harold's, so he woos Bonita. The sudden attention emboldens Bonita to ask Willie to help her murder Harold, but, before they can, Harold commits suicide and now Willie and Bonita must make it look like he died accidentally in order to collect the insurance money. When the insurance scam fails, Bonita is on her own until Harold's hand rises from the grave to offer both her and Willie a solution.

If the devil is in the details, *Jinxed!* was hell. It started when UA production vice president Steven Bach suggested Bette Midler to play Bonita and sent her a list of possible directors. Midler responded that she wanted only Don Siegel. Siegel recalled that he was sent the script and he rejected it saying that it was a third version of *The Postman Always Rings Twice*, but he agreed to meet with Midler to discuss it. When he

---

506. *Hollywood Reporter*, October 28, 1980.
507. At various other times it was also called *It's All in the Game* and *Three of a Kind*.
508. *Los Angeles Times*, June 28, 1981.
509. *The Reader*, October 22, 1982.

did, he and Bette agreed on two things: the script stank, and Bette would not sing. Several rewrites later by Jerry Blatt (Midler's associate), Carol Rydall (Siegel's associate), Midler herself, and Siegel, it was called *Hot Streak*.[510] At this point Siegel committed.[511]

Then casting began for Midler's two male leads. Rip Torn agreed to play Harold, and Midler approved of Ken Wahl as her romantic co-star. She also okayed the renowned cinematographer Vilmos Zsigmond as director of photography. UA's Bach agreed to these as he would to every other request Midler would make throughout what became a combative production. Confirmed Siegel, "Bette was 100 percent responsible for hiring me, 100 percent responsible for hiring Ken Wahl, and 100 percent responsible for hiring Vilmos Zsigmond, and she hated all three of us. She hated the script, all the scripts, we rewrote. Both of us tried to get off the picture before it started but we had signed contracts. I was afraid they'd sue."[512]

With a budget of $13,400,000, *Jinxed!* rolled on May 5, 1981 in Lake Tahoe, the scenic mountain community that straddles Nevada and California.[513] Four weeks later the company moved to the MGM Grand Reno, then to Bodie in the High Sierras, returning in late June for interiors at MGM (UA, which was then owned by MGM, did not have studio facilities). There were two hot nights shot in Joshua Tree National Park as well as three extra days shooting musical numbers at La Marita Civic Auditorium on direct orders from UA production executive Anthea Sylbert who ordered songs added to the picture.[514] For the scene in which Willie, acting in cahoots with Bonita, fakes Harold's death by sending his house trailer over a cliff in a fireball, Sam Peckinpah was called in. Although Peckinpah had entered film history by directing *The Wild Bunch*, *Ride the High Country*, and other pictures, he had also done more than his share of liquor and drugs which, followed by heart surgery, rendered him unemployable. Hiring the clearly overqualified Peckinpah was a way for Siegel to give his former apprentice a way to re-enter the industry. The trailer went off without a hitch.[515]

Unfortunately, the film itself did not. Even while it was still in production, a fusillade of brickbats flew from everyone except Ms. Midler who,

---

510. Don Siegel. *A Siegel Film: An Autobiography*. London and New York: Faber & Faber, 1993.
511. Army Archerd, *Variety*, February 11, 1981.
512. Lee Grant, *Los Angeles Times*, September 27, 1981.
513. *Weekly Variety*, September 22, 1982.
514. *Weekly Variety*, September 22, 1982.
515. Lee Grant, *Los Angeles Times*, September 27, 1980.

both by herself and through her representatives, maintained a discrete silence. Siegel called it "the worst experience of my life" and said, "I had to shoot some scenes three different ways. It wasn't so much that Bette wanted changes. It was that she didn't know *what* she wanted." The feisty veteran also had no love for UA's Steven Bach, though he didn't call him out by name. Instead, he said, "The brass there was so in awe of her that they let her do anything she wanted. Every time there was an argument — and there must have been 479 thousand of them — they sided with Bette." But then he allowed, "they'll be surprised at how good she turns out in this. I know [that] I am."[516] Offered Wahl, "In one scene I have to hit her in the face, and I thought we could save some money on sound effects here."[517] And Siegel concluded, "I've directed some pretty tough customers — John Wayne, Clint Eastwood, and Ronald Reagan among them. But the toughest star I ever directed…was Bette Midler. I'd let my wife, children, and animals starve before I'd subject myself to working with her again."[518]

Jinxed! lived up to its name. It's a star vehicle too misshapen to bear its own weight. Bette Midler could no sooner play a mediocre entertainer than Joan Crawford or Bette Davis could play mousy women or, say, Clint Eastwood or John Wayne could be CPAs. It's hard to accept Bette Midler as a loser, even reflected off of Rip Torn's brilliantly unctuous Harold. In real life at the time, Midler had just jettisoned her manager, Aaron Russo, who had also been her abusive lover, a character not far from Harold, so perhaps her decision to make *Jinxed!* was wish-fulfillment. According to a crew member interviewed by Lee Grant but not named, Midler was "difficult, but only because she wants certain things from the project… she's not a malicious or evil person." But then the crew member added, "This is not a Don Siegel movie. This is a Bette Midler movie, including the camera angles and everything."[519] There were reports, not substantiated, that Siegel had a heart attack after finishing the film. He lived for nearly ten years afterward, appearing as an actor in John Landis' 1985 thriller *Into the Night*, and prepared his memoir, which was published posthumously in 1993. He died on April 20, 1991 at 78.

516. *Los Angeles Herald-Examiner*, October 17, 1982.
517. David Shipman. *Movie Talk*. New York: St. Martin's Press, 1988.
518. Boze Hadleigh. *Celebrity Diss and Tell*. New Jersey: Andrews McMeel Publishing, 2005. The Author would like to note that he has spoken extensively with two directors who worked with Midler during this same period and not only did they report no conflicts, but the work they all did together was outstanding.
519. Grant, op. cit.

Siegel remains one of cinema's most fascinating directors because he spoke almost entirely through his films, yet saved his personal shots for the end. Though many people deemed him politically conservative because of the crime stories in his filmography, he considered himself liberal.[520] What it means at the finish line is that he was a man who got the job done against greater odds and with less recognition than his talent warranted. The lesson of his dedication and efficiency were not lost on Clint Eastwood, who learned much from working with him, and whose artistry is built upon Siegel's considerable foundation. He dedicated his Oscar®-winning *Unforgiven* to him in 1992.

---

520. Conversation with the Author.

GEORGE STEVENS
Jeu la est terminée

The Only Game in Town got made for the noblest of reasons but they weren't enough to make it as good as its creators wanted. The story behind it probably explains the dynamics of Hollywood filmmaking better than if it had turned out to be a classic, and speaks to the respect that everyone all down the line had for its director, George Stevens, perhaps to the point of clouding their judgment on the film he asked them to make.

A past master at every genre, and even having had a hand inventing one of them — Laurel and Hardy comedies — Stevens displayed immense craftsmanship, increasingly at the expense of spontaneity. Nothing seemed accidental in his movies, from the perfection of Astaire and Rogers in *Swing Time* (1936), the chemistry between Tracy and Hepburn in their first film together, *Woman of the Year* (1942), the iconic western *Shane* (1953), the tortured romance *A Place in the Sun* (1951), or, to a lesser extent, the rousing action-adventure *Gunga Din* (1939).

Stevens was sixteen when he began his film career as an assistant cameraman in 1921 and two years later joined Hal Roach to shoot short silent comedies, most of them starring Stan Laurel and Oliver Hardy. It had been Roach's idea (though Leo McCarey says it was his) to pair the physically dissimilar comedians, but it was Stevens — working under the varied direction of McCarey, James Parrott, Clyde Bruckman, Fred Guiol, and Lewis R. Foster — who brought a consistent look to The Boys' pictures. Not incidentally, it taught him the tricks of staging and capturing comedy. By the time he got to direct *Ladies Last* (1930), an entry in Roach's *The Boy Friends* series of domestic two-reelers, he thought he had a firm grasp of what works on screen.[521] But he was wrong, and in

---

521. *The Boy Friends* was described as a grown-up version of Roach's *Our Gang*.

correcting it he learned the secret of movies, which is not the individual shot but the succession of them. "I saw, when it was put together," he recalled, "that I had to save my professional life. The film couldn't be shown; it was impossible. I went in the cutting room and worked with it enough so that it could barely be accepted."[522]

He learned fast and, in 1932, moved to Universal, which was still struggling to survive despite the returns from its successful horror films. There he made his first feature, the sequel *The Cohens and the Kelley in Trouble*. It did not turn out to be the opportunity he sought, and not until he joined RKO in 1935 would he make a lasting break from short subjects. His RKO films were skillful and had a light touch, and when he started working with "A" level stars like Katharine Hepburn, Barbara Stanwyck, Ginger Rogers, and Fred Astaire he found that his craftsmanship gave them the assurance that they needed in order to excel. When he moved to Columbia Pictures he became his own producer, giving studio chief Harry Cohn fits over the excessive amount of footage he shot. They were mollified, however, by the Oscar® nominations the resulting films received, rivaling those of Columbia's other resident hit-maker, Frank Capra. For Cohn, Stevens made the outstanding pictures *Penny Serenade* (1941), *Talk of the Town* (1942), and *The More the Merrier* (1943). He also visited MGM to direct *Woman of the Year* as a favor to Katharine Hepburn, who had nurtured the script by fledgling writers Michael Kanin and Ring Lardner, Jr.[523]

Woman of the Year was a straightforward romantic comedy about an over-achieving female journalist, Tess Harding (Hepburn), whose marriage to blue collar sports writer Sam Craig (Spencer Tracy) is threatened by her stature. After screening the first cut, Stevens and producer Joseph L. Mankiewicz wondered whether Tess' superiority to Sam might offend the women in the audience who would invariably be watching it sitting next to their husbands. So Stevens and Mankiewicz, working with screenwriter John Lee Mahin, devised a scene at the end pitting Hepburn against her kitchen appliances, in which she tries and fails to cook a simple breakfast for Tracy.[524] The scene does the job of taking Tess down a few notches, but it is out of keeping with the tone of the rest of the film, not to mention Hepburn's character, even though Stevens staged it effectively. No matter; Stevens' handling won Kanin and Lardner an Oscar.®

522. Eric Sherman. *Directing the Film: Film Directors on Their Art*. Boston, Massachusetts: Little, Brown, 1976.
523. Lardner had actually been working in Hollywood for a decade and was responsible for, among other things, famous curtain line to the 1937 *A Star is Born*.
524. Kenneth L. Geist. *Pictures Will Talk*. New York: Charles Scribner, 1978.

If *Woman of the Year* marked Stevens' artistic transition, World War II caused his emotional one. As part of the government's motion picture unit, he directed the documentaries of German atrocities that were used in the Allies' prosecution of Nazi war criminals at the postwar Nuremberg trials. He returned to Hollywood changed. From this point he concentrated on films with "meaningful" subjects, and fewer of them, among them *A Place in the Sun* (1951), *Giant* (1956), and *The Diary of Anne Frank* (1959). By the time of *The Greatest Story Ever Told* (1965), which took him five years to prepare and felt that long to watch, he had lost his sense of humor, at least on screen.

The Only Game in Town (1970) began as a 1968 play by Pulitzer Prize-winning playwright Frank D. Gilroy. A lean three-hander about a Las Vegas chorus girl who takes up with a gambling musician when her long-time affair with a married man isn't working out, it is a chamber piece about two lonely people who cannot admit their loneliness. The characters reveal themselves through dialogue and behavior. Joe Grady is a glib piano player who works in a restaurant lounge and has been saving $5,000 so he can move to New York where he hopes to not only take off as a musician but escape the casinos that tempt his gambling addiction. Fran Walker is the chorus girl who lives on her own in a garden apartment where she waits for Thomas Lockwood, a businessman who would divorce his wife to be with her except "there are complications." Joe wins a fortune, loses it, and wins another one; likewise Fran wins Joe, loses him, and wins him back. It is a story told in nuance, decidedly unglamorous, and ultimately lightweight. But because Gilroy had what in Hollywood was known as "heat," he sent *Game* around in synopsis to the studios in late 1967 to close a film deal before starting its Broadway run.

On November 22, Richard D. Zanuck of Twentieth Century-Fox announced that his company won the bidding for $550,000 (Gilroy had asked for $700,000)[525] to be paid to the play's producing company and $150,000 to Gilroy himself to write the screenplay. They would also be on the line for an additional $3,500 for each profitable week of the play's Broadway run to a ceiling of $850,000 plus ten percent of the gross once the studio recouped its costs.[526] The overages became moot, however, when the play, starring Barry Nelson (who also directed), Tammy Grimes, and Leo Genn, closed after sixteen performances.

---

525. *Weekly Variety*, December 13, 1967.
526. *Hollywood Reporter*, November 29, 1967.

Zanuck handed the project to producer Fred Kohlmar and together they lured Elizabeth Taylor and Frank Sinatra to co-star.[527] Taylor, who had become a million-dollar star as *Cleopatra* (1963) and won her second Oscar® for *Who's Afraid of Virginia Woolf?* (1966), had been wandering through several pictures that were distinguished chiefly by her presence (*Boom!*, *Secret Ceremony*, *The Sandpiper*, *Reflections in a Golden Eye*, etc.) and had become more famous for appearing on supermarket tabloids than movie screens. *The Only Game in Town* had the potential to restore her acting credibility. When George Stevens agreed to direct, it conjured hope of repeating the luminous performance she had given him in *A Place in the Sun*.[528]

Stevens, then 66, hadn't made a film since the expensive flop *The Greatest Story Ever Told* three years earlier. It took him four months, working with Kohlmar and Gilroy, to rework the play into a script that was a movie. "Although I concede a certain lack of enthusiasm for the Broadway production," he said for the benefit of studio publicity notes, "I think the screenplay is much better with many of the kinks ironed out and the problems solved."[529] Stevens and Gilroy produced a detailed script with Stevens noting, for personal reference, each character's mood, motivation, and physical business at every important dialogue beat.[530] Filming was set for August, 1968 and immediately postponed for a month because Taylor needed an operation. Sinatra, however, was unable to shift his schedule — he had a locked-in opening at Caesar's Palace — so he dropped out. Kohlmar momentarily considered Rex Harrison.[531] This was just Hollywood hype, for Harrison was going to be appearing with Richard Burton in the Fox film *Staircase* that would be shooting at the same time in Paris. And because Burton would be in Paris, Taylor demanded that *The Only Game in Town* be shot there, too. A new start date of September 23 was announced and Stevens' creative team began building the City of Neon in the City of Lights where they would shoot by "French hours" of noon till 7 PM.[532]

Needing a male star who could match Taylor's stature, Stevens phoned Warren Beatty, who was in Chicago at the Democratic National Convention where the politically savvy actor was working behind the

527. *Hollywood Reporter*, April 16, 1968.
528. *Daily Variety*, April 23, 1968.
529. Twentieth Century-Fox presskit.
530. Stevens-Gilroy script conferences, particularly August 5, 1968. George Stevens papers, AMPAS.
531. *Hollywood Reporter*, May 16, 1968.
532. *Daily Variety*, July 4, 1968.

scenes to unify a shattered Democratic party. Beatty had become an even stronger power in Hollywood following the smash success of *Bonnie and Clyde* in 1967. When Stevens' call came, Beatty was fielding an offer to do *Butch Cassidy and the Sundance Kid*, which he turned down in order to work with the legendary director of *Giant* and *Shane*.

Production finally began on September 30, 1968 in Paris for 86 days. Production designer Herman Blumenthal and set dresser Jerry Wunderlich built Taylor's two-room apartment on a Boulogne studio sound stage. To make Paris look like Las Vegas they constructed a 160-foot animated cyclorama that would be seen through her windows, including a scaled-down construction site that would progress toward completion throughout the story's nine-month time span. Seventy-five percent of the movie would be shot on this set with additional scenes at Tony's Bar (built on Stage H), the Golden Nugget, and the Nevadan. Tensions arose — according to publicity, at least — when Taylor and Beatty filmed their love scenes. Burton was present on the set and reportedly objected to Beatty's ardor toward his wife.

Once the Parisian Las Vegas scenes were finished (and Burton had wrapped *Staircase*), the company laid off for three weeks, then moved to the real Las Vegas for ten days of night work starting January 6, 1969.[533] While Taylor was on set she had the use of the elaborate dressing room trailer that Fox had given Barbra Streisand during *Hello, Dolly!* (redecorated in Taylor's preferred "super-mod" style) while she, Burton, and their entourage occupied a four-bedroom suite atop Caesar's Palace. While she shot, he wrote his memoirs.

Strangely for such a small story, the picture took almost a year to edit and was released on January 21, 1970. The date is revealing: January is the traditional dumping month for pictures that a distributor thinks will die commercially, and die it did. Despite its star power, *The Only Game in Town* grossed only $1.5 million on an $11 million budget. The reasons can be found in the film itself: Beatty and Taylor have no chemistry. Beatty was thirty-three at the time, Taylor thirty-eight. The slight age difference isn't germane to the story — stars are ageless, aren't they? — but what truly separates them is the contrast in their acting styles. Taylor's movie artifice collides with Beatty's Method introspection; it's the same obstacle that Stevens ignored to the detriment of *Giant* where James Dean's stark realism was out of place against Taylor's and Rock Hudson's presentational performances.

---

533. September 5, 1968 schedule, George Stevens papers, AMPAS.

But even more destructive was the convention of star casting. A star brings an existing character with him or her, and *The Only Game in Town* spends its first half hour deconstructing Taylor's and Beatty's powerful screen presences. It's the same conundrum that killed *Frankie and Johnny* (1991), the screen version of off-Broadway's 1987 *Frankie and Johnny in the Clair de Lune* by putting Michelle Pfeiffer and Al Pacino into the Kathy Bates and Kenneth Welsh stage roles. In both cases the movies got made because of stars, but it was at the expense of the truth of the material.

An additional problem, and one that Mia Fonssagrives' and Vicki Tiel's costumes cannot disguise, is Taylor's chunky figure. It's hard to accept her as a chorus girl. Stevens shoots around this by showing an opening dance number in a casino in extreme long shot, cutting to an extreme close-up revealing Taylor bouncing up and down as one of the chorines, then cutting back to long shot where she is not recognizable. Beatty also has baggage. He has a fondness for playing characters who either die or are consumed by ennui. Here he is a loser who uses glibness to cover his insecurities and self-loathing, two traits that are at odds with the gifts that make him a star.

Despite trying to parallel park the movie equivalent of a battleship, Stevens brings consummate craft to the job. Famous for covering a scene from every angle, sometimes to the frustration of actors who loathe repetition, the variety of setups afforded him and editor John W. Holmes the ability to keep an otherwise static scene alive by constantly changing perspective. (Perhaps this accounts for the long post-production).

The Only Game in Town is a film that would be a credit to the resume of anyone who was just starting out in the business. Warren Beatty dismissed it as a "9,000-ton soufflé." Yet it was his regard for Stevens that made it possible.[534] That it became the last entry on the filmography of one Hollywood's greatest filmmakers shows what happens when the machinery consumes the artist.

George Stevens died March 8, 1975 following a heart attack.

---

534. Suzanne Finstad. *Warren Beatty: A Private Man*. New York: Harmony Books, 2005.

PRESTON STURGES
Genius-of-All-Trades

Whenever Hollywood lists its burnouts, Preston Sturges is usually Number One. They don't even blame Hollywood, they just cluck their tongues and lament that the man who wrote, directed, and sometimes produced seven extraordinary pictures between 1940 and 1944 — *The Great McGinty, Christmas in July, The Lady Eve, Sullivan's Travels, The Palm Beach Story, The Miracle of Morgan's Creek,* and *Hail the Conquering Hero* — couldn't go for eight, and they point to *The Great Moment* (1944) as proof. But *The Great Moment* — about W. T. G. Morton, the altruistic dentist who discovered ether as anesthesia — was shot in 1942 and held back two years after being changed by a studio that was afraid audiences wouldn't accept its daring blend of comedy and drama.

But there's an untold Sturges, too, because, as screenwriter Earl Felton noted, "He was too large for this smelly resort, and the big studios were scared to death of him. A man who was a triple threat (writing, directing, and producing!) kept them awake nights, and I'm positive they were all waiting for him to fall on his face so they could pounce on him and devour this terrible threat to their stingy talents…In this, alas, I was right. They pounced, and they got him good. But Preston knew the great days, when he was turning out marvelous pictures…those days when his can glowed like a port light from everyone kissing it!"[535]

Plainly stated, Preston Sturges enjoyed being Preston Sturges, and it annoyed a lot of people. Envy is not a disease confined to Hollywood, but in a town where the bar for talent is set high just for starters, someone who can hurdle it with apparent ease — and, worse, who knows he can — risks outright hatred. Sturges did not disappoint. He was erudite, having been

---

535. Quoted by James Curtis, letter, *The Los Angeles Times*, August 8, 2009.

raised, more or less, by his mother, Mary D'Este (*nee*: Dempsey), in the salons of Europe; he was an inventor (kiss-proof lipstick) that gave him an independent income; he spoke French when most of the men who ran the studios barely spoke English; he was prolific; and he had talent. What's so striking about Sturges' films is how he constructed a screen world, not of fantasy, but of a heightened reality, in which people spoke their minds and it resonated with audiences. It was both wise and giddy, both cynical and optimistic.[536]

He populated his screen world with a celebrated stock company of character actors and actresses that rivaled the denizens of Damon Runyon's fabled New York, and they looked like William Demarest, Franklin Pangborn, Robert Grieg, Allyn Joslyn, Thurston Hall, Akim Tamiroff, Alan Bridge, Jimmy Conlin, Robert Dudley, Porter Hall, Ernest Truex, Harry Rosenthal, Eugene Pallette, Elizabeth Patterson, Eric Blore, and Torben Meyer, among memorable others. They were the ones to whom Sturges gave many of his punch lines that not only took the puff out of his stars, they spoke the wisdom of the ages.

Examples: the notion of making a movie about poverty in *Sullivan's Travels:* "The poor know all about poverty and only the morbid rich would find the topic glamorous." Or in *Hail the Conquering Hero*: "Well, that's the war for you. It's always hard on women. Either they take your men away and never send them back at all, or they send them back unexpectedly just to embarrass you." Or in *The Miracle of Morgan's Creek*: "I don't deal with spooks. She doesn't need a lawyer, she needs a Medium." Or in *The Palm Beach Story*: "Cold are the hands of time that creep along relentlessly destroying slowly but without pity that which yesterday was young. Alone our memories resist this disintegration and grow more lovely with the passing years. That's hard to say with false teeth." What do these lines have in common? They are all spoken by supporting players, not the leads. Were a filmmaker dare to write them today, the stars would insist that they get all the funny lines.

Some critics have faulted Sturges' films for lacking depth, yet examination shows an economy of narrative that looks superficial but really isn't. He skillfully drew his characters with minimal exposition, relying on the actor to define the role. Then he kept his cockeyed caravan rolling

---

536. This may not be germane, but it is notable: in the early talkies when many writers and comic actors were Jewish, the Gentile Sturges had the humor of a patrician. His heroes seldom had oppressors against whom they rebelled; their fates were of their own making. Thus when Jerry Lewis and Frank Tashlin remade Sturges' *The Miracle of Morgan's Creek* into *Rock-a-Bye Baby*, in which Lewis played a relatively empowered character, it was among the least "ethnic" of Lewis' roles.

by plunging his leads into inextricable jams and springing them free in believable ways, relying on his secondary characters to focus the audience's point of view. He would play jokes, too, such as starting *The Palm Beach Story* with a montage of slapstick scenes that have nothing to do with what follows until the last 30 seconds. Or stopping the story entirely, such as Eddie Bracken's stirring barroom monologue about patriotism in *Hail the Conquering Hero*. He would let his shots run long, as he did when Bracken and Betty Hutton reminisce on a walk through town in *The Miracle of Morgan's Creek*. And he even referenced one film (*McGinty*) within another (*Morgan's Creek*) just for fun.

Where did it come from? And why hasn't anybody done it since?

Sturges fell into movies after wasting most of his life. Born in 1898 to an ambitious mother and a disinterested father, he was educated at boarding schools.[537] After service in World War I and several marriages, he drifted to New York where he achieved some success as a playwright, the greatest of which was 1929's *Strictly Dishonorable*.[538] The comedy about a speakeasy ran 557 performances and brought him to Hollywood with the general migration of Eastern literati when talkies came in. He was just one more writer making credited and uncredited contributions to such films in the early 1930s as *The Invisible Man*, *Twentieth Century*, *Imitation of Life*, *Next Time We Love*, and a few independents. He received sole screen credit for 1933's *The Power and the Glory* at Fox before digging in at Paramount.[539] There he established his reputation by writing *Easy Living* but, upset with how his script was toned down by director Mitchell Leisen, he began lobbying to direct his own material. This was simply not done in the compartmentalized studio system, but he offered Paramount's production chief William LeBaron a tempting deal: he would sell him his script *Down Goes McGinty* for $1 if he could direct it. The studio agreed.

With its title changed to *The Great McGinty* (1940), Sturges became the first writer-director at a major studio in the modern era. Its wry tale of a homeless man (Brian Donlevy) who is manipulated into elected office by a political boss (Akim Tamiroff) and then finds a way to outsmart his benefactor was not only a clever satire on machine politics, its success

537. It gets even more complicated, according to Sturges' biographer, James Curtis: Mary didn't even know she was pregnant until she went into labor; she thought she had a tumor and had decided to ignore it (James Curtis. *Between Flops*. New York: Harcourt, Brace, Jovanovich, 1982).
538. Sturges also wrote *The Guinea Pig*, *Recapture*, *The Well of Romance*, and *The Child of Manhattan*, all of which were produced on Broadway between 1928 and 1931.
539. An examination of the life of a railroad magnate told in multiple flashbacks by the people who loved and hated him, *The Power and the Glory* failed commercially but drew attention for Sturges. Scholars credit its structure with inspiring that of *Citizen Kane*.

empowered others such as Billy Wilder, John Huston, and Leo McCarey to join the ranks of Hollywood hyphenates.

Andrew Sarris has contended that comedy directors "decline" (his term) faster and more often than other directors. Why so with Sturges? Was he written out? Did audiences change? The fact that Sturges films continue to entertain suggests that humor is ongoing, if cyclical. It might also be said that Sturges benefited not only from his talent but from the people who were available to articulate it. It wasn't just the leads like Joel McCrea, Betty Hutton, Eddie Bracken, Ellen Drew, Veronica Lake, Henry Fonda, Claudette Colbert, etc. who made his films work, it was the colorful repertoire (see above) that studio factories kept on hand to fill character roles. This was what Sturges lost when he parted with Paramount in 1944 after the failure of *The Great Moment*, which had been shot in 1942 but not released until 1944 after he made *Hail the Conquering Hero*, which was a hit, but did not provide momentum to assure *The Great Moment*.

But before that happened he was one of Hollywood's highest-paid writers, wresting a profit percentage from his studio on top of salary. Never thinking it would ever stop, he sunk it into a yacht, an experimental lab, and a restaurant/theatre club called The Players above Sunset Boulevard where he played host, impresario, ringmaster, and *padrone*.

It couldn't last, and it didn't. In 1947 he became involved with semi-retired comedian Harold Lloyd and dilettante producer Howard Hughes in *The Sin of Harold Diddlebock*. A retread of Lloyd's 1923 building-scaling classic *Safety Last* and a continuation of his 1925 hit *The Freshman*, it was an uneasy collaboration whose failure drove him back into the studio system. Hoping that Sturges still had the touch, Darryl Zanuck at Twentieth Century-Fox backed two class-A productions: *Unfaithfully Yours* (1948), a labored comedy about a jealous symphony conductor (Rex Harrison) who fantasizes murdering his wife (Linda Darnell); and *The Beautiful Blonde From Bashful Bend* (1949), a western in which Betty Grable has the same sort of adulterous fantasies about her boyfriend (Caesar Romero). Forced to act instead of just showing her legs, Grable rebelled, and the studio took her side. After that, Sturges had to admit, "in twenty-two years I managed to alienate every one of the seven major studios and soon found myself out of work."[540]

In the summer of 1953, Sturges was writing the screenplay of Shaw's *The Millionairess* for Katharine Hepburn, who'd had a recent success with

---

540. James Curtis, op. cit.

it on the stage. He divided his time between her home in Turtle Bay and chasing the film's putative producer, Lester Cowan, for his weekly $1,000 paycheck. They made it to England when the project finally fell through, so he decided to take his wife, Sandy, and their newborn son, Preston, Jr., across the Channel to France to show them where he had been raised. While there he was contracted by Gaumont to adapt Pierre Daninos' popular *Le Figaro* column *Les Carnets du Major Thompson (The Diaries of Major Thompson)* into a screenplay. The popular column, in which a fictitious English Major Marmaduke Thompson voiced his observations about the French people, was originally to have been scripted by Daninos. When he failed to deliver, producer Alain Poire asked Sturges to take over, giving him permission to invent his own script.

Les Carnets du Major Thompson, known in America by the few who saw it (and many more who did not) as *The French They Are a Funny Race*, is actually three different films, two of which were shot. Sturges' concept, which he wrote in French and titled *Forty Million Frenchmen*, followed the misadventures of a French author who invents an English character who assumes a borrowed identity. Everyone seemed to be pleased with the script, but then Daninos published his columns in a book (*The Notebooks of Major Thompson*) to such acclaim that Gaumont changed its mind and demanded that Sturges write a new script that slavishly followed the best-seller. That one — about an English Major and his French wife — was called *Les Carnets du Major Thompson* in French and *The French They Are a Funny Race* in English. Sturges directed two different versions, one in French and one in English.[541] Casting was a bilingual nightmare. Martine Carol was France's most popular actress who, despite Gaumont's firm assurance that she could speak understandable English, could not. England's suave Jack Buchanan had the same problem *avec Français*. Filming their scenes together as husband and wife became its own comedy when neither could understand the other well enough to pick up cues. Needing money badly and aware that this was his last chance to resurrect his professional reputation in America, Sturges finished the film using two crews shooting at the same time and adapting his script to meet the shortfalls of the strapped studio facilities. The final budget was $540,000.

In his superb Sturges biography *Between Flops*, James Curtis reports that Sturges was uncomfortable with the film's French premiere, which was held without benefit of a test preview to adjust the film to an audience's

---

541. Curtis, ibid. Curtis has done a remarkable job of untangling these events only summarized here,

reaction. Although it grossed well on its home *territoire*, he had misgivings about its U.S. release, advising Walter Reade, whose Continental Distributing had bought the rights,[542] that not only did American audiences not know its stars, but that "everybody thinks I'm dead. I'm not kidding! They teach my scripts in the public schools, and some kid who had been studying me nearly fainted when he was introduced to me one day. He thought he was talking to a ghost!"[543]

By whatever title, *The French, They Are a Funny Race* did not do anyone any good. It opened at Reade's Baronet Theatre in New York on May 20, 1957 to generally unfavorable reviews. Perhaps the most stinging appraisal was rendered by the *Village Voice*'s Andrew Sarris in a retrospective piece in which he slapped Sturges as one of those artists "who are a little too smart for Hollywood, but not quite smart enough for anywhere else."[544]

Sturges had not made a film in six years and, though several projects hovered, none landed in his director's chair.[545] He died of a heart attack in New York City on August 6, 1959 at the age of sixty. At the time, he was working on his memoirs, which he titled *The Events Leading Up to My Death*. They were finished by his widow, Sandy Nagle Sturges, and published as *Preston Sturges by Preston Sturges* in 1990.

---

542. *Hollywood Reporter*, November 26, 1956.
543. Quoted in Curtis, op. cit.
544. Andrew Sarris, *The Village Voice*, September 10, 1979.
545. He had directed part of Howard Hughes' troubled 1946 production *Vendetta*, which was finally finished in 1950 and credited to Mel Ferrer, but his previous completed credit was 1949's *The Beautiful Blonde From Bashful Bend*, supposedly the only Betty Grable picture that lost money.

FRANK TASHLIN
Drawing to a Conclusion

When today's Hollywood blockbusters are slammed for being cartoons — not just because they're based on comic books or kiddie shows but because action trumps characterization and, sometimes, even coherence — it's ironic that one of the most talented directors of the 50s and 60s was praised for bringing a cartoon sensibility to live action movies. Frank Tashlin drew and directed cartoons for Warner Bros. and other studios during the heyday of the theatrical short in the 1930s and 40s. Although he's not as well known today as his peers Chuck Jones, Bob Clampett, Friz Freling, or Tex Avery, that's because he left the drawing board for the soundstage before scholars started noticing. But others did, most famously Jerry Lewis, who credits Tashlin — they worked together on eight pictures[546] — with teaching him the discipline of comic filmmaking. It was Tashlin who introduced asides and "in" jokes in his cartoons, a gimmick that Bob Hope would use his whole career. He would — and you really have to listen for it — sweeten sight gags with cartoony sound effects. It was Tashlin who made the screen safe for satire (*The Girl Can't Help It* and *Will Success Spoil Rock Hunter?*) when the prevailing wisdom was that satire was what closes on Saturday night.[547] And it was Tashlin who was consumed by his own creative fire.

"He seemed to burn out a lot quicker than a lot of directors did," said Joe Dante, whose *Gremlins* and general screen sensibility owe much to Tashlin. "He almost had a [Preston] Sturges-like career in that his later

---

546. Save yourself noodling *IMDb.com*: *Artists and Models* (1955), *Hollywood or Bust* (1956), *Rock-a-Bye Baby* (1958), *The Geisha Boy* (1958), *Cinderfella* (1960), *It's Only Money* (1962), *Who's Minding the Store* (1963), and *The Disorderly Orderly* (1964).
547. The bitter definition came from playwright/director George S. Kaufman who noted that most satirical plays flopped and folded after the Saturday night performance.

pictures — when you get to *The Private Navy of Sgt. O'Farrell* — it's pretty grim."[548]

Was "Tash" a victim of his own success or was he, like many early filmmakers, unable to compete with his own innovations once others adopted them? His gift, as animation historian Leonard Maltin has pointed out, was his interest in the cartoon as *film*: "He toyed with the possibilities of camera angles, cutting, montage, and other cinematic devices at a time when some of his colleagues were still taking a more prosaic approach to their work."[549]

Until he brought this perspective to Warner Bros. in the 1930s, cartoons had been at eye-level or slightly above; the gags merely happened. Tashlin — and later others, notably Avery — developed the technique of breaking gags into components to manipulate screen time and screen space. When he moved to live action, he brought that absurdity with him: by having Jerry Lewis impersonate TV commercials in *Rock-a-Bye Baby*; having Bob Hope and Trigger share a bed in *Son of Paleface*; and having Harpo Marx literally hold up a building in *A Night in Casablanca* (a gag that Tashlin contributed). In so doing, he lifted real people out of the realm of reality. None of this is high comedy, of course, but compared to the river of bodily functions that passes for comedy in the 2000s, Tashlin's guilelessness verges on nostalgia.

Francis Frederick von Tashlein (German father, French mother) was born in New Jersey in 1913 and raised on Long Island. He answered a "Can You Draw Me?" newspaper ad for a correspondence course while at P.S. 5 and, by the age of seventeen, with school behind him, was an animator at the Fleischer studios in New York. When his father died, Frank persuaded his widowed mother to move to Hollywood so he could follow his dream.[550] She did, and by 1933 he had taken up residence in Termite Terrace, the legendary shack where Leon Schlesinger was producing cartoons for Warner Bros. It was not a happy tenure; Tashlin left when Schlesinger found out he was moonlighting on a comic strip (called "Van Boring") and demanded a cut. That was all, folks.

It was at Paramount that Tashlin began submitting gags and writing scripts for Bob Hope (*Monsieur Beaucare* and *Paleface*) as well as freelancing for Lucille Ball, Eddie Bracken, Harpo Marx, Red Skelton, and Betty Hutton, and penned an unusual baseball satire for William

---

548. Quoted by Bill Krohn in *The Outsider: Frank Tashlin*. London: BFI, 1994.
549. Leonard Maltin. *Of Mice and Magic: The History of American Animated Cartoons*. New York: McGraw-Hill, 1980.
550. Bill Krohn, *Los Angeles Times*, January 18, 1995.

Bendix, *Kill the Umpire*. His material impressed Hope so much that the star asked Tashlin to direct retakes for *The Lemon Drop Kid* in 1951 and, when that became a hit, put him in full charge of *Son of Paleface* the next year. Paramount stars Dean Martin and Jerry Lewis, in the Hal Wallis unit, also benefited from Tashlin's talent, first with *Artists and Models* and more notably with *Hollywood and Bust* in 1956, the team's last film.[551]

In addition to his Martin and Lewis period, Tashlin's most notorious successes were *The Girl Can't Help It* and *Will Success Spoil Rock Hunter?*, both made for Twentieth Century-Fox and starring Jayne Mansfield. They're quite a pair (referring to the movies). The first is a send-up of the Mob's influence on rock and roll — you have to wonder how much was send-up and how much was exposé — as gangster Edmund O'Brien hires PR expert Tom Ewell to make a singing star out of his talentless moll, Mansfield. Tashlin had wanted Mansfield for *The Girl Can't Help It* after seeing her on stage in George Axelrod's *Will Success Spoil Rock Hunter?*, and the only way he got her for *Girl* was to buy *Hunter*. When he found a way to bend *Hunter* to his own taste, which turned out to be solid box office, the pair (still referring to the movies) were off and running. It might be said that the cantilevered Mansfield was her own satire, and in *Hunter* — in which advertising exec Tony Randall hires her to be the spokesvixen for his lipstick campaign — the irony is compounded when Mansfield insists that Randall also become her lover. By empowering a woman in a film about exploiting women, Axelrod and Tashlin pushed 1950s cinema to its limits. And they got away with it because it was "only" a comedy.

Bob Hope was an established Broadway and radio star when he came to Paramount in 1937 to make *The Big Broadcast of 1938*, the picture that introduced what became his theme song, "Thanks for the Memories." After that, whether solo or teamed with Bing Crosby (starting with 1940's *The Road to Singapore*), he swiftly established himself as not only a star but an American institution. He was also a brilliant businessman; in addition to buying vast amounts of San Fernando Valley real estate, he wisely limited his television exposure to hosting and guest appearances. In World War II he began the tradition of traveling with USO shows for which he came both beloved and rich.[552] By the time he enlisted his old friend

---

551. "They didn't speak to each other during the whole picture," Tashlin told Peter Bogdanovich. "It was a bitch." (*Who the Devil Made It*, op. cit.)
552. NBC had a long-term deal with Hope Enterprises which allowed Hope to retain ownership of the footage he shot. Much of it later appeared in Robert Mugge's 1994 documentary, *Entertaining the Troops*.

Frank Tashlin to direct him in the wartime service comedy *The Private Navy of Sgt. O'Farrell* (1968), Hope was more or less just going through the motions. Both he and Tashlin had made roughly a film a year away from each other since *Son of Paleface* in 1952, but even a cursory look at what each man was doing shows that Hope's movies were indifferent where Tashlin's continued to be inventive.

John Beck, who had produced *Kill the Umpire*, purchased the original John L. Greene/Robert L. Fresco story in late 1965 and began setting up the project at MGM. When he attached Bob Hope in March of that year, MGM withdrew and *O'Farrell* sailed over to United Artists where Hope Enterprises and NBC had a joint venture output deal. Tashlin became involved in January of 1967 as writer and director.[553]

The Private Navy of Sgt. O'Farrell is a shotgun marriage of *Mister Roberts* and *Whiskey Galore* set on an isolated Pacific Island called Funapee during an unspecified moment of World War II. Lacking women, the only thing that keeps the occupying American troops from requesting a transfer (Huh? They can transfer in wartime?) is beer. So when a shipment of brewskies is sunk by a Jap [sic] sub, there goes morale. By luck Sgt. O'Farrell (Hope) finds some of the cans that have washed ashore and, connecting with an American-born Japanese soldier (Mako) hiding on the island and with the collaboration of Lt. (j.g.) Lyman Jones (Jeffrey Hunter), a scheme emerges to find the rest of the beer. This is complicated by the suspicions of Navy Lt. Com. Snaveley (John Myhers) and the arrival of nurse Krauss (Phyllis Diller). There are also two shipwrecked anthropologists played by Mylene Demongeot and Miss Gina Lolobrigida (the *Miss* in the screen credits was contractual). Dick Sargent is the C.O. who just wants to write his novel.

Although there wasn't really a large enough role for Phyllis Diller, who had starred with Hope in 1966's *Boy Did I Get a Wrong Number!*, the role of the harridan nurse Krause was given to her. Diller, like so many up-and-coming comics, had earned a guest shot in movies to capitalize on her popularity as a TV variety show performer.[554] A genuinely sweet woman with talent in music and painting as well as comedy, Diller purposely trashed her looks in order to create a comic persona.[555]

There is nothing particular to recommend the results. Logic doesn't exist, which wouldn't matter if the jokes worked, but they play like dry

553. Roger Garcia. ed. *Frank Tashlin*. Editions du Festival Internationale du film de Locarno, 1994.
554. Examples include Don Rickles (*Pajama Party*, 1964); Bob Newhart (*Hell is for Heroes*, 1962), Shelley Berman (*The Best Man*, 1964), George Carlin (*With Six You Get Egg Roll*, 1968), etc.
555. Ruth Buzzi is another.

heaves: the motion is there but nothing comes up. There is a moment of clever visual ingenuity when the first dialogue among Japanese submariners appears in English with Japanese subtitles, but then it switches to Japanese dialogue and English subtitles. The rest is shopworn and strained.

After *O'Farrell*, Tashlin kept an office in Beverly Hills for four years where he wrote spec scripts, some of them with Allan Scott, and two plays (*What Are You Doing in My Life?* and *No Experience Necessary*), neither of which was produced. He also tried a mystery novel, as yet unpublished. On May 2, 1972 Tashlin was hit in his Beverly Hills home by a heart attack. It was his second; the first had occurred some time before and forced the six-foot, four-inch filmmaker to shed fifty pounds, bringing him down to 250. But this time there was no comic relief. The rescue squad stabilized him after an hour and then took him to Mt. Sinai Hospital in Hollywood.[556] He started to show improvement in the hospital but had another attack, this time fatally, three days later. He was fifty-nine.

556. *Weekly Variety*, May 10, 1972.

KING VIDOR
The Patience of Job

King Vidor deserves a Mulligan on *Solomon and Sheba*. That 1959 Biblical epic had about as much to do with the Bible as it did with Vidor's abilities as a filmmaker, which were legendary. This was the man who, after all, directed *The Crowd, Our Daily Bread, Hallelujah, Duel in the Sun, The Fountainhead*, and then, after he retired, solved one of Hollywood's most baffling and scandalous murders. But *Solomon and Sheba* exists, and what happened behind the camera is more exciting than what took place in front of it.

Like most wide-screen spectaculars of the era, *Solomon and Sheba* was a ploy to lure audiences away from television. And while it's tempting to say that the story of the Hebrew king and the Arab queen who loved him was inspired by the 1956 success of *The Ten Commandments*, in fact it was green-lighted in 1955 and was well on its way by the time Cecil B. DeMille freed the Hebrews from bondage. Why *Solomon and Sheba* didn't smite the Biblical trend is a mystery; costing $6 million and returning only slightly more than that in rentals, it was neither a commercial, critical, nor, need it be added, scholarly success.[557]

The Old Testament gives little space to Sheba. In I Kings 10:1-13 and 2 Chronicles 9:1-22 it is said that she heard of Solomon's wisdom and made the long trek from the land of Sheba to Jerusalem to meet him as a matter of state, not of seduction. Subsequent embellishments identify her as coming from Eritrea, Yemen, Ethiopia, or perhaps Saudi Arabia. In some versions (and the film chooses to portray them) she bore Solomon's son, beginning the line of Ethiopian kings. In others she just goes home.

---

557. Accurate budgets are smoky in Hollywood. Raymond Durgnat and Scott Simmons in *King Vidor: American* (Berkeley and Los Angeles, California: University of California Press, 1988) peg it at "ballooning from four million to six because of reshooting."

But in this case, script had to be stranger than scripture if it was going to flesh out a 139-minute movie.

The film has dying King David (Finlay Currie) naming his son, the poet Solomon (Yul Brynner) as his heir over the bitter objections of his other son, the military expert Adonijah (George Sanders) who feels he deserves the crown. But Adonijah has already misrepresented himself as king during a chance encounter with the Queen of Sheba (Gina Lollobrigida[558]), which makes him the dog in the manger (to mix metaphors). He seethes as Solomon endears himself to the twelve tribes of Israel by reminding them that they have enjoyed peace under David and shall continue to do so under him.

This Hebrew solidarity worries the leaders of Egypt, before whom Sheba promises Pharaoh (David Farrar) and his allies that she will conquer Israel by seducing Solomon and bring pagan gods to the monotheistic Israelites. In the course of wooing Solomon, however, Sheba truly falls in love with him, driving Pharaoh to jettison her and to seek an unholy alliance with Adonijah. In a final battle against Egypt, Solomon vanquishes Pharaoh's forces but disappears, allowing Adonijah to once again claim that he is king and to order the stoning of Sheba. Solomon suddenly appears, kills Adonijah, quells the crowd, and watches as Sheba — who is carrying his child — forsakes paganism and embraces a single God, who then miraculously heals her stoning injuries.

Producer Edward Small got the project going in 1954 when he brought it to United Artists along with seventy-five percent of the budget. UA put up the remaining twenty-five percent.[559] From there, like the Old Testament, *Solomon and Sheba* had many authors over several years. It was based on a play by Crane Wilbur, a silent movie actor turned writer, and adapted for the screen by Julius Epstein.[560] At some point not noted in trade reports, Epstein left the project and Anthony Veiller, Paul Dudley, and George Bruce went to work jointly and severally on the re-writing. Small also hired veteran studio producer Arthur Hornblow, Jr. to assist.[561] The start date was set for May of 1958, later revised to August 15.

Meanwhile, research raised a potential "race" issue. What color were Solomon and Sheba? Would there be an Arab-Jewish issue? Small averted controversy when he declared that "Sheba was Arabic, not Negroid [*sic*],

---

558. Unlike *The Private Navy of Sgt. O'Farrell*, it was just *Gina Lollobridiga*, not *Miss* Gina Lollobrigida.
559. *Los Angeles Times*, November 19, 1958.
560. *Daily Variety*, June 29, 1954.
561. *Hollywood Reporter*, November 4, 1955.

according to our researchers, so that rules out any controversy about miscegenation."[562]

Matters of showmanship were more easily settled. Scholars somehow vetted Sheba's twenty-four revealing costumes; construction crews converted cubits to feet when building their Biblically correct sets; the writers were careful to add a flashy pagan dance number and Ninja attack; and, in a more traditional vein, Solomon's well-known adjudication of the case of two mothers who both claim the same child would be reverently portrayed. Small and Hornblow added that they wanted to draw parallels between Biblical and modern relations between Israel and Egypt, but, just to cover all the bases, Small announced that King Solomon was "the greatest lover of his times."[563]

Consistent with Hollywood's portrayals of the Old Testament, all the Hebrews are played by Gentiles.

By this time the film's budget was a large but workable $3.5 million and Small started looking for a place to film it outside of the United States where crew salaries were lower.[564] He had originally thought of Spain, Italy, Egypt, or Israel but settled on Spain by what he called a process of elimination. Geopolitics excluded Egypt; Israel didn't have enough horses; and Italy was "tied in knots" because MGM's *Ben-Hur* was shooting there. So Spain it was. By this time Hornblow had departed, Ted Richmond had been hired in his place, and Tyrone Power was cast not only as King Solomon but as co-producer. Both Small and Lollobrigida forsook salaries in exchange for a percentage of net profits.[565] King Vidor agreed to direct, and a week before production was scheduled to start, Small delivered him the latest script.

King Vidor's immediately previous credit had been *War and Peace* (1956), a three-hour-plus adaptation of Tolstoy's dramatic chronicle of the Napoleonic wars. Vidor had been the first of eight writers who tackled that mammoth project, which star Henry Fonda admitted that he did just for the money and which suffered a box office Waterloo. A vigorous sixty-one at the time he shot the Russian epic throughout Italy, Vidor took pains to direct even the battle scenes himself, something a typical director might have left to any of the four second unit directors working under him. But Vidor was not a typical director. Always eager to push the cinematic envelope, the Texas-born Vidor was a self-taught cameraman

---

562. *Daily Variety*, March 4, 1958.
563. *Daily Variety*, July 15, 1957.
564. *Weekly Variety*, July 23, 1958.
565. Contrary to modern practice, in those days there actually were net profits.

who sold freelance footage to states rights distributors in his territory when he was barely a teenager in the early 1910s.

In 1915 he married his first wife, Florence, and together they drove to Hollywood, he to make movies, and she to act in them. All he could land were menial studio jobs, but his wife, using her married name, Florence Vidor, became a star and carried her struggling husband along. When she went to MGM, so did he. They soon divorced, but not before he had delivered Metro its biggest hit of 1925, *The Big Parade*. After that, he became a Metro mainstay for the next decade and a half, turning out such hits as *Show People*, *The Patsy*, and *The Champ*, and worked almost without salary in order to direct his passion projects, *The Crowd*, *Hallelujah* (the latter with an all-black cast), and *Our Daily Bread*. His independence made the moguls defensive, and his innovations — particularly camera mobility and subtle direction — frightened the creative *status quo*. For *The Fountainhead* (1949), he devised a stark design counterpart to the uncompromising Ayn Rand story; for *The Wizard of Oz* he directed (uncredited) the Kansas scenes including Judy Garland's "Over the Rainbow" number; and for *Duel in the Sun* he found a way to make the film itself look as hallucinogenic as his turbulent relationship with its driven producer, David O. Selznick.

Solomon and Sheba began as announced on September 15, 1958. The production immediately bogged down in rain, which softened and mildewed the plaster sets of Solomon's Temple that had been constructed at Sevilla studios in Madrid. Jet trails continually streaked the Biblical era skies, and costumes tended to disappear when people took them home as souvenirs. The extras posed a problem as most of them stood considerably shorter than Hollywood extras and their clothes and armor, which were off the rack in Los Angeles, had to be altered once they were unpacked on location.[566]

But such minor concerns went by the boards on November 15 after most of the picture had been shot. Vidor reached the climactic scene in which Tyrone Power and George Sanders settle their fraternal differences with swords. After eight takes, Power called for a break, lit a cigarette, and said, "I've got to stop. I don't feel well." For several days he had been complaining of an upset stomach and a pain in his left arm. He went to his dressing room. A nurse was called. Ten minutes later he was seen being helped into Lollobridgida's Mercedes with Ted Richmond taking the wheel and rushing him to the U.S. Air Force Base hospital in Torejòn.

---

566. Luis Canales. *The Imperial Gina*. Wellesley, Massachusetts: Branden Books, 1990.

Power had suffered a heart attack and — depending on reports — either died in the car en route to the hospital or passed as soon as he got there. It became Richmond's duty to tell Mrs. Power, Deborah Minardos, who was carrying their child. By haunting coincidence, Power's father, Frederick Tyrone Power, also an actor, had died on a movie set in 1931. Infant Tyrone Power IV was born on January 22, 1959.

Small, Richmond, and Vidor immediately assessed the damage. Should the picture be abandoned and let insurance cover the costs, or should they continue with a new Solomon? The picture had only two weeks left to shoot. They scrambled for a replacement; Gary Cooper, Charlton Heston, Robert Taylor, and William Holden were all called but were otherwise engaged. Finally Yul Brynner was enticed to come to Spain and re-do the Power footage, which turned out to be half of what was already shot, including, of course, all the scenes with Lollobrigida. For a while it was thought to keep Power in the film as "young Solomon" without a beard and have Brynner play "old Solomon" with a beard. Someone even suggested removing Solomon entirely.[567] Cooler heads prevailed and the retakes began, which turned out to be the best decision inasmuch as Brynner, covering his celebrated bald pate with a brown wig, delivered a more nuanced performance than Power.[568] Brynner arrived on December first after wrapping *Sound and Fury* at Fox. His salary and the cost of the retakes were covered by Fireman's Fund, the film's insurer, to the extent of over $1,300,000, the largest insurance payout in film history to that time.[569] Brynner's reshoots pushed the production into Spain's winter, which was so cold and wet that two filming units had to be maintained: indoors for bad weather, outdoors for clear skies, whichever happened to occur on any given day.

Lollobrigida, a legend in Italian cinema, was counting on *Solomon and Sheba* to expand her visibility in English-speaking movies. She brought her son, Milko, Jr. (by producer Milko Skofic) with her and spent time with Brynner, an expert photographer, learning about cameras. She was even photographed (not by Brynner) by *Life* magazine wiggling in a Hula-Hoop."[570] Her one objection came when she was asked to wear a scanty costume for Sheba's orgy dance. Fearing censorship, she showed up on the set in flesh-colored tights and demanded a brassiere. When Ted Richmond threatened to use a body double, the two of them agreed

567. *Los Angeles Times*, November 19, 1958.
568. Jim Powers, *Weekly Variety*, June 24, 1959.
569. Canales, op. cit.
570. *Life* magazine. New York: Time-Life, October 5, 1959.

to double-shoot the sequence: tame for America and the UK, and wild for Europe.[571]

Vidor kept his own counsel throughout the ordeal. "Someone once asked me if I would rather direct a battle scene with 6,000 soldiers or a love scene with two important stars," he said. "Without hesitation I answer, 'the battle scene.'"[572] He did just that in a memorable but contrived climax in which Solomon's army uses their polished shields to reflect the sun's rays into the eyes of the attacking Egyptian chariots and footsoldiers, blinding them to a cliff in their path and making them topple over the edge like lemmings. Without meaning it, rushing headlong into an abyss became a metaphor for the film itself, which finally cost $6 million and would return only $5 million in rentals.

Forced into *de facto* retirement after *Solomon and Sheba*, Vidor tried to get financing for a film based on the life of James Murray, the non-actor he picked off the street to star in *The Crowd* and who later disappeared just as fame and fortune were in his grasp.[573] In 1967 the director became fascinated with the events surrounding the 1922 murder of Paramount Pictures contract director William Desmond Taylor, a long-unsolved crime whose police investigation, at the time, included actress Mary Miles Minter, her mother Charlotte Shelby, comedienne Mabel Normand, and others in Taylor's life, which was revealed to have been uncommonly sordid. Sifting clues anew, Vidor identified the murderer as Minter's mother, Shelby, but also discovered that the crime scene had been so corrupted by Paramount's protective meddling that no one could ever be brought to justice. Vidor locked his investigation away and it was published four years after his death by his biographer, Sidney D. Kirkpatrick, in his fascinating 1986 book *A Cast of Killers*.[574]

In his interviews for Richard Schickel's 1973 PBS series *The Men Who Made the Movies*, Vidor, at seventy-nine, was still on the cutting edge of cinema. "I am very much interested in the new films because I don't feel any differently that I did when I was beginning," he proclaimed. "I haven't seen *Deep Throat* yet but I probably will. But I'm not going to call it bad; I'm going to call it progress and call it good, and I'm going to call it revealing and enlightening. It's got to be. I don't believe in a bad world."[575] He is

---

571. Canales, op. cit.
572. Joel W. Finler. *The Movie Directors Story*. New York: Crescent Books, 1985.
573. Ephraim Katz. *The Film Encyclopedia*. New York: HarperPerennial, 1994.
574. Sidney D. Kirkpatrick. *A Cast of Killers*. New York: E.P. Dutton, 1986. Vidor's conclusions have since been challenged.
575. Richard Schickel. *The Men Who Made the Movies*. New York: Atheneum, 1975.

credited with directing and writing a short subject about painter Andrew Wyeth called *The Metaphor* in 1980,[576] Vidor died November 1, 1982 at the age of eighty-eight, the longest-working director in Hollywood history, and, throughout, one of the most daring.

---

576. A conversation between Vidor and Wyeth, Vidor referenced Wyeth's landscapes when composing shots for *The Big Parade*.

RAOUL WALSH
Top o' the World

Jack L. Warner once said that Raoul Walsh's notion of a tender love scene was burning down a whorehouse.[577] Like most of Warner's humor it managed to be offensive without being either accurate or funny. But it does carry a germ of truth in that Walsh, one of the movies' most prolific and accomplished filmmakers, could wring sentiment out of action, comedy out of drama, and chicken salad out the chickenshit that Warner too often handed him to direct.

Raoul Walsh was a New Yorker, born there in 1887 to a mother whose family belonged to the D.A.R. and a father who had barely escaped from Ireland with his three brothers. When Raoul wasn't cutting school, he was fighting his classmates. What really intrigued him, though, were the people his father, a well-connected clothing designer and merchant, brought home to dinner, from Edwin Booth (brother of Presidential assassin John Wilkes, whom Walsh would portray in *The Birth of a Nation* in 1915), to fighters John L. Sullivan and "Gentleman Jim" Corbett (whom Walsh would immortalize in his 1942 film *Gentleman Jim*). He also got to meet such other Golden Age figures as Lillian Russell, Diamond Jim Brady, and Mark Twain. Together they taught him to respect talent, not celebrity.

By his late teen years Walsh had fled from the West Side of Manhattan for the west side of America, becoming a cowboy and horse handler, and then migrated into silent pictures. Through a series of adventures that could fill a Raoul Walsh movie, he joined D. W. Griffith, becoming the

---

577. In his autobiography, Walsh attributed the remark to Jack Pickford, and it went, "I always thought your idea of light comedy was to burn down a whorehouse." But he also quoted it as coming from Warner in *Film Crazy: Interviews with Hollywood Legends* (Patrick McGilligan. New York: St. Martin's Press, 2000).

great director's assistant. His first major job was chasing down Mexican revolutionary Pancho Villa in 1912 to shoot footage for a pseudo documentary.[578] Two years later he himself played Villa in a more formal movie biography. Until 1928, in fact, Walsh both acted and directed (such as in 1928's *Sadie Thompson*) until a freak road accident, in which a jackrabbit jumped through the windshield of his car, cost him his right eye. At the time, he was about to direct *In Old Arizona*, the first outdoor talking picture, and star in it as the Cisco Kid. In his absence, Irving Cummings did the former and Warner Baxter inherited the latter.

For the next decade Walsh worked for a succession of studios and independent companies, becoming known for his flair with strong action and memorable characters. In *The Thief of Bagdad* he catered to its star Douglas Fairbanks' passion for stunt work and special effects blended with fantasy and romance. For the silent *What Price Glory*, he mixed the Great War with ribald comedy, allowing lip readers to have a ball seeing what co-stars Victor McLaglen and Edmund Lowe were *really* saying between the clean subtitles. For Fox in 1930 he made an early widescreen epic, *The Big Trail*, for which he discovered John Wayne. And in *The Bowery* he recreated the Gay Nineties complete with the details he learned at the dinner table in his youth. Walsh made so many films, and the early record is so incomplete, that it will probably never be possible to tally all of them.

But it was at Warners that he delivered his most memorable pictures, starting in 1939 with the most romantic gangster film of them all, *The Roaring Twenties*. James Cagney and Humphrey Bogart — both of whom would break their own molds under Walsh's encouraging direction in this and subsequent pictures — played wartime buddies whose postwar gangster careers bring them into conflict. Bogart adapts to a new world, Cagney does not, and dies memorable, pieta-like, on the steps of a church in the arms of his girl.

Walsh's films always made emotional sense, even those that went over the top. There is no better example of this than *White Heat*. In its portrayal of the incendiary, psychopathic, mother-loving gang leader Cody Jarrett, Walsh and James Cagney fearlessly etched a screen killer who continues to amaze audiences. His fiery death on a gas refinery tank while shouting, "Top o' the world, Ma!" is an enduring screen moment. And then there was Cagney again in *Strawberry Blond* as Biff Grimes taking the fall for Hugo Barnstead (Jack Carson) because they both loved Virginia Brush

---

578. Walsh's escapades were recalled in Larry Gelbart's 2003 HBO movie, *And Starring Pancho Villa As Himself*.

(Rita Hayworth). Just as no crime film was simply a crime film for Walsh, neither was a romance just that. In the ironically titled *The Man I Love*, both nightclub owner Robert Alda and saxophonist Bruce Bennett want singer Ida Lupino, even though they treat her like a bar rag. Although the film didn't make history in its time, legend has it that its theme of abusive love inspired Martin Scorsese's dark 1977 musical, *New York, New York*.

Walsh was a man who had nothing to prove. When Humphrey Bogart asked him to take over the direction of *The Enforcer* in 1951 when its tyro director Bretaigne Windust fell ill, Walsh did most of the work but declined credit.[579] He had also refused credit the year before for *Montana*, starring another pal, Errol Flynn, deferring to Ray Enright. Neither film is mentioned in Walsh's enormously readable autobiography, *Each Man in His Time*.[580] Nor is his last film, *A Distant Trumpet*.[581]

Based on Paul Horgan's 1951 novel and scripted by John Twist from an adaptation by Richard Fielder and Albert Beich, its plot follows 2nd Lieutenant Matthew Hazard into the Arizona Territory in 1883 when Apache Chief War Eagle is resisting Major General Alexander Quait's efforts to confine him and his people to a reservation. But it isn't that simple because Quait considers himself a friend of the Cherikawa Apaches. He delegates Lt. Hazard to promise War Eagle that his people will be protected. As expected, Uncle Sam reneges on his word, but the crafty Quait calls on his old buddy, Chester A. Arthur, who happens to be President, to reinstate it over the objection of the War Department. This, the plot says, ends the Indian Wars.[582] Along the way Hazard falls in love with Suzanne Pleshette, who happens to be married to a superior officer, even though Hazard is betrothed to Diane McBain. Fortunately for the romance, Pleshette's husband is killed, and they all live opportunistically ever after.

Lest one get the impression that *A Distant Trumpet* is a revisionist western like 1970's *Soldier Blue* or *Little Big Man*, not so. The cavalry still gets to kill an incalculable number of Apache, each of whom falls to his death with a single gunshot while most white soldiers survive to tell the tale. On the other hand, the film has no qualms showing the pervasive

579. Based on the crime syndicate Murder, Inc., *The Enforcer* was Bogart's last picture for Warner Bros. and his intense dislike of J.L. may have required the more experienced Walsh to handle him instead of the less hardened Windust.
580. Raoul Walsh. *Each Man in His Time*. New York: Farrar, Strauss, Giroux, 1974.
581. Asked by Peter Bogdanovich why his autobiography lacked a filmography, Walsh said, "Cause then I'd have to put in all the turkeys, too." (*AP* obituary January 2, 1981,)
582. Not counting Geronimo and Naiche (son of Cochise), who held out until 1886, but there are too many other historical shortcomings in the film to even begin listing them.

racism among soldiers and politicians. It's an awkward combination as screenwriter Twist tries to reflect the complexity of Horgan's historical novel.

It began its Hollywood life in 1960 as the latter half of a two-picture deal at Warner Bros. with producer James Woolf and director Jack Clayton.[583] At some point the next year Laurence Harvey joined the team as star/co-producer and Alan LeMay was announced as screenwriter.[584] By the end of 1961 Burt Kennedy had replaced LeMay as writer[585] and as 1963 began Clayton was gone and Leslie H. Martinson was not only in the director's chair but scouting locations in Arizona and testing television actress Judee Morton for a role.[586] In short time the locations were set but everything else fell apart and the new team was producer William H. Wright, scripters John Twist *et al.*, and Raoul Walsh as director. Such maneuvers were not unusual for a studio film, especially under the contract system, which was vestigially in effect at Warners to service the studio's enormous television output.[587] Being able to switch employees was not only efficient, it hovered as a constant threat to the switchees that they were replaceable, which played to Jack Warner's sensitive handling of personnel.

Walsh was too busy to care. Although he was used to working by the seat of his britches, *A Distant Trumpet* demanded sleight-of-hand to disguise its uneasy menu of part cavalry western, part love story, and part political intrigue. Walsh settled on two location hubs: Flagstaff, Arizona and Gallup, New Mexico, from which he and cinematographer William Clothier would capture scenic action and dramatic sequences. Lacking the beauty of Monument Valley that John Ford used so well, Walsh stressed the visual isolation of the mounted troops set against the barren, notably un-fruited plains. Forty miles northeast of Flagstaff, studio crews built the main location, Fort Delivery, over a two-month pre-production period. The football field-sized fort was erected on the Navajo reservation and was turned over to the Navajo Tribal Council after filming with the sole covenant that it couldn't be rented to another movie company for one year. Following the fort scenes, the company relocated to Grand Falls on the Little Colorado River, six hundred feet high, a site that was so muddy that the lenses got splashed and had to be cleaned thoroughly

---

583. *Variety*, December 22, 1960.
584. Undated *Variety* notice. LeMay wrote the novel *The Searchers*.
585. *Variety*, December 9, 1961.
586. *Variety*, March 25, 1963.
587. *Surfside 6, Bronco, Cheyenne, Sugarfoot, Maverick, Roaring Twenties*, etc.

after every take. At Church Rock near Pyramid Peak east of Gallup in the Red Rock area the company set up a tent city and secured 700 horses and 675 people to ride them in the charges. Assistant directors William Kissell and Russ Saunders coordinated the Indian charges using the then-new device of short-wave receivers hidden in the long hair of charging Apaches to receive radio instructions during a take.[588] After five weeks at the Flagstaff location, the 150-person unit went back to Warner Bros. for three weeks of studio work.[589]

A Distant Trumpet hit general release on May 30, 1964 intended for summer hard-top and drive-in playoff. The largely uncritical reviews made no mention of Walsh's legacy as a horseman and, if anything, were dismissive of the "oater" genre except to point out the ludicrous accuracy of cavalry marksmen versus the hapless Apaches with such phrases as "Indians fall like ninepins."[590] Max Steiner wrote a playful score, the main theme of which — on trumpet, naturally — sounds like von Suppe's "Light Cavalry Overture" played by an oompah band. He even underscores the catty rivalry between Pleshette and McBain with "meow" sounds on the violin.

More than anything, though, *A Distant Trumpet* feels impatient. The Panavision frame is used merely to register action, not to create cinematic impact, staying in wide shots where interpretive close-ups or even simple medium shots would do the job better. There are narrative gaps that unnecessarily disorient the viewer, but there is also surprisingly crisp dialogue and moments of unexpected gruesomeness.

Walsh acknowledged he was disappointed in the results, starting with the cast. "Those people didn't belong in it," he told interviewers Patrick McGilligan and Debra Weiner. "No…no…didn't belong."[591] From its indifferent execution, neither did the great Raoul Walsh. After his retirement he toured college campuses where his humor, intelligence, and charisma made him a star all over again, He died at age 93 at the Simi Valley Adventist Hospital of a heart attack on the last day of 1980.

588. George H. Jackson, *Los Angeles Herald-Examiner*, August 31, 1963.
589. Studio presskit.
590. Robin Bean, *Films and Filming*, June, 1964.
591. Patrick McGilligan and Debra Weiner. "Interview with Raoul Walsh" (August, 1974), *Film Crazy: Interviews with Hollywood Legends*. New York: St. Martin's Press, 2000.

ORSON WELLES
Unfinished Symphony

The difficulty writing about Orson Welles' last film is that there are so many of them. It could be *Don Quixote* (1955-1992) which was put together seven years after his death. It could be *Touch of Evil*, which was released in 1958 in butchered form and restored in 1998 to his specs, but not to his inspection. It could be *It's All True* (1942) which was edited, but not by him, fifty years after it was shot. Some say *Filming Othello* (1978) or *Filming The Trial* (1981) were his last, but they are more properly colloquies than full-scale motion pictures. His last could even be the legendary *The Other Side of the Wind* that he began in 1972 and edited between paying jobs for the rest of his life, yet whose release has been delayed by rights issues.

So, for the record, Orson Welles' last officially released film was *F for Fake* (1973).[592] But like an avid reader who leaves books open all over the house intending to get to all of them, Welles was such a prolific creator while also being reluctant completer that bookending his career is as elusive as finding the real Welles himself.

The story of *F for Fake* begins, not with Welles, but with Elmyr de Hory (1905-1976), the Hungarian-born painter who became the world's most renowned art forger, but whose greatest forgery may have been his own life story. Raised middle class, he studied painting in Germany and then moved to Paris where he acquired a taste for fine art and fine living, yet learned that his own paintings had no sales appeal. He did discover, however, an amazing aptitude for being able copy not only the style but

---

592. A short subject called *Moby Dick Rehearsed* that Welles shot in 1971 but never edited was assembled in 1999 by Filmmuseum München. It was based on a play adapted by Welles from the Melville novel that opened and closed in 1962 and with which Welles was not otherwise involved, but for which he later shot footage for the TV series *Omnibus* but then abandoned.

the intimate brush strokes of the Masters and, by painting only "recently discovered originals" rather than copies of known works, he avoided being caught. By 1947 he had settled in America and was selling his product through a representative named Fernand Legros. He was always careful never to sign the name of the artist he was forging, because doing so would have been fraud, whereas painting in another artist's style was not. Legros may have added signatures on his own, however, because by the middle 1950s the art world started getting wise. During 1960s dozens of forgeries were detected, and de Hory served prison time in Spain (but not, apparently, for forgery). On release he moved to the island of Ibiza, off Spain, and continued to paint. In 1969 he collaborated with author Clifford Irving on a wishful autobiography, *Fake! The Story of Elmyr de Hory, the Greatest Art Forger of Our Time*. (McGraw-Hill). Not coincidentally, in 1971 Irving delivered another manuscript to McGraw-Hill that he insisted was the autobiography of reclusive billionaire Howard Hughes, a claim that was disproved a year later when Hughes contrived to testify *in absentia* to its falsehood and Irving went to jail for fraud. As for de Hory, on December 11, 1976, he died from an overdose of sleeping pills, after which, irony of ironies, his own paintings started to sell as briskly as his forgeries once had.

Both men figure prominently in *F for Fake*, a film that itself conjures the Welles essence by combining magic and chicanery, two talents that brought him to public notice and kept him a fascinating but elusive figure throughout his career. It's well known how he conned his way into the Gate Theatre in Dublin at the age of sixteen by claiming he was a Broadway star who happened to be visiting Ireland; how he became a popular voice talent and theatrical innovator in New York in his early twenties; and how he helped perpetrate a panic with a simulated Martian invasion on radio in 1938. Notoriety carried him to Hollywood where his first feature film, *Citizen Kane* (1941), both summarized the existing syntax of cinema and sent it in new and exciting directions.

The storm surrounding *Kane* rained on Welles' parade. Taken as a portrait of newspaper mogul William Randolph Hearst (which, c'mon, it was), it forever turned the press and the film industry against the then-26-year-old "boy wonder." Whether it was his subsequent marriages, his audacious theatrical enterprises, or his continuing innovations in screen storytelling (especially in turning low budgets into strengths), he was condemned by some, praised by many, and financed by few. Some even accused him of having a fear of completing anything lest it be compared unfavorably with *Kane*.

"It's not true that Orson didn't want to finish his films," counters Larry Jackson, who worked with him and is now an independent producer. "It's that he never got enough money to make a whole film at once, so he did them in bits and pieces." Thus did Welles sell himself as a commodity to finance his movies and to live like, well, like Orson Welles.[593] He was seventy when he died of a heart attack in 1985, but his films, quite literally, live on as new ones are discovered and old ones are completed.

Don Quixote, for example, is a project that Welles may have intended never to finish. Begun in 1955 with Francisco Reiguera as Quixote and Akim Tamiroff as Sancho Panza, it was designed as an odd juxtaposition of Cervante's windmill-tilter against modern civilization with the obvious moral being that, whatever era he is in, Quixote will always be defending traditions that were dead before he was born. That summer he shot footage of Micha Auer which he discarded.[594] He worked on the film sporadically as time and money allowed, and by 1960 had shot the bulk of it with himself as Narrator, Reiguera and Tamiroff as noted above, and Patty McCormick as Dulcie. By November of 1971 he playfully started calling the film *When Are You Going to Finish Don Quixote?* and began thinking of it not as Cervantes but as a filmed essay on Spain.[595] In 1992 a version of the footage was put together by chameleonic Spanish writer-director Jesus Franco, but the results are in question as to whether they reflect Welles' intent.

His legacy fared better in the 1993 release of *It's All True* (originally titled *Panamerican*) which had the pedigree of being rescued by film scholars and those who knew Welles. The backstory of that work stretches to the waning days of filming *The Magnificent Ambersons* at RKO in 1942. Welles was asked by Nelson Rockefeller, an RKO stockholder who was also working on "inter-American affairs" for the Roosevelt Administration, to take a goodwill trip to South America and shoot footage of Uncle Sam's World War II allies. Welles did just that, but the project quickly devolved into a succession of parties during Carnivale, and the backlash from *Kane* and *Ambersons* so tormented RKO that the trip was cancelled, Welles was summoned back to the States, and the footage was locked away. Come

---

593. "Orson's a whore," Brian de Palma once told me matter-of-factly. He'd directed him in *Get to Know Your Rabbit* (1972) and overcame Welles' reliance on cue cards by calling for so many takes that Welles couldn't help but learn his lines. Welles also appeared frequently on Dean Marin television shows produced by Greg Garrison.
594. Orson Welles and Peter Bogdanovich; Jonathan Rosenbaum, Editor. *This is Orson Welles*. New York: HarperCollins, 1992.
595. Welles and Bogdanovich, ibid.

1993 it was extricated from the UCLA Film & Television Archive vaults by film critic-turned-lawyer-producer Myron Meisel, writer-producer Bill Krohn, Cinematographer Gary Graver, and editor Ed Marx who attempted to complete Welles' original vision. A dramatic documentary, *It's All True* is a three-part film that was meant to give Americans a sense of the culture and personality of their allies in the global conflict.[596] The reconstruction uses interviews and period footage to relate not only what Welles tried to tell but the story of making the film itself.

In 1998 Welles' brilliant 1958 film noir *Touch of Evil* was reconstructed by editor Walter Murch, sound experts Bill Varney and Peter Reale, and picture restorer Bob O'Neil under the supervision of Rick Schmidlin and film critic Jonathan Rosenbaum, and released by Universal, the studio that had originally mutilated it. A hypnotically sleazy look at a political murder in a Mexican-U.S. border town (shot in the beach community of Venice, California), it was a four-decade *cause célèbre*. Welles rewrote the script and made it without studio interference, appearing memorably as corrupt police captain Hank Quinlan, but the moment filming wrapped, Welles was locked out of the editor room by Universal-International Pictures' production head Edward Muhl. In desperation, he composed a fifty-plus page memorandum delineating his editing instructions and offered it to the studio in a plea to have them reconsider. They refused. Murch *et al* discovered the memo years later along with much of the negative for the lost scenes. They used it to restructure and remix the film to come as possible to Welles' original vision. The results bear out the effort.

Welles' most famous unfinished film is, of course, *The Other Side of the Wind*, begun in 1972 with John Huston playing J. J. "Jake" Hannaford, an aging Hollywood director on the last night of his life. Everybody who was anybody in the exciting mid-1970s movie community became part of the cast ("You'd get a call to 'come be in the movie,'" filmmaker Paul Mazursky once recalled)[597] which included Peter Bogdanovich, Dennis Hopper, Oja Kadar (Welles' lover), Joseph McBride, Mercedes McCambridge, Edmund O'Brien, and Lili Palmer. The film's complex narrative style demanded intense editing, some of which took place at Peter Bogdanovich's home in Bel Air where Welles lived for a time during

---

596. The four segments were to have been *My Friend Bonito*, about a boy and his bull, directed by Disney veteran Norman Foster; *The Story of Samba*, set during Rio de Janeiro's Carnival and tracing the history of the dance; and *Four Men on a Raft* about a quartet of Brazilians who sailed 61 days and 1,660 miles to Rio without navigation equipment. A fourth segment, *The Story of Jazz*, with Duke Ellington and telling the story of Louis Armstrong, was never shot.
597. Conversation with the Author.

post-production. "I'm going to use several voices to tell the story," he explained to Bogdanovich. "You hear conversations taped as interviews, you see quite different scenes going on at the same time. People are writing a book about him — different books. Documentaries...still pictures, film, tapes. All these witnesses...the movie's going to be made up of all this raw material. You can imagine how daring the cutting can be, and how much film."[598]

By January of 1976 most of the editing had been completed, but other problems arose. As much as eighty percent of the financing had come from the brother-in-law of Reza Pahlavi, the Shah of Iran. In 1972 Welles had narrated a British documentary on the despot that was tolerant if not lauditory.[599] With the ouster of the Shah in 1979 came the entanglement of his family's finances and, with them, the rights to the film.

"The negative was locked in a lab in Paris," explains Larry Jackson, who had programmed and run the fabled Orson Welles Cinema in Cambridge, Massachusetts before becoming a producer in his own right, "but because the company was set up in France where the rights of the artist are protected over the rights of the financier, the Court said that Orson could finish the film if he had a plan and the money. He spent the rest of his life trying to raise the money." In 2002 it was announced that the Showtime cable television network would air the film once it was finished, but that deal dissolved under separate rights claims by Welles' heirs. At this writing there are rumblings of revival. According to sources, the film is complete. (Welles designated Huston or Bogdanovich to finish it if he was unable to do so; Huston died in 1987.)

One of the people whom Welles had come to know in his travels for *The Other Side of the Wind* was television producer François Reichenbach. Reichenbach had been working on a documentary about Elmyr de Hory for the BBC, which drew Welles' interest. The director's enthusiasm inspired Reichenbach to bring Welles into the project, which was variously entitled *?* (question mark), *Fake*, and *Hoax* before settling on *F for Fake*.[600] When Clifford Irving's Howard Hughes' hoax surfaced — and Reichenbach had interview footage with Irving regarding de Hory — Welles persuaded Reichenbach to reconfigure *F for Fake* as a theatrical feature. Because the Irving material was finite, Welles and Kadar contrived

---

598. Welles and Bogdanovich, op. cit.
599. Titled *The Shah of Iran*, the hour-long program does not appear on Welles' *IMDb.com* filmography.
600. The film itself has no formal main title but shows a question mark drawn on a Movieola screen and then cuts to the words *About Fakes* pasted on a film can.

a hoax of their own in which she would pose as a seller of fake Picassos. Shooting was completed in late summer/early fall of 1973 but took a year to edit because Welles was dealing not only with his own footage but also with something new for him: someone else's previously shot footage.[601] The results premiered September, 1973 at the San Sebastian Film Festival but took until January 9, 1977 for the American premiere: naturally, at the Orson Welles Cinema where Welles himself came, lectured, and shot footage for his later documentary, *Filming Othello*.

A cunning blend of drama and documentary, *F for Fake* presents three hoaxes and an audience double-cross that stings only in hindsight. At the very start of the picture Welles announces that everything he says for the next hour will be true.[602] And it is. But he depends upon the audience forgetting that the film runs 29 minutes beyond that hour, and that's when Welles starts spinning his gleefully distracting screen magic.

F for Fake is as revolutionary as anything Welles did at the beginning of his career. Kinetic in its editing and yet completely coherent, shot in widely disparate locations and yet constructed to fit together seamlessly, it is not only a well-told tale, it is a total fabrication using the very nature of film itself. Moreover, in blending truth and illusion — including outright lying and portraying dramatic encounters that never took place — Welles even presages by some twenty years the demon of reality television.

"In *F for Fake* I said I was a charlatan and didn't mean it," he told Mary Blume of the *International Herald Tribune*, "because I didn't want to sound superior to Elmyr, so I emphasized that I was a magician and called it a charlatan, which isn't the same thing. And so I was faking even then. Everything was a lie. There wasn't anything that wasn't."[603]

Welles was being hard on himself. There aren't many filmmakers who can turn Hollywood on its head with their first film and do it again with their last. Perhaps there was only one film all along, that being the chimera that was known as Orson Welles.

---

601. Barbara Leaming. *Orson Welles: A Biography*. New York: Viking Penguin 1985.
602. Actually, it isn't: Welles has Peter Bogdanovich and William Alland fabricate audio excerpts from the *Invasion From Mars* broadcast even though the actual aircheck recording has been widely (if illegally) available for decades. Whether this is to express his pique over the bootleg or to perpetrate a hoax of a hoax is a matter of playful conjecture.
603. December 9, 1983, quoted in Welles and Bogdanovich, op. cit.

William Wellman shows an actor how to punch.

WILLIAM WELLMAN
Silent Sentimentalist

For a guy who made pictures about war, gangsters, lynching, and con men, there is unexpected sentiment running through William Wellman's work, only it's played close to the chest, like the man himself. In a remarkable career than spanned some thirty-eight years, Wellman turned out, with a minimum of fuss and a maximum of skill, such films as the original *A Star is Born, The Public Enemy, Night Nurse, Wild Boys of the Road, Small Town Girl, Nothing Sacred, Beau Geste, Roxy Hart, Magic Town, Battleground, The Ox-Bow Incident, The Story of G.I. Joe,* and *The Next Voice You Hear*. He wanted to make pictures in nearly every genre: screwball comedies, social commentary, war, romances, satires, and one of the first and best gangster movies. More remarkably, "Wild Bill" Wellman himself may have been more dynamic than anything he put on the screen. His career even has an ironic closure, for his last film, 1958's *Lafayette Escadrille*, is an autobiographical work that harkens back to the movie that brought him to prominence in 1927, *Wings*. He earned the right to direct that one because of his experience in the French flying corps in World War I. His career is marked by fights with studio bosses (it was said that David O. Selznick was the only one who could get along with him), actors (he supposedly hated them and the feeling was often mutual despite seven of them getting Oscar® nominations under his direction), and censors (his 1931 *Night Nurse* is credited with helping to bring on the Production Code).

Wellman came to movies after a series of adventures that contradicted his upbringing in Brookline, Massachusetts, a gentle suburb of Boston. Born there in 1896, he was expelled from school when — with the accuracy that would distinguish him in World War I — he dropped a stink bomb on his principal's bald head. A succession of failed careers followed from chocolate salesman to worker in a shoe factory. A chance encounter with Douglas Fairbanks at an athletic field prompted the star to tell Wellman to get in touch if he made it to Hollywood. Then came the Great War. Wellman was barely eighteen when he joined the Norton-Harjes Ambulance Corps in France in June of 1917, having been snubbed by the U.S. Air Corps for lack of education (see: stink bomb). He then transferred to the French Foreign Legion's division in Alsace-Lorraine from December of 1917 to March of 1918.[604] More precisely, he flew for the Escadrille Américaine, for it was constructed of expatriate Americans who sought to stop the Kaiser while Congress was still making up its mind.[605] Wellman survived a wartime plane crash with a broken back and then, as many a rakish flyer did after the Armistice, headed for Hollywood. There he took Fairbanks up on his offer and, Fairbanks, good to his word, pushed him toward acting. But Wellman felt drawn more strongly behind the camera and by 1923 had earned the right from William Fox to direct Dustin Farnum and Buck Jones in westerns. When he heard that Paramount was embarking on their Great War epic in answer to MGM's *The Big Parade*, he campaigned with studio boss B.P. Schulberg to direct it. The result was *Wings* (1927), a film so realistic in its aerial battles (because the flying *was* real) that it won the first Academy Award® for Best Picture.

Wellman mastered an unusual number of genres from the devout cynicism of *Nothing Sacred*, in which a conniving reporter (Fredric March) persuades a desperate woman (Carole Lombard) to fake a lingering death in order to sell newspapers, to the deeply affecting and unflinching *A Star is Born* (both 1937). His *The Public Enemy* (1931) gave a career jump-start to James Cagney when he switched the charismatic actor from supporting to the lead a few days into shooting. The result became the seminal American gangster film with the seminal American gangster. *Beau Geste* (1939) is a grand desert adventure with a warm heart, while *Battleground* (1949) stands as a rousing war picture. Even more affecting was *The Story of G.I. Joe*, based on Ernie Pyle's intimate front line writing, which Wellman claimed to be his favorite picture.[606] It would seem that, in trying to avoid sentiment, Wellman sliced through to raw emotion and made his films all the more honestly moving.

He wrote *Lafayette Escadrille* (1958) himself under the title *C'est la Guerre*. Technically, the Lafayette Flying Corps is an outgrowth of the

---

604. Philip M. Flammer. *The Vivid Air: The Lafayette Escadrille*. Athens, Georgia: The University of Georgia Press, 2008.
605. William Wellman, Jr. *The Man and His Wings: William A. Wellman and the Making of the First Best Picture*. Santa Barbara, California: Greenwood Publishing Group, 2006.
606. Interviewed by Richard Schickel in *The Men Who Made the Movies*, Lorac Productions, 1973.

Escadrille Américaine. The young Yanks who flew in it were trained at Avord and then sent to Le Plessis Belleville where they waited until there was a vacancy, which meant that a flyer was killed, wounded, or missing from any of the sixty or so fight escadrilles along the front. *C'est la Guerre* was pattered, Wellman said, after a friend of his called "Joe" ("Thad" in the movie) who met a young French girl named "Joan" ("Renée" in the movie) who worked in a panel house (i.e. whorehouse, and maybe that's what drew the Jack Warner quote). The story it's based on is contorted and involved, but as it runs its course Joe goes to war, is put in the brig, escapes, finds Joan, and becomes her pimp. When he goes off and dies in combat, she drowns herself in the Seine.

Wellman sold the project to his old pal Jack Warner who saw it as a vehicle for his rising young contract star Tab Hunter (as the studio's *Fighter Squadron* had been for Rock Hudson in 1948 and in which Hunter had a small role) playing Thad. The catch was that Warner wouldn't let Wellman make it unless he agreed to do the more commercially promising *Darby's Rangers* (1958) too. Warner also wanted Tab Hunter to appear in *Darby,* but the actor staunchly refused. In *Lafayette*, Hunter gives a challenging performance as a self-centered young man prone to violent outbursts, presaging the work he would do to acclaim in 1958's *Portrait of a Murderer* on TV's *Playhouse 90.* The film's tyro cast included William Wellman, Jr. (playing his father), David Janssen, Brett Halsey, Tom Laughlin, and Clint Eastwood. Peerless pilot Frank Tallman coordinated the actual fleet of classic aircraft that included four Bieriot, two Nieuports, a Spad, Sopwith "Camel," Fokker, and Penguins.

Wellman's script was rewritten by Peter Paul Fix and dated July of 1954. It ended with Thad's death as Wellman intended. While *Lafayette* was in production from October 19 through December 8, 1956, rumors circulated that Wellman was making a dirty movie about the corps, probably because the plot had leaked about a prostitute and the boy who loved her. Negative reaction compounded from Tab Hunter fans; at a December sneak preview in Pasadena, Wellman was surrounded by hoards of bobbysoxers screaming, "You ought to be ashamed of yourself. Killing Tab Hunter! How dare you!"

Scalded by the reaction, Warner decreed that a happy ending would be shot in which both Thad and his girlfriend not only live but get married.[607] Hunter and Wellman reluctantly agreed, Wellman figuring that he would

---

607. A script rewrite from October of 1956 by Albert Sidney Fleischman (noted in the Warner Bros. files at USC by the AFI) changed the ending to a "happy" one. The dates don't mesh with the preview, but there it is.

rather deface his own film than let a stranger take a whack at it. The deed was done on April 26 and 27, 1957 and again on May 7. Making matters worse, Warner held up *Lafayette*'s release until Wellman fulfilled his promise to do *Darby's Rangers* (shot from April 22 to late June of 1957). *Darby* was released in February of 1958 just as *Lafayette* was having its private premiere in Washington, North Carolina. Surviving members of the squadron boycotted it, claiming, sight-unseen, that their corps was being exploited, which was not the case.

Wellman was shattered.[608] The supposedly tough-as-nails filmmaker became so dispirited over having to ruin his life's project that he swore off directing for the rest of his seventeen years. But he did not go quietly: "I told Warner that if I ever caught him alone, which in his case was damn near impossible, I would put him in the hospital. I have never hated a man as much as I hate him. On top of it all, he wouldn't let me kill Tab Hunter…after that phony Hollywood ending and the crappy title change, I just threw in the sponge."[609]

"A bad picture is like a frightened birthmark on your face," he added in his autobiography. "It never leaves you, first run, second run, reruns, TV prime time, late time, lousy time; it's always there for people to stare at unbelievingly or turn away from or worse still turn off, or should that be better still? It's your eternal badge of embarrassment."[610] The mutilation is tragic, especially because of the film's strengths, which combine the daringness of youth with the sure hand of experience. *Lafayette Escadrille* is a filmmaker's film. It takes off long before the first airplane does with a succession of sequences that tell the story economically and stylishly. Although there are some comic sequences that might charitably be called "robust," they pay off, as does the story itself, until the moment when it's obvious that the film is being forced into a flight path it was never designed to go.

Even with the retakes made with the director's own hand, it was not well received. William Augustus Wellman died on December 9, 1975 of leukemia. But in truth he died on February 28, 1958, the day that a sabotaged *Lafayette Escadrille* took off — and crashed.

608. Flammer, op. cit.
609. Quoted in Tab Hunter. *Tab Hunter Confidential: The Making of a Movie Star*. New York: Algonquin Books, 2006. Also: Frank Thompson. "Program for International Film Festival of San Sebastian" and the "Spanish Film Archive," Donaastia-San Sebastian, 1993.
610. William A. Wellman. *A Short Time for Insanity*. New York: Hawthorn Books, 1974. Adding insult to injury, Warner briefly wanted to call the film *With You in My Arms* in the U.S. and *Hell Bent for Glory* in the U.K.

Billy Wilder.

BILLY WILDER
You've Peed Enough

The night he was honored by the Writers Guild of America at their Golden Laurel Awards in 1997, sixteen years after he had last directed a picture, Billy Wilder, then ninety-one, declined to speak from the stage. Instead, he told a joke from the audience about an elderly man who sees a urologist. "The doctor asks him, 'What is your problem?' and he says, 'I can't pee.' And the doctor asks him, 'How old are you?' and he says, 'I'm ninety.' [The doctor] says, 'You've peed enough.'"

Wilder's last film, *Buddy Buddy* (1981), suggests the same advice about directing. It is a disappointing end to one of the most remarkable careers in Hollywood history, and it is baffling how it turned out as poorly it did. Wilder, who began writing Hollywood films in 1934 when Nazis pushed him out of his native Austria, was one of the first studio craftsmen to go from typewriter to director's chair, never letting go of either. Always working with a co-writer, he created a remarkable legacy of films that explore — sometimes with laughter and sometimes with knives — the darker side of human nature. It's generally agreed that his employer in those days, Paramount Pictures, paired him with patrician screenwriter Charles Brackett so the progressive Wilder could learn conservative politics as well as English. Only the latter stuck.

"[Brackett's] politics were to the right of Herbert Hoover," Wilder confirmed to a Writers Guild audience. "We just didn't think the same way at all. But this difference of opinions makes for good collaborators. If two collaborators think the same way, you don't need a collaborator. It's like pulling on one end of the rope: two men and no tension."[611] Brackett did his job until Wilder broke up the team and moved on to work with

---

611. Mel Stuart, *Billy Wilder: The Human Comedy*, American Masters, 1998.

Raymond Chandler, Walter Reisch, Walter Newman, Wendell Mayes, Harry Kurnitz, and, most notably, I.A.L. Diamond. The successive teams gave birth to an impressive number of films that crackled with style, wit, and character. They include *Sunset Boulevard*, *Ace in the Hole*, *The Lost Weekend*, *Double Indemnity*, *Love in the Afternoon*, *Stalag 17*, *Sabrina*, and *The Private Life of Sherlock Holmes*.

Holmes began Wilder's undeserved decline. If it's unfamiliar, even to Wilder buffs, it was even harder to take for its studio, United Artists, in 1970. UA had benefited grandly from Wilder's previous works which included the box office triumphs *The Apartment*, *Some Like It Hot*, and *Irma La Douce*. Even after the stumble of *Kiss Me Stupid* in 1964 he bounced back in 1966 with *The Fortune Cookie*. So committing $10 million to a three-hour reserved seat period piece about the world's first consulting detective seemed promising. Unfortunately, by the time *Holmes* was released, road-shows had fallen out of favor with the mercurial youth market and Wilder's magnum opus was slashed from nearly three hours to just over two in a desperate attempt to draw the kids. When it didn't, UA abandoned it.

The rejection crushed Wilder. It wasn't just that a film of his had failed; he'd had that happen before with *The Spirit of St. Louis*, *Ace in the Hole* and, most notoriously, *Kiss Me Stupid*. But *The Private Life of Sherlock Homes* was rejected not because it was bad but because it — and, by extension, its director — was deemed hopelessly old-fashioned. Wilder brushed it off with typical glibness: "I made *Sunset Boulevard*, *Some Like It Hot* and *The Apartment*, he said. 'I didn't suddenly get stupid."[612] Privately, however, he was deeply shaken. His kind of film had always counted on the public sharing his cynicism; how could he have been so far off base, not only with audiences but with the people who ran the film company? Quickly he and Diamond began putting together a more modest effort, one that would tap the rich resource of sassy romantic comedy that had given them so much past success.

Avanti! (1972) was based on an Italian play about a businessman who travels to a resort town to arrange for his vacationing father's funeral. Once there he discovers that the old man died in the sack with a woman who was not his wife. The daughter of his father's mistress has also arrived to supervise services, and the two offspring, after pro forma initial sparring, likewise have an affair. Jack Lemmon, then forty-seven, co-starred with Juliet Mills, then thirty-one. At two hours and forty minutes it was one of Wilder's longest pictures, particularly dangerous for a comedy. It took its time setting up and delivering situations, oblivious to the narrative

612. Attributed.

shorthand that had been introduced by the French New Wave, the British Invasion, and the impatient American film school generation. By acts of omission instead of commission Wilder was violating his own first rule of picture-making: "Don't bore."

The failure of *Avanti!* dissolved Wilder's fifteen-year relationship with United Artists. His next picture was made for Universal and producer Paul Monash. It was a remake of the Ben Hecht-Charles MacArthur newspaper drama, *The Front Page*. The project had initially been developed by director-writer Joseph L. Mankiewicz who left for undisclosed reasons, making way for Wilder and Diamond to rewrite Hecht and MacArthur. If that wasn't cheeky enough, the insertion of profanity was. Hecht and MacArthur had achieved the appearance of swearing in their Depression-era play by having their characters talk fast and spout wisecracks. Wilder and Diamond pushed it over the edge by having their 1929 reporters talk like those of 1974, the year it was shot. They may have thought they were being *au courant*, but the effect was anachronistic for a period piece. Once again the box office did not respond.

After that, Wilder and his agents found financing elusive. They managed to assemble a cartel of international backers to make *Fedora* (1978) from the quaternary *Crowned Heads* by best-selling writer (and former actor) Thomas Tryon. Its tale of a long-retired movie star who makes a comeback without apparently having aged was seen as a spiritual cousin to *Sunset Boulevard*, especially as both pictures starred William Holden. In fact, it was a love-hate letter to Hollywood's obsession with youth and the fragility of stardom. Little-seen in the states, *Fedora*, is a mature work by a filmmaker who was functioning again in his métier. It even suggested that, at seventy-two, Wilder was mellowing. Released the year after *Star Wars*, *Close Encounters of the Third Kind*, and *Saturday Night Fever*, however, *Fedora* faced a theatre-going public that had become even more immune to old-fashioned romance.

Three years later Wilder and Diamond embarked on an Americanization of a 1973 French film by Edouard Molinaro called *L'emmerdeur* ("*The Troublemaker*") based a Francis Veber play. Molinaro's stars were Lino Ventura and Jacques Brel. Agent Alain Bernheim, who repped Molinaro, enticed Wilder, Matthau, and Lemmon[613] into a $10 million package to remake it in America, and David Begelman — who had surfaced at MGM after defrauding Columbia — agreed to the deal.[614]

---

613. To appear in *Buddy Buddy*, Lemmon bailed on Blake Edwards' *S.O.B.*, in which he was to have played the Richard Mulligan role, reportedly telling friends, "Billy needs me."
614. Ed Sikov, *On Sunset Boulevard: The Life and Times of Billy Wilder*, New York: Hyperion, 1998).

In theory, the stars were perfectly cast: Matthau was droll and efficient, Lemmon neurotic and twittery. As in *The Odd Couple*, Lemmon was the fly to Matthau's rhinoceros, the squeaky wheel to the assassin's well-oiled killing machine. The film's humor is built around this chemistry of contrast. Matthau is a hit man named Trabucco who has been assigned to dispatch a witness scheduled to testify against the Mob. Staking out the courthouse from a hotel across the street, Trabucco is distracted by a neighboring guest, Victor Clooney (Lemmon), who is trying to kill himself because his wife (Paula Prentiss) left him for her sex therapist (Klaus Kinski). More out of efficiency than compassion, Matthau agrees to accompany Lemmon on a road trip to Kinski's clinic to effect a reconciliation. When Prentiss informs Lemmon that she intends to marry Kinski, he heads back to the hotel to finish his suicide. Kinski and Prentiss follow him intending to prevent this by giving him a sedative, but they give it to Matthau instead, and Lemmon, out of gratitude to his enabler, tries to help the hit man perform his duty. This restores Lemmon's purpose in life and everyone lives guiltily ever after.

It was the third pairing of Matthau and Lemmon (they would go on to make four more movies together post-Wilder). Matthau was a craggy sixty-one when shooting began and Lemmon a pulled-together fifty-six (his character says he is forty-eight). Somehow they appeared even older, slower, and more miscast than they'd been in *The Front Page*; what had been brash and endearing about them in their earlier comedies now seemed strained and life-threatening in *Buddy Buddy*, which is what the morbid comedy came to be called. Shot in and around the generic-looking central southern California town of Riverside starting on January 4, 1981, it wrapped in Hawaii on April 16 after interiors were completed at MGM.[615] Consistent with other Wilder-Diamond pictures, *Buddy Buddy* contains disguises: Matthau poses as a priest, mailman, and others as he kills his various victims. Unlike with other actors, Diamond and Wilder allowed Matthau to change his dialogue, not necessarily because his version was better but because they were tired of arguing with him. As Matthau recalled of Wilder during the filming, "He said, 'Each scene that you do must have some dramatic explosion, some astonishing things about it. Otherwise it falls down.' I said, 'How about if I build to that?' He said, 'No, forget about building. Building is for architects.'"[616]

---

615. Source: revised (January 29, 1981) production schedule in AMPAS files.
616. Stuart, op. cit.

Production was enlivened by Wilder's perception that women on location sought after him and by his penchant for giving line readings to his seasoned performers. Midway through filming, Matthau injured his neck doing a stunt (and attended the premiere still wearing a neck brace). Soon Wilder just seemed to want to just get it over with.[617] The finished film reflects his indifference. The dialogue is not so much acted as delivered. The pace is leaden and lines that should be tossed off lightly are driven home with deadly importance. Seasoned teammates Lemmon and Matthau miss beats picking up each other's cues, and because many of their scenes are held in master shots or two-shots, it's impossible to adjust their timing. It didn't help that Wilder's long-serving editor, Daniel Mandell, had retired after *The Fortune Cookie*.

It's hard to imagine how the man who was so deft in *Some Like It Hot* or so breathless in *One, Two, Three* could make a lugubrious picture like *Buddy Buddy*. The inclusion of profanity for the sake of profanity further alienates the viewer. Moreover, the logic by which Wilder's and Diamond's other works were driven to their inevitable conclusions — all the *I*s dotted, *T*s crossed, and *U*s umlauted — is painfully absent here. Why would Matthau choose such a clumsily obvious sniper post? Why doesn't he just kill Lemmon to get him off his back? Why did Lemmon have to return to the hotel to make his second suicide attempt? When the viewer asks such questions, it means that the film is not answering them peremptorily.

What is truly missing, though, is the directorial twinkle for which the razor-tongued but disarmingly charming Wilder was known. As Matthau remarked during Wilder's AFI honors in 1986, "in Billy's world, you can be sure that the situation is hopeless, but not serious." Except here.

"If there is a tragedy to Billy's life," offered another acclaimed director, William Friedkin, "it's that he wasn't born a painter or a composer because then all he would have needed was a blank sheet of paper or a blank canvas and a pencil to realize his creations. But if you want to be a film director in this country basically you need a one-ton pencil, and by that I mean you need a lot of money, a lot of equipment, a lot of support, and you can't just pick up that pencil yourself. You're dependent on the people who own the pencil, which is to say the major studios. And at a certain point they just stopped believing in Billy."[618]

Wilder may have ceased making films after *Buddy Buddy* but, fortunately for film history, he didn't stop talking about them. He maintained

---

617. Sikov, op. cit.
618. Stuart, op. cit.

an office in Westwood Village in the shadow of UCLA, a brisk walk from the apartment which he and his wife, Audrey Young, shared with one of the world's great Impressionist and Post-Impressionist art collections (he sold it in 1989 for over $32 million). No stranger to being fêted, he lived to be one of the last surviving directors of Hollywood's golden age, yet he refused to allow his autobiography to be published in English during his lifetime. (One marvels at the things a man who was so outspoken during his life could possibly have wanted hidden until it was over). Fortunately, he collaborated on a stunning biographical monograph with another gifted filmmaker, Cameron Crowe, in *Conversations with Wilder*, New York: Alfred P. Knopf, 1999.

"I just made pictures that I would like to see," he once stated in a 1998 retrospective interview. "And if I was lucky it coincided with the taste of the audience."

Most of the time it did. Billy Wilder died on March 27, 2002 of pneumonia. Not, it must be noted, of a cold heart.

ROBERT WISE
Institutional Memory

Nobody didn't like Robert Wise. Rarely has a filmmaker been so honored: Oscars® for directing *The Sound of Music* and for co-directing *West Side Story*, Oscar®-nominated for directing *The Sand Pebbles* and *I Want to Live*, and for editing *Citizen Kane*. Winner of the Irving G. Thalberg Award. Six awards from the directors Guild of America. President of the Academy of Motion Picture Arts and Sciences and of the DGA. And more honors and lifetime achievement plaques than would fit on a lifetime achievement plaque. By the time he died in 2005 at the age of 91 he had not only made film history, he had written it, not in the sense of having committed it to paper, but in telling it to other people. Robert Wise was among a handful of Hollywood veterans who, like Ishmael, survived to tell their stories. This is important. As Louise Brooks (who also survived) pointed out, "The tragedy of film history is that it is fabricated, falsified, by the very people who make film history. It is understandable that in the early years of film production, when nobody believed there was going to be any film history, most film magazines and books printed trash…. But since about 1950 film has been established as an art, and its history recognized as a serious matter."[619] Therefore it was important that Wise remembered, and even more important that he talked, and supremely important that he told the truth, because when your reputation is secure, your memory can afford to be. As Hollywood's premiere outstanding *eminence grise*, Wise was accessible, just like his films. They were all competent, beautifully mounted, and successful.

Wise was raised in, and was nurtured by, the studio system. Born in Winchester, Indiana in 1914, he dropped out of college in the Great

---

619. Louise Brooks. *Lulu in Hollywood*. New York: Alfred P. Knopf, 1974, 1982.

Depression and got a job as an assistant cutter at RKO Radio Pictures through the efforts of his older brother, who worked in the studio's accounting department. In 1940 he was seconded to a new unit headed by Orson Welles whom RKO had hired to do anything he wanted after scaring the pills off of America with his Martian invasion broadcast of Halloween, 1938. The result, in 1941, was *Citizen Kane*, which Wise and Mark Robson edited, followed by *The Magnificent Ambersons*. It was, alas, Wise who re-cut and directed new footage for *Ambersons*, offering the explanation for the rest of his career that he would do less damage than someone who didn't know the picture as well. It remains an asterisk on his reputation.

The association with Welles proved toxic, but Wise redeemed himself in the studio's eyes in 1944 when he took over Val Lewton's production of *The Curse of the Cat People* after its original director, Gunther von Fritsch, fell behind schedule. Wise guided the film efficiently to completion in ten days to become a landmark in psychological and atmospheric horror. Successive films like *The Body Snatcher* and *The Set-Up* (a boxing drama told in real time) marked him as an expert craftsman. But it was when he left RKO to become a journeyman and made *The Day the Earth Stood Still* (1951), *Executive Suite* (1954), *Somebody Up There Likes Me* (1956), *I Want to Live* (1958), and *Odds Against Tomorrow* (1959) that he was established as a deft, albeit not flashy, handler of actors and narrative. In the 1960s, he found himself the king of the roadshow. First with *West Side Story* (1961), then with *The Sound of Music* (1965), *Star!* (1966), and *The Sand Pebbles* (1968), he began to feel he would never be able to direct an intimate story again. So he pushed to make the intense science fiction thriller *The Andromeda Strain* (1971). "That picture was important for me," he said, "because, throughout the years before, I had been doing all these big pictures and I wanted a smaller one."[620] Despite *Andromeda*'s success, he agreed to make *The Hindenburg* (1975) a late-comer to the disaster film genre and a drama as hollow as the doomed gasbag itself. He followed it with *Audrey Rose* (1977) a modern-day horror story about reincarnation that went to such lengths to persuade the skeptics in the audience that it failed to suspend its own disbelief.

The Wise anomaly begins in 1979 and ends in 1989. It has never been satisfyingly resolved. When *Star Wars* and *Close Encounters of the Third Kind* (both 1977) demonstrated that there was a huge audience for science fiction special effect films, Paramount, which had been bungling

---

620. Interview with the Author, April 21, 1993.

its *Star Trek* franchise ever since the series ended on television in 1969, finally green-lighted *Star Trek: The Motion Picture* with Wise as director. The choice made perfect sense: Wise could handle huge budgets as well as the sf genre. What he couldn't handle, it turned out, was Star Trek®. Working with a script that was derivative at best, with a cast that had had seventy-nine episodes plus fifteen years of fan feedback as experience, the sixty-five-year-old Wise seemed to be from another planet. *ST:TMP* fell behind schedule, two visual effects directors (Douglas Trumbull and John Dykstra) worked together to complete it, and it barely made its release date.[621] Despite this, it returned $80 million against a $39 million outlay and resuscitated what has since become a multi-billion dollar franchise.

And yet Wise didn't direct another film for ten years. When he did, it was the unpretentious urban drama *Rooftops* (1989).

The plot of *Rooftops* is as shopworn as the Manhattan tenements in which it's set: a single-lettered street kid named "T" (Jason Gedrick) is a reclusive, orphaned, homeless youth who lives in an empty water tower atop an abandoned apartment building. When local drug dealer Lobo (Eddie Velez) and his two henchmen decide to set up their operations there, T — who doesn't involve himself in the neighborhood's tsuris — is forced out. T is also an expert at a kind of break-dancing called Combat, which is like kick boxing except the fighters don't make contact. At a block party T becomes attracted to a young woman named Elana (Troy Beyer) who is not only Lobo's cousin, she's his lookout. Lobo's murder of a young spray-painter who idolizes T forces T to take a stand, which he does using a Brazilian variation on Combat called Capoeira, where you actually kick the crap out of your opponent. Through a combination of guile, gravity, and police complicity, T prevails.

Rooftops began as a spec script by Terence Brennan from a story by Allan Goldstein and Tony Mark that director Taylor Hackford acquired for his New Visions Pictures once he, New Century Entertainment, and Cineplex Odeon landed $50 million to produce independent films.[622] Rather than helm it himself, Hackford accepted a suggestion to ask Robert Wise to do it, not only because of *West Side Story*'s similar milieu but because, "I wanted *Rooftops* to be tough, but also wanted it to have heart."[623] Wise differentiated between *Rooftops* and *West Side Story* by pointing out that the earlier film was about gangs while this was about

---

621. In 2001 Wise supervised an official "director's cut" on DVD that represented what he would have done in 1979 if the opening date hadn't been so pressing.
622. Will Tusher, *Daily Variety*, May 19, 1988.
623. Anne Thompson, *LA Weekly*, March 24, 1989.

homeless youth, drugs, prostitution, and violence. Budgeted at $8 million, the film shot in and around Alphabet City, the letter-numbered streets in lower Manhattan, beginning August 16, 1988 and wrapping nine weeks later. It was a smooth but complicated shoot. Because of decrepit conditions on location it was often necessary to film in front of one building, inside a second, and on the rooftop of a third, then cut them all together later to make them appear to be the same place. Days ran ten, twelve, and fourteen hours with one hitting the seventeen hour mark. It was shot under NABET, the television union, rather than the IATSE, the primary feature film union. According to colleagues, Wise was a gentleman throughout, acclimating to the independent spirit of smaller crews and tighter budgets. He encouraged suggestions while, at the same time, knowing precisely what shots he needed. He directed the dance and combat scenes without relying on a second unit director; John Carrafa and Jelon Vieira, respectively, choreographed them.

Despite such efforts, *Rooftops* was not well received. Although the filmmakers took its urban themes seriously, the presence of exhibition dancing, pop music (heavily promoted through commercial tie-ins), and slick production values ironically undercut its street cred. It grossed barely over $2 million. It's essentially a youth exploitation picture that looks like it was made by adults. In other words, it's too polished.

And there was something else that turned out to be fatal for a dance film: Wise had no particular skill in shooting dancing. In *West Side Story*, he had been called in to replace the film's original director, Jerome Robbins, who had directed and choreographed it on Broadway, when Robbins allowed the film to fall behind schedule. And despite directing two other musicals — *The Sound of Music* and *Star!* — Wise never developed a flair for dance, unlike, say, Bob Fosse (*Cabaret*, *All That Jazz*, *Sweet Charity*) or even MTV. *Rooftops'* choreography may have been exciting on the set, but on film it looks flat.

So, weirdly, is the film's occasional profanity. It's rare to hear people cuss in a classy Wise film, and its use here seems an obvious ploy to sound contemporary. But it comes off like grade-schoolers who've just learned dirty words on the playground but not yet what they mean. The characterizations are superficial; T has no particular goal in life, and though he opens up to Elana and rides off with her at the end, there's no indication that either of them have anything on their minds beyond survival, and the plot resolution brings no sense of unity among the young people who have survived.

In a way, this summarizes the career of Robert Wise. Everyone who ever worked with him liked and respected him. He helped others, was a genial ambassador for movies, made a lot of people a lot of money, and entertained audiences for four decades. But it's hard to name innovations that he brought to the art of cinema except to be the very best at what he did. His grace was in making everybody else look good even if he made himself look invisible. He died September 14, 2005 of heart failure at the age of 91.

WILLIAM WYLER
Just Do It Better

It sounds incredible, but the most honored director in the history of cinema apparently didn't know how to direct actors. Time and again, after the umpteenth take, performers from Laurence Olivier to Charlton Heston and Bette Davis to Barbra Streisand would ask William Wyler, "If I'm not doing it right, how do you want me to do it?" to which Wyler would invariably say, "just do it better." When they finally did — as long as he had the patience and the producer had the budget — he would say "print" and move on. And it was perfect.

"There was an instinct in him that told him when it was right, when it was true," Billy Wilder tried to explain, as did John Huston who said, tantalizingly, "It would be a value so fine that it would drown in the discussion of it." "He was an amazingly inarticulate man about what he wanted," Bette Davis said. "But when he saw it he knew that's what he wanted but it was very hard for him to say it. He would just have us do it again."[624] "Being directed by Willy[625] Wyler is like getting 'the works' at a Turkish bath," Charlton Heston famously summarized about the man who guided him to his 1959 Oscar® for *Ben-Hur*. "You nearly drown but you come out smelling like a rose."

Heston, Davis, et al spake truth. Because, despite being virtually inarticulate, Wyler's impressive bouquet includes *The Best Years of Our Lives, Jezebel, Friendly Persuasion, Ben-Hur, The Little Foxes, Dodsworth, Dead End, Wuthering Heights, The Heiress, Memphis Belle, Roman Holiday,* and *Detective Story* — some of the most consummate and timeless works in cinema. So it's hard to understand how he could have ended his career

---

624. Interviews from *Directed by William Wyler*. Aviva Slesin, A. Scott Berg, 1986.
625. His friends wrote to him as both *Willy* and *Willie*.

with *The Liberation of L.B. Jones* (1970), a film that is both troubling and troublesome.

Born in Alsace-Lorraine in 1902, Wyler came to America in 1920 when his mother's cousin, Carl Laemmle, offered him a job at the New York office of his company, Universal Pictures. He started as a publicist, a job that was equal parts diplomacy and fabrication. Both talents served him well as he moved a year later to Universal City in California. By 1925, he had become an assistant director at the semi-rural studio, which was known for cheap westerns. He even moonlighted at MGM that same year on the chariot race for the silent *Ben-Hur* (by fate or coincidence, Wyler would direct the talkie remake of that film in 1959). He began as a full director on his return to Universal with *The Crook Buster*, a two-reeler. The good news about Universal was that they gave newcomers the opportunity to work. The bad news was that they were so cheap that couldn't hold onto those that were any good. Because he was very good, Wyler left Universal by 1935 and wound up at Samuel Goldwyn's company.

The mercurial Goldwyn was known for three things: mangling English, fierce independence, and superb taste.[626] Wyler basked in the third, directing his finest work while Goldwyn fumed at how slow he was. Somehow the symbiosis paid off; Wyler's output during his seven Goldwyn years from 1935 to 1942 was remarkable: *These Three*, a gutted but spiritually faithful adaptation of Lillian Hellman's *The Children's Hour*; *Dodsworth*, from the Sinclair Lewis novel, remarkable for putting divorce on the screen; *Dead End*, Sidney Kingsley's slum drama with outstanding performances by Humphrey Bogart and Marjorie Main; *Jezebel*, on loan-out to Warners, with Bette Davis, with whom Wyler had an affair; *Wuthering Heights*, in which he made Laurence Olivier realize the potential of screen acting; and *The Little Foxes*, a riveting adaptation of the Hellman classic with Davis and Herbert Marshall.

Wyler served with valor in World War II directing combat films, among them *Memphis Belle* (1944), about a seemingly charmed bomber and its brave crew. It was during the war that he was shelled and suffered irreparable hearing loss, eventually going deaf in one ear. He returned to Goldwyn after the war and made *The Best Years of Our Lives*, a timeless drama about World War II veterans returning to a home front to which they can no longer relate.

Wyler's skills did not go unrewarded by the industry. He was nominated for twelve directing Oscars® and won three (*Mrs. Miniver*, *The Best*

---

626. Many people ascribe much of Goldwyn's taste to his beloved second wife, Frances.

Years of Our Lives, and *Ben-Hur*), the latter an uncharacteristic epic for Hollywood in that it focused on human elements rather than the clash of armies.

A Wyler film was a meticulous film. His best early work was photographed by Gregg Toland, the lighting and deep focus artist who gave *Citizen Kane* its timeless look. For Wyler, Toland shot *These Three, Dead End, Wuthering Heights, The Cowboy and the Lady, The Westerner*, and more. Their chemistry was legendary, but their process is unknown. Did Toland read Wyler's mind where to place the camera? Was Wyler focused on the actors while Toland chose the angle? Or was it a pure collaboration? Neither man left records beyond the films themselves, which are inventive and precise.

"I've been accused of having no signature," Wyler said, acknowledging the mystery, "because you cannot tell a Wyler film from another man's film by just looking at it. To me it's more challenging, and more fun, too, to do different types of pictures."[627]

In 1949, Wyler played the field and had his choice of projects, all of which further distinguished him. *The Heiress, Detective Story, The Desperate Hours, The Collector, Friendly Persuasion,* and *The Big Country* show his range: period, crime, psychological, bucolic, war, and western. The only thing he never tried was a musical-comedy. Oh, wait, he did: *Funny Girl*, Barbra Streisand's 1968 screen debut (replacing Sidney Lumet, who backed out following differences with Streisand and producer Ray Stark). Not surprisingly, tensions were reported from the set. After all, Streisand had played the role over 1,348 times on Broadway and Wyler was directing his first musical. Initially, the star balked at the prospect — Wyler was partially deaf — but after a while she found herself wanting to please him. That didn't mean that she would be a pushover; according to legend, one day Wyler became upset with his young star's insistence and somebody took him aside to say, "Be tolerant of her, Willy, she's never directed a picture before."[628]

The advance excitement for *Funny Girl* inspired Columbia Pictures, its studio, to offer Wyler a five-picture contract the month before its premiere.[629] At age sixty-six, Wyler was to produce two pictures and direct

---

627. Interviewed in *Directed by William Wyler.*
628. An unsourced quote has Ms. Streisand rebutting, "I didn't give Mr. Wyler instructions. I did play *Funny Girl* on stage for three years. I know every line, every word, everything. It's part of myself and I had the right to voice an opinion." In the end, Streisand won her first Oscar®.
629. William Wyler and Axel Madsen. *William Wyler: The Authorized Biography.* New York: Thomas Y. Crowell Company, 1973.

three, the first of which was to be *The Liberation of Lord Byron Jones*. The project had been brought to Columbia by producer Ronald Lubin who had secured the rights to Jesse Hill Ford's controversial novel of the same name in 1969 while he was at MGM. It seemed an odd choice, but Lubin had been chasing Wyler for twenty years to make a film together when *LBJ* presented itself. [630] Still, Wyler was known for stately elegance, and *LBJ* was about sex and southern racism that escalated into deadly violence.

Set in Ford's home town of Humboldt, Tennessee (called Somerset in the script), a dignified black undertaker Lord Byron ("L.B.") Jones (Roscoe Lee Browne) hires an old-line white lawyer, Oman Hedgepath (Lee J. Cobb), to handle his uncontested divorce from his wife (Lola Falana), who is having an affair with a white policeman (Anthony Zerbe). Problems erupt when Falana fights the divorce and the white community pressures the ordinarily docile Jones to back off. Standing up for his dignity as a black man, Jones announces, "to hell with the white man," a decision that costs him his manhood and his life. Jones' murder is avenged indirectly by Sonny Boy Mosby (Yaphet Kotto), but the legacy or racism has been renewed.

When Ford submitted an unsuccessful first draft, Lubin brought in Stirling Silliphant, for which the Oscar®-winning screenwriter of *In the Heat of the Night* was paid $200,000 (Wyler received $600,000; the total budget was $3.5 million). Wyler originally wanted Henry Fonda to play the competent but disagreeable lawyer, Hedgepath, but he was unavailable. In February of 1969, Wyler traveled to Humboldt to meet Ford and scout locations. One of his first questions to the author was why he exaggerated the situations in the story. Only then did Ford advise him of what everybody in town already knew, which is that it was all sadly true.[631]

While he was still finalizing production, Wyler met Roy Wilkins, the head of the NAACP, at a luncheon in Wilkins' honor hosted by Lew Wasserman (MCA/Universal) and Jack Valenti (MPAA). The two men briefly discussed *Jones*, after which Wyler sent Wilkins a script asking for his "frank and candid reaction" to the racially-charged material.[632] After he had read it, by which time Wyler was already shooting, Wilkins responded positively and likened its potential power to that of *In the Heat of the Night*.[633]

---

630. Letter to Wyler from Lubin, May 16, 1968. William Wyler papers, AMPAS.
631. Jan Herman. *A Talent for Trouble*. New York: G. P. Putnam's Sons, 1995.
632. The luncheon was held on April 21, 1969 at the Beverly-Wilshire Hotel. Wyler wrote Wilkinson April 25, 1969. William Wyler papers, AMPAS.
633. Wilkins letter to Wyler, June 4, 1969. William Wyler papers, AMPAS.

Location filming began on June 2, 1969 with word spreading through town that the film would be dropping $250,000 to local businesses. In order to avoid friction with Jim Crow, the racially mixed cast and crew was billeted in a color-blind Holiday Inn outside of town. No incidents were reported, but it was only after everyone returned to Los Angeles that Wyler learned that the black members of the company had been wary not to venture out at night in Humboldt. In addition to Humboldt, filming was conducted at nearby Gibson, Trenton, and Brownsville, Tennessee.

Almost as soon as cameras turned, Wyler succumbed to the heat and humidity of the Tennessee summer. He tired easily and needed naps. His two assistant directors Anthony Ray (Nick Ray's son) and Robert Swink covered for him by persuading Columbia that the shoot was so complex it would need two separate crews. In this way, Wyler and his ADs confounded the studio bean-counters.[634] After two weeks, the company returned to Columbia's studio facility on Gower Street in Hollywood where the production spread over five soundstages and wrapped, apparently on schedule, on July 11. Remarkable for a Wyler film, principle photography was completed in 38 days.

By November, editor Carl Kress had a first cut ready for screening. Almost immediately rumors began circulating that the film was so inflammatory that it would spark race riots in theatres. Whether these were launched by Ford's Humboldt enemies or the Columbia publicity department is not certain. Wyler insisted that no compromises had been made in the hard-hitting story, although he and Ford did at one time discuss an alternate ending in which, after Jones had been killed, a train arrives in town and a number of Black Panthers disembark to give the town the lesson it needs. It never went past the brainstorm stage.[635]

The Liberation of L.B. Jones (shortened title) was not a commercial hit and fared poorly with critics. Perhaps coming two years after the assassinations of Martin Luther King, Jr. and Robert Kennedy, two months after the FBI's killing of activist Fred Hampton, and the expansion of the Black Panther Party, a movie made by white people — no matter how liberal their racial views or how fervent their support of civil rights — seemed out of step with the times. "When I wrote *The Liberation of L.B. Jones,*" recalled screenwriter Stirling Silliphant, "I was up to my gills with the prevailing wisdom that race relations in the USA were now okay…when, in fact, the only thing that had changed, deep down in the white hearts of my

---

634. Jan Herman, op. cit.
635. Wyler and Madsen, op. cit.

countrymen, was their delusion that they had at last accepted any person of a different skin color or ethnic background as a fellow human being. *LBJ* in its own dark heart is saying only one thing: "F**k all of you, all you white bastards, all you black bastards, f**k you for hating each other, for hating yourselves!' The film is unremitting, inexorable, without pity or compromise or solution. It simply states that hatred prevails."[636]

There is also the possibility that Wyler, already deaf in one ear and losing hearing in the other in addition to being fatigued by location conditions, was unable to exercise his legendary taste and patience on a limited budget, and may have lacked the ability, or the will, or the tenacity, to accept his usual standard.

"True," Silliphant confirmed, "Mr. Wyler was nearing the end of his brilliant career — and the end of his life span — but Willy cared passionately about this film. After I had finished my screenplay and the changes he requested, he still wanted more. He wanted me on the set. He wanted to bounce ideas. At the time, I was becoming involved in another project — Lord only remembers what it could have been — so I told Willy I would not be available. I guess my passion for the finished film is based on the fact that the picture was uncompromising. It offered no solutions, no hope — it simply said this is what happens when two sides hate each other. I value the film because in the period when it was made it was decades ahead of all the other 'safe' Hollywood black-white themes. We dared to say that racial hatreds run *deep* in America — for that matter, all over the world. We scorned the happy ending — the ray of hope. This is why to me *LBJ* is one of the works of which I am the most satisfied. It is sans bullshit."[637]

William Wyler lived until July 7, 1981 and died in his Beverly Hills home at age seventy-nine one day after returning from a career tribute in London and three days after filming his interview for *Directed by William Wyler* (1986).[638] The documentary was co-produced by his oldest daughter, Catherine, and took five years after his passing to complete.

It had been Wyler's stated personal goal to make one kind of every genre of picture and, in his final interview, when he says, "Now I've done everything," no one could have known how much closure he had achieved. Like the actors in his films, there was no way that William Wyler could have done it better.

636. Interview with the Author, *Backstory 3*, op. cit.
637. Interview with the Author, ibid.
638. AP obituary July 29, 1981.

Peter Yates.

PETER YATES
Mister Versatile

Peter Yates' filmography defines the thin difference between *eclectic* and *diverse*. Both words mean *varied*, but the former implies a random range while the latter addresses a broad, interrelated selection. Adherents to the *auteur* theory have tried to reconcile the two by insisting that directors display themes and trademarks despite the subject matter of their films. Counter-*auteurists* claim that anybody who has ever tried to make a film knows that you only get to make what they let you make, and if you need to convince yourself that it was your choice and not theirs, hey, whatever floats your director's finder.

In thirty-five years and twenty-three feature films, Yates indeed made the pictures they let him make while infusing even those that, perhaps, he didn't want to make (*Krull*? *Mother Jugs and Speed*? Oh c'mon) with enough of what interested him that the results invariably wound up holding an audience. His strongest work was in the crime and character arenas, but a couple of quirky comedies crop up, too, including his last, *Curtain Call* (1998).

Yates was unpretentious but firm, a quiet professional who adjusted his style to the film-at-hand rather than forcing the work to adhere to a pre-configured vision. He also got his actors to deliver their best by meeting them on their own terms.

"I was trained as an actor," Yates said. "I think that helps. It gives me a sympathy with actors' problems. Sometimes I think it gives me *too* much sympathy. They're capable of doing quite a lot of things technically which they *don't* do. What I try to do when casting is find actors who I feel are going to bring something to their characters, who are doing observation on their own. Robert Shaw said that [English actors] get away with murder. We sit there and look off camera and raise one eyebrow, and think about when our lunch break is going to be, and they all believe we're giving incredible performances."[639]

Yates adapted to his material. The slick, super-cool, efficiency of *Bullitt* (1968) matched the slick, cool efficiency of its star, Steve McQueen, while the somber, brooding *The Friends of Eddie Coyle* (1973) seemed to flow from the like qualities of its star, Robert Mitchum. Likewise, the popcorn thriller *The Deep* (1977, his biggest hit) is as shamelessly manipulative as its cheesy Peter Benchley source material, while *Breaking Away* (1979), ostensibly a drama about teenage bicycle racers, becomes one of the finest statements of mid-twentieth century American anguish in any medium.

Born into the worldwide Great Depression in 1929 in the British army town of Aldershot, England, Yates attended the Royal Academy of Dramatic Art with aspirations to act. RADA's training also exposed him to stage managing and directing, and he soon found the latter more to his liking. Then history helped; in 1960 England's film industry was freed from constraints of the low-budget, short-scheduled "quota quickies" it had been forced to churn out and, almost immediately, such blossoming filmmakers as Lindsay Anderson, Tony Richardson, John Schlesinger, Terrence Young, and Guy Hamilton began bringing real-life concerns to the screen.[640] Yates was attached to a succession of their productions as assistant director before being handed singing star Cliff Richard's 1963 romp *Summer Holiday* (replacing, according to legend, the incongruous choice for its original director, Ken Russell). It may not have been a quota quickie, but it was handled in the U.S. by American International Pictures who specialized in horror, beach blanket, and pop music releases. From 1963 through 1967, Yates busied himself with television episodics in the UK but, in 1967, drew attention for the feature *Robbery*, a fictionalized account of the great 1964 British train robbery (fictionalized again in 1988's *Buster*, with Phil Collins). Largely a procedural, it featured a car chase that so impressed Steve McQueen that he asked Yates to direct his upcoming production of *Bullitt*, bringing the filmmaker to America and jump-starting his A-list career. Coincidentally, Yates had briefly been a race car driver in England.

---

639. Interview with the Author July, 1979. Yates and Shaw made *The Deep*.
640. Sometimes called "kitchen sink" dramas because of their unflinching portrayal of working class life, early-60s titles include *A Taste of Honey*, *The Loneliness of the Long-Distance Runner*, *Billy Liar*, *The Entertainer*, and *This Sporting Life*. They paralleled a similar trend in American television drama (*Philco-Goodyear Playhouse*, *Studio One*, *Armstrong Circle Theatre*, etc.), eventually breaking out into independent theatrical films like *Marty* and *David and Lisa*.

Bullitt's nearly eleven-minute chase through San Francisco's twisted, vertiginous streets was a movie milestone. For the first time a car chase wasn't used as a free-standing action sequence, but was integrated into the plot, summoning emotion as well as thrills. Yates, producer Phil D'Antoni (who later produced *The French Connection,* 1972, with its still-unmatched car/subway pursuit), stunt coordinator Carey Loftin, and stunt drivers Bud Ekins and Bill Hickman spent five weeks of Sunday mornings (note that the streets are practically empty) to pin viewers alternately to the backs of their chairs and the edges of their seats.

With *Bullitt* a $42 million hit, Yates defied expectations by next making what could be considered a chamber romance, *John and Mary* (1969), starring Dustin Hoffman and Mia Farrow. Quiet to the point of obscurity, it disappointed audiences who were awaiting Hoffman's follow-up to *Midnight Cowboy* and *The Graduate* and Farrow's next after *Rosemary's Baby*. But it cleverly established Yates' directorial chops with actors and led him to a pair of quirky pictures: *Murphy's War* (1971), with Peter O'Toole as a World War II soldier who obsessively wants to sink the U-Boat that killed the rest of his crew; and *The Hot Rock* (1972), a screwy heist written by William Goldman and starring Robert Redford and George Segal.[641]

The Friends of Eddie Coyle, adapted by producer Paul Monash from George V. Higgins' low-key blue-collar crime novel, is Yates' masterpiece. Subtle and intense, it stars Robert Mitchum as a mid-level Boston hood who gets squeezed between gun runners, bank robbers, and the Feds. A spiritual forerunner to *The Sopranos, Coyle* had gone unseen for decades before Paramount Pictures deigned to let Criterion video rescue it from vault hell, and to this day it remains one of the finest performances of the capable, but often lazy, Robert Mitchum, thanks to Yates' savvy guidance.[642]

The twenty years after *Eddie Coyle* brought Yates to alternately commercial and risky projects. *The Deep* (1977) was first cousin to *Jaws* (1975) and had to do with diving for sunken treasure in Bermuda, but most moviegoers — especially a generation of teenage boys — remember it for co-star Jacqueline Bisset's wet T-shirt. And that's a shame, because films like *The Deep* can easily go off-kilter if their tone is wrong. Yates

---

641. Three words: Afghanistan banana stand.
642. The Author was permitted to watch Yates at work on what became a classic film. Assigned to cover the filming of *The Friends of Eddie Coyle* for a Boston newspaper, I was told to sit in a barroom booth with Joe Santos who was playing a scene with Peter Boyle. Only afterward did Yates learn that I was not an extra but was there to interview him. "I needed somebody with long hair to play a barfly," Yates later explained over lunch.

and cinematographer Christopher Challis wrought a glossy yet controlled thriller from formulaic material. A nearly $75 million gross — and a vast sale of Bisset posters — was the result. It was also Yates' first big-budget film.

As if seeking to offset his acquired reputation as an action director, others of Yates' films concentrate on character. *Breaking Away*, written by Steve Tesich, became a surprise hit. In addition to fine central performances by Dennis Christopher, Dennis Quade, and Daniel Stern, it featured immensely moving work by Barbara Barrie and Paul Dooley as the parents of bicycle racer Christopher who, although proud of their small town of Bloomington, Indiana, yearn for him to make something more of his life than they did of theirs. This turned out to be a universal theme and audiences of all ages were drawn to it. "I think that's what movies are about," Yates has said. "To create an experience that one can identify with, hopefully, and also to maybe get some ideas, examine some feelings of your own. It should be very personal, I think."[643]

His expert direction of Sigourney Weaver and William Hurt (*Eyewitness*, 1981), of Albert Finney and Tom Courtney (*The Dresser*, 1983), of Kate Nelligan (*Eleni*, 1985), Cher (*Suspect*, 1987), and of Jeff Daniels, Kelly McGillis, and the Red Scare (*The House on Carroll Street*, 1988) comprise a series of performance-driven films that is rare, if not heroic, at a time when the American film industry was dominated by action and special effect blockbusters. Somehow, Yates managed to find money to make movies about people and ideas. His versatility was further demonstrated with *The Year of the Comet* (1992) that brought him back to England; *Needful Things* (1993) to British Columbia; and *The Run of the Country* (1995) to Ireland. The first was a drama about a bottle of rare wine and an approaching cosmic fireball; the second a Satanic fable; and the third a superbly well-observed story of father-son tension in a provincial village.

But anyone trying to extrapolate the arc of Yates' career would be baffled by what became his last film, *Curtain Call*, released briefly in 1998. A self-proclaimed "spirited romance," it was shot under the improbable title *Later Life* and then *It All Came True* but, unfortunately, nothing came true for the producers and it quickly found an afterlife on home video. Which is a shame because it's a capable rom-com about a bickering ghost couple (Maggie Smith and Michael Caine) who help a young living couple (James Spader and Polly Walker) realize that they're in love, and vice versa. It shares ectoplasm with *Blithe Spirit*, *Topper*, and *Dona Flor*

---

643. Ibid.

and Her Two Husbands, among other spiritual fantasies, and it succeeds on the strength of its casting and performances rather than on special effects.

The picture was announced in early 1997 as the first joint venture for Quadra, a distribution company that bought the international rights from producer Andrew Karsch and Sidney Kimmel.[644] Peter Bogdanovich was first considered to direct, but Yates wound up with the assignment. Interestingly, the first announcements identified Michael Caine as a friendly neighbor "who was a bachelor until he met a woman who made him commit: Maggie Smith." There was no mention of Caine, Smith, or ghosts.[645]

In the loosely hung story, Spader is the heir to a publishing dynasty and believes in quality, unlike the crass conglomerate led by Buck Henry that has acquired his company. Walker is his significant other who wants them to marry, but when he moves into an elegant Manhattan brownstone he sends vibes that she will be only a guest there, not his wife. This drives her into the arms of a U.S. Senator played nobly by Sam Shepard. Meanwhile, the house's previous residents, the showbiz duo of Max Gale and Lily Marlowe (Caine and Smith), who are dead, make themselves visible to Spader, but only to him (of course). This allows for a number of well-worn "who's that guy talking to?" gags. Max and Lily, who are playfully aware that they're deceased, were theatrical stars whose shtick was bickering on stage, but after a while their married life began to imitate art and the curtain came down on their mutual affection. Or so it seems, because the audience knows it's just a question of time before they reconcile with one another and lead Spader to see Walker in their new light.

Yates faced an interesting challenge. While *Curtain Call* hardly matches wits with Noel Coward or Philip Barry, its dialogue is brittle enough to require actors who can sell it properly. Caine and Smith were past masters; they traded similar barbs in 1978 in Neil Simon's *California Suite*, which won Smith an Oscar®. Spader had an equally tough task. While he's an intelligent actor, he can also be an abrasive one, yet he had to appear charming and a match for his co-stars. The problem was solved by having him shamelessly debase himself in a masterful falling-down drunk sequence with Caine. The bottom line is that *Curtain Call* earns points for being about bright people whom you want to spend time with and watch them straighten out their lives so they can get on with their deaths.

644. *Daily Variety*, January 29, 1997. It's possible that the lack of an American distributor also limited its potential despite having European release.
645. Michael Fleming, *Daily Variety*, January 20, 1997.

Peter Yates made two TV movies after *Curtain Call*: a fantasy-rich adaptation of *Don Quixote* in 2000 and a remake of John Knowles' strange prep school novel *A Separate Peace* in 2004. He died of heart failure in England on January 9, 2011 at age eighty-one.

"It's fun enough making pictures without making a lot of money on it as well," he once said. It's not a bad epitaph.[646]

---

646. Interview with the Author November 1, 1972.

Fred Zinnemann.

FRED ZINNEMANN
You First, Sonny

The story may be apocryphal, but it's told most often about Fred Zinnemann: an older but still vital director is pitching a project to a young vice president of production at a major Hollywood studio. "It's very interesting," the twenty-something says with feigned interest. "But tell me, what films have you made?" At this remark Zinnemann — whose credits include *High Noon, From Here to Eternity, The Nun's Story, Oklahoma!* and a couple Oscars® — leans forward and says to the lad, "You first, Sonny."

Zinnemann isn't the only experienced director who has come face to face with "embryos in three-piece suits," as writer Larry Gelbart called them: executives who occupy positions of power without having the slightest knowledge of, or interest in, the history of their own profession. The kind of people who make remakes instead of originals, who mine comic books and old TV shows because that's what they grew up on, and who try to ensure success by depending on market research instead of their guts.

A careful constructionist whose good taste kept incendiary subjects from becoming lurid, Zinnemann slipped violence and adultery past the censors in *From Here to Eternity* (1953); sympathized with a novitiate who rejects her vows in *The Nun's Story* (1959); created exquisite tension from a sheriff abandoned by the town he is sworn to protect in *High Noon* (1952); and took an unflinching look at paraplegic World War II veterans in *The Men* (1950), among other challenges. Whether drama, musical, western, or thriller, Zinnemann attacked each genre on its own terms, sometimes succeeding, sometimes uncovering flaws that he was not able to surmount; and sometimes outright failing. His last film, *Five Days One Summer*, is an unfortunate example of the last.

The distinguished filmmaker was born in Vienna in 1907 and grew up as the Austro-Hungarian Empire was declining. Raised on American movies more than European cinema after World War I crushed the European film industry, he moved to Paris when he gave up study of the law in favor of learning film. With the arrival of sound, he came to America and landed at MGM where he entered the short subject department, an apprenticeship that served as training ground for feature directors. When one of his shorts — *That Mothers Might Live* — won the 1938 Oscar®, MGM moved him to the big league. His 1944 feature *The Seventh Cross* not only won him good reviews, it won him its star, Spencer Tracy, as an advocate. By 1948 and war's end he made *The Search*, a documentary-style drama of a couple of American GIs (one of whom was Montgomery Clift in his first movie) helping a war orphan look for his family. He also was Marlon Brando's first director in *The Men*, giving him a galvanizing screen debut.

Even though Zinnemann's 55-year career is prolific in retrospect, it slowed down as it went on. His directing Oscar® for the taut and lively *From Here to Eternity* led him to the plum *Oklahoma!*. The Rodgers and Hammerstein stage success may have revolutionized Broadway musicals, but its lugubrious screen treatment set *movie* musicals back twenty years.[647] In 1958 he was reunited with Spencer Tracy for *The Old Man and the Sea* but left the production midway (it was finished by John Sturges), and the results only prove how good the book was. *The Nun's Story* (1959), with Audrey Hepburn as the real life Sister Luke (Marie-Louise Habets), who finds medicine more sacred than her vows, was a hit, perhaps because Zinnemann added a sexual tension not present in the Kathryn Hulme best-seller on which it was based. The Spanish Civil War was the subject of Zinnemann's *Behold a Pale Horse* (1964) that didn't gel dramatically, but his stately *A Man for All Seasons* (1966), about the conflict between Thomas More and Henry VIII over church vs. state, was a box office and Oscar® triumph.

Despite all the awards, it was seven years before Zinnemann made — or was allowed to make — another movie. *The Day of the Jackal* (1973), based on Frederick Forsythe's yarn about a terrorist who tries to assassinate Charles de Gaulle, achieved the impossible: it generated tension despite being completely unbelievable. He took another four years to make *Julia*, adapted by Alvin Sargent from Lillian Hellman's embroidered memoir

---

647. This may be partly the fault of the unwieldy new Todd-AO 70mm format in which *Oklahoma!* was shot but, considering how Rouben Mamoulian liberated the then-new sound cameras in *Applause*, it's worth noting.

Pentimento. The film was unaccountably difficult to cast even though it had two compelling women's parts; Barbra Streisand, Julie Christie, and Faye Dunaway reportedly turned down the starring roles eventually played to acclaim by Jane Fonda and Vanessa Redgrave. Abetted by Jason Robards, Jr. as Hellman's lover Dashiell Hammett, the screen alchemy was magical and *Julia* was an immense success.

Nevertheless, Zinnemann couldn't get another picture together. He was 70 when *Julia* came out and 75 when the stars finally aligned for what became his final film, *Five Days One Summer*. Completed in 1982, five years after *Star Wars'* seismic impact destroyed the system under which directors like Zinnemann had flourished, it was both a struggle and a disappointment. It was based on Kay Boyle's 1934 *Harper's Bazaar* story *Maiden, Maiden,* in which Zinnemann found an intriguing articulation of his recurring theme, "a crisis of conscience." In 1932, an older man (Sarat in the story, Douglas in the film; Sean Connery) arrives at an Alpine hotel with a younger woman (Willa in the story, Kate in the movie; Betsy Brantley) posing as his wife. They are there for a mountain climbing holiday and enlist the help of a local guide (unnamed in the story, Johann in the film; Lambert Wilson). After an early team foray, the girl waits below as the two men attempt to climb a menacing peak called the Maiden. One of them accidentally falls to his death, but we and the girl don't know which it is. Finally we see that it was the guide. Then it comes out that Douglas is Willa's uncle, not her husband, and that he is still married, casting doubt on the integrity of their relationship. In the story (but not the film) Douglas stands trial for the death of the guide, whom he suspected of having an affair with Willa. "She cares about *both* of them," Zinnemann declared, "but she is in love with *one* of them."[648]

"It was not the characters in the short story that interested me," Zinnemann continued, "but the short story's final situation of a girl sitting in a hut waiting for two men to come back from a mountain. Only one of them comes back, but from the distance she doesn't know which one."[649]

The director had wanted to shoot *Five Days* in black and white, believing that mountains look more "dramatic" when photographed that way, but he yielded to the commercial demand for color.[650] Determined to make his film as authentic as possible, Zinnemann made his screenwriter

648. Presskit from The Ladd Company/Warner Bros.
649. Zinnemann to Alan Arnold, Fred Zinnemann papers, AMPAS.
650. Alan Arnold, op cit.

Michael Austin take climbing lessons with mountaineering advisor Norman Dyhrenfurth, who became second unit director. They practiced the climbing methods of the 1930s, when the story is set, rather than modern techniques. Zinnemann also took pains to ensure that his actors and crew acclimated themselves to the thin air, cold temperature, and high altitudes at 6,500 feet by, first, making sure that he, himself, could still do it at age seventy-four. Connery, then fifty-one, eagerly accepted the role as a break from playing James Bond (which he would do again the next year in *Never Say Never Again*).[651] Zinnemann cast North Carolinian Betsy Brantley after seeing her in only one film, the completely unrelated *Shock Treatment* (1981), the unsuccessful sequel to *The Rocky Horror Picture Show*. And he chose Lambert Wilson, with whom he had worked briefly in *Julia*, as Johann.

In the days before CGI, the scenery was more difficult to cast. Boyle had invented it for her story; the "Maiden" she described did not exist. The company based itself in Pontresina near St. Moritz after getting permission from the Swiss to shoot in the Engadine region of the Alps. The Maiden became three peaks shot from different angles: Piz Costello, Piz Badile, and Piz Palu. Production extended from August 3, 1981 on a glacier below Diavolezza to September 19. In July, an unusually heavy snow storm had made it impossible to ascend the mountain, so cover sets were used for interior scenes. When filming on the glacier resumed, cast and crew were given detailed surface maps noting where the crevices were and sporting the warning "Do not wander."[652]

Because of assurances given the Swiss authorities that they would maintain the pristine nature of the countryside, the company used helicopters to make daily trips from the location to the town below to dispose of trash from dishes to gum wrappers. Two additional choppers were employed to bring cast and crew back and forth to the otherwise-inaccessible peaks.

In late July, the crew made a grizzly discovery: they found the body of a police officer who had fallen down a steep crevice thirty-one years earlier. As happens in such tragedies, the glacier moves slowly but inexorably down, finally depositing the perfectly preserved body on the ground. The incident inspired Zinnemann and Austin to script a scene in which the Johann describes a local mountain legend in which a glacier similarly reveals the body of a man who disappeared while climbing it 40 years

---

651. Fred Zinnemann, *A Life in Movies*. New York: Charles Scribner's Sons, 1992.
652. Fred Zinnemann papers, AMPAS.

earlier. The villagers gather and a white-haired woman is brought up to identify him: it turns out that he was her fiancé who disappeared while climbing years ago.[653]

On September 19, the company returned to England where shooting was completed at Shepperton Studios from September 22 to October 22.

Five Days One Summer was released on November 12, 1982 and received a reception as chilly as its setting. "Polite and tasteful," remarked *The Hollywood Reporter* politely.[654] *L.A. Magazine* added that it is "such a well-made, well-acted, well-photographed film that it's easy to overlook the fact that it has virtually no point at all."[655] And *Weekly Variety* was characteristically blunt calling it: "Glacially slow."[656] It's hard to think of a movie about mountain climbing that has neither tension nor conflict, but *Five Days One Summer* is so low-key and interior that it works against its own ingredients.

With a budget of $15,375,000 and a gross of less than $200,000 it was an ignominious capper for a distinguished resume. Zinnemann was never able to get another project made. He published an elaborate memoir in 1992 and died in England, where he had moved in the late 1950s, on March 14, 1997.

Perhaps because he attempted so many genres, Zinnemann was never able to establish a style in any of them, the kind of thing that auteurists look for and say, "Aha!" Of course, "style" can have many meanings. If it's low-angle tracking shots into faces rapt in wonderment, or slow-motion carnage, that's one kind. Showing ceilings is another. So are smoke and backlighting. But if it means taste, restraint, sharp casting, and consummate acting, then Zinnemann was at the summit all along.

---

653. It's a touching tale but nobody seems to have mentioned in the publicity or the reviews that the same legend had aired on October 4, 1959 as an *Alfred Hitchcock Presents* television episode called *The Crystal Trench*. Stirling Silliphant scripted it from A.E.W. Mason's short story and Hitchcock himself directed it with a wicked twist: When the old woman, who has remained single all these years out of loyalty to her dead fiancé, is shown his body, he is wearing a locket. When she opens it, it contains the picture of another woman.
654. *Hollywood Reporter*, October 29, 1982.
655. *Los Angeles* Magazine, October, 1982.
656. *Weekly Variety*, October 27, 1982.

Selected Bibliography

Acker, Ally. *Reel Women: Pioneers of the Cinema 1896 to the Present*. New York: Continuum, 1991.

Anderson, Lindsay. *About John Ford*. New York: McGraw-Hill, 1981.

Bach, Steven. *Final Cut: Dreams and Disaster in the Making of Heaven's Gate.* New York: William Morrow, 1985.

Barry, Iris. *D.W. Griffith: American Film Master*. New York: The Museum of Modern Art, rev. 1965.

Bart, Peter. *Fade Out: The Calamitous Final Days of MGM*. New York: William Morrow & Co., 1990.

Bergan, Ronald. *The United Artists Story*. New York: Crown Publishers, 1986.

Birchard, Robert S. *Cecil B. DeMille's Hollywood*. Lexington, Kentucky: University Press of Kentucky, 2004.

Bogdanovich, Peter. *Who the Devil Made It*. New York: Alfred A. Knopf, 1997.

Brownlow, Kevin. *David Lean, a Biography*. New York: St. Martin's Press, 1996.

Byman, Jeremy. *Showdown at High Noon: Witch-hunts, Critics, and the End of the Western.* Lanham, Maryland: Scarecrow Press, Inc., 2004.

Capra, Frank. *The Name Above the Title: An Autobiography*. New York: MacMillan and Company, 1971.

Capua, Michelangelo. *William Holden: A Biography*. Jefferson, North Carolina: McFarland & Company, 2009.

Carey, Gary and Joseph L. Mankiewicz. *More About All About Eve*. New York: Random House, 1972.

Ceplair, Larry and Steven Englund. *The Inquisition in Hollywood: Politics in the Film Community, 1930-1960* (rev.). Urbana and Chicago, Illinois: University of Chicago Press, 2003.

Chaplin, Charles. *My Autobiography*. New York: Simon & Schuster, 1964.

———. *My Life in Pictures*. New York: Grossett & Dunlap, 1975.

Curtis, James. *Between Flops: A Biography of Preston Sturges*. New York: Harcourt, Brace, Jovanovich, 1982.

Daniel, Douglass K. *Tough as Nails: The Life and Films of Richard Brooks.* Madison, Wisconsin: University of Wisconsin Press, 2011.

DeMille, Cecil B., Donald Hayne, ed. *The Autobiography*. London: W. H. Allen, 1960.

Dmytryk, Edward. *It's a Hell of a Life, But Not a Bad Living*. New York: Times Books, 1978.

———. *Odd Man Out: A Memoir of the Hollywood Ten*. Illinois: Southern Illinois University Press, 1996.

Eames, John Douglas. *The MGM Story*. New York: Crown Publishers, 1975.

Jerry Epstein and Geoff Brown. *Remembering Charlie, a Pictorial Biography*. New York: Doubleday, 1989.

Fine, Marshall. *Bloody Sam*. New York: Donald I. Fine, 2006.

Finler, Joel. *Movie Directors' Story*. New York: Crescent Books, 1985.

Flammer, Philip M. *The Vivid Air: The Lafayette Escadrille*. Athens, Georgia: The University of Georgia Press, 2008.

Flom, Eric L. *Chaplin in the Sound Era*. Jefferson, North Carolina: McFarland Press, 1997.

Ford, Dan. *Pappy: The Life of John Ford*. Englewood Cliffs, New Jersey: Prentice-Hall, 1979.

Freeman, David. *The Last Days of Alfred Hitchcock*. Woodstock, New York: The Overlook Press, 1984.

Fuller, Samuel, Christa Fuller and Jerome Rhodes, *A Third Face: My Tale of Writing, Fighting, and Filmmaking*. Montclair, New Jersey: Hal Leonard Company, 2004.

Garcia, Roger, ed. *Frank Tashlin*. Editions du Festival Internationale du film de Locarno, 1994.

Gehring, Wes D. *Leo McCarey: From Marx to McCarthy*. Lanham, Maryland: Scarecrow Press, 2005.

Geist, Kenneth L. *Pictures Will Talk: The Life and Films of Joseph L. Mankiewicz*. New York: Charles Scribner's Sons, 1978.

Giddins, Gary. *Natural Selection: Gary Giddins on Comedy, Film, Music, and Books*. New York: Oxford University Press, 2006.

Gill, Brendan; Robert Kimball, ed. *Cole: A Biographical Essay*. New York: Holt, Rinehart and Winston, 1971.

Gish, Lillian, and Ann Pinchot. *The Movies, Mr. Griffith, and Me*. Englewood Cliffs, New Jersey: Prentice-Hall, 1969.

Goodman, Ezra. *The Fifty-Year Decline and Fall of Hollywood*. New York: Simon & Schuster, 1961.

Grobel, Laurence. *The Hustons*. New York: Charles Scribner's Sons, 1989.

Hadleigh, Boze. *Celebrity Diss and Tell*. New Jersey: Andrews McMeel Publishing, 2005.

Hamblin, Dora Jane. "It May Be Funny but No Laughter, Please, We're Serious." *Life* New York: Time-Life, January 1, 1966.

Haver, Ronald. *A Star is Born: The Making of the 1954 Movie and Its 1983 Restoration*. New York: Alfred A. Knopf, 1988.

Henderson, Robert M. *D.W. Griffith: His Life and Work*. New York: Oxford University Press, 1972.

Herman, Jan. *A Talent for Trouble*. New York: G. P. Putnam's Sons, 1975.

Heston, Charlton; Hollis Alpert, ed. *The Actor's Life: Journals 1956-1976*. New York: Dutton, 1976.

Higham, Charles. *Cecil B. DeMille*. New York: Da Capo Press, 1980.

Hunter, Tab. *Tab Hunter Confidential: The Making of a Movie Star*. New York: Algonquin Books, 2006.

Jackson, Carlton. *Picking Up the Tab: The Life and Movies of Martin Ritt*. Bowling Green, OH: Bowling Green State University Popular Press, 1994.

Kaminsky, Stuart M. *Don Siegel: Director*. New York: Curtis Books, 1974.

Katz, Ephraim. *The Film Encyclopedia* (Second ed.). New York: Harper Perennial, 1994.

Kazan, Elia. *A Life*. New York: Alfred A. Knopf, 1988.

Kirkpatrick, Sidney D. *A Cast of Killers*. New York: E.P. Dutton, 1986.

Koch, Howard. *As Time Goes By: Memoirs of a Writer*. New York: Harcourt Brace Jovanovich, 1979.

Kramer, Stanley with Thomas M. Coffey. *Mad Mad Mad Mad World: A Life in Hollywood*. New York: Harcourt, Brace and Company, 1997.

Leaming, Barbara. *Orson Welles: A Biography*. New York: Viking Penguin, 1985.

Leff, Leonard J. and Jerold L. Simmons. *The Dame in the Kimono: Hollywood, Censorship, & The Production Code from the 1920s to the 1960s*. New York: Grove Weidenfeld, 1990.

Link, Mardi. *Isadore's Secret: Sin, Murder, and Confession in a Northern Michigan Town*. Ann Arbor, Michigan: University of Michigan Press, 2009.

Maltin, Leonard. *Of Mice and Magic: A History of American Animated Cartoons*. New York: McGraw-Hill, 1980.

Mankiewicz, Joseph L. *More About All About Eve: A Colloquy with Gary Carey*. New York: Random House, 1972.

McBride, Joseph. *Frank Capra: The Catastrophe of Success*. New York: Simon & Schuster, 1992.

——————. *Searching for John Ford, A Life*. New York: St. Martin's Press, 2001.

—————— and Michael Wilmington, *John Ford*. New York: Da Capo Press, 1974.

McClintick, David. *Indecent Exposure*. New York: William Morrow, 1982.

McGilligan, Patrick. *Alfred Hitchcock: A Life in Darkness and Light*. New York: Regan Books, 2003.

——————ed., *Backstory 2*. Berkeley and Los Angeles: University of California Press, 1992.

——————. *George Cukor: A Double Life*. New York: St. Martin's Press, 1981.

Meisner, Sanford and Dennis Longwell. *Sanford Meisner on Acting*. New York: Random House, 1987.

Miller, Gabriel. *The Films of Martin Ritt: Fanfare for the Common Man*. Jackson, Mississippi: The University Press of Mississippi, 2000.

Mosley, Leonard. *Zanuck: The Rise and Fall of Hollywood's Last Tycoon*. Boston, Massachusetts: Little, Brown Company, 1984.

Navasky, Victor. *Naming Names: Afterword to the Third Edition*. New York: MacMillan and Company, 2003.

Powell, Michael. *Million Dollar Movie*. New York: Random House, 1992.

Pratley, Gerald. *The Cinema of Otto Preminger*. New York: Castle Books, 1971.

Robertson, James C. *The Casablanca Man: The Cinema of Michael Curtiz*. London and New York: Routledge, 1993.

Rosten, Leo. *The Joys of Yiddish*. New York: McGraw-Hill, 1968.

Russo, Vito. *The Celluloid Closet: Homosexuality in the Movies*. New York: Harper & Row, 1981.

Sarris, Andrew. *The John Ford Movie Mystery*. Bloomington, Indiana: The Indiana University Press, 1975.

———. *The American Cinema: Directors and Directions 1929-1968*. New York: E. P. Dutton & Co., 1968.

Schickel, Richard. *D.W. Griffith: An American Life*. Milwaukee, Wisconsin: Hal Leonard Corporation, 1996.

Segaloff, Nat. *Arthur Penn: American Director*. Kentucky: The University Press of Kentucky, 2011.

———. *Hurricane Billy: The Stormy Life and Films of William Friedkin*. New York: William Morrow and Co., 1990.

———. *Mr. Huston/Mr. North*. Unpublished manuscript. Academy of Motion Picture Arts and Sciences, 1987.

Server, Lee. *Ava Gardner: Love is Nothing*. New York: MacMillan, reprint, 2007.

Shearer, Stephen Michael. *Patricia Neal: An Unquiet Life*. Lexington, Kentucky: The University Press of Kentucky, 2006.

Siegel, Donald. *A Siegel Film: An Autobiography*. London: Faber & Faber, 1993.

Sikov, Ed. *On Sunset Boulevard: The Life and Times of Billy Wilder*. New York: Hyperion, 1998.

Silverman, Stephen M. *The Fox That Got Away*. Secaucus, New Jersey: Lyle Stuart, Inc., 1988.

Sinclair, Andrew. Sam Spiegel: The Man Behind the Pictures. Boston, Massachusetts: Little, Brown & Company, 1987.

Spada, James. *The Divine Bette Midler*. New York: MacMillan and Company, 1994.

Spoto, Donald. *The Dark Side of Genius: The Life of Alfred Hitchcock*. Boston, Massachusetts: Little-Brown, 1983.

Sragow, Michael. *Victor Fleming: An American Movie Master*. New York: Pantheon Books, 2008.

Sturges, Preston. *Preston Sturges: His Life in His Words,* adapted and edited by Sandy Sturges. New York: Simon & Schuster, 1990.

Tonguette, Peter Prescott. *The Films of James Bridges*. Jefferson, NC: McFarland & Co., 2011.

Wagner, Walter. *You Must Remember This*. G. P. Putnam's Sons, 1975.

Walsh, Raoul. *Each Man in His Time: The Life Story of a Director*. New York: Farrar, Strauss and Giroux, 1974.

Welles, Orson, Peter Bogdanovich, Jonathan Rosenbaum, ed. *This is Orson Welles*. New York: HarperCollins, 1992.

Wellman, William A. *A Short Time for Insanity*. New York: Hawthorn Books, 1974.

Wyler, William and Axel Madsen. *William Wyler: The Authorized Biography*. New York: Thomas Y. Crowell Company, 1973.

Zinnemann, Fred. *A Life in Movies*. New York: Charles Scribner's Sons, 1992.

Zolotow, Maurice. *Billy Wilder in Hollywood*. New York: Putnam, 1977.

Credits

This page should be considered an extension of the Copyright page.

William Allyn papers; Charles Chaplin papers; Jon Davison papers; Linwood G. Dunn papers; Alfred Hitchcock papers; Joseph L. Mankiewicz papers; Metro-Goldwyn-Mayer Wardrobe Department records; Motion Picture Association of America, Production Code Administration records; Sam Peckinpah papers; authorial Arthur Penn material; Martin Ritt papers; Peggy Robertson papers; George Stevens papers; William Wyler papers; Fred Zinnemann papers courtesy of the Margaret Herrick Library, Academy of Motion Picture Arts and Sciences (AMPAS).

Authorial interviews with Robert Altman, James Bridges, John Huston family; Sidney Lumet, Joseph L. Mankiewicz, John Milius, Michael Powell, Michael Ritchie, Martin Ritt, John Schlesinger, and Peter Yates courtesy of Nat Segaloff Special Collection, UCLA Performing Arts Library. © Nat Segaloff.

"OSCAR®," "OSCARS®," "ACADEMY AWARD®," "ACADEMY AWARDS®," "OSCAR NIGHT®," "A.M.P.A.S.®" and the federally registered "Oscar" design mark are registered and copyrighted by the Academy of Motion Picture Arts and Sciences.

Bear Manor Media

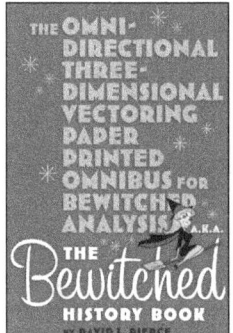

Classic Cinema.
Timeless TV.
Retro Radio.

WWW.BEARMANORMEDIA.COM

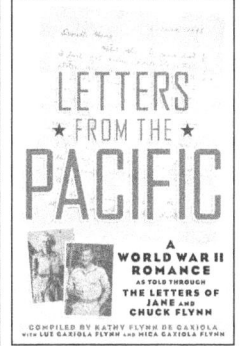

www.ingramcontent.com/pod-product-compliance
Lightning Source LLC
Chambersburg PA
CBHW070228230426
43664CB00014B/2237